IDEA

Amendments of 1997:

Practice Guidelines for School-Based Teams

NATIONAL
ASSOCIATION OF
SCHOOL
PSYCHOLOGISTS

Edited by: Cathy F. Telzrow, Ph.D. ABPP and Melody Tankersley, Ph.D.

| IDEA Amendments of 1997:
Practice Guidelines for School-Based Teams

Copies may be ordered from:
NASP Publications
4340 East West Highway, Suite 402
Bethesda, MD 20814
(301) 657-0270
(301) 657-0275, fax
e-mail: *publications@naspweb.org*
www.naspweb.org

ISBN 0-932955-88-6

Printed in the United States of America

First Printing, Fall 2000

10 9 8 7 6 5 4 3 2 1

From the NASP Publications Board Operations Manual
The content of this document reflects the ideas and positions of the authors. The responsibility lies solely with the authors and does not necessarily reflect the position or ideas of the National Association of School Psychologists.

TABLE OF CONTENTS

CHAPTER CONTRIBUTORS

Christine Balan
Assistant Professor
Kent State University

E. M. Bard
Coordinator of School Psychologists
Akron Public Schools
Akron, Ohio

George M. Batsche
Professor, School Psychology Program
University of South Florida

Andrea Canter
Lead Psychologist
Minneapolis Public Schools
Minneapolis, Minnesota

Bryan G. Cook
Assistant Professor
Kent State University

Richard J. Cowan
Doctoral Student
University of Nebraska-Lincoln

Michael J. Curtis
Chair, Department of Psychological
and Social Foundations
University of South Florida

Erik Drasgow
Assistant Professor
University of South Carolina

John W. Eagle
Doctoral Student
University of Nebraska-Lincoln

Laurie Ford
Assistant Professor
University of South Carolina

Allison L. House
Graduate Research Assistant
University of Minnesota and National
Center on Educational Outcomes
Minneapolis, Minnesota

Christine M. Hurley
School Psychologist
Minneapolis Public Schools
Minneapolis, Minnesota

Martin J. Ikeda
Coordinator of Research and
Special Projects
Heartland Area Education Agency 11
Johnston, Iowa

Timothy P. Knoster
Program Director/Instructional
Support System of Pennsylvania
Lewisburg, Pennsylvania

Robert J. Kubick, Jr.
School Psychologist
Akron Public Schools
Akron, Ohio

Timothy J. Landrum
Associate Professor
Cleveland State University

Eric M. Mesmer
Research Analyst
American Institutes for Research
Washington, D.C.

Kershini Naidu
Doctoral Student
School Psychology Program
Kent State University

J. Ruth Nelson
Graduate Research Assistant
University of Minnesota and National
Center on Educational Outcomes
Minneapolis, Minnesota

Joseph D. Perry
Associate Professor of School Psychology
Barry University

Cheryl L. Reid
School Psychologist
Minneapolis Public Schools
Minneapolis, Minnesota

Daniel J. Reschly
Professor of Education and Psychology
Vanderbilt University

Susan M. Sheridan
Professor
University of Nebraska-Lincoln

Mark R. Shinn
Professor of Special Education
University of Oregon

Michelle M. Shinn
Research Associate
University of Oregon

Melody Tankersley
Associate Professor
Kent State University

Cathy F. Telzrow
Professor
Kent State University

W. David Tilly III
Coordinator of Assessment Services
Heartland Area Education Agency 11
Johnston, Iowa

Mitchell L. Yell
Associate Professor
University of South Carolina

James E. Ysseldyke
Birkmaier Professor of Educational
Leadership
University of Minnesota and National
Center on Educational Outcomes

EXTERNAL REVIEWERS

Jennifer J. Beebe
Doctoral Student
School Psychology Program
Kent State University

Servio Carroll
School Psychologist
Sheridan County School District
Sheridan, Wyoming

George M. Csanyi
Coordinator
Educational Assessment Project
Mid-Eastern Ohio Special Education
Regional Resource Center
Cuyahoga Falls, Ohio

Linda Garrison-Harrell
Associate Professor/Reading, Special
Education, and Instructional Technology
Southwest Missouri State University

Antonis Katsiyannis
Professor
Clemson University

Joseph Kovaleski
Director of Pupil Services
Cornwall-Lebanon School District
Lebanon, Pennsylvania

Timothy J. Landrum
Associate Professor
Cleveland State University

John W. Maag
Professor
University of Nebraska-Lincoln

Leslie Z. Paige
Project Director, R.U.R.A.L. Safe
Schools/Healthy Students Initiative
Hays Unified School District
Hays, Kansas

Kathy Pluymert
School Psychologist
Crystal Lake Elementary School
District 47
West Dundee, Illinois

Kevin P. Quinn
Associate Professor
University of Albany, SUNY

Jane Rhys
Executive Director
Kansas Council on Developmental
Disabilities
Topeka, Kansas

Jacqueline Schakel
Assessment Coordinator
Anchorage School District
Anchorage, Alaska

Julie Schendel
Coordinator, Southern Zone
Heartland Area Education Agency 11
Indianola, Iowa

James G. Shriner
Assistant Professor
University of Illinois at Urbana

Diane Smallwood
School Psychologist
South Brunswick Board of Education
Plainsboro, New Jersey

Stephen B. Thomas
Professor
Kent State University

Peter Tolan
Consultant
Ohio Department of Education
Columbus, Ohio

Joseph Wehby
Assistant Professor of Special Education
Peabody College at Vanderbilt University

INTRODUCTION

Kevin P. Dwyer, NCSP
Past President NASP, 1999-2000

Approximately 6 million children in the United States receive special education and related services each year. Their entitlement to a free appropriate public education (FAPE) was the result of parent efforts and court decisions that moved Congress to action and in 1975 culminated in P.L. 94-142, subsequently renamed the Individuals with Disabilities Education Act (IDEA).

Although this legislation has been amended and expanded several times since passage, the latest reauthorization process, which was to be completed in 1995, was one of the most contentious.

In July 1995 the House Committee on Economic and Educational Opportunities presented a draft bill. A number of children's rights advocates had major disagreements with the bill as proposed. Differences included discipline, funding, parental protections, professional standards waivers, and discretionary programs. More important, FAPE was threatened by all of those proposed amendments and most seriously by the discipline amendments that allowed expulsion without education.

What was first perceived as a slight delay in the reauthorization and amendment of IDEA turned into a multi-year battle. Several of the contentious issues were tackled during tense meetings of all stakeholders at the National Education Association's headquarters, with the Consortium for Citizens with Disabilities on one side and the National School Boards Association, among others, on the other. Numerous issues were resolved, but several more harmful loopholes remained in the bill.

Many felt that if the bill being proposed were passed by this Congress, then it would be an injustice to thousands of children. There was anger and rancor on both sides, and some feared that several of IDEA's fundamental principles would be abandoned. The following year a small group of advocates that included Madeleine Will (past Assistant Secretary for Special Education and Rehabilitative Services in the U.S. Department of Education under the Reagan Administration, and parent of a child with a disability), Patty Smith (Will's former assistant and a disability/parent advocate), and Stephanie Lee (National Down Syndrome Society), along with the co-chairs of the Consortium for Citizens with Disabilities— Justine Maloney (Learning Disability Association), Katy Beh Neas (Easter Seal Society), Paul Marchand (The Association for Retarded Citizens), and myself (as NASP governmental liaison)—met with Senator Trent Lott's (R-Miss.) staff. Senator Lott was the Republican majority leader of the Senate, and a proponent of the initiative to amend IDEA. We argued that the best thing for the children of the country was for the Congress to let the proposed bill die; that is, that no bill was better than this proposed bill. We prevailed. The 104th Congress adjourned without a bill's being sent to President Bill Clinton.

In early 1997 the House re-submitted its 104th Congress "dead draft," now called H.R. 5. An historic bill-writing process was established. Senate and House staff held town hall meetings. Those weekly meetings, led by David Hoppe, staff director for Senator Lott, continued until all issues, contentious and otherwise, were addressed. Compromises were made and reluctantly accepted, and Congressional staff submitted new drafts of all sections of the law. In May 1997 the amended IDEA was passed by both houses of Congress and sent to President Bill Clinton for signature.

The bill supports continued education for all children with disabilities. It structures discipline procedures. It supports mediation over appeals. It supports the implementation of effective positive interventions and strategies and aid for children needing those services. It gives the schools latitude to develop school-wide programs and to collaborate with other agencies to ensure adequate services. It suggests that the evaluation process minimize labeling and emphasize processes to assist the individualized education program team in determining how the child's "general curriculum" success could be improved by special education and related services. It replaces psychological reevaluations based on mechanical timelines by a problem-solving process to determine what if any assessments are required to address the student's academic and behavioral needs. These are but a few examples of the significant changes in the IDEA Amendments of 1997 (IDEA 97) that will affect the practices of school psychologists and other members of school-based teams.

The leadership that the National Association of School Psychologists has shown in child advocacy and best professional practice, evident throughout the reauthorization process and development of regulations, continues with the publication of this volume, which brings together the most current information about key provisions of IDEA 97.

I am confident that these practice guidelines will be useful and thought provoking for school-based teams as they continue their work on behalf of children, families, and schools.

Kevin P. Dwyer, NCSP
NASP Governmental Liaison, 1982–1997
NASP Assistant Executive Director, 1993–1998
NASP President, 1999–2000

These remarks were based on "Implementing IDEA 97: An Historical Perspective," published in Communiqué, *December 1999.*

PREFACE

Twenty-five years ago, P.L. 94-142 was passed *in perpetuity*, changing forever the educational landscape for children and youth with disabilities. Within months of the law's enactment, thousands of children, including those who had previously been excluded from school because of the profound nature of their disabilities, were provided access to a free appropriate public education that was individually designed to meet their needs. The original statute was amended several times during the intervening 25 years, becoming first the Education of the Handicapped Act (EHA) and, subsequently, the Individuals with Disabilities Education Act (IDEA). During this period, as children's access opportunities were successfully maximized, greater emphasis was placed on the quality of their educational experiences and the effects of these in enhancing student performance. This focus is particularly evident in the IDEA 1997 (IDEA 97) amendments, which introduced some of the most significant changes in the federal law since its original enactment.

Many of the IDEA 97 amendments have direct implications for members of school-based teams, who are largely responsible for the identification, evaluation, program planning, service delivery, and program evaluation activities that comprise the special education delivery system. Although local education agencies have been legally responsible to meet the requirements of most of the new amendments since July 1997, few practice guidelines are available to assist school-based teams in effective implementation of those new provisions. This volume is intended as a practical resource that can fill that gap.

The volume is designed to provide practical guidelines, model forms, concrete exemplars, and other direct practice strategies associated with quality service delivery within prescribed areas of practice. It is anticipated that it will be a valuable resource for members of school-based teams, including school psychologists, special education and general education teachers, counselors, speech-language pathologists, occupational therapists, physical therapists, and other related service personnel. Because the volume also provides an excellent summary of many of the changes included in IDEA 97, building and district administrators, in particular, may find it an excellent reference for many of the changes that must be initiated in their schools. Given that the volume provides both practice implications and an overview of the IDEA 97 amendments, this resource also may be utilized by college and university faculty for pre-service and in-service training of special education and related service personnel.

The edited volume consists of 11 chapters concerning the IDEA 97 amendments. Nine of the 11 chapters are devoted to key themes in the 1997 amendments that are judged to most directly affect the practice of educational professionals. These chapters describe practice guidelines for (a) student participation in statewide and districtwide assessments; (b) new approaches to assessment and eligibility determination and to conducting reevaluations (c) various aspects of student discipline (e.g., manifestation determination, behavioral plans, functional behavioral assessment, and interim alternative educational settings); (d) expanded opportunities for parent involvement; and (e) strengthening of the IEP to enhance results for students. An introductory chapter providing an overview of the IDEA 97 amendments and a closing chapter devoted to managing and leading school-based change frame those topic-specific chapters.

With the exception of the introductory and closing chapters, which address the 1997 amendments more globally, each chapter employs a common organizational structure. Each of the topical chapters begins with a brief overview concerning the background/purpose of the provision in IDEA 97 to provide an historical and political context for its addition. This is followed by a discussion of the issues and considerations that school-based teams must address when implementing the specific provision on which the chapter focuses, including the relevant research from which practice recommendations can be derived. A section devoted to best practice strategies follows, in which specific practice guidelines for school-based teams are described. Whenever appropriate, this section incorporates lists, charts, examples, forms, and processes that concretely demonstrate the recommended practices. Because of the significant practice changes associated with IDEA 97, a brief section on professional development implications is included in each of the topical chapters. This section outlines the kinds of new learning and new practices that school-based teams need to acquire as individuals, as well as those systemic issues that need to be addressed within educational organizations. Each chapter includes an annotated bibliography considered to be central to the specific provision, particularly as related to implementation by school-based teams.

The contributors to this volume represent leaders in the disciplines of school psychology and special education. They are among the most knowledgeable individuals nationally about the practice implications of the IDEA 97 amendments, as is evident from their previous publications and presentations on these topics as well as their direct practice experience in educational settings.

Successful completion of a volume of this scope requires the collaboration and support of many individuals. First, we thank the National Association of School Psychologists (NASP), whose Publications Board recognized the need for such a volume in the field and committed to its development and publication. Special thanks are extended to Leslie Paige, Chairperson of the NASP Publications Board during the contract negotiation period, who provided us timely and personal feedback; to Veronica Evans Lewis, our liaison from the NASP Publications Board, who provided us with consistent and efficient guidance during the development phase; and to Linda Morgan, Production Manager in the NASP office, who expedited the production of the volume. We also thank several key individuals within our institution for their support. Dr. Barbara Schirmer, a special educator by training and experience who serves as the Department Chairperson of the Department of Educational Foundations and Special Services, provided us both practical and moral support throughout the project. Department secretary, Marcia Kibler, provided efficient clerical support; and graduate students Amanda Tandy and Cari Ritzman contributed valuable editorial assistance.

In addition, we acknowledge the valuable contributions of our external reviewers, who provided proficient and constructive comments on each chapter during its development. These individuals, who represent excellence in scholarship, deserve special distinction for their service to this project.

Finally, we thank the chapter authors. We are immensely privileged to serve as editors of this volume, whose contributing authors represent prominent researchers, practitioners, and leaders in the field of educating and providing services to students with disabilities. We are most grateful to these chapter authors, who contributed their expertise and time at the expense of many competing forces to produce this timely and comprehensive publication. We sincerely appreciate their commitment to and enthusiastic participation in creating this volume.

Cathy Telzrow, Professor of School Psychology
Melody Tankersley, Associate Professor of Special Education
Kent State University

CHAPTER 1

The Individuals with Disabilities Education Act Amendments of 1997:
Implications for School-Based Teams

Mitchell L. Yell
Erik Drasgow
Laurie Ford
University of South Carolina

IDEA '97

PURPOSE

On June 4, 1997, President Bill Clinton signed the Individuals with Disabilities Education Act Amendments of 1997 (IDEA 97) into law. This law amended and reauthorized the Individuals with Disabilities Education Act of 1990 (IDEA) by adding a number of major provisions that likely will result in substantial changes in the education of students with disabilities. The additional provisions of IDEA 97 have the potential to increase the participation of teachers and other service providers in the special education process. IDEA 97 also brings with it an opportunity for members of school-based teams to expand their roles by translating the requirements of IDEA 97 into practice.

The purpose of this chapter is to describe the major changes that appear in IDEA 97 and the effects that these changes will have on members of school-based teams. The chapter begins with a presentation of a brief history of IDEA. The history is followed by a discussion of the changes in IDEA 97 that will have the greatest influence on education personnel. The discussion is followed by an analysis of the changes to determine the possible effects on the roles of school personnel in the special education process. The chapter concludes with recommendations to assist school psychologists and other education personnel in meeting the challenges and opportunities of IDEA 97. Readers should note that many of the changes that are briefly discussed in this chapter will be examined in greater depth in the chapters that follow.

HISTORY OF THE INDIVIDUALS WITH DISABILITIES EDUCATION ACT

President Gerald Ford, signed the Education for All Handicapped Children Act (EAHCA; also called P.L. 94-142) into law on November 29, 1975. The EAHCA combined an educational bill of rights for students with disabilities with the promise of federal financial incentives to assist states in providing appropriate educational programming for eligible students. The EAHCA required participating states to provide a free appropriate public education (FAPE) by September 1, 1978, for all qualified students with disabilities between the ages of 3 and 18 and by September 1, 1980, for all students between the ages of 3 and 21. Furthermore, the EAHCA mandated that eligible students with disabilities had the right to (a) a complete and individualized evaluation using nondiscriminatory testing and evaluation procedures, (b) a free appropriate public education consisting of special education and related services, and (c) educational placement in programs with nondisabled students to the maximum extent appropriate. Additional legislation since the passage of EACHA in 1975 has served to clarify and extend the requirements of EAHCA. These laws and amendments are summarized in Table 1.

Congress passed IDEA 97 to reauthorize and make improvements to IDEA. In the next section the reauthorization process that leads to laws that amend and refund IDEA is described briefly. This will be followed by a description of IDEA 97 with an emphasis on those changes of greatest importance to school-based teams.

REAUTHORIZATION AND IDEA

Congress passes laws that appropriate money in several ways. First, Congress may fund the law on a permanent basis. If it is permanent, then funding will continue as long as the law remains unchanged. Thus, Congress must repeal or amend the law to remove funding. Second, Congress may fund the statute on a limited basis, with the specific funding period designated in the statute. When this period of time expires, Congress must reauthorize funding or the law will expire. Third, Congress may fund parts of a law on a permanent basis and parts of the law on a limited basis.

IDEA has four parts, and falls into the third category. Thus, parts of IDEA are funded permanently and parts of it are funded on a limited basis.

TABLE 1: Major Amendments to the IDEA

Title and Number of Law	Major Changes
The Handicapped Children's Protection Act of 1986; P.L. 99-372	• Courts were granted authority to award attorney's fees to parents or guardians if they prevailed in lawsuits under the IDEA
The Infants and Toddlers with Disabilities Act of 1986; P.L. 99-457	• Provided new funding for programs for children with disabilities from ages birth through age 2 (infant and toddler programs) • Created additional financial incentives for states to make children eligible for special education programs at age 3 (preschool programs)
The Individuals with Disabilities Act of 1990; P.L. 101-476 *EAHCA → IDEA*	• Changed the name of the law from the Education for All Handicapped Children Act (EAHCA) to the Individuals with Disabilities Education Act (IDEA) • Added two categories of disability: Autism and Traumatic Brain Injury • The IEPs of students with disabilities, age 16, must include transition services
The Individuals with Disabilities Act Amendments of 1997; P.L. 105-17	• Made changes to the IEP team and document • Added disciplinary changes to the IDEA

Table 2 lists and describes the four parts of IDEA. Part A contains the general provisions of the statute and does not contain funding. This section of the law, therefore, does not require reauthorization. Part B, the section of IDEA that creates the entitlement to a FAPE and provides federal monies to the states, is funded permanently. This means that the funding for state programs in Part B can be changed only if Congress repeals or amends that section. Parts C and D of IDEA 97 contain discretionary or support programs. These parts support the primary purpose of the law, which is to provide appropriate educational programming for students with disabilities through funding activities such as research, personnel preparation programs, and infant and toddler programs. Specifically, Part C addresses the needs of young children with disabilities; and Part D contains activities, such as personnel preparation, technical assistance, and research grants. Parts C and D are authorized on a limited basis. In the past, Congress has authorized funding for these programs for periods of 4 or 5 years, necessitating periodic reauthorization.

TABLE 2: **Four Parts of the IDEA**

Subchapter	Title	Purpose and Contents
1-Part A	General Provisions	Purposes, definitions
2-Part B	Assistance for Education for All Children with Disabilities	State formula grant program, FAPE entitlements, and procedural safe guards
3-Part C	Infants and Toddlers with Disabilities	Requires that states serve preschool students with disabilities (3 to 5) and authorizes grants to states to provide early intervention services to infants and toddlers (birth to 2)
4-Part D	National Activities to Improve Education of Children with Disabilities	State improvement grants, technical assistance, dissemination of information, funding research and demonstration projects, and training personnel for educating students with disabilities

Previous reauthorizations of IDEA have often been accompanied by amendments to the statute. Some of these amendments have been minor. For example, in 1988, P.L. 100-630 altered some of the law's language; and in 1991, P.L. 102-119 modified parts of the infants and toddlers program. Some amendments, however, have made important changes to IDEA by expanding the rights of students with disabilities and the responsibilities of school districts. Four laws that made significant changes since EAHCA was originally enacted were the Handicapped Children's Protection Act (P.L. 99-372), the Infants and Toddlers with Disabilities Act (P.L. 99-457), the Individuals with Disabilities Education Act Amendments of 1990 (P.L. 101-476), and the Individuals with Disabilities Education Act Amendments of 1997 (P.L. 105-17). The changes made in these laws were incorporated into IDEA as amendments.

IDEA 97 made a number of important changes to the federal special education law that will have a major impact on the ways in which students with disabilities are educated, and thus, on the professional roles of educators and other educational personnel. Indeed, the changes in IDEA 97 represent the most significant changes to special education law since its original passage in 1975.

IDEA 97

In passing IDEA 97, Congress noted that IDEA had been very successful in ensuring access to a free appropriate public education and improving educational results for students with disabilities. Nevertheless, the implementation of IDEA had been impeded by (a) low expectations, (b) insufficient focus on translating research to practice, and (c) too much emphasis on paperwork and legal requirements at the expense of teaching and learning (Yell & Shriner, 1997). The changes incorporated into the law by IDEA 97 were seen as the next important step in providing special education and related services by ensuring that students with disabilities received a quality public education that emphasized the improvement of student performance. The major purpose of IDEA was ensuring access to educational services for students with disabilities, whereas the major purpose of IDEA 97 is to ensure that special education programming for students with disabilities allows them to make *meaningful* educational progress.

Congress' major purposes for making the changes in IDEA 97 are summarized in Table 3. Of these changes, IDEA 97 requirements regarding evaluation, the individualized education program (IEP), and the discipline of students with disabilities will most directly affect educational personnel. Further discussion of requirements associated with these areas follow.

IEP – indiv. edu. prgm

TABLE 3: Congress' Goals in Passing IDEA 97

Major Goal	Explanation
Increasing parental participation	Parents must be more fully involved in the special education process through involvement in evaluation, program planning, and placement decisions
Ensuring student access to the general curriculum	Students with disabilities have an opportunity to be involved in the general education curriculum and be educated with their nondisabled peers
Decreasing inappropriate labeling	State education agencies give increased attention to racial, ethnic, and linguistic diversity to prevent inappropriate identification and mislabeling
Using mediation to resolve disputes	Parents and educators are encouraged to work out their differences using nonadversarial means
Improving educational results	Unnecessary paperwork requirements reduced to free teachers to focus on teaching and learning. Accountability mechanisms are incorporated in IDEA 97 (e.g., measurable annual goals)
Increasing school safety	IDEA 97 now includes disciplinary requirements

Evaluation

Special education begins with the referral and evaluation process that may lead to the provision of specially designed instruction and related services. School psychologists historically have been actively involved with evaluation in the special education process. The reader is referred to Reschly in this volume for additional discussion about the evaluation requirements in IDEA 97. Table 4 contains IDEA 97's requirements regarding evaluations.

The formal assessment and evaluation procedures of IDEA are intended to ensure that (a) complete and individualized evaluations are conducted, (b) special education services are provided to students who demonstrate the need for such services, and (c) requirements for evaluations are implemented consistently in all districts and states and monitored for appropriateness and compliance (Yell &

TABLE 4: IDEA 97's Evaluation Procedures

Area	Explanation
Consent	• If parents fail to respond to school's efforts to secure consent, the school may evaluate the student • If parents refuse consent, the school may use mediation or due process procedures to secure permission to evaluate
Test administration	• Tests must be administered in the child's native language or other mode of communication • Standardized tests must be administered by trained personnel in conformity with the publisher's instruction
Evaluation instruments	• Standardized tests must have been validated for the specific purpose for which they are intended
Procedures	• No single procedure can be used as the sole criterion for determining the presence of a disability or the student's program or placement • The evaluation team must be composed of a multidisciplinary team group, at least one of whom has knowledge in the student's suspected area of disability • The evaluation must be tailored to assess the child's specific areas of educational need, includ-

What about issues of dialects?

Table 4 continued on p. 8

Table 4 continued

	ing information provided by the parent that may assist in determining the student's disability and the content of his or her IEP
Reevaluations	• At least every 3 years (or more frequently if conditions warrant it or parents request a reevaluation) a student in special education must be reevaluated
	• School districts must obtain parental consent to conduct a reevaluation
	• The revaluation must conform to the same procedural criteria as the original evaluation (e.g., tests must not be discriminatory)
	• The IEP team may determine that no additional data are needed, and the reevaluation should focus on collecting information about how to teach the child
	• If the IEP team determines that no additional data are needed, parents must be notified that they have the right to request and receive a full evaluation

Shriner, 1997). IDEA 97 included three major changes to the evaluation process. First, parents must grant consent before schools can reevaluate a student in special education. Second, evaluations must now include information regarding a student's progress in the general education curriculum. Third, IEP teams now can determine the necessity of a complete reevaluation every 3 years. A brief explanation of these three changes is contained in the following section.

Parental Consent for Reevaluations

Parental consent is now required for *reevaluations* unless the school can determine that the parents failed to respond to reasonable attempts to obtain their consent. This means that before a student can be given a complete reevaluation, the school must inform the parents about the nature of the reevaluation and obtain written permission to conduct the reevaluation. Note that consent is not required for routine formative evaluation procedures conducted by school psychologists or by teachers to assess a student's progress toward his or her educational goals. Rather, consent pertains to the complete and individualized reevaluation conducted to determine if the child is still eligible for special education services. If parents do not respond to a school district's efforts to secure their permission, then a school district may proceed with the reevaluation. In such situations it is important to document the efforts to contact the parents.

Involvement and Progress in the General Education Curriculum

All evaluations must include information about the student's involvement and progress in the general curriculum or, for preschoolers, in appropriate activities. This required information has the potential to change the manner by which multidisciplinary teams conduct evaluations. With greater emphasis on the general curriculum, the use of alternative assessment procedures such as curriculum-based assessment or curriculum-based measurement assumes greater importance (see Shinn and Shinn, this volume). Such procedures will likely promote additional communication with family members and teachers as a part of the evaluation process, thus providing families data-based details concerning their child's progress. The additional information requirement provision is intended to force considerations of all factors that might be affecting a student's performance, to facilitate a more ecological approach to the evaluation process, and to reduce the number of students who are improperly placed in special education.

Triennial Reevaluation

The reevaluation process has been streamlined in IDEA 97. Prior to reauthorization, the 3-year revaluation process required an extensive assessment of students in special education. Typically, to satisfy this requirement, a complete assessment battery consisting primarily of standardized tests was administered to students. Under the new law, a 3-year evaluation may rely on existing information and previous evaluations. If the IEP team believes that no additional information is needed, then the team must notify the parent that no further assessment is recommended. In such instances, it is possible that the reevaluation can be conducted with no new assessments being given. The parents must concur with this plan, however, or the school must demonstrate that the parents did not respond to notifications for consent to carry out a no-assessment evaluation.

It is also possible that the parent or team members may conclude that it is best to conduct an assessment in any or all areas of development if it would provide useful information about how to best teach the child. In this regard, the reevaluation process is more purposeful, because then assessment occurs only when it is judged to be necessary. Because many school psychologists report that they spend a significant portion of their time conducting reevaluations (Reschly & Wilson, 1995), this change in reevaluation requirements may permit them to engage in other non-assessment–related activities. The reader is referred to Canter, Hurley, and Reid in this volume for additional discussion about the reevaluation requirements in IDEA 97.

Individualized Education Program

To achieve the purposes of the EAHCA, Congress concluded that the requirement of a written IEP was crucial (Zettel & Ballard, 1982). The IEP became the cornerstone of the law. The primary people in a student's educational environment, including his or her parents, were given an opportunity to participate in planning the educational program. Thus, the IEP itself became the educational blueprint tailored to meet a student's unique needs. All aspects of a student's special education program are directed by the IEP and monitored throughout the IEP process (Smith, 1990). The IEP is so crucial that the failure to develop and implement an IEP properly may render a student's entire special education program legally invalid (Yell, 1998).

The IEP is the key to serving all eligible students with disabilities. The "IEP process ... is devoted to determining the needs of the child and planning for the child's education with the parents and school personnel" (Senate Report, 1997, p. 28). IDEA requires that school districts hold IEP planning meetings for students who are eligible for special education services. The purpose of the IEP planning process is to develop a student's special education program. To ensure that the parents and school personnel develop an appropriate educational program, IDEA mandates rigorous procedural requirements to be followed in the IEP process. Strict adherence to these procedural requirements (e.g., notice, consent, and participants) is extremely important. Major procedural errors on the part of a school district may render an IEP inappropriate (Bateman & Linden, 1998; Yell & Drasgow, 2000). When procedural violations have been detected in the IEP process, courts have scrutinized the effects of the violations. If the violations interfere with the development of the IEP, and a student did not receive an appropriate education as a result, then the IEP and the student's program of special education will be ruled inappropriate. Therefore, it is critical that administrators and special education teachers understand their responsibilities with respect to planning, developing, and reviewing the IEP (Senate Report, 1997).

Preceding reauthorization, Congress heard testimony indicating that IDEA had been extremely successful in improving students' access to public schools. However, concerns were expressed about the performance and educational achievement of students with disabilities in both the special and general education curricula. To address these concerns, Congress mandated a number of changes to both to the IEP process and contents. Major changes are related to (a) the participants who are required to be at the IEP meeting and (b) the content of the IEP.

Participants in the IEP Process

There are two changes in IDEA 97 with respect to the composition of the IEP team. Table 5 lists and describes the requirements regarding participants on the IEP team.

The involvement of a general education teacher in the IEP meeting is required if a student participates or may participate in the general education environment. The school district has the discretion to determine which teachers should be on the IEP team. Only one general education teacher has to be on the team. The

TABLE 5: **The IEP Team**

Participants	Explanation
Parents	The school is required to follow specific procedures to ensure that parents attend and fully participate in the IEP meeting. These procedures include (a) notifying parents enough in advance to ensure that they will have an opportunity to attend the meeting, (b) scheduling meetings at a mutually agreeable time and place, and (c) arranging other methods of including parents if they cannot attend the IEP meeting (e.g., conference calls). The parent can be the biological parent, a guardian, or a surrogate.
Local educational agency representative	A representative of the school or school district must be (a) qualified to provide or supervise the provision of the special education, (b) able to commit school district resources, and (c) able to ensure that the educational services specified in the IEP will be provided.
The student's special education teacher	The special education teacher with primary responsibility for implementing the IEP should attend the IEP meeting.
The student's general education teacher	The general education teacher participating in the meeting should be the teacher who is, or may be, responsible for implementing the IEP. If a student has more than one general education teacher, the LEA may designate which

Table 5 continued on p. 12

Table 5 continued

	teacher or teachers will participate. The LEA is also encouraged to seek contributions from a student's general education teachers who are not on IEP team.
An individual who can interpret the instructional implications of the evaluation results	This individual must attend all IEP meetings. Requiring someone with knowledge and expertise in evaluation at each IEP meeting provides a clearer link between evaluation results and instruction. This person may be someone already on the IEP team (e.g., special education teacher).
Other individuals at the discretion of the parent or school	Either the school or the parents may invite others to the meeting. Confidentiality rules may prevent the attendance of those who are not employed by the school district unless the parents give consent in writing. This may include related services personnel, transition providers, counselors, school social workers.
The student, if appropriate	The school must inform the parents that the student may attend the meeting. Beginning at age 14, the student is an important member of the IEP team because of transition considerations.

teacher should usually be the general education teacher who will be implementing the IEP, although in instances where multiple teachers are involved, the input of all of a student's teachers should be sought and documented. This change reflects the emphasis on general education curricular involvement found throughout IDEA 97. Most students with disabilities receive instruction in the general education classroom for at least part of their day, so general educators usually will be involved in the IEP process. However, the general education teacher may not need to be involved in "*all* aspects of the IEP team's work" (Senate Report, 1997, p. 26). For example, there may be individual tasks (e.g., related services coordination) that do not require regular education participation. The IDEA 97 regulations also indicate that a student's IEP must be made available to all of his or her general education teachers so that they know what modifications are necessary to ensure involvement in general education. School-based teams, therefore, should establish procedures to meet those requirements of the IEP.

The second addition to the IEP team is a member who has knowledge and expertise in evaluation *and* who can interpret the instructional implications of the evaluation results. This requirement provides a clearer link between evaluation results and instruction (Huefner, 2000). The law requires that this member of the IEP team be selected by area of expertise and not by area of discipline. If there are others who can interpret the instructional implications of the evaluation results, then the school psychologist is available to engage in other activities such as intervention, consultation, and work with families.

Finally, a representative of the local educational agency (LEA) has always been required to participate in the IEP meeting. The reason for his or her presence is to ensure that schools provide the educational services specified in the IEP. The school principal, or any member of the school staff designated by the principal, may fill this position. IDEA 97 now requires that the LEA representative must be (a) qualified to provide or supervise special education, (b) knowledgeable about the general education curriculum, and (c) authorized to commit school district resources. In the past, school psychologists and other service providers have often served as the LEA representative on IEP teams; however, now these new requirements must be met before school personnel other than a principal can assume this role.

Content of the IEP Document

According to IDEA 97 the purpose of the IEP "is to tailor the education to the child; not tailor the child to the education" (Senate Report, 1997, p. 27). Special education programming must be different from programming that a student would typically receive in general education. The IEP document codifies the decisions arrived at in the IEP planning process, and new requirements regarding the content of the IEP are specified in IDEA 97. Congress' primary purpose in making these additions was to improve educational results for students with disabilities by ensuring access to the general education curriculum and any general education reforms. Furthermore, IDEA 97 increases accountability by requiring that (a) IEPs contain measurable goals, (b) parents receive regular reports on their children's progress toward achieving these goals, and (c) students with disabilities are included in districtwide and statewide assessment systems. Additionally, when a student's behavior impedes his or her learning or the learning of others, the student's IEPs must address problem behavior, regardless of his or her disability category. In the following sections the required components of the IEP document are explained and the ways in which they may affect school-based teams are discussed.

Present levels of educational performance. The first required component in an IEP is a statement of the student's present level of educational performance. The purpose of the statement is to describe the problems that interfere with the student's education so that annual goals can be developed (Gorn, 1997). In effect, the present levels of performance represent the starting point or baseline by which teams develop and measure the success of the IEP. The statement should contain information about the student's academic performance, test scores (with an explanation of those scores), physical health, sensory status, emotional development, social development, and prevocational and vocational skills. Additionally, this statement should include academic areas and such nonacademic areas as behavioral problems, daily life activities, and mobility. IDEA 97 also requires that this statement include information concerning how students' disabilities affect their involvement and progress in the general education curriculum. Labels (e.g., learning disabled, emotionally disturbed) are not appropriate substitutions for descriptions of educational performance because they have no direct relationship to individualized and effective instruction (Ysseldyke, Algozzine, & Thurlow, 2000).

The statement of needs should be written in objective terms by using information from a student's evaluation. When test scores are included in this section, an explanation of the results understandable to all parties should be provided.

Clearly, the present level of educational performance section will be based on the evaluation conducted prior to the development of the IEP. It is important, therefore, that the evaluation be directed at more than determining eligibility. The evaluation also must provide information that the IEP team can use in determining the appropriate educational program, goals and objectives, special education and related services, and a student's placement. Such requirements mean that the IEP team must include members who are familiar with curriculum in both the special and general education environments. Further, comprehensive evaluations may require that the team members interview teachers and observe students in relevant settings.

Measurable annual goals, benchmarks, and short-term objectives. Further changes to the IEP content require the development of measurable annual goals, including benchmarks or short-term objectives. This is intended to enable parents and educators to accurately determine a student's progress. The goals are written by the IEP team (a) to enable students to be involved and progress in the general education curriculum and (b) to address educational needs related to the disability. As before, these goals focus on remediation of academic or nonacademic problems, and are based on the student's present levels of educational performance.

Annual goals are projections that the team makes regarding the progress of the student in one school year. Annual goals, correctly written, allow the IEP team to monitor a student's progress in a special education program and then to make educational adjustments when necessary (Bateman & Linden, 1998; Deno, 1992; Salvia & Ysseldyke, 1998; Yell, 1998). The primary difference in the statement of goals as required by IDEA 97, relative to the original IDEA, is the emphasis on accurately measuring and reporting a student's progress toward the annual goals.

Benchmarks or short-term objectives (STOs) are written for each annual goal. These are markers that enable educators, parents, and others to monitor a student's progress toward the annual goals. The benchmarks and STOs tell us how far a student has progressed toward meeting his or her annual goal by a specified date (Bateman & Linden, 1998). According to IDEA 97, benchmarks are "major milestones" toward achieving a goal. For example, benchmarks could be written to measure a student's progress toward his or her annual goal every 9 weeks. STOs are also progress markers and are written for shorter time periods. In IDEA 97, STOs are referred to as "intermediate steps" toward meeting the annual goals. STOs are measured more frequently than are benchmarks; for example, they may be measured every 6 weeks. Benchmarks and STOs are not synonymous. Both are used for monitoring a student's progress, but the frequency of measurement is different. If measurement of a benchmark or STO indicates that a student's progress makes it unlikely that the annual goal will be met, then the teacher must use this information to make an instructional or programmatic change. Congress viewed the requirement of "measurable" annual goals and benchmarks or STOs as "crucial to the success of the IEP" (Senate Report, 1997, p. 25). If a student achieves the individual benchmarks or STOs, then he or she logically must achieve the annual goals.

IEP teams may need to make adjustments to their assessment procedures to ensure that the annual goals, benchmark, and STO requirements are met. These adjustments include a greater understanding of the student's abilities compared not only with same age peers but also compared to their performance relative to the school program in which their instruction occurs. This is necessary because educational programming should be individual to a student and be built upon his or her unique pattern of strengths in a particular educational environment.

Reporting requirements. There is an accountability provision built into the annual goal-benchmark-STO strategy that reflects Congress' intent to increase accountability. IDEA 97 requires that parents be informed of their child's progress toward annual goals as often as parents of a nondisabled child are informed of their child's progress. For example, if a school normally sends home interim marking period reports at 4 1/2 weeks and report cards at 9 weeks for each quarter of the school year, then special educators must report progress at the same frequency. The Senate suggested a method of providing feedback to parents about their child's progress, such as providing an IEP Report Card with "checkboxes or equivalent options that ... enable the parents and the special educator to review and judge ... performance on a ... multipoint continuum" (Senate Report, 1997, p. 25). A student's progress and ratings on the goals, benchmarks, and STOs might be communicated on a scale ranging from "No Progress" to "Completed." In this way, the effects of the general education, special education, and related services a student receives can be evaluated in concert so that the student's total school experience is considered.

Special education and related services. The third major component in the IEP is a statement of the specific educational services to be provided by the school. This includes special education, related services, and supplementary aids and services that are required to assist a student to attain the IEP goals and objectives. Services provided to students should enable the student to (a) advance appropriately toward attaining the annual goals, (b) be involved in and show progress in the general education curriculum and to participate in extracurricular and other nonacademic activities, and (c) be educated with students without disabilities. Furthermore, the amount of time that is committed to each service must be appropriate to the student's needs and clear to those who developed the IEP (Bateman & Linden, 1998). Related services are any services that are necessary for a student to benefit from his or her education. Examples of related services are speech and language services, physical and occupational therapy, orientation and mobility services, assistive technology services and devices, psychological services, and counseling services.

Supplementary aids and services and program modification or supports. IDEA 97 added a requirement that the IEP document should contain program modifications or supports for school personnel. These modifications and supports are defined as "aids, services, and other supports that are provided in regular education classes or other education-related settings to enable children with disabilities to be educated with same age peers to the maximum extent appropriate" [IDEA 20 U.S.C. § 1401(25)]. This section is included so that the IEP team will not only consider those services needed to enable the student to benefit from special education but also will consider services necessary to maintain the student in an integrated setting.

Transition services. The purpose of including transition services is to infuse a long-range perspective into the IEP process and to help students to better reach their potential in post-school life (Yell, 1998). According to Maag and Katsiyannis (1998), the transition process must be outcome-oriented and encompass a broad array of services and experiences that lead to employment and must promote movement from school to other post-school outcomes. An IEP that includes transition services must include the areas that are listed in IDEA's definition (i.e., instruction, community services, and employment and other adult-living objectives). In IDEA 97 an additional transition requirement specified that certain transition services begin at age 14. A statement must be included in the IEP focusing primarily on a student's courses of study (e.g., vocational education classes) so that the student's curriculum will mesh with the transition services to be offered when the student turns 16. Additionally, this statement must be updated annually.

Participation in statewide and districtwide assessments. IDEA 97 includes several new requirements concerning the participation of students with disabilities in statewide or districtwide assessments with or without modifications (see Ysseldyke, Nelson, and House, this volume). It is the task of the IEP team to determine if a student can participate in statewide assessments. Because students with disabilities may need individual modifications and accommodations to participate in these assessments, the IEP must include a statement detailing all such modifications. However, the Office of Special Education Programs in the U.S. Department of Education has advised that states may restrict the types of modifications or accommodations they allow to be used in statewide testing (Shriner, 2000). When considering the use of modifications in statewide testing programs, therefore, IEP teams should be familiar with state rules and regulations. If the IEP team determines that a student cannot be accurately assessed in statewide or districtwide assessments, even with modifications, then the IEP must contain a statement explaining why the assessment is not appropriate. The statement also must identify an alternative assessment that will be used in place of the statewide or districtwide assessments.

These requirements reflect the logic the Senate committee used in its explanation of participation considerations: "The majority of children identified as eligible for special education are capable of participating in the general curriculum to varying degrees. The new focus is intended to produce ... access for appropriate participation in particular areas of the curriculum" (Senate Report, 1997, p. 22). If, after discussing the student's program with those familiar with the general curriculum, it is determined that no portion of the curriculum is appropriate, even with modification, then the decision to use an alternate assessment strategy is indicated.

Addressing problem behavior in the IEP. IDEA 97 requires that if a student with disabilities has behavior problems that impede his or her learning or the learning of others, then the IEP team shall consider strategies, including positive behavioral interventions, strategies, and supports, to address these problems. These requirements will affect the IEP planning process for students with disabilities who have a history of, or are currently displaying, problem behavior. Congress clearly intended that IEP teams approach problem behavior in an educational and proactive manner rather than by reacting with punishment. This means that when problem behavior is evident, the IEP team must conduct an assessment to determine the function the behavior serves and develop a plan to teach appropriate socially acceptable replacement behaviors. Thus, the IEPs of students with disabilities who exhibit problem behavior, regardless of category, should address the behaviors in the present levels of educational performance, the goals and objectives, and the special education services section. Furthermore, if the behavior plan involves program modification to the general education classroom, then these modifications must be included in the IEP.

Neither IDEA 97 nor the regulations detail what problem behaviors are covered under the law. Drasgow, Yell, Bradley, and Shriner (1999) contend that these behaviors include (a) disruptive behaviors that distract the teacher from teaching and students from learning, (b) noncompliance, (c) abuse of property, (d) verbal abuse, and (e) aggression toward students and staff. Moreover, Drasgow et al. (1999) state that if an IEP team fails to address problem behaviors in the student's IEP, then that failure would deprive the student of a FAPE, which could result in application of the law's sanctions against the school district.

Additionally, when a school suspends or places a student with disabilities in an interim alternative educational setting for 10 or more days and the school has not conducted a functional behavioral assessment and implemented a behavior intervention plan, then the IEP team must do so within 10 days. If such a plan is already included in the IEP, the team must meet to review the plan to determine its appropriateness and modify it if necessary.

These requirements will affect the IEP planning process for students with disabilities who have a history of, or are currently displaying, problem behavior. Congress clearly intended that IEP teams approach problem behavior in a proactive rather than reactive manner. The IDEA 97 requirements regarding functional behavioral assessments and behavior intervention plans are examined in the following sections.

Functional behavioral assessment. Functional behavioral assessment (FBA) refers to gathering information about factors that reliably predict and maintain problem behavior to develop more effective intervention plans (Horner & Carr, 1997; O'Neill et al., 1997). The factors related to the occurrence of problem behavior consist of (a) setting events (i.e., events that make it more likely that problem behavior will occur), (b) antecedents (i.e., events or actions that precede and trigger problem behavior), and (c) consequences (i.e., events or actions that occur as a result of problem behavior). In essence, an FBA is used to develop an understanding of the cause and purpose of problem behavior (Drasgow et al., 1999). (See Tilly, Knoster, and Ikeda, this volume.)

Horner and Carr (1997) state that an FBA has two important implications for developing interventions for problem behavior. First, it focuses on environmental events (i.e., antecedents, consequences, and setting events). Thus, problem behavior is viewed as the result of challenging social situations for which the problem behavior represents an attempted solution (e.g., yelling is one way to get attention) rather than viewing problem behavior as the result of invisible, dynamic forces residing within a person. Second, intervention is not focused on managing or controlling a person but instead on redesigning the environment and on building new skills that make the problem behavior irrelevant, inefficient, and ineffective in that environment.

Horner, O'Neill, and Flannery (1993) suggest that an FBA should achieve four outcomes: (a) operational definition of the problem behavior or problem behaviors; (b) identification of the factors that predict the occurrence and nonoccurrence of the problem behaviors (e.g., times, places, activities); (c) identification of, or hypotheses about, the consequences responsible for the problem behavior; (d) verification of the predictors and consequences through direct observation.

Behavior intervention plans. The IEP team designs a behavior intervention plan (BIP) based on the FBA (see Tankersley, Landrum, Cook, and Balan, this volume). The BIP is a behavior change program that emphasizes teaching prosocial behaviors to replace a student's inappropriate behaviors (Drasgow et al., 1999). The key component of the BIP is the use of positive behavioral interventions that do not rely on coercion or punishment for behavior change (Dunlap & Koegel, 1999).

Beyond indicating that a BIP has to be individualized to meet the needs of different students in different educational environments, IDEA 97 does not provide details about the composition of the plan. However, O'Neill et al. (1997) suggest that all BIPs should contain the following generic key features: (a) an observable and measurable description of the problem behavior; (b) an identified purpose of problem behavior as a result of the FBA; (c) a general strategy, or combination of strategies, for changing the problem behavior; (d) a game plan for when, where, and how often the strategy will be implemented; and (e) a consistent system of monitoring and evaluating the effectiveness of the plan.

Disciplining Students in Special Education

Perhaps the most widely discussed change in IDEA 97 relates to the discipline of students with disabilities. Congress heard testimony regarding the lack of parity school officials faced when making decisions about disciplining students with and without disabilities who violated the same school rules (Senate Report, 1997). That is, school officials were concerned that some disciplinary actions (e.g., long-term suspension) that could be used when students in general education committed certain violations of school rules were prohibited when students in special education committed the same violations. This dual disciplinary standard was seen as restricting school administrators' options when disciplining students. To address these concerns, Congress added a section to IDEA 97 that was intended to balance school officials' obligation to ensure that schools are safe and orderly environments conducive to learning with their obligation to ensure that students with disabilities receive a free appropriate public education.

Disciplinary Procedures

School officials may discipline a student with disabilities in the same manner as they discipline students without disabilities with two notable exceptions. First, school officials may unilaterally change the placement of a student for disciplinary purposes to an appropriate interim alternative educational setting (IAES), another setting, or by suspending the student to the extent that these disciplinary methods are used with students without disabilities. The primary difference between disciplining students with and without disabilities is that students who are disabled must receive educational services from the school if their suspension or placement change exceeds 10 school days. This means that the school must continue to implement the IEP (e.g., goals and objectives, related services) when a student is suspended in excess of 10 school days during *a school year*.

Second, school officials may unilaterally place a student with disabilities in an appropriate IAES for up to 45 days if the student brings a weapon to school or a school function. There are no laws regarding suspension or expulsion if a student without disabilities brings a weapon to school or a school function. For purposes of IDEA 97, Congress defines a weapon as a "... device, instrument, material, or substance, animate or inanimate, that is used for, or is readily capable of, causing death or serious bodily injury, except that such term does not include a pocket knife with a blade of less than 2 1/2 inches in length" (Senate Report, 1997). Schools also may place a student with disabilities in an IAES if the student knowingly possesses, uses, or sells illegal drugs or sells or solicits the sale of a controlled substances at school or a school function. Controlled substances are any drugs that have a high potential for abuse. (For the list of controlled substances see the Controlled Substances Act, 21 U.S.C. § 812(c).)

A hearing officer may order a 45-day change in placement when a student with disabilities presents a substantial risk to the safety of others. In such situations, school officials may request an expedited hearing to have a student removed from school. School officials must present evidence to the hearing officer that maintaining the student with disabilities in the current placement is substantially likely to result in injury to the student or to others and that school officials have made reasonable efforts to minimize this risk of harm. A hearing officer will order such a change in placement if he or she determines that the school has "substantial evidence" that demonstrates that (a) maintaining the current placement is substantially likely to result in injury to the student or others, (b) the IEP and placement are appropriate, (c) the school has made reasonable efforts to minimize the risk of harm, and (d) the IAES meets the criteria set forth in IDEA 97. IDEA 97 define substantial evidence as being a "beyond a preponderance of evidence" (Sec. 615 (k)(10)(C)).

Additionally, the school must have an appropriate IEP and placement, and must place the student in an IAES that meets the requirements of IDEA 97. This means that the school must continue to provide the special education services, supplementary aids and services, program modifications, and related services listed in the IEP, including the interventions to address the student's problem behavior.

Manifestation Determination

A manifestation determination (i.e., a review of the relationship between a student's disability and misconduct) must be conducted within 10 days of the action when school officials seek a change of placement, suspension, or expulsion in excess of 10 school days (see Kubick, Bard, and Perry, this volume). A student's IEP team must conduct the manifestation determination. If the determination is made that no relationship exists between the misconduct and disability, then the same disciplinary procedures that would be used with students who are not disabled may be used for a student with disabilities (i.e., long-term suspension, expulsion). Educational services, however, must be continued. If the team finds a relationship between a student's disability and misconduct, school officials may still seek a change of placement but cannot use long-term suspension or expulsion. The parents of the student may request an expedited due process hearing if they disagree with the results of the manifestation determination. The student's placement during the hearing will be in an IAES.

When conducting the manifestation determination, the IEP team must consider all relevant information regarding the behavior in question. This includes evaluation and diagnostic results, information supplied by the parents, and direct observations of the student. Furthermore, the team must examine the student's current IEP and placement to determine if they are appropriate. The IEP team can determine that the misconduct was *not* a manifestation of a student's disability only when the following four criteria are met: (a) the student's IEP and placement were appropriate (including the behavior intervention plan), (b) the IEP was implemented as written; (c) the student's disability did not impair the ability of the student to understand the impact and consequences of the behavior subject to the disciplinary sanction; and (d) the student's disability did not impair the student's ability to control the behavior at issue.

Interim Alternative Educational Setting

The school must assure that the student with disabilities continues to receive special education and related services in a setting other than the public school when that student is removed from school for more than 10 days (see Telzrow and Naidu, this volume). This setting is referred to in IDEA 97 as the IAES. The law describes the standards that the IAES must meet. First, the IEP team must determine the setting. Although the IAES may not necessarily be in the school environment, the student must be able to continue to participate in the general education curriculum and continue to receive the services and modifications listed in the IEP. Moreover, the student must continue to work toward his or her goals and objectives of the IEP, including goals that address the behavior problems that led to the placement.

Legal challenges to school district's IAES placements have focused on the quality of educational services that are provided to students in these settings (Yell, Katsiyannis, Bradley, & Rozalski, 2000). These challenges have been successful when the school districts have failed to provide appropriate special education and related services to students when they were in an IAES. It is, therefore, vital that IEP teams understand and apply the law, when making such placements.

IMPLICATIONS OF **IDEA 97** FOR SCHOOL-BASED TEAMS

IDEA 97 will have a significant impact on the way that students with disabilities are served in public education. The new requirements place a greater emphasis on improving educational services for students with disabilities. Thus, the roles of school-based team members will be expanded and altered to meet these new requirements. These changing roles have important implications for the preparation of school personnel at both the preservice and inservice levels. Members of school-based teams need to be trained in (a) meeting the requirements of IDEA 97, (b) developing effective programs for students with disabilities, and (c) preventing and remediating problem behaviors. The following guidelines are offered to help prepare members of school-based teams to meet the requirements of IDEA 97.

Training in the Requirements of IDEA 97

IDEA 97 contains the most important changes to federal special education law since the original passage of the EAHCA in 1975. These changes include new evaluation procedures, a tighter connection between the evaluation results and educational programming, an emphasis on measurable goals and meaningful educational benefits, and a more proactive approach to addressing problem behavior. Members of school-based teams will be responsible for ensuring that these changes in the law are implemented in public schools throughout the United States. Preparation at the preservice level, therefore, must place greater emphasis on preparing professionals to meet the requirements of IDEA 97.

The failure of school-based teams to apply the law's requirements to students' educational programs likely will result in inappropriate IEPs and, thus, in the denial of a FAPE. The denial of a FAPE may, in turn, lead to due process hearings, litigation, and legal sanctions against the offending school districts. Preservice and inservice educational opportunities should be provided to ensure that members of school-based teams thoroughly understand their responsibilities under IDEA 97 to meet the legal requirements of the law.

Training in Developing Effective Programs for Students with Disabilities

According to IDEA 97, effective programs for students with disabilities (a) are based on a full and individualized evaluation of a student's needs; (b) contain measurable goals, benchmarks, and short-term objectives that are appropriate given a student's ability; and (c) provide special education services and general education program modifications that will result in a student making meaningful and measurable progress toward his or her goals. There are three implications for training members of school-based teams to develop effective programs. First, school-based team members must achieve a better understanding of conducting meaningful assessments that lead directly to educational programming. The purpose of the evaluation is to gather information (a) to determine if a student is eligible for services in special education and (b) to develop the student's educational program. Assessment begins with a determination of eligibility and continues by contributing useful *and* functional information about a student's needs and how best to meet them.

Second, team members must write *measurable* annual goals, benchmarks, and objectives that are appropriate given a student's skills and abilities. Annual goals are statements of what the team believes a student can reasonably accomplish in one year with effective educational programming. Benchmarks and objectives are statements of how far a student will progress toward his or her goal by a specified date. To ensure that this part of a student's program is appropriate, members of school-based teams will need training in using the results of assessments to write annual goals that can be measured at the end of a school year. Furthermore, teams need training in monitoring a student's progress during the school year to determine if it is sufficient to allow him or her to achieve the annual goals. Clearly, team members must also be able to adjust instructional programs if formative data indicate that a student's progress is not sufficient.

Third, team members must be knowledgeable about the full range of special education services, related services, and general education programs to ensure that educational programs will facilitate a student's advancement toward his or her goals. Moreover, these special education and general education services must result in meaningful educational benefit.

Preventing and Remediating Problem Behavior in the Classroom

If a student with a disability has behavior problems, regardless of his or her category of disability, then the IEP team should consider strategies, including positive behavior supports and interventions to address those problem behaviors. This new requirement reflects an empirically driven proactive approach to reducing problem behavior combined with an increase in school accountability for implementing these procedures (Drasgow et al., 1999).

Addressing problem behaviors in a proactive manner requires IEP teams to conduct FBAs, write measurable goals, benchmarks, and objectives, and develop proactive BIPS. Moreover, these proactive procedures require that BIPS include prevention components (e.g., teaching socially acceptable replacement behaviors) rather than reacting to problem behavior with punishment procedures. Punishment is aimed at behavioral reduction, whereas BIPS are aimed at increasing skills. The provisions for students with significant behavior problems likely will require a behavioral assessment that includes direct observation in multiple environments, on-going program development and monitoring, and well-developed consultation skills.

Members of school-based teams should be trained in the use of behavioral assessments and positive behavioral programming. Such training should include the appropriate use of disciplinary procedures as well as legal ramifications of these procedures. A policy letter from the U.S. Department of Education notes the importance of training teachers and educational personnel in the effective use of behavior management strategies, indicating that the appropriate use of these strategies is essential to ensure the success of interventions to ameliorate problem behavior (*OSEP Discipline Guidance*, 1997).

Summary

IDEA 97 will require changes in the ways that students with disabilities are educated. These changes have the potential for expanding and enhancing the ways that educators deliver services to students with disabilities. At present, states are in the process of revising rules and guidelines so that these conform to the new law and its regulations. Therefore, teachers and other professionals should consult the rules and regulations in their respective states. The courts will also further clarify the meaning of the changes in IDEA 97. Nevertheless, in their current form, these changes portend significant alterations in the roles of educators and other members of school-based teams. The chapters that follow will provide in-depth discussions of many of these changes.

REFERENCES

Bateman, B., & Linden, M. (1998). *Better IEPS* (3rd ed.). Longmont, CO: Sopris West.

Deno, S. L. (1992). The nature and development of curriculum-measurement. *Preventing School Failure, 36,* 5–11.

Drasgow, E., Yell, M. L., Bradley, R., & Shriner, J. G. (1999). The IDEA amendments of 1997: A school-wide model for conducting functional behavioral assessments and developing behavior intervention plans. *Education and Treatment of Children, 22,* 244–266.

Dunlap, G., & Koegel, R. L. (1999). Welcoming introduction. *Journal of Positive Behavior Interventions,1,* 2–3.

Gorn, S. (1997). *The answer book on individualized education programs.* Horsham, PA.: LRP.

Horner, R. H., & Carr, E. G. (1997). Behavioral support for students with severe disabilities: Functional assessment and comprehensive intervention. *The Journal of Special Education, 31,* 84–104.

Horner, R. H., O'Neill, R. E., & Flannery, K. B. (1993). Effective behavior support plans. In M. E. Snell (Ed.), *Instruction of students with severe disabilities* (4th ed.). (pp.184-214). New York: Macmillan.

Huefner, D. S. (2000). The risks and opportunities of the IEP requirements under IDEA 97. *Journal of Special Education, 33,* 194–206.

Individuals with Disabilities Education Act Regulations, 34 C. F. R. § 300, 301, Appendix C to Part 300: Notice of Interpretation.

Individuals with Disabilities Education Act, 20 U.S.C. § 1401-1485.

Maag, J. W., & Katsiyannis, A. (1998). Challenges facing successful transition for youth with E/BD. *Behavioral Disorders, 23,* 209–221.

O'Neill, R. E., Horner, R. H., Albin, R. W., Sprague, J. R., Storey, K., & Newton, J. S. (1997). *Functional assessment and program development for problem behavior.* Pacific Grove, CA: Brooks/Cole.

OSEP Discipline Guidance, 26 IDELR 923 (OSEP 1997).

Reschly, D.J., & Wilson, M. S. (1995). School psychology faculty and practitioners: 1986 to 1991 trends in demographic characteristics, roles, satisfaction, and system reform. *School Psychology Review, 24,* 62–80.

Salvia, J., & Ysseldyke, J. E. (1998). *Assessment.* Boston: Houghton Mifflin.

Senate Report (1997). Senate Report of the Individuals with Disabilities Act Amendments of 1997 available at *http://wais.access.gpo.gov.*

Shriner, J.G. (2000). Legal perspectives on school outcomes assessment for students with disabilities. *Journal of Special Education, 33,* 242–256.

Smith, S. W., (1990). Individualized education programs (IEPs) in special education-from intent to acquiescence. *Exceptional Children, 57,* 6–14.

Yell, M. L. (1998). *The law and special education*. Upper Saddle River, NJ: Merrill/ Prentice-Hall.

Yell, M. L., & Drasgow, E. (2000). Litigating a free appropriate public education: The Lovaas hearings and cases. *Journal of Special Education, 33*, 206–215.

Yell, M. L., Katsiyannis, A., Bradley, R., & Rozalski, M. F. (2000). Ensuring compliance with the disciplinary provisions of IDEA '97: Challenges and opportunities. *Journal of Special Education Leadership, 13*, 204-216.

Yell, M. L., & Shriner, J. G. (1997). The IDEA amendments of 1997: Implications for special and general education teachers, administrators, and teacher trainers. *Focus on Exceptional Children, 30,* 1–19.

Ysseldyke, J. E., Algozzine, B., & Thurlow, M. L. (2000). *Critical issues in special education*. Boston: Houghton Mifflin.

Zettel, J. J., & Ballard, J. (1982). The Education for All Handicapped Children Act of 1975 (P. L. 94-142): Its history, origins, and concepts. In J. Ballard, B. Ramirez, & F. Weintraub (Eds.), *Special education in America: Its legal and governmental foundations* (pp. 11-22), Reston, VA: The Council for Exceptional Children.

ANNOTATED BIBLIOGRAPHY

Drasgow, E., Yell, M.L., Bradley, R, & Shriner, J.G. (1999). The IDEA amendments of 1997: A school-wide model for conducting functional behavioral assessments and developing behavior intervention plans. *Education and Treatment of Children, 22,* 244–266.

This article outlines a model for forming school-based teams to work with IEP teams in conducting FBAs and developing BIPs.

Huefner, D.S. (2000). *Getting comfortable with special education law: A framework for working with children with disabilities*. Norwood, MA: Christopher-Gordon.

This textbook covers all aspects of special education law. It includes coverage of the IDEA 97 regulations released in 1999.

Journal of Special Education, Vol. 33(4), Winter, 2000. This is a special issue edited by Mitchell L. Yell and Erik Drasgow.

The issue is devoted to legal issues in special education. It includes coverage of IDEA 97 (e.g., IEPs, discipline).

Yell, M.L. (1998). *The law and special education*. Upper Saddle River, NJ: Merrill/ Prentice-Hall.

This textbook covers all aspects of special education law. It was published prior to the release of the IDEA 97 regulations in 1999.

Yell, M. L., & Shriner, J. G. (1997). The IDEA amendments of 1997: Implications for special and general education teachers, administrators, and teacher trainers. *Focus on Exceptional Children, 30,* 1–19.

This issue covers all aspects of the IDEA 97. However, it was published before the final regulations were released in 1999.

CHAPTER 2

Statewide and Districtwide Assessments:
Current Status and Guidelines for Student
Accommodations and Alternate Assessments

James E. Ysseldyke
J. Ruth Nelson
Allison L. House
National Center on Educational Outcomes
University of Minnesota

BACKGROUND/PURPOSE OF ASSESSMENT PROVISIONS IN IDEA 97

With the intensified attention to the performance of students on state achievement tests and probing questions directed at our educational leaders and systems, there has been an increasing push for educational accountability and for direct communication between those inside and outside the educational arena about how students are doing locally, nationally, and even internationally. Since 1985, researchers have responded to concerns raised by legislators, bureaucrats, and policy makers about the extent to which *students with disabilities* were profiting from their educational experiences. As well as expected? Better than expected? Worse?

Examination of the major national databases, such as the National Assessment of Educational Progress (NAEP) and the National Education Longitudinal Study (NELS), revealed that scores of students with disabilities were excluded from those reports, and, worse yet, the students were excluded from the opportunity to participate in national assessments (McGrew, Algozzine, Spiegel, Thurlow, & Ysseldyke, 1993; McGrew, Thurlow, Shriner, & Spiegel, 1992). It was estimated at that time that "approximately 40% to 50% of all school-age students with disabilities" were excluded from these national data collection programs (NAEP, NELS) (McGrew et al., 1992, p. 18). Indications were that students were excluded because of an absence of available accommodations or in an effort to keep scores high.

As a direct result of these investigations, focus groups were conducted with representatives from national data collection agencies (e.g., National Center of Education Statistics, NCES) and with state assessment and special education directors to develop approaches to increase participation of students with disabilities in large-scale assessments. A self-study guide was developed to help states, districts, and federal agencies increase participation of students with disabilities (Thurlow, Ysseldyke, & Olsen, 1996; Ysseldyke, Thurlow, McGrew, & Vanderwood, 1994). Journal articles, policy briefs, technical reports, and conference presentations increasingly addressed the inclusion of students with disabilities in large-scale assessment.

In the current reauthorization of Individuals with Disabilities Education Act (IDEA 97) (Individuals with Disabilities Education Act Amendments, 1997), the U.S. Congress included new statements about the participation of students with disabilities in large-scale assessment, their inclusion in reports of test results, and the creation of alternate assessments. Some of the key IDEA 97 provisions that now directly affect assessment practice and are the subject of this chapter include:

- Participation in state assessments: Students with disabilities will be included in general statewide and districtwide assessments with appropriate accommodations. For those unable to participate in general assessments, the state education agency (SEA) or the local education agency (LEA) shall develop guidelines for participation in alternate assessments and conduct those assessments no later than July 1, 2000.

- Reporting of state assessment results: The SEA was required to report with the same frequency it does for nondisabled students (a) the number of children participating in the regular and alternate assessments and (b) the performance on regular assessments by July 1, 1998. The SEA must also report, with the same frequency it does for nondisabled students, performance on alternate assessments by July 1, 2000.

These new IDEA 97 requirements occurred after a great deal of independent progress within states to include students with disabilities in statewide assessments.

ISSUES AND CONSIDERATIONS FOR SCHOOL-BASED TEAMS IN IMPLEMENTING THE ASSESSMENT PROVISIONS

Why the concern about including all students with disabilities in assessment? For just a moment, consider the following scenario. A building principal, Karen, picks up a copy of her local paper and reads a front page article on the performance of the students in her school. The students in her school scored thirty-seventh in the state in mathematics and twenty-eighth in the state in reading. She is concerned about these results and contacts the district's director of research to ask about why her school did not perform better. In a neighboring school, the principal, Sam, picks up the same newspaper and is pleased to see that students in his school scored third in mathematics and second in reading. Discussions in the first school led to the discovery that all students were included in their assessments, but that the schools at the top of the list (such as Sam's school) excluded 20% or more of their students. The Director gives Karen exemption information provided by the district that reveals that Sam's school excluded students receiving services in special education, English language support, and Title I. They also exempted any students on free and reduced price lunches from participating in their state assessment. Karen's office receives hundreds of angry calls about the results, and Sam's office receives primarily congratulatory calls about the results. How does Karen feel? Does she believe that the playing field is level?

In early 1998, SEA, LEA, and testing personnel met to discuss issues that states confront in efforts to implement the assessment provisions of the revised IDEA. One issue highlighted was the exclusion of various types of students from large-scale testing (Ysseldyke, Thurlow, Kozleski, & Reschly, 1998). The group argued that exclusion from large-scale assessment occurs at three points. First, the needs of students with disabilities are not necessarily considered when developing test items. Bias review panels may not include persons with disabilities or those who can advocate for students with disabilities. During test administration, students with disabilities may be asked to stay home or to go on a field trip when all the other students are testing (*Why Johnny Stayed Home*, 1997). Finally, even if students with disabilities were tested, many times, then their results are not publicly reported (Ysseldyke, Thurlow, Kozleski et al., 1998). When consequences to educational systems follow results, there is a perception that negative consequences will follow the reporting of results on the performance of students with disabilities. It is assumed that their scores will "drag down other scores." Rewards are in place for some schools that manage to achieve high levels of performance. However, as the scenario described earlier illustrated, rarely does one stop and take a moment to ponder the accuracy of such results (e.g., Who is actually included in the test results?).

Issues Relative to Standards

Many states have brought together various stakeholder groups to identify the outcomes they would like their high school seniors to achieve, and have translated these outcomes into state standards. Nearly all states ($N = 49$) have or are developing standards for their educational systems (American Federation of Teachers, 1998). Only half of these states say that their standards are for "all students," and only 8% define "all students" as including students with disabilities (Thurlow, Ysseldyke, Gutman, & Geenen, 1998). States have seen the need for students to develop other skills beyond academics. Over 95% of states have standards that focus on areas beyond academics. When states conducted design groups for their standards, only eight states included special education personnel in the development of their standards. This has led to standards that are overly narrow and aren't inclusive of all students with disabilities' needs or goals (Thurlow, Ysseldyke, Gutman et al., 1998).

Large-Scale Assessment Issues

The issues concerning students with disabilities participating in large-scale assessment are listed in Table 1. These are divided into general issues, and specific considerations related to participation, accommodation, reporting, and alternate assessment. In the sections that follow, the current status in each of these areas is summarized, followed by a description of relevant issues.

General Issues

Four general issues are listed in Table 1. The first challenge for many state departments of education is to ensure that their assessments and content or curricular standards are aligned. Teachers regularly express concerns about whether students are being given an opportunity to learn the content of the tests and about whether tests measure what students are being taught. This is a concern, in part, because many state assessments were in place before states had standards. Currently, 39 states are focusing much attention on aligning their assessments and standards (Ysseldyke, 1998).

Many states have high stakes accountability systems on the basis of which positive or negative consequences are delivered to systems or students. Student performance on assessments is usually one factor considered in making system accountability decisions. An accountability system, by definition, requires that there are consequences attached to the results. Approximately 40 states have consequences for schools or staff when targets are not attained. These include negative consequences like probation or watch lists, warnings, loss of accreditation, takeover by the state, funding loss, and dissolution of individual schools, or positive consequences like funding gains and regulatory waivers (Bond, Roeber, & Connealy, 1998).

Another general large-scale assessment issue for students with disabilities is graduation exams. Twenty states require students to pass a graduation exam to receive a standard diploma, and three more states have graduation exams pending for future years (Guy, Shin, Lee, & Thurlow, 1999). All of these states allow students with disabilities to earn a standard diploma by passing the exam. In

TABLE 1: **Large-Scale Assessment Issues**

General Issues
- Alignment of assessments with standards
- High stakes
- Graduation/diploma issues
- Cost

Participation Issues
- Absence of data on participation
- Participation rates
- Definitional confusion
- Responsibility for results
- Decision making

Accommodation Issues
- Disability-specific versus need-driven
- Variability among states
- Discrepancy between policy and practice
- Lack of empirical data

Reporting Issues
- Aggregation versus disaggregation
- Types of scores used
- Status of public reports

Alternate Assessment Issues
- Eligibility
- Nature of state or school district standards
- Selection of data for alternate assessment
- Reporting results
- Scores
- Link to standards

nearly all states, students have multiple opportunities to pass the exam. However, modifications to the exam requirements were available to students with disabilities in only four states (Minnesota, New Jersey, Ohio, Texas). For three of the states, students with disabilities could be exempted from the test and still receive a standard diploma by meeting Individualized Education Program (IEP) goals.

Minnesota was the only state that allowed students with disabilities to pass the exit exam with different scores (Guy et al., 1999).

The cost of including students with disabilities in large-scale assessment is another frequently cited general concern, although limited information about the costs of accommodations is available at this time. A study of the assessment systems in Maryland and Kentucky examined the resources required for implementation of an alternate assessment (Ysseldyke, Thurlow, Erickson et al., 1996). In Maryland, the pilot version of their alternate assessment cost approximately $31.25 per student for basic and ongoing costs, and $191.25 per student for startup costs. When compared to the $5000–8000 spent for educating a student for a year, this cost is relatively nominal. Fewer than 0.5% of all students in Kentucky participate in the alternate assessment, with a total yearly cost of $75,000–90,000. More research on the costs of including students with disabilities in assessments is clearly needed, but as of now the costs are not extraordinary.

Participation Issues

IDEA 97 requires that all students with disabilities participate in state and district large-scale assessments. There are three ways in which students with disabilities can participate: They may take the regular assessments without accommodations, take the regular assessment with accommodations, or take an alternate assessment (Thurlow, Elliott, & Ysseldyke, 1998). Figure 1 (Participation Decision Tree) can aid school-based teams (IEP teams) in deciding which of the three ways of large-scale test participation is most appropriate for an individual student with a disability.

The first question of the Participation Decision Tree (see Figure 1) the IEP team can discuss is whether the student is working toward the same state standards specified for general education students. If not, then the student should be working on an alternate or expanded set of standards that are more appropriate to the student's needs, and should participate in an alternate assessment that addresses these standards. If the student is working toward the same set of standards as specified for general education students, then the team must decide if the student requires accommodations to demonstrate proficiency such as those given within the classroom setting. If so, then the student should be allowed to participate in the regular assessment with such accommodations. If the student does not need accommodations (e.g., does *not* receive any accommodations in the classroom) and is working toward the same standards as general education students, then the student should participate in the regular assessment.

Not only can school-based practitioners use this Participation Decision Tree, but it can also aid state department personnel in the development of state participation guidelines. Nearly every state has revised its participation guidelines or has developed new ones since the passage of IDEA 97 (Thurlow, Seyfarth, Boys, &

FIGURE 1: **Participation Decision Tree**

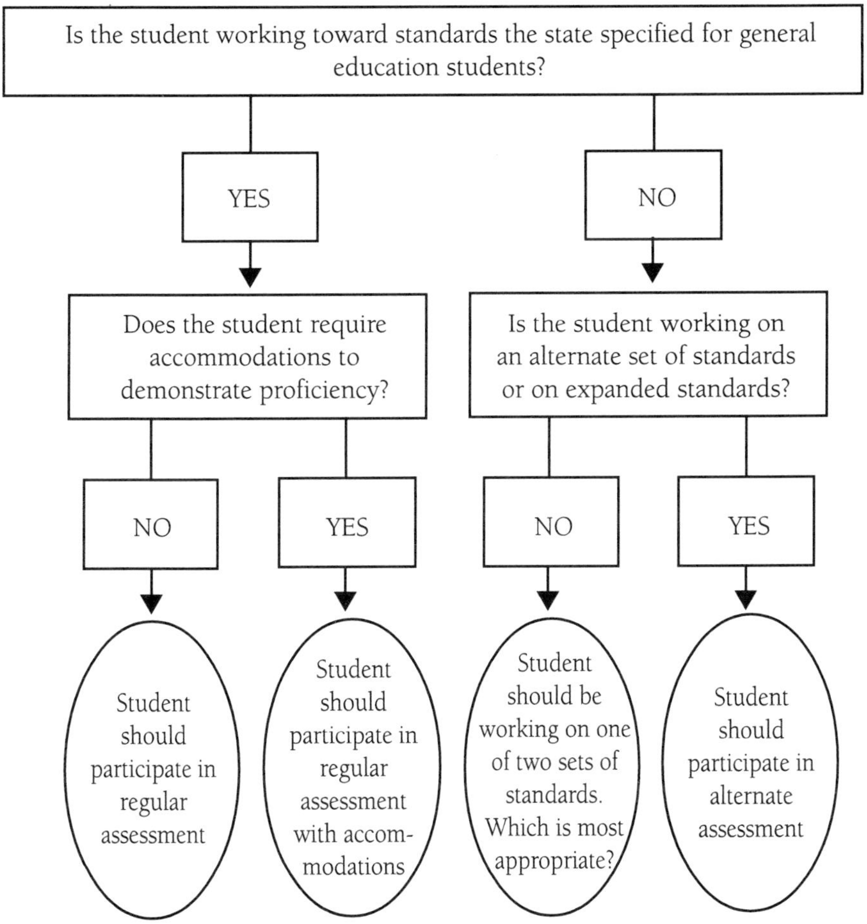

```
┌─────────────────────────────────────────────────────────────┐
│ Is the student working toward standards the state specified  │
│              for general education students?                 │
└─────────────────────────────────────────────────────────────┘
```

| YES | NO |

| Does the student require accommodations to demonstrate proficiency? | Is the student working on an alternate set of standards or on expanded standards? |

| NO | YES | NO | YES |

- **Student should participate in regular assessment**
- **Student should participate in regular assessment with accommodations**
- **Student should be working on one of two sets of standards. Which is most appropriate?**
- **Student should participate in alternate assessment**

Scott, 2000). Most states rely heavily on the IEP team to make decisions about the most appropriate way to include students with disabilities in large-scale assessments (Thurlow et al., 2000). When making decisions, states often recommend that the IEP team examine a student's individual needs and learning characteristics rather than the student's educational placement. Additionally, many states are developing or have developed eligibility guidelines for their alternate assessment system, and unless a student meets those guidelines, it is expected that the student will take the regular assessment.

Five participation issues are listed in Table 1. First, it is difficult to obtain data on how students with disabilities participate in state assessments. For example, in a recent study in which files of general and special education students were examined, it was unclear whether students with disabilities had taken the state assessments (Ysseldyke et al., 1999). Furthermore, many states have indicated that they do not have data that indicate the number of students with disabilities who participated in their assessments (Erickson, Thurlow, & Thor, 1995).

In the early 1990s, only 28 states had policies on participation of students with disabilities in assessments (Thurlow, Ysseldyke, & Silverstein, 1993). By 1997, all states had policies in place or in development (Thurlow, Seyfarth, Scott, & Ysseldyke, 1997). From a more recent, but limited, sample of 17 states that reported data on participation of students with disabilities in public accountability reports, it appeared that there was a wide range of participation: between 33% and 97% of students with disabilities actually participated in statewide assessments with or without accommodations (Ysseldyke, Thurlow, Nelson, & Teelucksingh, 2000). It is recommended that 85% of students with disabilities should be participating in typical statewide assessments (Ysseldyke, Thurlow, McGrew, & Shriner, 1994), and 100% should be included in statewide educational accountability systems.

A second participation issue is one of calculating rates. Not only can it be difficult to establish the number of students with disabilities participating in statewide assessments, but different definitions of who is eligible to participate in the various kinds of assessment lead to confusion about how inclusive a system really is: Did all students participate, or did all *eligible* students participate (Erickson, Thurlow, & Ysseldyke, 1996)? Many states describe their participation rate as a fraction, with the number of students with disabilities who took the exam as a numerator, and the total number of students with disabilities as the denominator. In some cases the denominator consists of the students included in a state's special education child count, while in other states or districts the denominator is the number of students with disabilities on the day of the test. This results in a condition Erickson et al. (1996) called drifting denominators.

In the 1997 State Special Education Outcomes Survey, 22 of 56 state special education directors reported that they do not currently collect or receive information on the number or rate at which students with disabilities participate in their statewide assessments (Erickson & Thurlow, 1997). In the follow-up 1999 State Special Education Outcomes Survey, 45 state special education directors of indicated that they have data on the number of students with disabilities tested in their statewide assessments. Yet only 23 states provided actual participation data (Thompson & Thurlow, 1999).

Definitional confusion occurs when discussing participation rates. Some states discuss participation in terms of the percentage of *all students in the population*, while others discuss it in terms of *all students with disabilities*. It is widely thought that 85% of *students with disabilities* are capable of participating meaningfully in state tests, with or without accommodations, while 15% would more appropriately take an alternate assessment (Elliott, Thurlow, & Ysseldyke, 1996). This translates to 1–2% of all students.

Once a student is included in the *assessment* system, there is no guarantee that the student's results will be part of the *accountability* system (Thurlow, Elliott, Scott, & Shin, 1997). This leads to debate about responsibility for results. Regular and special educators regularly debate assignment of accountability for results, especially when students with disabilities are educated in general education classes.

The process of making decisions about participation in statewide assessment is debated. Most often the IEP team makes such decisions, though in some states school principals or other school officials make the final decision (Thurlow et al., 2000). This means that many different individuals and groups are interpreting states' guidelines about participation, and this can result in inconsistent application of the guidelines. Exemption of students with disabilities from large-scale testing will likely be monitored more in the future, due to the new requirements of IDEA 97, but until now there has not been a mechanism to ensure that participation decisions are being made appropriately (Ysseldyke, Thurlow, Kozleski et al., 1998).

Accommodation Issues

The revision to IDEA is intended to ensure that states are finding more ways to *include* all students in their assessments and accountability systems. This means that state personnel must ensure that students have access to the assessments without having the student's disabilities impede the student's ability to demonstrate academic progress. Accommodations are intended to remove the effect of the disability from the testing or to "level the playing field," while maintaining test validity and reliability to the extent possible. Unfortunately, due to the paucity of research on testing accommodations, these judgments are generally made based on opinion rather than empirical findings (Thurlow, Elliott, & Ysseldyke, 1998).

IDEA 97 requires states and districts to provide appropriate accommodations to students with disabilities participating in large-scale assessments. Policies on accommodations and modifications to testing have followed a trend similar to policies on participation. In the early 1990s, 21 states reported having policies on accommodations (Thurlow, Ysseldyke, & Silverstein, 1993), although in 1997 only one state did not have accommodations guidelines in place or under development (Thurlow, Seyfarth, Scott & Ysseldyke, 1997). More importantly, the ways students qualify for accommodations have changed significantly, moving from a focus on the type of disability the student has to the student's individual learning characteristics and needs (Thurlow, Seyfarth, Scott et al., 1997). This has led to a groundswell of new accommodation policies, with nearly every state changing its policy since passage of IDEA 97 (Thurlow et al., 2000). States are often including decision-making criteria for identifying accommodations, are generally requiring that the IEP teams make the decision, and often are requiring that the teams attempt to match testing accommodations to those used in instruction.

The basis for an accommodation is a major issue. Though the law encourages a focus on individual learning needs, recent trends in accommodation policies have resulted in some states providing accommodations based on students' specific disability classification (Thurlow et al., 2000). For example, a student who has a physical disability may be allowed to use a scribe, while a student with a learning disability in writing may be required to write out his or her responses. Many states are determining appropriate accommodations by examining the accommodations used for instruction (Thurlow et al., 2000). However, other states are indicating that although this can be a guide, there may be requirements within a standardized testing situation that are not like those of the instructional environment, and, as such, there may need to be different accommodations provided in each situation.

One of the best ways to characterize the status of accommodation policies is to recognize that there is a great deal of variability among states in what is permitted (Thurlow, Seyfarth, Scott et al., 1997). This includes specific accommodations, such as reading the test aloud and providing a spell-check device, as well as categories of accommodations, such as setting accommodations (e.g., preferential seating) and scheduling accommodations (e.g., extended time). Adding to the variability among states is the fact that different states use different terms. "Accommodation" is generally used to indicate a change to the test or test environment to remove the effect of a student's disability (Thurlow, Seyfarth, Scott et al., 1997). Some states, such as Minnesota, add another term, "modification," to indicate a change that is believed to change the construct measured by the test (Thurlow et al., 2000). At the same time, states such as Florida have used the term "modification" to mean any change to the test.

A third issue is the disparity between accommodations policies and practice. Many states' policies permit a wide variety of accommodations to their state and district tests (Thurlow et al., 2000). Yet, recent findings have indicated that just because accommodations are permitted does not mean that they are used in practice. This discrepancy between state policies and actual practices may arise from an unwillingness to provide allowable accommodations, lack of training in decision making, or a perception that the accommodations are too difficult to implement. Many state policies indicate that reasonable accommodations should be provided, but there is no clarification about what "reasonable" means. Further, some educators believe that accommodations provide students with disabilities an unfair advantage when the intent is to offer students with disabilities a level playing field to demonstrate their abilities.

Once the decision is made to offer an accommodation, each specific accommodation comes with a set of issues, and there is little research to help answer the questions that educators raise. For example, extending the time for testing is a fairly common accommodation; however, research findings concerning this accommodation have been contradictory. In some cases, there is evidence that extending the time results in incompatible scores between those who received the accommodations and those who did not. Other research has indicated that it makes no significant difference (Thurlow, Hurley, Spicuzza, & El Sawaf, 1996). At this time there is very limited information on the extent to which provision of accommodations alters what is assessed.

Reporting Issues

The law and accompanying regulations about public reporting of results for students with disabilities has changed significantly. IDEA 97 requires that states report aggregated and disaggregated data on the performance results of students with disabilities on regular and alternate assessments, as well as the number of students with disabilities participating in such assessments.

The reporting of scores obtained by students with disabilities on large-scale assessments is hotly debated and not clearly understood. Disaggregating data on the performance of students with disabilities refers to separating out those results from the entire student population and reporting their scores as a group of students with disabilities. Some states (e.g., North Carolina) disaggregate by federal special education categories. Sometimes states report scores separately for those students who took the test under standard and nonstandard administrations. Some states have chosen not to include any results of students with disabilities if they used any accommodations. Very few states publicly report the exemption rates of students with disabilities on statewide tests ($N = 10$) (Ysseldyke et al., 2000).

There is also considerable discussion about the kinds of scores to report. Some states report norm-referenced scores, or scores that are compared to those obtained by a national sample of students of the same age or grade. Others report standards-based scores (sometimes labeled criterion-referenced), which compare a student's performance to an absolute standard set by the district or state. Additionally, some states report scores that are compared to an absolute level, such as 75% of math problems correct, while others look at relative level, such as percent growth since last testing. Adding to the confusion is the fact that many of the scores can be reported in more than one way. For example, norm-referenced scores can be reported as standard scores (mean of 100, standard deviation of 15), *T*-scores (mean of 50, standard deviation of 10), stanines, percentile ranks, or many other ways. Criterion-referenced scores can be reported as percent correct, number who passed or failed, score on a 4-point rubric, and dozens of other ways. Finally, some states only report raw scores for students with disabilities who received accommodations to the assessment. This variability in the types of scores used can make comparison across states or districts difficult, as well as confusing those who most need the information, such as educators, families, and the public at large.

In an earlier review of 115 public accountability report documents, only 12 states provided outcome data on students with disabilities beyond that required for federal reporting (e.g., achievement test data) (Ysseldyke, Thurlow, Langenfeld et al., 1998). When states provided information on students with disabilities, the majority (N = 33) reported enrollment data. This 1998 review was completed before the publication of regulations for the reauthorization of IDEA 97. In a more recent review of over 165 public accountability reports completed after the reauthorization, the number of states providing performance data on students with disabilities had increased to 17 (Ysseldyke et al., 2000).

Though one might have expected more states to be reporting such data because of the federal mandates, states may have been in a quandary about how to interpret and implement the delayed regulations that followed the 1997 Reauthorization of IDEA (Individuals with Disabilities Education Act Regulations, 1999). It is expected that more states will begin to report disaggregated performance data on students with disabilities and these changes in reporting practices will provide the data needed to monitor the progress and performance of students with disabilities.

Alternate Assessment Issues

Thurlow, Elliott, and Ysseldyke (1998) referred to alternate assessment as the "ultimate accommodation." In the past, students with disabilities for whom an alternate assessment would be appropriate were excluded from the general curriculum, state and district assessments, and accountability systems (Elliott & Thurlow, 1997; Erickson & Thurlow, 1997; Roach & Raber, 1997). As a result of IDEA 97, the spirit and intent of the law is to promote an inclusive look into how *all* students are performing, including those for whom the state and district assessments were not appropriate.

The development of alternate assessments has progressed in a manner similar to the development of accommodation and participation guidelines, albeit somewhat slower. Kentucky and Maryland were among the first states to implement an alternate assessment for students unable to participate meaningfully in the regular assessments (Ysseldyke, Thurlow, Seyfarth et al., 1996). In 1997, only eight states reported having an alternate assessment in place or in development (Thurlow, Seyfarth, Scott et al., 1997). However, more recent examinations of states' activities have found that 32 states are currently working on developing an alternate assessment (Thompson, Erickson, Thurlow, Ysseldyke, & Callendar, 1999).

It is reasonable to imagine a student in a district or school building for whom none of the available testing accommodations would provide the means needed to assess the student's true abilities and progress. This student might have significant support needs or might not be working on the same set of skills or standards as the majority of students. In fact, this student may need a different way to demonstrate learning and to be accounted for in state and district accountability systems. Thus, alternate assessment can be a more appropriate tool to measure and demonstrate the student's growth.

As a result of the IDEA 97 mandate to provide alternate assessments, there are a number of issues for school-based teams to consider as they begin to implement alternate assessment in their schools (see Table 1 on page 32). Eligibility for an alternate assessment is the first consideration. The school team that collaborates to make participation and accommodation decisions could decide that a student may be best served by participating in an alternate assessment. In some states, not only are teams responsible for deciding that a student needs alternate assessment, they also are responsible for deciding which tasks comprise an individual student's alternate assessment.

Nationwide, many SEAs have taken preliminary and formal steps to establish eligibility guidelines for alternate assessments. In the latest status report of a national alternate assessment cybersurvey released by the National Center on Educational Outcomes (NCEO), 34 states reported that they were establishing eligibility guidelines that will assist local educational agencies in determining which students should take the alternate assessment (Thompson et al., 1999). In fact, most of these guidelines were in draft form at the time the NCEO report was published. Eligibility guidelines are crucial so that alternate assessments do not become a dumping ground for large numbers of students with or without disabilities.

Alternate assessments are intended for those students who have an alternate or more individualized curriculum. For those students with more severe cognitive disabilities and significant support needs, and who are not able to participate in the same course requirements and assessments as students without disabilities, an alternate assessment may be more appropriate. NCEO has suggested that the alternate assessment is primarily designed for students with severe cognitive impairments; that is, 1–2% of an entire student population, or about 15–20% of students with disabilities (Ysseldyke, Thurlow, Kozleski et al., 1998). However, the regulations for IDEA 97 do not specify that only students with severe cognitive disabilities should take the alternate assessment.

Because most states appear to be placing the decision to participate in an alternate assessment in the hands of the IEP team, it is helpful to have a formal decision-making process that can be used every time a participation decision must be made. Thurlow, Elliott, and Ysseldyke (1998) proposed a series of four questions that a team can work through in deciding which assessment is appropriate for an individual student. This form, however, must be adapted to individual state assessments and standards (see Table 3 on page 46). Such standard forms can ensure that basic questions are asked and answered for *each* individual student.

A second issue involves relevance of state standards for students with significant disabilities. The nature of state standards is important to consider when developing IEP goals for a student with a disability. The broader the standards originally developed, the easier it is to include all students in the same accountability system. When standards are broad, a student can still be working toward attainment of the standard but appropriately participate in the alternate assessment.

A good example of broad standards can be found in Kentucky where teachers and others who provided services to students with severe cognitive disabilities examined the standards to ensure that at least a portion (28 of 60 standards) would apply as well to their students (Thurlow, Elliott, & Ysseldyke, 1998). An example of an academic expectation or standard in reading is: "Students construct meaning from a variety of printed materials for a variety of purposes through reading." An indicator of this standard for students with severe disabilities is: "Reads environmental, pictorial print." If a state's standard is sufficiently broad, creating goals to measure growth via an alternate assessment can be relatively easy. Broad standards help to maintain a unified educational system with all students being held accountable to the same standards.

Most states have used task forces or groups of stakeholders to consider the standards needed to be addressed by alternate assessment (Thompson et al., 1999). The most common approach was to use a subset of the general state standards; additionally, a number of states added standards in the areas of social skills, communication, independent functioning, and career development (Thompson et al., 1999).

So what should be measured in alternate assessments? Gathering data on the performance of students with disabilities through alternate assessments requires a "rethinking of traditional assessment methods" (Thompson et al., 1999, p. 2). Alternate assessments are neither large-scale assessments nor individualized assessments. Alternate assessments are a hybrid; that is, a common assessment that can be administered to students who have unique backgrounds and educational goals and who differ greatly in their ability to respond to stimuli, solve problems, and provide responses (Ysseldyke & Olsen, 1999). However, alternate assessments can be completed with the same methodology as other assessments (e.g., norm-referenced, criterion-referenced, and performance assessments).

Statewide assessments usually focus on academic areas. The most common areas are language arts, mathematics, and writing (Ysseldyke, Thurlow, Langenfeld et al., 1998). Yet, stakeholders actually identified eight domains of essential and desirable outcomes or results when the NCEO conducted a national consensus-building process (Vanderwood, Ysseldyke, & Thurlow, 1993; Ysseldyke, Krentz et al., 1998). Most assessments fall in one of those eight domains; that is, Academic and Functional Literacy. Other programs or curricula for students with severe cognitive disabilities focus more attention on the other educational outcome domains (e.g., Personal and Social Adjustment, Contribution and Citizenship, Responsibility and Independence, Physical Health). These skills may occur as a result of incidental learning, but for some students, they must be taught directly and systematically. Other functional living frameworks include Choosing Options and Accommodations for Children (COACH) (Giangreco, Cloniger, & Iverson, 1993), the Syracuse Community-Referenced Curriculum Guide (Ford et al., 1989), Community-Based Curriculum (Falvey, 1989), Career Education for Handicapped Individuals (Kokaska & Brolin, 1985), and Addressing Unique Educational Needs (AUEN) (Frey, Burke, Jakworth, Lynch & Sumpter, 1996a; Frey, Burke, Jakworth, Lynch & Sumpter, 1996b; Frey, Burke, Jakworth, Lynch & Sumpter, 1996c; Frey, Burke, Jakworth, Lynch & Sumpter, 1996d).

Another consideration related to alternate assessment concerns reporting issues. There are a number of views about how states should report results from an alternate assessment. One method is to compile the results from the alternate assessment and report these results separately from those of the general assessment. Yet, the necessity to maintain confidentiality may limit disaggregation by individual school or even school district, depending on the size. Another method is to aggregate the alternate assessment results with the results from the general assessment system and then report an aggregate score that includes all students.

Currently, Kentucky and Maryland are the only states that have a fully implemented alternate assessment (Ysseldyke, Thurlow, Erickson et al., 1996). Kentucky has attempted to create equitable proficiency levels between their general and alternate assessments. In that state, data from the Alternate Portfolio Assessment are scored using the same 4-point rubric (novice, apprentice, proficient, distinguished) as is employed in the general assessment, so that a score of 3 on the regular assessment is considered to be equivalent to a score of 3 on the alternate assessment (Ysseldyke, Thurlow, Seyfarth et al., 1996).

The advantage to disaggregating the results of the alternate assessment is that such results can be used to improve special education services and provide accountability for these students' performance. However, this approach continues to separate students with disabilities from the majority of students. The goal, again, is to maintain a unified accountability system in which all students' needs and results are addressed.

Almost half of the states ($N = 21$) have reported that they are in the process of determining how scores from an alternate assessment should be disaggregated or aggregated with scores from special education and general education students (Thompson et al., 1999). Only 13 states have begun to consider how scores from students taking the alternate assessment may be included in their high stakes systems; that is, those that have perceived or real consequences for students, staff, or schools (Thompson et al., 1999).

The challenge for states and practitioners is to link the alternate assessment to the common core of learning. Because it is assumed that all students who participate in alternate assessments are not working toward general education goals or standards or a standard diploma, some may argue that all assessments are individual appraisals of how students are achieving IEP objectives. The problem with this approach is that IEP goals are not equivalent among students, and attainment of IEP goals cannot easily be aggregated for accountability purposes. There are common domains of learning that all students should be working toward, and there is a need for a common measurement across general and alternate assessments for accountability purposes.

BEST PRACTICE STRATEGIES FOR IMPLEMENTING THE ASSESSMENT PROVISIONS

In implementing the assessment provisions, the following recommendations can serve as a starting point for school personnel. These recommendations are listed in Table 2.

Getting Stakeholder Commitment

Though these assessment provisions are federal requirements, it is even more imperative that everyone who has a "stake" in this process—stakeholders—be involved at the outset of implementation (Ysseldyke & Thurlow, 1993). Not only do stakeholders encompass teachers, supervisors, and related services personnel, they should also include parents. Involving all stakeholders on the front end of development helps school-based teams consider the range of perspectives and needs that will have to be addressed as educators work together to implement the assessment provisions. When stakeholders are involved from the very beginning, they will have a better understanding of the rationale for and issues in implementation of the new provisions.

TABLE 2: Best Practices for Implementing the Assessment Provisions

- Getting stakeholder commitment
- Providing rationale for new assessment provisions
- Being clear about definitions and guidelines
- Getting to know your state's guidelines
- Making participation decisions
- Making accommodation decisions
- Making reporting decisions
- Alternate assessment practices
- Professional development implications for educators and systems
  - Communication with families
  - Setting high expectations
  - Referral to existing resources

Providing Rationale for New Assessment Provisions

NCEO personnel have demonstrated that various types of students have routinely been excluded from assessments, including students on IEPs, students who speak English as a second language, and low-achieving students. Why is it important to include these students in statewide and districtwide assessments as now mandated by IDEA 97?

It is clear that when students with disabilities are excluded from large-scale assessments, an inaccurate understanding of student progress is achieved (Zlatos, 1994). Referral rates to special education, as well as grade retentions, climb when there is an opportunity to exclude students from accountability systems (Allington & McGill-Franzen, 1992). By including students with disabilities in state and district assessments and their corresponding educational accountability systems, educators, families, and policymakers have an accurate picture of education and are able to make appropriate comparisons (Thurlow, Elliott, & Ysseldyke, 1998).

Changes in education are frequently driven by the results obtained from these accountability systems. If students with disabilities are not included in such systems, then it is highly unlikely that their needs will be considered when creating and implementing reforms. Many times students who are "out of sight, out of mind" are forgotten when decisions are being made. The final reason for including students with disabilities in large-scale testing and accountability systems is to promote high expectations for *every* individual student. When students are excluded from a test, the underlying message to the student is that they are *not able* to meet the expectations of the test.

Being Clear About Definitions and Guidelines

Terms such as "accommodations," "modifications," "alternate assessment," and "alternative assessment" have multiple meanings in professional and popular literature. One of the most helpful first steps one can take to improve communication and avoid misunderstandings is to come to agreement with stakeholders on definitions of these and other terms that might cause confusion. Some other troubling terms that can cause confusion include: "accountability," "all students," "outcomes," "indicators," "benchmarks," "content standards," "public accountability reporting," "partial exclusions," "exclusion," and "limited participation."

Getting to Know Your State's Guidelines

In the process of clarifying definitions, one will more than likely consult with school district and state department guidelines and personnel. Getting to know your own state's guidelines is critical to successful implementation of the assessment provisions. How these assessment provisions correlate with one's current state standards should be explored as well as guidelines and practices of participation, accommodation, and reporting decisions.

Making Participation Decisions

In addition to the participation decision tree (Figure 1) discussed earlier, investigators and policy makers have been developing best practice strategies for the participation of students with disabilities in large-scale assessment. Data from focus groups, surveys, and national meetings have been used in these efforts (e.g., Elliott, Thurlow, & Ysseldyke, 1996; Seyfarth, Ysseldyke, & Thurlow, 1998; Ysseldyke, Thurlow, Kozleski et al., 1998). Through this process, a number of recommendations have been developed (see Table 3).

TABLE 3: Best Practice Criteria for Students with Disabilities in Large-Scale Assessments

1. All students, including students with disabilities and students in nontraditional settings, are to participate in state and district assessments.
2. The decisions about participation and accommodations are made by a person (or a group) who knows the student.
3. The decisions about participation and accommodations are based on the student's current level of functioning and learning characteristics.
4. A form is used that lists the variables to consider in making participation and accommodations decisions and documents the decisions and the reasons behind the decisions.
5. A student must participate in an assessment if the student receives any instruction on the content assessed, regardless of where instruction occurs.
6. Decisions about assessment accommodations link to instructional accommodations.
7. Decisions about how students participate and about accommodations are not based on the category of disability, program setting, or percentage of time in the general education environment.
8. Only a small percentage of students with disabilities need to participate in an alternate assessment (e.g., those with severe disabilities, <1% of all students).
9. Parents understand the state/district accountability system, the participation options, the accommodations options, and the reporting policy for their child's assessment results and also understand the implications of choices they make for their child.
10. Parents, educators and administrators receive information about participation in assessments and training mechanisms are in place for these groups.

11. A written policy exists about who is included when calculating participation or exclusion rates.
12. Rates of exclusion that are specific to students with disabilities, and reasons for the exclusion, are reported when assessment results are reported.
13. Data reports include information from all test takers, including those students receiving federally funded educational services in nontraditional settings such as those who are home-schooled or attending private schools, charter schools, or residential treatment centers.
14. Records are maintained in a manner that permits data for students with disabilities to be reported separately, overall, or by other distributions.
15. Records are maintained of the use of accommodations by students with disabilities so that the assessment information can also be disaggregated by accommodation use by individual student or by the entire population of students with disabilities.

(Adapted from Elliott, Thurlow, & Ysseldyke, 1996; Thurlow, Elliott, & Ysseldyke, 1998; Ysseldyke, Thurlow, Kozleski, & Reschly, 1998; Ysseldyke, Thurlow, McGrew, & Shriner 1994; Ysseldyke, Thurlow, McGrew, & Vanderwood 1994)

These recommendations begin with the premise that all students, including students with disabilities and those in nontraditional settings, should participate in the district or state accountability system. These best practice recommendations also ensure that as many students as possible participate in large-scale assessments and, if not appropriate for 1–2% of the student population, in an alternate assessment. It is recommended that a team that knows the child well consider the student's current level of functioning and learning characteristics when making participation decisions. The student should participate in the assessment if the student receives *any* instruction on the content assessed, regardless of where instruction occurs.

Participation decisions should *not* be based on program setting, category of disability, or percentage of time spent in the regular education environment. The team should be considering the individual strengths and needs of each student. School professionals also have the responsibility to describe participation options to parents and to assist those parents in fully understanding the implications of their child's not being included in an assessment or accountability system. Finally, these decisions need to be documented on the student's IEP. For more detail, the reader is referred to Elliott, Thurlow, and Ysseldyke (1996) and Thurlow, Elliott, and Ysseldyke (1998).

When these recommendations were presented to educators in the field for validation, there was generally widespread endorsement of them (Seyfarth, Ysseldyke, & Thurlow, 1998). The least popular of the criteria were those that required full participation of students, and the criteria seen as most difficult to implement were those that required parents to fully understand the decisions being made and the implications of those decisions. However, although the criteria were seen as desirable, and some were seen as feasible, they were not widely used at the time.

Given that the new requirements for IDEA 97 in many ways closely mirror the NCEO recommendations, there is now a legal mandate to implement many of them, particularly those regarding participation of all students, accommodations, alternate assessment availability, and reporting of results. The next step for school-based practitioners is to implement best practices in making participation, accommodation, and reporting decisions.

Making Accommodation Decisions

School-based teams must determine whether and how to provide accommodations for each individual student. The following recommendations can facilitate this decision-making process. By considering the individual student's current level of functioning and learning characteristics, school professionals can begin to consider whether accommodations are appropriate for the student and, if so, which kinds of accommodations. NCEO has recommended an alignment between instructional and assessment accommodations, such that if the accommodation is being provided in the classroom it also should be provided for the statewide assessment. It is also advised that teams create a district/state form that lists variables to consider in making the accommodation decisions and documents for each student the decision and reasons for it (Elliott, Thurlow, & Ysseldyke, 1996).

Thurlow, Elliott, and Ysseldyke (1998) have composed a list of "Do's and Don'ts in Testing Accommodations." These authors do not encourage the introduction of a new accommodation for the first time in an assessment. Instead, they suggest that instructional accommodations should be carried through the assessment process. It is suggested that school-based teams should not begin their decision-making process about a student's needed accommodations by consulting the district or state list of approved accommodations. If, after contemplating the student's need for a particular accommodation, the team finds that the district/state does not approve of such an accommodation, then approval of the accommodation can be requested from the district or state. Finally, it is suggested that decisions about accommodations be based on student needs rather than their category of disability.

Making Reporting Decisions

When researchers have examined state accountability reports, it has been difficult to ascertain whether or not students with disabilities were included in the compilation of state results in reviewing public accountability reports (Ysseldyke, Thurlow, Langenfeld et al., 1998). It is recommended that a written policy specifying who is included when reporting assessment performance and participation data be made available. The federal law guides state personnel to disaggregate data on students with disabilities. Therefore, database systems need to be revised or designed so that the performance and participation of students with disabilities can be disaggregated. Some states are currently investigating ways to change their computerized management information systems to permit them to integrate data on students with disabilities at the state level. These decisions about data gathering and distribution require coordination and integration (Nelson, Ysseldyke & Thurlow, 1998). There is an excellent resource by Jaeger and Tucker (1998) that school-based practitioners can use for the analysis, disaggregation, reporting, and interpretation of student achievement test results.

Reading states' public accountability reports has been difficult due to vague statements, insufficient definitions and explanations, and hard-to-read database presentations (Ysseldyke, Thurlow, Langenfeld et al., 1998). When designing state reports, it is imperative to consider the needs of the consumers and ways to report the information in a clear and concise manner. Layout should not be cluttered or complex, but should provide executive summaries, reader's guides, tables of contents, indices, and glossaries. Good organization of information and interesting styles of presentation will help ensure that educators and other stakeholders will actually read and use these reports. Ysseldyke and Nelson (1998) have suggested that to increase clarity and usefulness for intended readers, reports need to be targeted toward specific audiences, and systems may want to develop a pyramid of reports, ranging from those who want less detailed information to those who may need more substantial details.

In collaboration with the Reporting Study Group within the Council of Chief State School Officers' (CCSSO) State Collaborative on Assessment and Student Standards, Assessing Special Education, Ysseldyke and Nelson (1998) formulated a checklist of guidelines to be used when preparing state and district educational accountability reports. This checklist highlights the various characteristics that all reports should strive to contain: clarity (e.g., with regard to purpose, intended audience, state standards, conceptual model of accountability, description of population of students being reported on), comprehensiveness (e.g., data on *all* students), fair comparative information (e.g., fair judgments over time), concise presentation (e.g., pyramid of reports for specific audiences), cautions (e.g., avoiding scapegoating, unintended consequences, negatives), and confidentiality (e.g., no reporting on groups of 10 or fewer). For the Checklist of Guidelines for State and District Educational Accountability Reports, refer to Ysseldyke and Nelson (1998).

Alternate Assessment Practices

Because alternate assessments are just beginning to be implemented, it is difficult to summarize best practice strategies at this point in time. From a broad perspective, a few assumptions offered by focus groups of teachers may have relevance for implementing alternate assessment (Ysseldyke & Olsen, 1999):

- The focus of an alternate assessment should be on authentic skills and on assessing experiences in community and real life environments. Students who are expected to function in a community should be asked to perform in actual community situations. For example, a task for a junior high student might involve being able to choose and pay for items at a grocery store with a specified amount of money. The term "community" can assume different forms at the elementary, middle and secondary levels. Community for a senior may include the grocery store or bank whereas a second grader's community might include daycare and the playground.

- School personnel should measure integrated skills across domains. For example, assessing personal and social skills separately from academic skills might result in redundant teaching or ineffective instruction in isolated skills. The student needs to be able to attend to all of these skills within a given situation (e.g., paying for an item).

- To provide more accurate and reliable information than single snapshots of performance, Ysseldyke and Olsen (1999) recommend assessment methods that incorporate continuous measures over time. Students with severe disabilities have greater variability in their skills from day to day than do students without disabilities or students with milder disabilities. Practitioners should select methods that reflect student change to monitor the progress of the individual student. For example, a student may be able to complete three steps of a task today and yet skip one step of the same task tomorrow (e.g., 8 out of 10 days the student was able to complete all three steps of checking her daily schedule).

- Not only should alternate assessment be designed to reflect the progress of individual students, but the extent to which the school system provides the needed assistive devices, people, and other supports to allow students to function as independently as possible should be reported. Adding an accommodation/support criterion to alternate assessments helps to level the playing field and ensure that students with the most severe impairments do not always receive the lowest scores. Kentucky included this criterion in their alternate assessment system, and has shown that it enhances effective school and classroom practice (Kleinert, Kearns, & Kennedy, 1996).

- The key to effective alternate assessments is the link between results and instructional practice for the students who take them. If school personnel are continuously monitoring the progress of students in an appropriate manner, but do not use these data to make instructional changes based on the performance results, then the alternate assessment becomes a simple measure of the status quo and the student's supposed lack of progress. To ensure student progress, assessment data need to be reviewed, and instructional adaptations should occur as necessary. For example, a student continues to walk across the street without taking the time to check his surroundings for indicators that he is safe to cross the street. The teacher takes this into consideration and provides instruction along with a picture/symbol flipbook illustrating the simple steps to follow when preparing to cross the street.

Sources of Data

Salvia and Ysseldyke (1998) have identified the four kinds of approaches that are used to gather data on students: observation, recollection (via interview or rating scale), record review, and testing. Ysseldyke and Olson (1999) further described how school-based team members can gather those four sources of data for alternate assessments of student performance (see Table 4 on page 52).

Observation. Observations can provide highly accurate and detailed information about student performance (Salvia & Ysseldyke, 1998). Data may be collected by using systematic or nonsystematic procedures. Observations can be conducted at school, home, or in a community setting depending on the type of behavior(s) being observed. Observations can be staged, or they may occur in the natural environment. A disadvantage of observational data is that the observer must have clearly defined scoring rubrics and a good working knowledge of typical development (Ysseldyke & Olsen, 1999).

Recollection. Persons familiar with a student may be asked to recall observations and interpretations of behavior and events and can complete interviews or rating scales based on such recollections (Ysseldyke & Olsen, 1999). Those measures may be collected from the student, from peers, from teachers, from work-study coordinators, from employers, or from family members. Interviews can be conducted face-to-face, over the telephone, or in small groups. In general, when one wants to aggregate data from interviews of several students, it is best to use a structured interview (Ysseldyke & Olsen, 1999).

Record review. Five kinds of existing information about students may be used as data for an alternate assessment: student cumulative records, school databases, student products, anecdotal records, and non-school records (Salvia & Ysseldyke,

TABLE 4: Summary of Assessment Methods for Alternate Assessments

Observations: Teachers or third party informant watching student exhibit the behavior

- Staged or natural
- Taped or live
- Segmented or continuous

Interviews/surveys: Gathering information by interviews or surveys with people who know the student (caregiver, parent, student, teacher, therapist, work-study coordinator, employer)

- Face-to-face or phone interviews (group or individual)
- Mail surveys
- Standard checklists, rating scales, adaptive behavior records

Record reviews: Using a structured procedure to extract information

- Cumulative files/IEPs
- Databases
- Student products
- Teacher/therapist anecdotal records
- Nonschool records (e.g., parents' files, medical records)

Tests: Putting a challenge in front of students and having the student solve the problem

- Adaptations of the state assessment
- Battery of published instruments
- Performance events
- Portfolios
- Close- or open-ended
- Norm or criterion referenced
- Variety of options for communicating responses

(Taken from Ysseldyke & Olsen, 1997, p. 12; For specific examples of adaptive behavior checklists, consult Chapter 26 of Salvia & Ysseldyke, 1998)

1998; Ysseldyke & Olsen, 1999). Record review requires the development of standardized record extraction forms and procedures to ensure consistency and utility of information. There are a number of limitations in using existing data. It is time-consuming to examine a volume of information in order to gather information that answers assessment questions. The assessor also has no control over data collected in the past, and critical context information is typically not included in student records.

Testing. Testing students is the most common method for gathering achievement information. Testing is the process of measuring student competencies, attitudes, and behaviors by presenting a challenge or problem and having the student generate a response (Salvia & Ysseldyke, 1998). Many states now use either norm-referenced tests or performance-based measures to assess student progress toward the attainment of standards. In general, these tests used by states are not appropriate assessments for students with severe cognitive disabilities due to the complexities of the tasks, the cognitive skills involved, and the content addressed by the tests.

Some have suggested using the tests designed to measure standards and gather information on beginning components of the standards (Ysseldyke & Olsen, 1997). A second option might be to collect a battery of existing standardized measures that address various domains. A portfolio system has also become a popular option, yet there is little consensus on how to use portfolios on a large-scale basis. A summary of assessment methods and examples appears in Table 4.

PROFESSIONAL DEVELOPMENT IMPLICATIONS FOR EDUCATORS AND SYSTEMS

When new federal regulations are put in place, the next key step is providing training for educators. Suggested strategies for providing professional development include involving the key stakeholders, defining terms, providing basic assessment background information, and revisiting the purposes of the revisions to ensure that all school personnel share a common understanding about these new assessment provisions and their implementation.

One professional development implication of the new provisions pertaining to large-scale assessment is the need for basic assessment literacy. Educators will need to fully understand the various purposes of assessment. Salvia and Ysseldyke (1998) describe 13 different purposes of assessment. These include instructional decision making, eligibility decisions, and also educational accountability. Large-scale assessment, as discussed in this article, is generally expected to be used for educational accountability, though it sometimes is intended to provide information for instructional decision making.

Stiggins (1995) points out that many educators graduate from their higher-education training programs with little to no knowledge of assessment in any form. Further, few districts or states require assessment literacy when hiring teachers or other educators. Stiggins suggests that educators must know what they are assessing, why they are performing the assessment, how to best assess the content of interest, and potential problems in the assessment. It would be ideal if higher education institutions required basic assessment literacy to ensure fully competent educators at all levels; however, this may not occur for some time.

School psychologists, who usually have more assessment background than other school-based personnel, can play an integral role in assisting the development of assessment literacy. They can train teachers, parents, administrators, and other educators about assessment in general, and about large-scale assessments in particular. In performing the training, school professionals must differentiate between the various purposes for engaging in the practice of large-scale assessments. The use of data for accountability and quality evaluation must be differentiated from the eligibility testing many school psychologists and other educators engage in and also must be differentiated from testing for instructional decision making.

In describing large-scale assessments, school-based practitioners must know what is being assessed in their state or district (e.g., which content areas and how these areas are assessed). As was mentioned earlier, this is often related to the standards states have established for their students, although this is not always the case.

School professionals also will need to describe the population being tested. Some accountability systems test only a carefully selected portion of the students in a state, and other states intend to test all students. The use of the term "all" in the state needs to be defined. Does "all" include students with disabilities, and if so, does it mean every student with a disability will be tested? Does "all" include students who are English language learners?

Integrally linked to the question of who is being tested is how to test the students. If all students with disabilities are to be included, then how do we test the students who have no meaningful communication system? If students who are English language learners are included, then does that mean that the test will be administered orally in Hmong if needed? Further, if accommodations are to be provided, then there can be logistical difficulties with accessing appropriate accommodations. Careful advance planning can sometimes be required, and school-based practitioners can inform colleagues about how to access accommodations in a timely fashion.

Communication With Families

Decision-making skills will be important throughout this process as well as communication with families. School professionals (e.g., teachers, school psychologists, testing specialists) can assist with such areas, both through their own problem-solving and communication skills as well as by helping to develop effective decision making and communication systems that can be used to help prevent miscommunication (Ysseldyke, Dawson et al., 1997).

The information gathered on the assessments will vary by the assessment, but school professionals can assist in the training of how to use the information presented. This is important for families so they can understand their child's scores and any consequences attached to such scores. Teachers and other educators may be able to use the information to improve or refocus classroom instruction, but may not understand how to do so without additional training.

Setting High Expectations

Related to the use of the assessment data is the general approach to the education of students with disabilities. School professionals can help set a tone of high expectations for all students. They can encourage the belief that all students can learn and focus on the provision of supports needed by students to learn successfully. Effective instructional techniques should be an area school psychologists and other school-based teams are already consulting about, but the presence of accountability systems and large-scale assessments may help bring this issue to the forefront again.

Referral to Existing Resources

School personnel can also act as resources in this process, referring families and educators to the appropriate existing materials in this area. Some of these resources are available through NCEO, but other research centers and agencies (e.g., Consortium for Policy Research in Education, Education Commission of the States), parent projects on large-scale assessments, regional resource centers, conferences on large-scale assessment, and topic-specific websites also are available. A list of resources on large-scale assessment and students with disabilities is included in Table 5 on page 56.

As large-scale assessments continue to focus attention on providing a quality education to all students, there will be many opportunities for school professionals to provide leadership. This will include decision making, facilitating communication, training, and providing resources. By serving in these important roles, school-based teams can help ensure equitable access to school reform; that is, improvement for all, not just for some.

TABLE 5: List of Resources on Large-Scale Assessment and Students with Disabilities

- *Office of Educational Research and Improvement (OERI)*
  http://www.ed.gov/offices/OERI
  OERI is a federal government agency that provides national leadership for educational research and statistics. This agency conducts research, funds demonstration projects, collects statistics on the status and progress of schools, and distributes information and provides technical assistance to education personnel.

- *Office of Special Education Programs (OSEP)*
  http://www.ed.gov/offices/OSERS/OSEP
  OSEP is a component of the Office of Special Education & Rehabilitative Services (OSERS) of the U.S. Department of Education. OSEP's mission and organization focus on the free appropriate public education of children and youth with disabilities through age 21. Provides overheads from OSEP Regional Trainings on IDEA 97 and a website for IDEA 97 regulations (*www.ed.gov/offices/OSERS/IDEA/*).

- *National Center on Educational Outcomes (NCEO)*
  http://www.coled.umn.edu/NCEO
  NCEO provides national leadership in the identification of outcomes and indicators to monitor the educational results of all students, including students with disabilities. NCEO addresses the participation of students with disabilities in national and state assessments, standards-setting efforts, and graduation requirements. NCEO also has a national alternate assessment cybersurvey that can be reviewed for each state.

- *Council of Chief State School Officers (CCSSO)*
  http://www.ccsso.org
  CCSSO is a nationwide, nonprofit organization composed of the public officials who head departments of elementary and secondary education in the states, District of Columbia, the Department of Defense Education Activity, and five extra-state jurisdictions. The State Education Assessment Center of CCSSO provides a clearinghouse to improve data acquisition, monitoring, and the assessment of education. CCSSO publishes an annual survey of state student assessment programs.

- *Center for Research on Evaluation, Standards, and Student Testing (CRESST)*
  http://cresst96.cse.ucla/
  This research center conducts research on important topics related to K–12 educational testing. Researchers have specifically created and evaluated approaches and accommodations that promote equity of assessment. This site includes a parent page with helpful information.

- *Consortium for Policy Research in Education (CPRE)*
  http://www.upenn.edu/gse/cpre/
  CPRE unites researchers from five of the nation's leading universities to improve elementary and secondary education through research on policy, finance, school reform, and school governance. CPRE researchers are currently examining alternative approaches to reform; that is, new accountability policies, whole-school reform efforts, and the contracting out of instructional services.

References

Allington, R. L., & McGill-Franzen, A. (1992). Unintended effects of educational reform in New York. *Educational Policy, 6,* 397–414.

American Federation of Teachers. (1998). *Making standards matter: 1998.* Washington, DC: Author.

Bond, L., Roeber, E., & Connealy, S. (1998). *Annual survey of state student assessment programs.* Washington, DC: Council of Chief State School Officers.

Elliott, J., & Thurlow, M. (1997). *Opening the door to educational reform: Understanding educational assessment and accountability.* Boston, MA: The Federation for Children with Special Needs.

Elliott, J., Thurlow, M., & Ysseldyke, J. (1996). *Assessment guidelines that maximize the participation of students with disabilities in large-scale assessments: Characteristics and considerations* (Synthesis Report 25). Minneapolis, MN: University of Minnesota, National Center on Educational Outcomes.

Erickson, R., & Thurlow, M. (1997). *1997 state special education outcomes.* Minneapolis, MN: National Center on Educational Outcomes, University of Minnesota.

Erickson, R.N., Thurlow, M. L., & Thor, K.A. (1995). *State special education outcomes 1994.* Minneapolis, MN: University of Minnesota, National Center on Educational Outcomes.

Erickson, R., Thurlow, M., & Ysseldyke, J. (1996). *Neglected numerators, drifting denominators, and fractured fractions: Determining participation rates for students with disabilities in statewide assessment programs* (Synthesis Report 23). Minneapolis, MN: University of Minnesota, National Center on Educational Outcomes.

Falvey, M. (1989). *Community-based curriculum: Instructional strategies for students with severe handicaps* (2nd ed.). Baltimore, MD: Brookes.

Ford, A., Schnorr, R., Meyer, L., Davern, L., Black, J., & Dempsey, P. (1989). *The Syracuse community-referenced curriculum guide.* Baltimore, MD: Brookes.

Frey, W., Burke, D., Jakworth, P., Lynch, L., & Sumpter, M. (1996a). *Addressing unique educational needs of individuals with disabilities: Educational performance expectations for achieving full independence in major life roles: AUEN 3.0.* Lansing, MI: Disability Research Systems.

Frey, W., Burke, D., Jakworth, P., Lynch, L., & Sumpter, M. (1996b). *Addressing unique educational needs of individuals with disabilities: Educational performance expectations for achieving functional independence in major life roles: AUEN 3.0.* Lansing, MI: Disability Research Systems.

Frey, W., Burke, D., Jakworth, P., Lynch, L., & Sumpter, M. (1996c). *Addressing unique educational needs of individuals with disabilities: Educational performance expectations for achieving supported independence in major life roles: AUEN 3.0.* Lansing, MI: Disability Research Systems.

Frey, W., Burke, D., Jakworth, P., Lynch, L., & Sumpter, M. (1996d). *Addressing unique educational needs of individuals with disabilities: Educational performance expectations for achieving participation in major life roles: AUEN 3.0.* Lansing, MI: Disability Research Systems.

Giangreco, M., Cloninger, C., & Iverson, V. (1993). *Choosing options and accommodations for children: A guide to planning inclusive education.* Baltimore, MD: Brookes.

Guy, B., Shin, H., Lee, S., & Thurlow, M. (1999). *State graduation requirements for students with and without disabilities.* Minneapolis, MN: University of Minnesota, National Center on Educational Outcomes.

Individuals with Disabilities Education Act Amendments of 1997, 20 U.S.C. § 1400 *et seq.* (West 1997).

Individuals with Disabilities Education Act Regulations, 34 C.F.R. § 300 and 303. (1999).

Jaeger, R., & Tucker, C. (1998). *Analyzing, disaggregating, reporting, and interpreting students' achievement test results: A guide to practice for Title I and beyond.* Washington, DC: Council of Chief State School Officers.

Kleinert, H., Kearns, J., & Kennedy, S. (1996). Accountability for all students: Kentucky's Alternate Portfolio Assessment for students with moderate and severe disabilities. *Journal of the Association for Severe Handicaps, 22*, 88–101.

Kokaska, C., & Brolin, D. (1985). *Career education for handicapped individuals* (2nd ed.). New York: Merrill/Macmillan.

McGrew, K., Algozzine, B., Spiegel, A., Thurlow, M., & Ysseldyke, J. (1993). *The identification of people with disabilities in national databases: A failure to communicate.* Minneapolis, MN: University of Minnesota, National Center on Educational Outcomes.

McGrew, K., Thurlow, M., Shriner, J., & Spiegel, A. (1992). *Inclusion of students with disabilities in national and state data collection programs.* Minneapolis, MN: University of Minnesota, National Center on Educational Outcomes.

Nelson, J. R., Ysseldyke, J., & Thurlow, M. (1998). *Desired characteristics for state and school district educational accountability reports.* Minneapolis, MN: University of Minnesota, National Center on Educational Outcomes.

Roach, V., & Raber, S. (1997). *State educational reform: District response and the implications for special education. A cross-site analysis based on four case studies.* Alexandria, VA: Center for Policy Research on the Impact of General and Special Education Reform, National Association of State Boards of Education.

Salvia, J., & Ysseldyke, J. (1998). *Assessment* (7th ed.). Boston: Houghton Mifflin.

Seyfarth, A., Ysseldyke, J., & Thurlow, M. (1998). *An analysis of perceived desirability, feasibility, and actual use of specific criteria for large-scale assessment and accountability systems* (Technical Report 21). Minneapolis, MN: University of Minnesota, National Center on Educational Outcomes.

Stiggins, R. (1995). Assessment literacy for the 21st century. *Phi Delta Kappan, 77*(3), 238.

Thompson, S., Erickson, R., Thurlow, M., Ysseldyke, J., & Callendar, S. (1999). *Status of the states in the development of alternate assessments.* Minneapolis, MN: University of Minnesota, National Center on Educational Outcomes.

Thompson, S., & Thurlow, M. (1999). *1999 state special education outcomes: A report on state activities at the end of the century.* Minneapolis, MN: University of Minnesota, National Center on Educational Outcomes.

Thurlow, M., Elliott, J., Scott, D., & Shin, H. (1997). *An analysis of state approaches to including students with disabilities in assessments implemented during educational reform.* Minneapolis, MN: University of Minnesota, National Center on Educational Outcomes.

Thurlow, M., Elliott, J., & Ysseldyke, J. (1998). *Testing students with disabilities: Practical strategies for complying with district and state requirements.* Thousand Oaks, CA: Corwin.

Thurlow, M., Hurley, C., Spicuzza, R., & El Sawaf, H. (1996). *A Review of the Literature on Testing Accommodations for Students with Disabilities* (Minnesota Report 9). Minneapolis, MN: University of Minnesota, National Center on Educational Outcomes.

Thurlow, M., Seyfarth, A., Boys, C., & Scott, D. (2000). *State assessment policies on participation and accommodations for students with disabilities: 1999 update.* Minneapolis, MN: University of Minnesota, National Center on Educational Outcomes.

Thurlow, M., Seyfarth, A., Scott, D., & Ysseldyke, J. (1997). *State assessment policies on participation and accommodations for students with disabilities: 1997 update* (Synthesis Report 29). Minneapolis, MN: University of Minnesota, National Center on Educational Outcomes.

Thurlow, M., Ysseldyke, J., Gutman, S., & Geenen, K. (1998). *An analysis of inclusion of students with disabilities in state standards documents.* Minneapolis, MN: University of Minnesota, National Center on Educational Outcomes.

Thurlow, M., Ysseldyke, J., & Olsen, K. (1996). *Self-study guide for the development of statewide assessments that include students with disabilities.* Minneapolis, MN: University of Minnesota, National Center on Educational Outcomes.

Thurlow, M., Ysseldyke, J., & Silverstein, B. (1993). *Testing accommodations for students with disabilities: A review of the literature.* Minneapolis, MN: University of Minnesota, National Center on Educational Outcomes.

Vanderwood, M., Ysseldyke, J., & Thurlow, M. (1993). *Consensus building: A process for selecting educational outcomes and indicators (Outcomes and Indicators No. 2).* Minneapolis, MN: University of Minnesota, National Center on Educational Outcomes.

Why Johnny stayed home. (1997, Oct. 6). *Newsweek,* p. 60.

Ysseldyke, J. (1998). *Results of the 1997 national survey of state assessment practices for students with disabilities.* Paper presented at the 28th Annual National Conference on Large Scale Assessment, Colorado Springs, CO, June 14–17.

Ysseldyke, J., Dawson, P., Lehr, C., Reschly, D., Reynolds, M., & Telzrow, C. (1997). *School psychology: A blueprint for training and practice II.* Bethesda, MD: National Association of School Psychologists.

Ysseldyke, J., Krentz, J., Elliott, J., Thurlow, M., Erickson, R., & Moore, M. (1998). *NCEO framework for educational accountability.* Minneapolis, MN: University of Minnesota, National Center on Educational Outcomes.

Ysseldyke, J., & Nelson, R. (1998). *Enhancing communication: Desirable characteristics for state and district educational accountability reports* (Synthesis Report 30). Minneapolis, MN: University of Minnesota, National Center on Educational Outcomes.

Ysseldyke, J., & Olsen, K. (1999). Putting alternate assessments into practice: What to measure and possible sources of data. *Exceptional Children, 65* (2), 175–185.

Ysseldyke, J., & Olsen, K. (1997). *Putting alternate assessments into practice: What to measure and possible sources of data* (Synthesis Report 28). Minneapolis, MN: University of Minnesota, National Center on Educational Outcomes.

Ysseldyke, J., & Thurlow, M. (1993). *Self-study guide to the development of educational outcomes and indicators: A companion piece to the six levels of educational outcomes and indicators for use by state departments of education, school districts, and local schools.* Minneapolis, MN: University of Minnesota, National Center on Educational Outcomes.

Ysseldyke, J., Thurlow, M., Erickson, R., Gabrys, R., Haigh, J., Trimble, S., & Gong, B. (1996). *A comparison of state assessment systems in Kentucky and Maryland with a focus on the participation of students with disabilities* (State Assessment Series, Maryland/Kentucky Report 1). Minneapolis, MN: University of Minnesota, National Center on Educational Outcomes.

Ysseldyke, J., Thurlow, M., Kozleski, E., & Reschly, D. (1998). *Accountability for the results of educating students with disabilities: Assessment conference report on the new assessment provisions of the 1997 amendments to the Individuals with Disabilities Education Act.* Minneapolis, MN: University of Minnesota, National Center on Educational Outcomes, Council of Chief State School Officers, National Association of School Directors in Special Education.

Ysseldyke, J., Thurlow, M., McGrew, K., & Shriner, J. (1994). *Recommendations for making decisions about the participation of students with disabilities in state assessment programs.* Minneapolis, MN: University of Minnesota, National Center on Educational Outcomes.

Ysseldyke, J., Thurlow, M., McGrew, K., & Vanderwood, M. (1994). *Making decisions about the inclusion of students with disabilities in large-scale assessments.* Minneapolis, MN: University of Minnesota, National Center on Educational Outcomes.

Ysseldyke, J., Thurlow, M., Langenfeld, K., Nelson, R., Teelucksingh, E., & Seyfarth, A. (1998). *Educational results for students with disabilities: What do the data tell us?* Minneapolis, MN: University of Minnesota, National Center on Educational Outcomes.

Ysseldyke, J., Thurlow, M., Nelson, R., & Teelucksingh, E. (2000). *Where's Waldo?: A third search of state accountability reports.* Minneapolis, MN: University of Minnesota, National Center on Educational Outcomes.

Ysseldyke, J., Thurlow, M., Seyfarth, A., Bielinski, J., Moody, M., & Haigh, J. (1999). *Instructional and assessment accommodations in Maryland.* Minneapolis, MN: University of Minnesota, National Center on Educational Outcomes.

Zlatos, B. (1994). Don't test, don't tell: Is 'academic red-shirting' skewing the way we rank our schools? *The American School Board Journal, 181*(11), 24–28.

ANNOTATED BIBLIOGRAPHY

Thompson, S., Erickson, R., Thurlow, M., Ysseldyke, J., & Callendar, S. (1999). *Status of the states in the development of alternate assessments.* Minneapolis, MN: University of Minnesota, National Center on Educational Outcomes.

This synthesis report summarizes the responses generated by 37 states and three other educational entities that receive U.S. funding for special education services to an on-line alternate assessment cybersurvey produced by the National Center for Educational Outcomes. Although 32 states are currently working on identifying the curricular or content standards for which an alternate assessment will be developed, a number of states are identifying specific instruments and approaches for collecting alternate assessment data. Individuals can also view other states' answers to such alternate assessment issues as eligibility guidelines, the decision-making process to participate in such an assessment, the link of state or school district standards to alternate assessment, the selection of data for an assessment, and the reporting of such assessment results and how to aggregate/disaggregate such results.

Thurlow, M., Elliott, J., & Ysseldyke, J. (1998). *Testing students with disabilities: Practical strategies for complying with district and state requirements.* Thousand Oaks, CA: Corwin.

This essential resource for school professionals describes accountability systems, participation and accommodation decisions, alternate assessment, the reporting of assessment results, school staff collaboration, rethinking of the IEP, and involving parents in testing decisions. To help implement practical strategies, a number of forms, checklists, and transparency masters are available in reproducible formats. To further facilitate the implementation of assessment provisions, another portion of the book, "Conducting Staff Development," is designed to help in the delivery and dissemination of information about the what, why, how, and what-ifs of assessment programs and accommodations decisions for students with disabilities. Finally, this resource also contains a list of technical assistance and dissemination networks that can provide information relevant to large-scale assessment issues.

Thurlow, M., Seyfarth, A., Boys, C., & Scott, D. (2000). *1999 state assessment policies for students with disabilities: Participation and accommodations.* Minneapolis, MN: University of Minnesota, National Center on Educational Outcomes.

This document contains the most current information concerning state participation and accommodations policies for students with disabilities. The National Center on Educational Outcomes has been tracking these state policies for the past seven years, and a chronology of changes/trends is noted. Thorough tables provide a national look at the variables included in state participation and accommodations decision criteria, testing options, broad areas of accommodations, and the specific types of accommodations permitted by individual states.

Ysseldyke, J., Thurlow, M., Kozleski, E., & Reschly, D. (1998). *Accountability for the results of educating students with disabilities: Assessment conference report on the new assessment provisions of the 1997 Amendments to the Individuals with Disabilities Act.* Minneapolis, MN: University of Minnesota, National Center on Educational Outcomes.

Recognizing the challenges to be faced with the new assessment provisions, the U.S. Department of Education's Office of Special Education and Rehabilitative Services (OSERS), and its component Office of Special Education Programs (OSEP) requested that the National Center on Educational Outcomes convene a working conference in Washington, D.C., to define issues and develop recommendations related to statewide and districtwide assessments and accountability. This report summarizes the 3-day working conference covering the assessment provisions. Issues such as lack of consistency or consensus, assessment design and administration, and consequences of the IDEA provisions are summarized. Recommendations regarding assessment practices, research and development, technical assistance, professional development, and monitoring are included.

Ysseldyke, J., & Olsen, K. (1999). Putting alternate assessments into practice: What to measure and possible sources of data. *Exceptional Children, 65* (2), 175–185.

The authors define alternate assessment, describe methods that can be used to collect data, and describe domains in which data should be collected. A helpful matrix is provided to help school professionals think about the types of data they may collect for the various domains. This article was developed from the results of a focus group study in which teachers delineated ways in which data might be collected by using each of the methods in each of the domains. An initial set of thoughts can serve as a starting point for the creation of alternate assessments.

CHAPTER 3

Assessment and Eligibility Determination in the Individuals with Disabilities Education Act of 1997

Daniel J. Reschly
Vanderbilt University

Significant legal influences on the practice of school psychology and the delivery of special education have been increasingly recognized over the past quarter century (Fagan, 1992, 1995). Although all aspects of the practice of school psychology are influenced by legal requirements (Reschly & Bersoff, 1999), the areas most affected are the assessment of children and youth with disabilities and the determination of eligibility for special education or related services. These activities constitute the majority of school psychologists' current professional roles (Curtis, Hunley, Walker, & Baker, 1999; Reschly, 2000; Reschly & Wilson, 1995). In this chapter the origins, current interpretations, and practice implications of the federal regulations concerning eligibility determination and assessment will be discussed within the context of the Individuals with Disabilities Education Act Amendments of 1997 (IDEA 97) and subsequent regulations (Individuals with Disabilities Education Act Amendments, 1997; Individuals with Disabilities Education Act Regulations, 1999).

BACKGROUND/PURPOSES OF ASSESSMENT/ELIGIBILITY PROVISIONS IN IDEA 97

The development of school psychology in this century has closely followed the establishment of state legislation establishing special education programs and classification criteria requiring psychological assessment (Fagan, 1987a, 1987b, 1992). Since 1975 school psychology has grown rapidly as a result of the enactment of mandatory special education laws at the state and federal levels in the early to mid-1970s. Current legal requirements regarding assessment and eligibility determination originated in this legislation. A brief review of that litigation and legislation provides an appreciation of *why* certain IDEA requirements exist today.

Litigation

The fascinating history of litigation in special education and school psychology is beyond the scope of this chapter. Interested readers are referred to Reschly and Bersoff (1999) and Reschly, Kicklighter, and McKee (1988a, 1988b, 1988c). The litigation prior to 1975 has the most relevance to the IDEA 97 provisions concerning assessment and eligibility; hence, this brief review will focus on that litigation.

Four class-action court cases markedly influenced the mandatory state and federal special education legislation that was established first in the 1970s and is reflected most prominently in IDEA 97. The first cases are called the "right to education" in that they established the rights of students with disabilities (SWD) to free and appropriate public educational services (FAPE) in the least restrictive environment (LRE), procedural safeguards, and individualized programming (*Mills v. Board of Education*, 1972; *Pennsylvania Association for Retarded Children v. Commonwealth of Pennsylvania*, 1972). Pennsylvania Association for Retarded Children (PARC) and Mills involved parent groups interested in SWD who sued state educational agencies over the practice of allowing local school districts discretion in whether they permitted SWD to attend public schools and whether special education programs were provided to them if they were admitted to school.

The Mills and PARC courts reasoned that because children and youth with disabilities could learn and profit from educational services, it was a violation of their equal protection and due process constitutional rights if states required and financially supported the education of students without disabilities but denied access to educational services to SWD. The courts reasoned that state and local educational agencies treating children and youth with disabilities differently by denying educational access to them was not a rational or permissible form of differential treatment. The PARC and Mills courts went further in mandating that the educational programs for children and youth with disabilities meet critical standards. Those standards are now represented in IDEA 97 provisions regarding the principles of an appropriate education at no cost to the parents (FAPE), least restrictive environment (LRE), procedural safeguards, individual evaluation of disability status and educational needs, and individualized education program (IEP) (Reschly & Bersoff, 1999).

A second type of case with equally important implications for special education appeared in the federal courts at the same time as the PARC and Mills cases.

These cases established the rights of all children to nondiscriminatory assessment in the consideration of their special education needs and in their placement in special education programs (*Diana v. State Board of Education,* 1970; *Guadalupe Organization v. Tempe Elementary School District No. 3,* 1972). Disproportionate minority representation in special education programs was the impetus for the Diana and Guadalupe cases. Both established important protections in assessment and decision making by using unequivocal language that was tracked nearly verbatim in later federal regulations. Some of the important principles established in these cases were nondiscrimination in testing, evaluation, and special education decision making; use of multiple measures of student performance; consideration of multiple domains of behavior, not just IQ; consideration of primary language in evaluations; and decision making by a team composed of parents and professionals such as teachers and school psychologists. The issue of disproportionate minority representation has not been resolved successfully over the nearly quarter century of federal legislation guaranteeing nondiscrimination in special education assessment and decision making (Reschly, 1997; Reschly & Bersoff, 1999), prompting further federal regulations that will be reviewed later.

The early litigation exerted enormous influence on subsequent legislation and on the requirements that professionals such as school psychologists must meet in assessing children and youth suspected of or having disabilities and in determining that such students are eligible for special education services. Today it is impossible to ignore this legislation in the practice of school psychology and special education. Litigation since 1975 (*Hendrick Hudson Board of Education v. Rowley,* 1982; *Honig v. Doe,* 1987; *Larry P. v. Riles,* 1979, 1984, 1992; *Marshall et al. v Georgia,* 1984, 1985) also has had important influences on special education; however, none of the recent litigation had the truly revolutionary effects of the litigation that occurred in the late 1960s and early 1970s.

Legislation

The litigation just reviewed was instrumental in the development of state and federal legislation regarding the educational rights of children and youth with disabilities. The Education of All Handicapped Children Act (EHA) (1975) was the touchstone federal legislation that appears in an updated form today as IDEA 97. All of the major principles of IDEA 97—free appropriate education at public expense, least restrictive environment, individualized educational program, procedural safeguards, and nondiscrimination and appropriate assessment—appeared in the EHA (1975) (see Table 1 on page 68). The amendments to EHA since 1975 have been in the form of extending the ages of children covered by the Act, adding provisions such as transition programming, and clarifying and extending the meaning of certain principles such as rights to procedural safeguards and to individualized education programs.

TABLE 1: EHA/IDEA Principles: Effects on Schools and Impact on Special Education

1. Right to a Free Appropriate Education at Public Expense

Effects: All students with disabilities (SWD) guaranteed educational rights leading to (a) more students in the existing population of students classified as having mild disabilities such as specific learning disabilities and (b) students with complex multiple disabilities and severe disabilities gain access to public schools.

Impact: Greater demand for special education teachers and related services personnel to provide instructional and other services to SWD; greater need for highly specialized skills in working with students with low incidence and severe disabilities such as autism.

2. Least Restrictive Environment

Effects: More SWD served in general education environments or in part-time resource teaching programs. Special education is increasingly becoming a range of services brought to children and youth in natural environments rather a place where educational services are provided.

Impact: More emphasis on assessment and delivery of services in natural settings and greater emphasis on providing supplementary supports and services in general education classrooms to SWD.

3. Individualized Educational Program (IEP)

Effects: Development of detailed plans to guide the provision of special education and related services, including general goals and specific objectives, assessment of progress, focus on progress in the general education curriculum, and annual review of the IEP.

Impact: More emphasis on identifying specific educational needs during evaluations and on monitoring progress toward goals.

4. Procedural Safeguards

Effects: Formal procedures to protect rights and to involve parents in decision making through requirements of informed consent, rights to appeal decisions, and impartial hearings.

Impact: Greater scrutiny of the work of special educators and related services personnel as well as more emphasis on communicating with parents. Increased likelihood of legal challenges to decisions made by special educators and psychologists.

5. Protection in Evaluation and Determination of Eligibility

Effects: Nondiscrimination in evaluation and decision making, multifactored assessment and decision making by a team that includes various professionals and parents, valid assessment that focuses on educational need, primary language, and educational programming.

Impact: Some traditional prerogatives of related services and special education personnel were limited. Less emphasis on IQ and greater emphasis on assessment with direct applications to IEP development. Assessment of multiple domains of behavior required along with a focus on functional, intervention-related assessment. Emphasis on consideration of language differences and sociocultural status.

6. Confidentiality of Records and Parental Access to Records

Effects: Access to records controlled by client/parent. School officials' access to records determined by a need-to-know principle. Parents or youth of legal age are guaranteed access to records.

Impact: The work and records of special educators and psychologists open to parental inspection including test protocols and treatment notes (unless excluded under state law), raising legal issues about violation of copyright laws and professional ethical issues regarding disclosure of sensitive information. In some instances schools required to make copies of copyrighted test protocols for parental inspection.

This brief review of litigation and legislation establishes the background for consideration of the legal requirements in IDEA 97 pertaining to assessment and eligibility determination with children and youth suspected of having disabilities. Several layers of legal influence involving both court precedent and statute at the state and federal levels establish these general requirements, making them relatively stable and unlikely to change dramatically in the immediate future.

Two sources of law typically are needed to implement the will of Congress or state legislatures. The first is the statute or law as passed by the legislative body. The federal IDEA statute is found in the United States Code (USC) at Chapter 20, beginning with Section 1400 (*http://www.ideapolicy.org/*; Individuals with Disabilities Education Act Amendments, 1997). A typical federal or state statute establishes general principles that are implemented through more detailed federal regulations or state rules. The federal regulations implementing IDEA 97 were first published in a final form on March 12, 1999. They appear in the Code of Federal Regulations (CFR), Chapter 34, beginning with Section 300 (*http://www.ideapolicy.org/*; Individuals with Disabilities Education Act Regulations, 1999).

Federal regulations or state rules, such as the state special education rules, typically are developed by the executive branch of government responsible for implementing the law, submitted for public comment, revised one or more times, approved by an oversight committee of the legislative branch, and then published officially. Federal regulations or state rules are part of the law; that is, they are law in the same way that the statute is law. State special education rules cannot be inconsistent with federal IDEA regulations. IDEA 97 regulations were developed and monitored by the Office of Special Education and Rehabilitation Services, a division of the U.S. Department of Education. The Division or Bureau of Special Education, a unit of the State Department of Education or State Department of Public Instruction, typically develops state special education rules.

The analyses of assessment and eligibility determination in this chapter focuses on federal regulations. Practitioners are cautioned, however, to consult relevant special education rules in their state to become fully informed about the legal requirements pertinent to the services they provide to children and youth with disabilities.

CONSIDERATIONS FOR SCHOOL-BASED TEAMS IN IMPLEMENTING ASSESSMENT/ ELIGIBILITY PROVISIONS

In this section, the IDEA 97 regulations pertaining to assessment, eligibility determination, and disproportionality are reviewed. Changes in the existing regulations as a result of IDEA 97 are emphasized. Before reviewing these regulations it is important to note that the assessment and eligibility determination regulations are interconnected to other regulations governing individualized education programs, placement in the least restrictive environment, due process procedural safeguards, and confidentiality. Some of those interconnections will be discussed as appropriate.

Assessment Regulations

Regulations governing assessment and decision making with children and youth with disabilities were first promulgated by the U.S. government on August 23, 1977, as the Protection in Evaluation Procedures Provisions (PEP) (EHA, 1975, 1977). Specific features of the PEP regulations were derived, often verbatim, from the prior consent decrees that settled class action court cases (*Diana, Guadalupe, PARC,* and *Mills*). Incorporated into PEP from these cases were regulations requiring a comprehensive, individualized evaluation; nondiscriminatory evaluation; consideration of multiple domains of behavior, not just a single measure such as IQ; and decision making by a team of professionals with the participation of parents.

The PEP regulations were not changed from 1977 until March 12, 1999, when the regulations for IDEA 97 (Individuals with Disabilities Education Act Regulations, 1999) were published as the Procedures for Evaluation and Determination of Eligibility (PEDE) (34 CFR 300.530 to 34 CFR 300.543; see Table 2). The change in title was accompanied by expansion from approximately 1100 to approximately

1900 words. The section of the regulations devoted to Additional Procedures for Evaluating Children with Specific Learning Disabilities (34 CFR 300.541 through 300.543) did not change and has not changed since first published in 1977 (see Table 2). All of the PEP regulations were incorporated into PEDE, along with several new regulations that reflect increasing concerns with the quality and usefulness of the information gathered during the full and individual evaluation.

TABLE 2: IDEA (1997, 1999) Procedures for Evaluation and Determination of Eligibility (PEDE)

§300.530 General

Each SEA shall ensure that each public agency establishes and implements procedures that meet the requirements of §§300.531300.536.

§300.531 Initial evaluation

Each public agency shall conduct a full and individual initial evaluation, in accordance with §§300.532 and 300.533, before the initial provision of special education **and related services** to a child with a disability under Part B of the Act.

(Authority: 20 U.S.C. 1414(a)(1))

§300.532 Evaluation procedures

Each public agency shall ensure, at a minimum, that the following requirements are met:

a. 1. Tests and other evaluation materials used to assess a child under Part B of the Act—

   (i) Are selected and administered so as not to be discriminatory on a racial or cultural basis; and

   (ii) Are provided and administered in the child's native language or other mode of communication, unless it is clearly not feasible to do so; and

2. **Materials and procedures used to assess a child with limited English proficiency are selected and administered to ensure that they measure the extent to which the child has a disability and needs special education, rather than measuring the child's English language skills.**

b. **A variety of assessment tools and strategies are used to gather relevant functional and developmental information about the child, including in-**

Table 2 continued on p. 72

Table 2 continued

formation provided by the parent, and information related to enabling the child to be involved in and progress in the general curriculum (or for a preschool child, to participate in appropriate activities), that may assist in determining—

1. Whether the child is a child with a disability under §300.7; and

2. The content of the child's IEP.

c. 1. Any standardized tests that are given to a child—

      (i) Have been validated for the specific purpose for which they are used; and

      (ii) Are administered by trained and knowledgeable personnel in accordance with any instructions provided by the producer of the tests.

    2. If an assessment is not conducted under standard conditions, a description of the extent to which it varied from standard conditions (e.g., the qualifications of the person administering the test, or the method of test administration) must be included in the evaluation report.

d. Tests and other evaluation materials include those tailored to assess specific areas of educational need and not merely those that are designed to provide a single general intelligence quotient.

e. Tests are selected and administered so as best to ensure that if a test is administered to a child with impaired sensory, manual, or speaking skills, the test results accurately reflect the child's aptitude or achievement level or whatever other factors the test purports to measure, rather than reflecting the child's impaired sensory, manual, or speaking skills (unless those skills are the factors that the test purports to measure).

f. No single procedure is used as the sole criterion for determining **whether a child is a child with a disability** and for determining an appropriate educational program for the child.

g. The child is assessed in all areas related to the suspected disability, including, if appropriate, health, vision, hearing, social and emotional status, general intelligence, academic performance, communicative status, and motor abilities.

h. **In evaluating each child with a disability under §§300.531-300.536, the evaluation is sufficiently comprehensive to identify all of the child's special education and related services needs, whether or not commonly linked to the disability category in which the child has been classified.**

i. **The public agency uses technically sound instruments that may assess the relative contribution of cognitive and behavioral factors, in addition to physical or developmental factors.**

j. The public agency uses assessment tools and strategies that provide relevant information that directly assists persons in determining the educational needs of the child.

(Authority: 20 U.S.C. 1412(a)(6)(B), 1414(b)(2) and (3))

§300.533 Determination of needed evaluation data

a. Review of existing evaluation data. As part of an initial evaluation (if appropriate) and as part of any reevaluation under Part B of the Act, a group that includes the individuals described in §300.344, and other qualified professionals, as appropriate, shall—

1. Review existing evaluation data on the child, including—

    (i) Evaluations and information provided by the parents of the child;

    (ii) Current classroom-based assessments and observations; and

    (iii) Observations by teachers and related services providers; and

2. On the basis of that review, and input from the child's parents, identify what additional data, if any, are needed to determine—

    (i) Whether the child has a particular category of disability, as described in §300.7, or, in case of a reevaluation of a child, whether the child continues to have such a disability;

    (ii) The present levels of performance and educational needs of the child;

    (iii) Whether the child needs special education and related services, or in the case of a reevaluation of a child, whether the child continues to need special education and related services; and

    (iv) Whether any additions or modifications to the special education and related services are needed to enable the child to meet the measurable annual goals set out in the IEP of the child and to participate, as appropriate, in the general curriculum.

b. Conduct of review. The group described in paragraph (a) of this section may conduct its review without a meeting.

c. Need for additional data. The public agency shall administer tests and other evaluation materials as may be needed to produce the data identified under paragraph (a) of this section.

d. Requirements if additional data are not needed.

1. If the determination under paragraph (a) of this section is that no additional data are needed to determine whether the child continues to be a child with a disability, the public agency shall notify the child's parents—

Table 2 continued on p. 74

Table 2 continued

(i) Of that determination and the reasons for it; and

(ii) Of the right of the parents to request an assessment to determine whether, for purposes of services under this part, the child continues to be a child with a disability.

2. The public agency is not required to conduct the assessment described in paragraph (d)(1)(ii) of this section unless requested to do so by the child's parents.

(Authority: 20 U.S.C. 1414(c)(1), (2) and (4))

§300.534 Determination of eligibility

a. Upon completing the administration of tests and other evaluation materials

1. A group of qualified professionals and the parent of the child must determine whether the child is a child with a disability, as defined in §300.7; and

2. The public agency must provide a copy of the evaluation report and the documentation of determination of eligibility to the parent.

b. A child may not be determined to be eligible under this part if—

1. The determinant factor for that eligibility determination is—

(i) Lack of instruction in reading or math; or

(ii) Limited English proficiency ; and

2. The child does not otherwise meet the eligibility criteria under §300.7(a).

c. 1. A public agency must evaluate a child with a disability in accordance with §§300.532 and 300.533 before determining that the child is no longer a child with a disability.

2. The evaluation described in paragraph (c)(1) of this section is not required before the termination of a student's eligibility under Part B of the Act due to graduation with a regular high school diploma, or exceeding the age eligibility for FAPE under State law.

(Authority: 20 U.S.C. 1414(b)(4) and (5), (c)(5))

§300.535 Procedures for determining eligibility and placement

a. In interpreting evaluation data **for the purpose of determining if a child is a child with a disability under §300.7, and the educational needs of the child,** each public agency shall—

1. Draw upon information from a variety of sources, including aptitude and achievement tests, parent input, teacher recommendations, physical condition, social or cultural background, and adaptive behavior; and

2. Ensure that information obtained from all of these sources is documented and carefully considered.

b. If a determination is made that a child has a disability and needs special education and related services, an IEP must be developed for the child in accordance with §§300.340300.350.

(Authority: 20 U.S.C. 1412(a)(6), 1414(b)(4))

§300.536 Reevaluation

Each public agency shall ensure—

a. That the IEP of each child with a disability is reviewed in accordance with §§300.340300.350; and

b. That a reevaluation of each child, in accordance with §§300.532-300.535, **is conducted if conditions warrant a reevaluation, or if the child's parent or teacher requests a reevaluation, but at least once every three years.**

(Authority: 20 U.S.C. 1414(a)(2))

Additional Procedures for Evaluating Children with Specific Learning Disabilities

§300.540 Additional team members

The determination of whether a child suspected of having a specific learning disability is a child with a disability as defined in §300.7, must be made by the child's parents and a team of qualified professionals which must include—

a. 1. The child's regular teacher; or

2. If the child does not have a regular teacher, a regular classroom teacher qualified to teach a child of his or her age; or

3. For a child of less than school age, an individual qualified by the SEA to teach a child of his or her age; and

b. At least one person qualified to conduct individual diagnostic examinations of children, such as a school psychologist, speech-language pathologist, or remedial reading teacher.

§300.541 Criteria for determining the existence of a specific learning disability

a. A team may determine that a child has a specific learning disability if—

1. The child does not achieve commensurate with his or her age and ability levels in one or more of the areas listed in paragraph (a)(2) of this section,

Table 2 continued on p. 76

Table 2 continued

if provided with learning experiences appropriate for the child's age and ability levels; and

2. The team finds that a child has a severe discrepancy between achievement and intellectual ability in one or more of the following areas:

    (i)   Oral expression.

    (ii) Listening comprehension.

    (iii) Written expression.

    (iv) Basic reading skill.

    (v)   Reading comprehension.

    (vi) Mathematics calculation.

    (vii) Mathematics reasoning.

b. The team may not identify a child as having a specific learning disability if the severe discrepancy between ability and achievement is primarily the result of—

    1. A visual, hearing, or motor impairment;

    2. Mental retardation;

    3. Emotional disturbance; or

    4. Environmental, cultural or economic disadvantage.

§300.542 Observation

a. At least one team member other than the child's regular teacher shall observe the child's academic performance in the regular classroom setting.

b. In the case of a child of less than school age or out of school, a team member shall observe the child in an environment appropriate for a child of that age.

    (Authority: Sec. 5(b), Pub. L. 94-142)

§300.543 Written report

a. For a child suspected of having a specific learning disability, the documentation of the team's determination of eligibility, as required by §300.534(a)(2), must include a statement of—

    1. Whether the child has a specific learning disability;

    2. The basis for making the determination;

    3. The relevant behavior noted during the observation of the child;

    4. The relationship of that behavior to the child's academic functioning;

5. The educationally relevant medical findings, if any;

6. Whether there is a severe discrepancy between achievement and ability that is not correctable without special education and related services; and

7. The determination of the team concerning the effects of environmental, cultural, or economic disadvantage.

b. Each team member shall certify in writing whether the report reflects his or her conclusion. If it does not reflect his or her conclusion, the team member must submit a separate statement presenting his or her conclusions.

Notes: 1. The Protection in Evaluation and Eligibility Determination Regulations (PEDE) first appeared on March 12, 1999 in the *Federal Register, 64*(48). The forerunner to PEDE was the Protection in Evaluation Procedures Provisions which first appeared on August 23, 1977 in the *Federal Register, 42*(163) as part of the Regulations Implementing the Education for All Handicapped Children Act of 1975 (PL 94-142). The PEP regulations were not changed from 1977 to 1999.
2. The Procedures for Evaluating Specific Learning Disabilities, section 300.540 through 300.543, first appeared in the *Federal Register*, 1977, December 29, *42*(250), pp. 65082–65085. These provisions remain the same in the IDEA (1997) Regulations [*Federal Register, 64*(48), March 12, 1999].

Readers are urged to review carefully the PEDE regulations in Table 2. The changes and additions that are new in the 1999 PEDE regulations are in bold type. All of the regulations represent important decisions by Congress regarding the characteristics of the evaluation and decision making provided by schools to children and youth with disabilities. All have the force of law. Moreover, the bolded content represents efforts to improve the nature of the evaluation and decision making provided to students with disabilities.

Continuing EHA Regulations

In this section the IDEA PEDE regulations that were continued from the EHA (1977) regulations are discussed. Like EHA, IDEA 97 continues to place responsibility on states to ensure that the PEDE regulations are implemented by local educational agencies.

Full and Individual Evaluation

The EHA regulations regarding assessment, eligibility, and placement provide the essential background for consideration of the new IDEA PEDE regulations. Perhaps the most important provision is the continuing requirement that every child must receive a *full and individual evaluation* prior to the provision of special education and related services (for a description of related services, see 34 CFR 300.24). The implication of this regulation continues to be that a thorough evaluation, tailored to the individual child, is needed prior to decisions about determination of disability or the development of an individualized education program (IEP).

Best practice requires the individualization of the evaluation, which involves matching it carefully and precisely to referral concerns and the student's learning and behavior patterns. These requirements imply the avoidance of standard batteries of tests or the use of a common set of procedures, such as an IQ test, a test of visual-motor perception, and a brief screening test of achievement, for all children. Recent survey data suggest that a standard battery is still prominent in school psychology practice, though perhaps less common in the 1990s than in prior decades (Reschly, 1998). Such standard evaluation approaches do not adequately implement the ideas of a full and *individualized* evaluation.

Multiple Domains

Other regulations continued in IDEA 97 from the EHA regulations include the requirements that multiple domains of behavior be considered and, *if appropriate*, assessed thoroughly. This regulation, as well as many other parts of IDEA, require professional judgments and individualization. This regulation does not require that every domain of functioning—intelligence, vision, health—be assessed with every child; rather, that all relevant domains be considered. For many children, there is ample existing evidence regarding one or more of the domains mentioned in 34 CFR 300.532 such that new information is unneeded in that domain. For others, brief screening measures may be sufficient, depending on the referral problems and the child's educational needs.

The exercise of judgment in designing evaluations has been problematic since the inception of EHA. Individualization means much more than using individually administered tests. Individualization means matching the evaluation to the nature of the problem, the characteristics of the child, and the likely educational needs. Individualization and administration of a standard battery to all children are contradictory practices. Treating all alike by using a standard battery is the antithesis of the meaning of this requirement and the spirit of the law. Best practices involve well-informed judgments and differential decisions, not standard batteries of assessment procedures.

Team Decision Making

In addition to individualization and multiple domains of behavior, the IDEA continues the EHA requirements that a team of persons, including professionals, parents, and, if appropriate, the child, be involved with the full and individual evaluation (34 CFR 300.533). Eligibility and placement decisions are viewed in the law as being too complex and important to allow reliance on a single specialty such as school psychology or on professionals without the involvement of parents. A continuing challenge is to adopt strategies that fully capitalize on the expertise of different professional specialties and the insights of parents in eligibility and intervention decisions.

IDEA 97 also continues the EHA regulations that (a) tests must be valid for the specific purpose for which they are used, (b) tests and evaluation procedures must be nondiscriminatory and administered in the child's native language unless clearly not feasible to do so (see later discussion), (c) no single test or procedure can be the sole basis for eligibility or placement, (d) tests are administered by trained and knowledgeable persons consistent with the instructions of the test author(s), and (e) an IEP must be developed that meets extensive requirements if the child is eligible for special education. It is important to note that these regulations have been in place without any changes since 1977.

Specific Learning Disabilities (SLD)

Additional procedures regarding the evaluation of children with SLD appeared in the *Federal Register* in December 1977 three months after the regulations first appeared for the remainder of the EHA. Congress in the mid-1970s was concerned about the absence of agreement among scholars and practitioners regarding what constituted a learning disability, the wide variations in estimated prevalence rates, and poorly operationalized and subjective classification criteria.

Congress challenged the Federal Bureau of Education for the Handicapped (BEH) to formulate evaluation procedures and classification criteria that would separate true from pseudo learning disabilities and that would limit SLD prevalence. Failure to publish the SLD regulations would have led to a de facto limit of 2% on LD prevalence with respect to federal funding of special education programs. The SLD regulations provoked intense debate among practitioners and professionals, but no consensus was reached as the deadline approached for the publication of the SLD regulations. Finally, BEH published a set of regulations that in essence defined SLD as an unexplained learning problem (see the exclusion factors in Regulation 300.541) reflected in one of several areas of achievement, resulting in a severe discrepancy between achievement and intellectual ability (see Regulation 300.541).

No one was pleased with the SLD regulations in 1977, and no one is pleased with them today. Although there is dissatisfaction with these regulations, there never has been, nor is there today, consensus on how SLD is to be defined or criteria for classification. The same regulations have existed verbatim now for two decades, and they were not changed in IDEA 97. There is, however, increasing consensus that the current SLD rules in the states have undesirable effects on the treatment of reading problems (see later discussion). This dissatisfaction will almost certainly change how SLD is diagnosed, at least in the early school grades.

New IDEA Assessment Regulations

IDEA 97 added several important regulations regarding assessment and decision making. Study of these regulations provides insight into areas seen by Congress as problematic in the implementation of mandatory special education legislation.

Nondiscrimination

Nondiscrimination and consideration of the child's native language clearly receive greater emphasis in IDEA 97, requiring additional practitioner efforts to avoid discriminatory practices or unwise decisions with limited English proficient (LEP) children. The nondiscrimination clause has been and continues to be problematic. There is no consensus in the law or in the professional literature on a definition of discrimination or on criteria to judge specific practices as discriminatory (Reschly & Bersoff, 1999; Reynolds, Lowe, & Saenz, 1999; *Journal of Special Education*, 1998). A subtle form of further direction to the states regarding nondiscrimination is provided in IDEA 97 through a set of regulations dealing with disproportionality (34 CFR 300.755), signaling that disproportionate minority enrollment in special education may be one criterion for the determination of discrimination (see later discussion).

Concerns about inappropriate decisions are reflected in 34 CFR 300.534, where the "determinant factor" for eligibility cannot be the absence of instruction in basic academic skills or limited English proficiency. The latter provision undoubtedly reflects the concern that LEP children/youth are penalized on tests because of language differences that can result in inappropriate eligibility and placement decisions.

Practitioners can expect greater scrutiny of the "fairness" of assessment, eligibility determination, and placement. Special education is not seen positively by many professionals who see disability status and special education placement as continuations of historical patterns of race discrimination. Strident criticism is often directed at special educators suggesting that eligibility is determined by discriminatory tests and that the programs are stigmatizing and ineffective.

Minority overrepresentation in special education is seen increasingly as a symptom that provokes additional scrutiny by state and federal agencies. That scrutiny will take the form of questioning traditional assessment practices, especially those tied to standardized intelligence and achievement tests, along with demands that the effectiveness of special education programs be documented for individuals and groups. Several subsequent regulations appear to be directed specifically to the concerns about fairness of assessment and effectiveness of programs. Generally, assessment procedures that do not rely on IQ tests and, instead, focus directly on educational needs and intervention design will be more acceptable to minority critics of current special education practices.

Functional Assessment and IEP Relevance

Part b of Regulation 532 (see Table 2 on page 71) is new and significant. First, a clear emphasis is placed on functional and developmental information gathered from a variety of sources including the parents. The *functional* requirement implies greater emphasis on gathering information in the natural setting that is directly relevant to the problem behavior and to interventions addressing the problem behavior. The requirement that the evaluation procedures address progress in the general education curriculum further solidifies the emphasis on natural setting and interventions. Although the term "functional" has varied meanings (see Tilly, Knoster, & Ikeda, this volume), all of the meanings in the literature have important implications for the implementation of the law.

Practitioners are challenged to develop and tailor assessment procedures to more clearly reflect the problem behavior in natural classroom, other school, and home settings. Behavior assessment and curriculum-based assessment methodologies typically provide information from the natural setting that is directly relevant to problem definition, special education need, and the design and evaluation of interventions. This section of the regulations, along with other sections discussed shortly, push the field toward problem-solving approaches featuring behavioral and curriculum-based assessment with less emphasis on standardized tests (Reschly, 1988; Reschly & Tilly, 1999; Reschly & Ysseldyke, 1995; Tilly, Reschly, & Grimes, 1999). These approaches have the advantages of being more acceptable to minority critics of special education and more closely related to ensuring effective programs.

The three new regulations at the end of this section, 532 (h), (i), and (j), appear to be directed toward ensuring that the assessment procedures are closely related to the development of the special education program. Emphasis is placed on identifying all of the child's special education needs, assessment of the relative contribution of cognitive and behavioral factors, and, most importantly, the collection of "relevant information that directly assists persons in determining the educational needs of the child." Clearly, IDEA 97 places significant emphasis on determining educational needs and not just disability classification and eligibility determination.

Divergence From Standardized Procedures

A new regulation addresses the clearly important issue of divergence from standardized procedures in administering and interpreting assessment results (34 CFR 300.532). When divergence from standardized procedures occurs or is required due to the characteristics of the child or the setting, it is the practitioner's responsibility to address these variations in a report and, presumably, to evaluate the likely effects of the variations on the assessment results.

Determination of Eligibility

Several new regulations stress the procedures by which children may be diagnosed as having a disability. First, according to 34 CFR 300.534 the diagnosis has to be made by a "group of qualified professionals and the parent of the child...." Second, the school or other public agency must share with parents an evaluation report and the documentation regarding eligibility determination (whether the child is eligible). The reporting requirement was regarded as best professional practice for many years, although the kind and amount of information that is shared with parents are sometimes disputed.

Judgments About Needed Data and Reevaluations

In EHA all children with disabilities were required to be reevaluated triennially or, if requested or needed, more frequently. Moreover, the reevaluation was widely and perhaps erroneously interpreted to require an evaluation closely patterned after the initial eligibility evaluation. That interpretation often led to a retesting exercise in which the continued eligibility was examined, with little focus on the effectiveness of the special education program, specific educational needs, and other information useful in forming a new IEP (see Canter, Hurley, & Reid, this volume).

Changes in IDEA 97 clearly indicate that judgments should be made about what data are needed to make the necessary decisions (34 CFR 300.533). An important step in these judgments about further data collection is reviewing existing data including "evaluations and information provided by the parents of the child; current classroom-based assessments and observations; and observations by teachers and related services providers."

Clearly, the old interpretation of the reevaluation requirement as automatic "retesting" is not consistent with the current regulations and, arguably, was not consistent with the old regulations. Moreover, the reevaluation is to be guided by the informed judgments of professionals regarding the kind of information needed in order to make informed decisions. Under these regulations different cases will require different kinds of data collection depending on the key decisions to be made. For example, for a child with a profound cognitive disability, for whom special education eligibility is not questioned, the original evaluation and the reevaluation might focus exclusively on programming issues such as the acquisition of self-help skills and the *experimental* functional analysis of specific problematic behaviors. For another child, special education eligibility due to an emotional or behavioral disorder may be a significant issue along with programming concerns in both the initial evaluation and the reevaluation. The evaluations for these students should look very different if they are *individualized* as well as focused on specific educational needs.

Integration of PEDE With Other IDEA Regulations

It is important to understand that the PEDE regulations do not stand alone. A good illustration of the interconnectedness of all of the IDEA 97 regulations is apparent from studying the PEDE regulations in conjunction with the IEP regulations (34 CFR 300.340 to 300.350). First, the IEP regulations require the participation of someone on the IEP team who can interpret the *instructional* implications of the evaluation results. That person can be and often is a school psychologist. The IEP must include a statement of the child's or youth's present levels of *educational* performance including how the disability affects involvement with and progress in the general education curriculum. The IEP also must address the student's participation in the statewide and districtwide assessment programs including any modifications of the assessment procedures to accommodate the needs of the student with a disability. Finally, the IEP must include information on the annual goals, short-term objectives, and measurement of progress toward these goals and objectives. IDEA 97 suggests that all of these IEP requirements should be addressed in the full and individual evaluation governed by the PEDE regulations.

Disability Classification and Disproportionality

Definitions for the 13 disability categories have changed only slightly since the 1991 revisions to IDEA when two categories were added, "Traumatic Brain Injury" and "Autism." Conceptual definitions are provided for each of the categories in the regulations; however, specific classification criteria are not provided (see Table 3). In fact, the federal definitions do not constitute a national classification system, because the states are permitted wide discretion in the names and numbers of disability categories, conceptual definitions, and classification criteria (Mercer, Jordan, Allsopp, & Mercer, 1996; Patrick & Reschly, 1982).

TABLE 3: IDEA Definitions of Disabilities (IDEA, 1999)

§300.7 Child with a disability
a.   General.

1.   As used in this part, the term child with a disability means a child evaluated in accordance with §§300.530300.536 as having mental retardation, a hearing impairment including deafness, a speech or language impairment, a visual impairment including blindness, serious emotional disturbance (hereafter referred to as emotional disturbance), an orthopedic impairment, autism, traumatic brain injury, an other health impair-

Table 3 continued on p. 84

Table 3 continued

ment, a specific learning disability, deafblindness, or multiple disabilities, and who, by reason thereof, needs special education and related services.

2. (i) Subject to paragraph (a)(2)(ii) of this section, if it is determined, through an appropriate evaluation under §§300.530-300.536, that a child has one of the disabilities identified in paragraph (a)(1) of this section, but only needs a related service and not special education, the child is not a child with a disability under this part.

    (ii) If, consistent with §300.26(a)(2), the related service required by the child is considered special education rather than a related service under State standards, the child would be determined to be a child with a disability under paragraph (a)(1) of this section.

b. Children aged 3 through 9 experiencing developmental delays. The term child with a disability for children aged 3 through 9 may, at the discretion of the State and LEA and in accordance with §300.313, include a child—

    1. Who is experiencing developmental delays, as defined by the State and as measured by appropriate diagnostic instruments and procedures, in one or more of the following areas: physical development, cognitive development, communication development, social or emotional development, or adaptive development; and

    2. Who, by reason thereof, needs special education and related services.

c. Definitions of disability terms. The terms used in this definition are defined as follows:

    1. (i) Autism means a developmental disability significantly affecting verbal and nonverbal communication and social interaction, generally evident before age 3, that adversely affects a child's educational performance. Other characteristics often associated with autism are engagement in repetitive activities and stereotyped movements, resistance to environmental change or change in daily routines, and unusual responses to sensory experiences. The term does not apply if a child's educational performance is adversely affected primarily because the child has an emotional disturbance, as defined in paragraph (b)(4) of this section.

        (ii) A child who manifests the characteristics of "autism" after age 3 could be diagnosed as having "autism" if the criteria in paragraph (c)(1)(i) of this section are satisfied.

    2. Deaf-blindness means concomitant hearing and visual impairments, the combination of which causes such severe communication and other developmental and educational needs that they cannot be accommodated in special education programs solely for children with deafness or children with blindness.

3. Deafness means a hearing impairment that is so severe that the child is impaired in processing linguistic information through hearing, with or without amplification, that adversely affects a child's educational performance.

4. Emotional disturbance is defined as follows:

    (i) The term means a condition exhibiting one or more of the following characteristics over a long period of time and to a marked degree that adversely affects a child's educational performance:

    (A) An inability to learn that cannot be explained by intellectual, sensory, or health factors.

    (B) An inability to build or maintain satisfactory interpersonal relationships with peers and teachers.

    (C) Inappropriate types of behavior or feelings under normal circumstances.

    (D) A general pervasive mood of unhappiness or depression.

    (E) A tendency to develop physical symptoms or fears associated with personal orschool problems.

    (ii) The term includes schizophrenia. The term does not apply to children who are socially maladjusted, unless it is determined that they have an emotional disturbance.

5. Hearing impairment means an impairment in hearing, whether permanent or fluctuating, that adversely affects a child's educational performance but that is not included under the definition of deafness in this section.

6. Mental retardation means significantly subaverage general intellectual functioning, existing concurrently with deficits in adaptive behavior and manifested during the developmental period, that adversely affects a child's educational performance.

7. Multiple disabilities means concomitant impairments (such as mental retardation-blindness, mental retardation-orthopedic impairment, etc.), the combination of which causes such severe educational needs that they cannot be accommodated in special education programs solely for one of the impairments. The term does not include deaf-blindness.

8. Orthopedic impairment means a severe orthopedic impairment that adversely affects a child's educational performance. The term includes impairments caused by congenital anomaly (e.g., clubfoot, absence of some member, etc.), impairments caused by disease (e.g., poliomyelitis, bone tuberculosis, etc.), and impairments from other causes (e.g., cerebral palsy, amputations, and fractures or burns that cause contractures).

Table 3 continued on p. 86

Table 3 continued

9. Other health impairment means having limited strength, vitality or alertness, including a heightened alertness to environmental stimuli that results in limited alertness with respect to the educational environment, that—

   (i) Is due to chronic or acute health problems such as asthma, attention deficit disorder or attention deficit hyperactivity disorder, diabetes, epilepsy, a heart condition, hemophilia, lead poisoning, leukemia, nephritis, rheumatic fever, and sickle cell anemia; and

   (ii) Adversely affects a child's educational performance.

10. Specific learning disability is defined as follows:

   (i) General. The term means a disorder in one or more of the basic psychological processes involved in understanding or in using language, spoken or written, that may manifest itself in an imperfect ability to listen, think, speak, read, write, spell, or to do mathematical calculations, including conditions such as perceptual disabilities, brain injury, minimal brain dysfunction, dyslexia, and developmental aphasia.

   (ii) Disorders not included. The term does not include learning problems that are primarily the result of visual, hearing, or motor disabilities, of mental retardation, of emotional disturbance, or of environmental, cultural, or economic disadvantage.

11. Speech or language impairment means a communication disorder, such as stuttering, impaired articulation, a language impairment, or a voice impairment, that adversely affects a child's educational performance.

12. Traumatic brain injury means an acquired injury to the brain caused by an external physical force, resulting in total or partial functional disability or psychosocial impairment, or both, that adversely affects a child's educational performance. The term applies to open or closed head injuries resulting in impairments in one or more areas, such as cognition; language; memory; attention; reasoning; abstract thinking; judgment; problem-solving; sensory, perceptual, and motor abilities; psychosocial behavior; physical functions; information processing; and speech. The term does not apply to brain injuries that are congenital or degenerative, or to brain injuries induced by birth trauma.

13. Visual impairment including blindness means an impairment in vision that, even with correction, adversely affects a child's educational performance. The term includes both partial sight and blindness.

(Authority: 20 U.S.C. 1401(3)(A) and (B); 1401(26))

The identification of a child or youth as needing special education is a two-pronged determination: (a) A disability in obtaining an education must be documented, and (b) a need for special education must be established. Meeting one prong without meeting the other renders the child or youth not eligible for special education and related services. The federal definitions generally include the phrase "adversely affects educational performance" to communicate the latter requirement as well as the language "... and who by reason thereof, needs special education and related services" [See Table 3, 34 CFR 300.7(a)(1)]. In future conceptions of best practices, more emphasis on the special-education–need component of eligibility is likely through strengthening interventions before referral and determining empirically that well-designed and properly implemented interventions in general education are not sufficient to enable the student to receive an appropriate education.

Disability Classification Policy and Noncategorical Changes

Contrary to the interpretation of many professionals, IDEA does not now, nor has it ever, required the use of the federal definitions or even a disability classification scheme using traditional categories. System change to a non-categorical approach along with other reforms has significant promise to make special education programs more effective and to reduce the excessive reliance on standardized tests in the full and individual evaluations (Graden, Zins, & Curtis, 1988; Reschly, 1988; Reschly, Tilly, & Grimes, 1999; Reschly & Ysseldyke, 1995). In a policy clarification letter from OSEP, Hehir (1996) noted what follows as the federal interpretation of the regulations regarding disability identification:

> Part B does not require States to label children. The definitions of "children with disabilities" at 34 CFR §300.7 must be used by states to prepare annual data reports for the U.S. Department of Education regarding the number of children in the state receiving "special education" and "related services" under the Part B program requirements. The Department has no objection to a state's use of categories which differ from those specified in Part B or, if it elects, the use of a noncategorical approach *so long as those children eligible under Part B are appropriately identified and served* (23 IDELR 341; emphasis added).

The possibility of non-categorical special education eligibility was made even more explicit with the following IDEA (1999) regulation:

> Nothing in the Act requires that children be classified by their disability so long as each child who has a disability listed in §300.7 and who, by reason of that disability, needs special education and related services is regarded as a child with a disability under Part B of the Act (34 CFR 300.125).

States and local districts must serve all children with disabilities who are in need of special education, but they do not have to use disability labels or categories, an insight that has vast implications for the delivery of special education and school psychology services.

State Discretion in the Use of IDEA Disability Categories

States do, in fact, use broad discretion in the disability category names, definitions, and classification criteria. Some states do not use disability categories at all, only the broad designation that the child is eligible for special education based on educational need and very low performance in relevant domains of behavior (Tilly et al., 1999). Further evidence of state variations in the use of disability categories is apparent from a review of prevalence data reported by the states to the U.S. Department of Education (1998) (see Table 4). Perhaps the most convincing evidence of state variations in the use of the categories appears in the last three columns, the lowest and highest prevalence for various categories and the multiplicative factor by which they differ. For example, there are 33 times as many children eligible under the category of emotional disturbance (ED) in Minnesota as in Mississippi. There are about nine times as many children reported under the category of mental retardation (MR) in Alabama as in New Jersey.

TABLE 4: Distribution of Disabilities by Category (U. S. Department of Education, 1998)

Category	Age 6–17 Number	Age 6–17 Percent of Enroll	Age 6–17 Percent of SWD	State: Lowest Percent	State: Highest Percent	Factor
High incidence						
SLD	2,536,359	5.53	51.07	GA: 2.94	RI: 9.09	3.09
ED	421,701	0.92	8.49	MS: 0.06	MN: 1.98	33.00
MR	530,116	1.16	10.67	NJ: 0.31	AL: 2.85	9.19
Sp/language	1,044,616	2.28	21.03	HI: 1.25	NJ: 3.86	3.09
Total high incidence	4,532,792	9.89	91.26			
Low incidence						
Autism	31,456	0.07	0.63	CO/OH: 0.02	OR: 0.24	12
Hearing impaired	64,042	0.14	1.29	ND: 0.08	WA: 0.21	2.63
Visual impaired	23,938	0.05	0.48	7 at: 0.03	TN: 0.09	3
Orthopedic	62,110	0.14	1.25	AR/UT: 0.03	MI: 0.51	17
OHI	155,249	0.34	3.13	4 at: 0.00	WA: 1.44	144
Multiple disabilities	86,946	0.19	1.75	9 at: 0.00	NJ: 0.99	99
Deaf blind	1,077	0.00	0.02	40 at: 0.00	ND: 0.04	4
TBI	9,166	0.02	0.18	3 at: 0.00	PA/WY: 0.07	7
Total low incidence	433,984	0.95	8.73			
Grand totals	4,966,776	10.84	99.99	HI: 7.94	RI: 15.09	

These huge variations in prevalence show definitively that the categories are used differently and inconsistently by the states. Some of these differences occur because of idiosyncratic state funding mechanisms, variations in state classification criteria for the various disabilities, and other local, poorly understood, influences. The classification criteria beyond the category name or the conceptual definition for the disability are important influences. Some states require a discrepancy of 15 standard score points between intellectual ability and achievement as part of their SLD classification criteria while other states use discrepancy criteria such as 12 or 22 points (Mercer et al., 1996). The maximum IQ score used by states for determination of MR varies from 69, 70, 75, and even 80. Other state variations of this kind exist, leading to large differences in the prevalence of different categories. Clearly, it is possible for a student to be classified as eligible for special education in one state and not in another, or for the disability category to change with a move across state lines.

Although less well documented, in-state variability in the prevalence of different categories of disabilities also exists. Some of the variations may reflect different levels of performance in urban and suburban districts (Gottlieb, Alter, & Gottlieb, 1999; Gottlieb, Alter, Gottlieb, & Wishner, 1994), while others may be explained by the degree of rigor in applying state classification criteria in decisions about eligibility. Some of the intra-state variations likely reflect real differences in district student populations, while others cannot be explained easily.

For the reasons just described, practitioners must focus primarily on state rules regarding the use (or nonuse) of disability categories, definitions of disabilities, and classification criteria. This information typically appears in the State Department of Education Special Education Rules and also in policy interpretation or guidelines documents.

Disproportionate Minority Representation

One of the most controversial issues in general and special education for at least 40 years is minority overrepresentation in some programs (e.g., special education MR and ED) and underrepresentation in other programs (e.g., gifted and talented) (Harry, 1994; Heller, Holtzman, & Messick, 1982; MacMillan & Reschly, 1998; Reschly, 1997). Disproportionate representation was a significant concern in the early litigation and in EHA and IDEA (see earlier discussions). From 1977 to 1999 there was a strong nondiscrimination clause in the PEP and PEDE regulations, but no further elaboration on what discrimination was or how it should be examined.

IDEA 97 changed the legal landscape regarding the nondiscrimination requirement by establishing regulations that establish implicitly one meaning of nondiscrimination; that is, equal proportions of all racial/ethnic groups in special education (see Table 5 on page 90). These regulations require the states to collect and report information on the distribution of children/youth across special education categories and the LRE alternatives (e.g., regular class, resource room, special class). These data were first collected in December 1998 and reported to OSEP in February 1999. At the time of this writing, the disproportionality data are not available; however, data collected by the Federal Office for Civil Rights (OCR) since 1968 confirm that minority children are disproportionately represented in special education programs, with some groups markedly *under*represented (Asian-Pacific Islander), two groups very near the national average (Hispanic and Caucasian), and two groups slightly overrepresented (African-American and Native American Indian) (see Table 6). The overrepresentation data are very easily misunderstood and exaggerated (MacMillan & Reschly, 1998; Reschly, 1997).

TABLE 5: **Disproportionality Regulations in IDEA 97**
(34 CFR 300.755)

Section 300.755 Disproportionality

a. General. Each State that receives assistance under Part B of the Act, and the Secretary of the Interior, shall provide for the collection and examination of data to determine if significant disproportionality based on race is occurring in the State or in the schools operated by the Secretary of the Interior with respect to

   1. The identification of children as children with disabilities, including the identification of children as children with disabilities in accordance with a particular impairment described in section 602(3) of the Act; and

   2. The placement in particular educational settings of these children.

b. Review and revision of policies, practices, and procedures. In the case of a determination of significant disproportionality with respect to the identification of children as children with disabilities, or the placement in particular educational settings of these children, in accordance with paragraph (a) of this section, the State or the Secretary of the Interior shall provide for the review and, if appropriate revision of the policies, procedures, and practices used in the identification or placement to ensure that the policies, procedures, and practices comply with the requirements of Part B of the Act.

(Authority: 20 U.S.C. 1418(c))

TABLE 6: Distribution of Three Disabilities by Group in the United States (OCR, 1994, 1997)

Category	Native American Indian		Asian/Pacific Islander		Hispanic		African-American		Caucasian	
	Percent of Program	Percent of Group	Percent of Program	Percent of Group	Percent of Program	Percent of Group	Percent of Program	Percent of Group	Percent of Program	Percent of Group
Mental Retardation	1.18	1.61	1.35	0.52	8.25	0.92	31.45	2.65	57.77	1.25
Emotional Disturbance	1.29	0.95	0.85	0.18	7.80	0.47	24.53	1.12	65.53	0.76
Learning Disability	1.37	7.28	1.35	2.01	13.01	5.68	17.22	5.67	67.05	5.66
Total: MR, LD, ED	1.33	9.84	1.30	2.71	11.62	7.07	20.56	9.44	65.19	7.67
Percent of general population by group		1.04		3.72		12.71		16.85		65.68

Understanding disproportionality necessitates careful examination of the statistical data typically reported by agencies such as the OCR and State Departments of Education. A critical distinction required for accurate interpretation of these data is the difference between the percent of a program by group and the percent of a group in a program. Data from the most recent OCR survey are presented in Table 6 to illustrate these differences for the five major ethnic/racial groups in the United States. In the last row, the percent of the general student population by group in the OCR national survey is provided. African-American students comprised 16.85% of the total student population in the OCR survey. However, they constituted over 31% and nearly 25% of the population of MR and ED students, respectively (see column labeled percent of program by group). These data indicate that African-American students are overrepresented in the MR and ED categories nationally.

The results just reported often are misunderstood to mean that large proportions of African-American students are classified as MR or ED. In fact, the actual percentages of African-American students in MR and ED are 2.65% and 1.23%, respectively (see column labeled percent of group in program). The OCR survey was restricted to three categories of disabilities, MR, ED, and SLD, because the agency has concluded from earlier surveys that these are the categories in which disproportionate group representation occurs. The sum of those three categories by group is presented in the fourth row of data in Table 6 on page 91. The overall national mean for those three categories across all groups in the OCR (1994) survey was 7.74. Variations exist across groups with Asian-Pacific Islanders significantly underrepresented (2.71%), Hispanics (7.07%) and Caucasians (7.67%) close to the national average of 7.74%, and Native American Indians (9.84%) and African-Americans (9.44%) slightly above the national average.

The IDEA 97 regulations on disproportionality require the states to provide for "review and, if appropriate revision of the policies, procedures, and practices used in the identification or placement ..." if significant disproportionality is found (Individuals with Disabilities Education Act Regulations, 1999). The criteria for "significant disproportionality" are not established in the law, nor is there consensus about this issue in the professional literature (Reschly, 1997). The appearance or perception of "significant disproportionality" will be influenced by the overrepresentation statistic used; that is, percent of program by group versus percent of group in program (see Table 6 on page 91).

Efforts to comply with the disproportionality regulations are likely to place more emphasis on nontraditional assessment approaches such as curriculum-based and behavioral assessment and less emphasis on traditional standardized tests of achievement and ability. Implementation of the new PEDE regulations will be especially important with minority children and youth, particularly if minorities were over represented in special education. Practitioners will be challenged in these situations to show that the classification as disabled and the placement in special education was *educationally* necessary and that documentable benefits were derived from the special education program.

The overall effects of the increased scrutiny of state policies that will be prompted by the nearly inevitable finding of disproportionate representation in some if not most states are difficult to anticipate. The policy changes contemplated will likely focus at least in part on assessment procedures and eligibility determination practices. Special education professionals must monitor these statistics and policy changes carefully to ensure that they are in the best interests of children.

BEST PRACTICE STRATEGIES FOR IMPLEMENTING THE IDEA ASSESSMENT/ ELIGIBILITY PROVISIONS

IDEA 97 establishes the legal foundation for special education and much of school psychology practice for the next decade. School psychologists are likely to continue to spend a significant amount of time with various aspects of services to students with disabilities. Changes may occur, however, in how eligibility determination is conducted, in the types of assessment procedures used, and in the degree to which they are involved with intervention services.

Disability Categories and Assessment Procedures

As noted in the previous section, both the statute and regulations are permissive regarding state variations in the use of disability categories and the assessment procedures used to determine eligibility. In a profound way, state rules drive practice regarding assessment and eligibility determination. If the state statute and rules adopt traditional categories such as MR and SLD with classification criteria specifying intellectual ability and achievement standards for eligibility, then the use of traditional, standardized IQ and achievement tests is extremely difficult to avoid. Administration of such tests, requiring typically two to three hours of direct child/youth contact, plus additional time for scoring and report writing, are virtually required by traditional state statute and rules that define certain high incidence disabilities by IQ and achievement.

A variety of well-known best professional practices exist regarding the use and interpretation of standardized IQ and achievement tests (e.g., Reschly & Grimes, 1995). These best practices are not always followed rigorously, causing concern for the quality of assessment practices in at least some situations. Implementation of best practices when using standardized tests is an obvious necessity and challenge for all school psychologists and special educators.

Many of the traditional assessment procedures used in addition to conventional intelligence and achievement tests have questionable technical properties. Many of these more subjective or "clinical" instruments, despite their popularity, do not meet well-established standards for test development and use. Practitioners are cautioned regarding *any* use of the various "Draw-A-Something" instruments (e.g., Draw-A-Person, Kinetic Family Drawings), brief achievement screening measures such as the Wide Range Achievement Test, and abstract inferences about cognitive style or neurological functioning based on the interpretations of test battery profiles (Barnett & Macmann, 1992a, 1992b; Macmann & Barnett, 1994a, 1994b, 1997). These assessment practices have little or no empirical support, and it is impossible for them to meet the IDEA provision of "valid for the specific purpose." The persistence of these instruments and procedures in school psychology practice, although declining, is troubling in view of legal requirements and best professional practices.

Dissatisfaction With Current Disability Categories

Increasing dissatisfaction with traditional disability categories has been evident from the school psychology and special education literatures for many years (Hobbs, 1975a, 1975b; NASP-NCAS, 1985; Reschly et al., 1999; Reschly & Ysseldyke, 1995). Recent concern has been expressed about the SLD category by a group of researchers funded by the National Institute of Child Health and Development (Lyon, 1996). The most widely used classification criterion for determining SLD eligibility—the severe discrepancy between intellectual ability and achievement—is increasingly regarded as invalid for establishing a group of low achievers with unique needs. In fact, children with low reading achievement have the same needs and respond to the same treatments regardless of their IQ levels, according to these researchers (Fletcher, Francis, et al., 1998; Fletcher, Shaywitz, et al., 1994; Vellutino, Scanlon, & Lyon, 2000).

Even more damaging to traditional SLD discrepancy determination practices is the unintended effect of using a discrepancy requirement with children in the early grades. It is nearly impossible for young children to meet the state mandated discrepancy criteria before grade 3 or 4. Use of the discrepancy criteria that are based on standardized IQ-achievement test differences delays treatment to later grades when the problems are more severe and treatment less effective (Fletcher, Francis, et al., 1998; Fletcher, Shaywitz, et al., 1994).

> Classifications of children as discrepant versus low-achievement lack discriminative validity.... However, because children can be validly identified on the basis of a low-achievement definition, it simply is not necessary to use an IQ test to identify children as learning disabled (Fletcher, Francis, et al., 1998, p. 200). For treatment, the use of the discrepancy models forces identification to an older age when interventions are demonstrably less effective (Fletcher, Francis, et al., 1998, p. 201).

Increasing advocacy for changes in how SLD is conceptualized and diagnosed is apparent in the literature and in discussions of professional practice. It is probable that significant changes will occur in the states' SLD conceptions and classification criteria over the next decade. Elimination of the IQ testing and severe discrepancy determination associated with SLD eligibility determination likely would have a profound impact on school psychology and special education. SLD constitutes the largest of the disability categories, accounting for over half of all children and youth receiving special education in the United States (see Table 4 and U.S. Department of Education, 1998). The minimal effect of changes in SLD classification criteria likely will be markedly reduced demand for standardized IQ and achievement testing accompanied by increased demand for direct assessment of academic skills and greater involvement with the design and evaluation of interventions.

Cognitive Process Assessment

Many psychologists and special educators attempt to use traditional standardized procedures to determine the underlying processes related to learning and to learning problems. These processes have been variously described as learning modalities, channels of information processing, cognitive style, and neuropsychological strengths and weaknesses. The use of the information on processing varies with the different schools of thought regarding cognitive functioning. Some traditional and contemporary authors advocate attempting to improve the processing in deficit areas as a means of improving educational achievement (e.g., Kephart, 1960; Kirk & Kirk, 1971; Naglieri & Das, 1997), while other processing advocates dismiss efforts to remediate processing deficits as futile (Reynolds, 1981, 1992). Other advocates of process or modality assessment stress the matching of modality or process strengths to teaching methodology (Kaufman, Goldsmith, & Kaufman, 1984; Reynolds, 1992), assuming that teaching methods that capitalize on "intact" neurological processes or modality strengths will produce the best achievement outcomes.

Enormous problems exist for the advocates of cognitive process assessment and interventions driven by inferred cognitive process constructs. The empirical evidence does not support the reliability and validity of the inferences about the processes and, most damaging, the interventions predicated on the process constructs are not effective (Kavale & Forness, 1999). Training the processes is difficult, and process training typically does not transfer to different situations requiring the use of the process. Matching teaching methodology to processing strengths, assuming the existence of an aptitude by treatment interaction, likewise does not fare well in empirical studies (Arter & Jenkins, 1977, 1979; Ayers & Cooley, 1986; Ayers, Cooley, & Severson, 1988; Good, Vollmer, Creek, Katz, & Chowdhri, 1993; Hammill & Larsen, 1974, 1978; Kavale, 1981; Kavale & Forness, 1987, 1990, 1999; Ysseldyke & Mirkin, 1982).

Some of the professional practice regarding cognitive process interpretation is predicated on what is a futile attempt to gain more useful information from the traditional tests that psychologists already have to use to comply with state statute and rules for SLD and MR eligibility determination. That is, once an IQ test is required, why not attempt to derive more information from the test data through making inferences about cognitive processing? These inferences are believed by advocates to lead to increased understanding of the child. Unfortunately, this increased understanding is more ephemeral than real, and no matter how satisfying to psychologists, the empirical evidence reveals no benefits to children or the teachers and parents who work with them.

The interpretation of cognitive processes is potentially damaging. Focusing on process deflects attention from potentially useful data that can be gathered through direct measures of academic skills and social behaviors. It is not simply a benign activity that hurts no one. Attention paid to variables that lead to ineffective practices are harmful to children. Moreover, there is nothing in IDEA 97 that requires process assessment and intervention and much that, interpreted in light of the evidence just cited, discourages these practices.

Reliable, Valid, and Useful Assessment

IDEA 97 clearly mandates the collection of reliable, valid, and intervention-related assessment information. The assessment conducted as part of eligibility determination is expected not only to determine whether the student meets the criteria for a disability but also to determine need for special education and related services, present levels of educational performance, and information that assists with program development. Requirements in the PEDE regulations (see Table 2 on page 71) that support this interpretation include (a) "specific areas of educational need," (b) "functional and developmental information," (c) "relevant information that directly assists persons in determining the educational needs of the child," and (d) "classroom-based assessments and evaluations." Models of how such assessments can be gathered and used in interventions are available in a number of sources (Gresham & Noell, 1999; Howell & Nolet, 2000; Kern & Dunlap, 1999; Shinn, Good, & Parker, 1999).

PROFESSIONAL DEVELOPMENT IMPLICATIONS FOR EDUCATORS AND SYSTEMS

The IDEA statute and regulations (Individuals with Disabilities Education Act Amendments, 1997; Individuals with Disabilities Education Act Regulations, 1999) regarding assessment, eligibility determination, and disproportionality provide impetus for system change. Efforts in the states are supported to a greater extent than ever before to establish delivery systems based on non-categorical classification, functional assessment, problem solving, and empirically validated academic, behavioral, emotional, and social interventions (Reschly et al., 1999; Reschly & Tilly, 1999; Tilly et al., 1999). A nontraditional system with these elements is now in the state special education rules (Iowa Rules of Special Education, 1995) as the official state system in Iowa, and at least a dozen other states are in various stages of implementing delivery system reforms that are consistent with those principles. The Federal Office of Special Education has approved the Iowa rules as complying with IDEA.

The possibilities exist today for a special education system and school psychology practice focused primarily on empirically supported interventions for children and youth that are evaluated frequently and rigorously to ensure effective outcomes. The federal law permits changes that will further system reform. State laws can and should be changed to support the practices that produce better outcomes for students with disabilities. Assessment changes will be crucial in achieving the better outcomes.

Most professionals involved with providing services to students with disabilities have enormous continuing education needs. These needs exist equally at all levels, including university faculty, state department of education officials, and school district practitioners. The broad themes in continuing education will include the identification and implementation of empirically supported treatments through a self-correcting problem solving methodology (Tilly & Flugum, 1995; Tilly et al., 1999). Problem solving is crucial because even interventions with strong empirical validation do not always work with individual children. Therefore, a method of examining results frequently and making intervention changes when results do not meet goals is crucial. Problem solving methodologies provide the structure for those evaluations and intervention changes.

The content of those continuing education needs is well described in *School Psychology: A Blueprint for Training and Practice II* (Ysseldyke et al., 1997). Continuing education consistent with the *Blueprint II* domains is fundamental to system change. Moreover, approaches to system change are increasingly understood and explained in the literature, along with descriptions of models in which the change process has occurred successfully (Curtis, Batsche, & Mesmer, this volume; Knoff & Batsche, 1995; Tilly et al., 1999). Today, to a greater degree than before, there is the knowledge base for a special education system and school psychology practices that achieve well-documented and positive outcomes for individual children. Today, to a greater extent than previously, the federal legal requirements regarding students with disabilities support and encourage system reforms. These changes increase the likelihood of achieving the goals of the advocates and professionals that resulted in the original EHA legislation 25 years ago, an appropriate (and effective) education for all students with disabilities.

References

Arter, J. A., & Jenkins, J. R. (1977). Examine the benefits and prevalence of modality considerations in special education. *Journal of Special Education, 11*, 281–298.

Arter, J. A., & Jenkins, J. R. (1979). Differential diagnosis—Prescriptive teaching: A critical appraisal. *Review of Education Research, 49*, 517–555.

Ayers, R., & Cooley, E. J. (1986). Sequential versus simultaneous processing on the K-ABC: Validity in predicting learning success. *Journal of Psychoeducational Assessment, 4*, 211–220.

Ayers, R. R., Cooley, E. J., & Severson, H. H. (1988). Educational translation of the Kaufman Assessment Battery for Children: A construct validity study. *School Psychology Review, 17*, 113–124.

Barnett, D. W., & Macmann, G. M. (1992a). Aptitude-achievement discrepancy scores: Accuracy in analysis misdirected. *School Psychology Review, 21*, 494–508.

Barnett, D. W., & Macmann, G. M. (1992b). Decision reliability and validity: Contributions and limitations of alternative assessment strategies. *Journal of Special Education, 25*, 431–452.

Curtis, M. J., Hunley, S. A., Walker, K. J., & Baker, A. C. (1999). Demographic characteristics and professional practices in school psychology. *School Psychology Review, 28*, 104–116.

Diana v. State Board of Education, No. C-70-37 RFP U. S. District Court, Northern District of California, Consent Decree, February 3, 1970.

Education of the Handicapped Act. (1975, 1977). PL 94-142, 20 U.S.C. 1400-1485, 34 CFR-300.

Fagan, T. K. (1987a). Gesell: The first school psychologist, Part I. The road to Connecticut. *School Psychology Review, 16*, 103–107.

Fagan, T. K. (1987b). Gesell: The first school psychologist. Part II: Practice and significance. *School Psychology Review, 16*, 399–409

Fagan, T. K. (1992). Compulsory schooling, child study, clinical psychology, and special education: Origins of school psychology. *American Psychologist, 47*, 236–243.

Fagan, T. K. (1995). Trends in the history of school psychology in the United States. In A. Thomas & J. Grimes (Eds.), *Best practices in school psychology III* (pp. 59-67). Washington, DC: National Association of School Psychologists.

Fletcher, J. M., Francis, D. J, Shaywitz, S. E., Lyon, G. R., Foorman, B. R., Stuebing, K. K, Shaywitz, B. A.(1998). Intelligent testing and the discrepancy model for children with learning disabilities. *Learning Disabilities Research and Practice, 13*, 186–203.

Fletcher, J. M., Shaywitz, S. E., Shankweiler, D. P., Katz, L., Liberman, I. Y., Fowler, A., Francis, D. J., Stuebing, K. K., & Shaywitz, B. A. (1994). Cognitive profiles of reading disability: Comparisons of discrepancy and low achievement definitions. *Journal of Educational Psychology, 85,* 1–23.

Good, R. H., Vollmer, M., Creek, R. J., Katz, L., & Chowdhri, S. (1993). Treatment utility of the Kaufman Assessment Battery for Children: Effects of matching instruction and student processing strength. *School Psychology Review, 22,* 8–26.

Gottlieb, J., Alter, M., & Gottlieb, B. W. (1999). General education placement for special education students in urban schools. In M. J. Coutinho & A. C. Repp (Eds.), *Inclusion: The integration of students with disabilities* (pp. 91-111). Belmont, CA: Wadsworth Publishing Co.

Gottleib, J., Alter, M., Gottlieb, B., & Wishner, J. (1994). Special education in urban America: It's not justifiable for many. *Journal of Special Education, 27,* 453–465.

Graden, J. L., Zins, J. E., & Curtis, M. J. (Eds.). (1988). *Alternative educational delivery systems: Enhancing instructional options for all students.* Washington, DC: National Association of School Psychologists.

Gresham, F. M., & Noell, G. H. (1999). Functional assessment as the cornerstone for noncategorical special education. In D. J. Reschly, W. D. Tilly III., & J. P. Grimes (Eds.), *Special education in transition: Functional assessment and noncategorical programming* (pp. 49–80). Longmont, CO: Sopris West.

Guadalupe Organization v. Tempe Elementary School District No. 3, No. 71-435 (D. Ariz., January 24, 1972) (consent decree).

Hammill, D., & Larsen, S. (1974). The effectiveness of psycholinguistic training. *Exceptional Children, 41,* 5–14.

Hammill, D., & Larsen, S. (1978). The effectiveness of psycholinguistic training: A reaffirmation of position. *Exceptional Children, 44,* 402–414.

Harry, B. (1994). *The disproportionate representation of minority students in special education: Theories and recommendations.* Alexandria, VA: National Association of State Directors of Special Education.

Hehir, T. (1996). Office of Special Education Policy Letter. *Individuals with Disabilities Education Report, 23,* 341.

Heller, K., Holtzman, W., & Messick, S. (Eds.). (1982). *Placing children in special education: A strategy for equity.* Washington, DC: National Academy Press.

Hendrick Hudson District Board of Education v. Rowley, 45f U.S. 176, 179 (1982).

Hobbs, N. (1975a). *The futures of children.* San Francisco: Jossey-Bass.

Hobbs, N. (Ed.) (1975b). *Issues in the classification of children, Vol. I and II.* San Francisco: Jossey-Bass.

Honig v. Doe, 56 S. Ct. 27 (1988).

Howell, K., & Nolet, V. (2000). *Curriculum-based evaluation: Teaching and decision making* (3rd ed.). Atlanta, GA: Wadsworth.

Individuals with Disabilities Education Act Amendments of 1997, 20 U.S.C. § 1400 *et seq.* (West 1997).

Individuals with Disabilities Education Act Regulations, 34 C.F.R. § 300 and 303. (1999).

Iowa Rules of Special Education (1995). Des Moines, IA: Department of Education, Bureau of Special Education.

Journal of Special Education, 32(1). Entire issue.

Kaufman, A., Goldsmith, B. Z., & Kaufman, N. L. (1984). *K-SOS: Kaufman sequential or simultaneous.* Circle Pines, MN: American Guidance Service.

Kavale, K. A. (1981). Functions of the Illinois Test of Psycholinguistic Abilities: Are they trainable? *Exceptional Children, 47,* 496–510.

Kavale, K. A., & Forness, S. R. (1987). Substance over style: Assessing the efficacy of modality testing and teaching. *Exceptional Children, 54,* 228–239.

Kavale, K. A., & Forness, S. R. (1990). Substance over style: A rejoinder to Dunn's animadversions. *Exceptional Children, 56,* 357–361.

Kavale, K. A., & Forness, S. R. (1999). Effectiveness of special education. In C. R. Reynolds & T. B. Gutkin (Eds.) *The handbook of school psychology* (3rd ed.). New York: John Wiley.

Kephart, N. (1960). *The slow learner in the classroom.* Columbus, OH: Merrill.

Kern, L., & Dunlap, G. (1999). Developing effective program plans for students with disabilities In D. J. Reschly, W. D. Tilly III., & J. P. Grimes (Eds.), *Special education in transition: Functional assessment and noncategorical programming* (pp. 213–232). Longmont, CO: Sopris West.

Kirk, S. A., & Kirk, W. (1971). *Psycholinguistic learning disabilities: Diagnosis and remediation.* Champaign, IL: University of Illinois Press.

Knoff, H. M., & Batsche, G. M. (1995). Project ACHIEVE: Analyzing a school reform process for at risk and underachieving students. *School Psychology Review, 24,* 579–603.

Larry P. v. Riles (1979, 1984, 1992). 495 F. Supp. 926 (N. D. Cal. 1979) (decision on merits) aff'd (9th cir. no. 80-427 Jan. 23, 1984). Order modifying judgment, C-71-2270 RFP, September 25, 1986. Memorandum and Order, August 31, 1992.

Lyon, G. R. (1996). Learning disabilities. *The Future of Children: Special Education for Students with Disabilities, 6,* 56–76.

Macmann, G. M., & Barnett, D. W. (1994a). Some additional lessons from the Wechsler scales: A rejoinder to Kaufman and Keith. *School Psychology Quarterly, 9,* 223–236.

Macmann, G. M., & Barnett, D. W. (1994b). Structural analysis of correlated factors: Lessons from the verbal-performance dichotomy of the Wechsler scales. *School Psychology Quarterly, 9,* 161–167.

Macmann, G. M., & Barnett, D. W. (1997). Myth of the master detective: Reliability of interpretations for Kaufman's "intelligent testing" approach to the WISC-III. *School Psychology Quarterly, 12,* 197–234.

MacMillan, D. L., & Reschly, D. J. (1998). The disproportionate representation of African-Americans in special education: The case for greater specificity or reconsideration of the variables examined. *Journal of Special Education, 32,* 15–24.

Marshall et al. v. Georgia. (1984, 1985). U. S. District Court for the Southern District of Georgia, CV482-233, June 28, 1984; Affirmed (11th Cir. No. 84-8771, Oct. 29, 1985). (Appealed as NAACP v. Georgia). Note: The court of appeals decision was published as *Georgia State Conference of Branches of NAACP v. State of Georgia.*

Mercer, C. D., Jordan, L., Allsopp, D. H., & Mercer, A. R. (1996). Learning disabilities definitions and criteria used by state education departments. *Learning Disability Quarterly, 19,* 217–232.

Mills v. Board of Education, 348 F. Supp. 866 (D. D. C. 1972)

Naglieri, J. A., & Das, J. P. (1997). *Cognitive Assessment System.* Itasca, IL: Riverside.

NASP-NCAS. (1985). Position Statement: *Advocacy for appropriate educational services for children.* (1985). Washington, DC: National Association of School Psychologists/National Coalition of Advocates for Students.

Patrick, J., & Reschly, D. (1982). Relationship of state educational criteria and demographic variables to school-system prevalence of mental retardation. *American Journal of Mental Deficiency, 86,* 351–360.

Pennsylvania Association for Retarded Children v. Commonwealth of Pennsylvania, 343 F. Supp. 279 (E. D. Pa. 1972).

Reschly, D. J. (1988). Special education reform: School psychology revolution. *School Psychology Review, 17,* 459–475.

Reschly, D. J. (1997). *Disproportionate minority representation in general and special education programs: Patterns, issues, and alternatives.* Des Moines, IA: Mountain Plains Regional Resource Center.

Reschly, D. J. (1998). *School psychology practice: Is there change?* Paper presented at the Annual Convention of the American Psychological Association, August, San Francisco.

Reschly, D. J. (in press). The present and future status of school psychology in the United States. *School Psychology Review.*

Reschly, D. J., & Bersoff, D. N. (1999). Law and school psychology. In C. R. Reynolds & T. B. Gutkin (Eds.) *The handbook of school psychology* (3rd ed.). New York: John Wiley.

Reschly, D. J., & Grimes, J. P. (1995). Intellectual assessment. In A. Thomas & J. Grimes (Eds.), *Best practices in school psychology III.* Washington, DC: National Association of School Psychologists.

Reschly, D. J., Kicklighter, R. H., & McKee, P. (1988a). Recent placement litigation. Part I, Regular education grouping: Comparison of *Marshall* (1984, 1985) and *Hobson* (1967, 1969). *School Psychology Review, 17,* 7–19.

Reschly, D. J., Kicklighter, R. H., & McKee, P. (1988b). Recent placement litigation. Part II, Minority EMR overrepresentation: Comparison of *Larry P.* (1979, 1984, 1986) with *Marshall* (1984, 1985) and *S-1* (1986). *School Psychology Review, 17,* 20–36.

Reschly, D. J., Kicklighter, R. H., & McKee, P. (1988c). Recent placement litigation. Part III, Analysis of differences in *Larry P., Marshall,* and *S-1* and implications for future practices. *School Psychology Review, 17,* 37–48.

Reschly, D. J., & Tilly, W. D. III. (1999). Reform trends and system design alternatives. In D. J. Reschly, W. D. Tilly III, & J. P. Grimes (Eds.), *Special education in transition: Functional assessment and noncategorical programming* (pp. 19–48). Longmont, CO: Sopris West.

Reschly, D. J., Tilly, W. D. III, & Grimes, J. P. (Eds.). (1999). *Special education in transition: Functional assessment and noncategorical programming.* Longmont, CO: Sopris West.

Reschly, D. J., & Wilson, M. S. (1995). School psychology faculty and practitioners: 1986 to 1991 trends in demographic characteristics, roles, satisfaction, and system reform. *School Psychology Review, 24,* 62–80.

Reschly, D. J., & Ysseldyke, J. E. (1995). School psychology paradigm shift. In A. Thomas & J. Grimes (Eds.), *Best practices in school psychology III* (pp. 17–31). Washington DC: National Association of School Psychologists.

Reynolds, C. R. (1981). Neuropsychological assessment and the habilitation learning: Considerations in the search for aptitude x treatment interaction. *School Psychology Review, 10,* 343–349.

Reynolds, C. R. (1992). Two key concepts in the diagnosis of learning disabilities and the habilitation of learning. *Learning Disability Quarterly, 15,* 2–12.

Reynolds, C. R., Lowe, P. A., & Saenz, A. L. (1999). The problem of bias in psychological assessment. In C. R. Reynolds & T. B. Gutkin (Eds.), *The handbook of school psychology* (3rd ed.) (pp. 549–595). New York: John Wiley.

Shinn, M. R., Good, R. H. III, & Parker, C. (1999). In D. J. Reschly, W. D. Tilly III, & J. P. Grimes (Eds.), *Special education in transition: Functional assessment and noncategorical programming* (pp. 81–106). Longmont, CO: Sopris West.

Tilly, W. D., III, & Flugum, K. R. (1995). Ensuring quality interventions. In A. Thomas & J. Grimes (Eds.), *Best practices in school psychology III* (pp. 485–500). Washington DC: National Association of School Psychologists.

Tilly, W. D., III, Reschly, D. J., & Grimes, J. P. (1999). Disability determination in problem solving systems: Conceptual foundations and critical components. In D. J. Reschly, W. D. Tilly III. & J. P. Grimes (Eds.), *Special education in transition: Functional assessment and noncategorical programming* (pp. 285–321). Longmont, CO: Sopris West.

U.S. Department of Education (1998). *To assure the free appropriate public education of all children with disabilities: Twentieth annual report to congress on the implementation of the Individuals with Disabilities Education Act.* Washington, DC: Office of Special Education Programs, Author.

Vellutino, F. R., Scanlon, D M., & Lyon, G. R. (2000). Differentiating between difficult-to-remediate and readily remediated poor readers: More evidence against the IQ-achievement discrepancy definition of reading disability. *Journal of Learning Disabilities, 33,* 223–238.

Ysseldyke, J., Dawson, P., Lehr, C., Reschly, D., Reynolds, M., & Telzrow, C. (1997). *School psychology: A blueprint for training and practice II.* Bethesda, MD: National Association of School Psychologists.

Ysseldyke, J. E., & Mirkin, P. K. (1982). The use of assessment information to plan instructional interventions: A review of the research. In C. R. Reynolds & T. B. Gutkin (Eds.), *The handbook of school psychology* (pp. 395–409). New York: John Wiley.

ANNOTATED BIBLIOGRAPHY

Yell, M. L. (1998). *The law and special education.* Upper Saddle River, NJ: Merrill/Prentice Hall.

A very readable discussion of the law and special education with emphasis on IEP development and inclusion.

Individuals with Disabilities Law Report (IDELR). Palm Beach Gardens, FL: LRP Publications.

IDELR is the most useful source for those conducting research on litigation pertaining to students with disabilities. The complete texts of due process and state and federal court decisions are available. Commentary is provided on major decisions. IDELR is available online to subscribers. This resource is expensive; however, local, regional, and state education agencies often subscribe to the hard copy and the online versions of IDELR, as do many university law libraries and some general libraries.

Reschly, D. J., & Bersoff, D. N. (1999). Law and school psychology. In C. R. Reynolds & T. B. Gutkin (Eds.), *The handbook of school psychology* (3rd ed.) (pp. 1077–1112). New York: John Wiley.

Litigation that influences practices in school psychology and special education is discussed along with explanations of how various legal mechanisms affect local and state education agencies and practitioners.

IDEA Practices *http://www.ideapractices.org/*

IDEA Practices is a free online resource developed by the Education Development Center, Inc., Newton, Mass. This site provides a wide range of resources including copies of the IDEA statute and regulations, descriptions of federally funded projects, and guidelines for parents and professionals.

CHAPTER 4

A Better IDEA for Reevaluation

Andrea S. Canter
Christine M. Hurley
Cheryl L. Reid
Minneapolis Public Schools
Minneapolis, Minnesota

BACKGROUND OF REEVALUATION REQUIREMENTS IN IDEA 97: CREATING A MORE FUNCTIONAL REEVALUATION

The mandatory 3-year reevaluation of students with disabilities is perhaps one of the least preferred and most perfunctory professional tasks of school psychologists and other special educators. Often indistinguishable in purpose and content from the initial assessment (Ross-Reynolds, 1990), reevaluations have been part of special education law since the passage of P.L. 94-142. Yet, this required practice has been given little attention in research, training, or even in recent discussions of "best practice," as the topic was dropped in the third edition of *Best Practices in School Psychology* (Thomas & Grimes, 1995) and given no mention at all in the revised *School Psychology: A Blueprint for Training and Practice II* (Ysseldyke et al., 1997).

Indeed, previous regulations (U.S. Department of Education, 1977) were typically interpreted as requiring a repetition of the initial comprehensive eligibility evaluation, meaning that "intelligence tests, as well as other somewhat redundant techniques, had to be readministered to redetermine if the child was still disabled and eligible for special education" (Dwyer, 1996, p. 1). Although some practitioners and programs certainly adopted a broader approach to reevaluation as an opportunity to evaluate student progress, and although school psychologists demonstrated some decrease in their use of IQ tests for reevaluation during the 1980s (Reschly & Grimes, 1995), previous federal and state regulations provided little incentive to consider issues other than gatekeeping and a reaffirmation of the previous collection of data. With a significant number of school psychology practitioners reporting that they complete 50 or more reevaluations per year (Curtis, Hunley, Walker, & Baker, 1999), it seems critical that time spent in such activities results in meaningful outcomes for students, leading to problem solving and program improvement. "Time that could be spent on instruction and learning is currently wasted on unnecessary repetitive testing" (Council for Exceptional Children, 1998, as found at *www.cec.sped.org/pp.testmny.htm*).

The lowly status of the special education reevaluation has been given a boost with the adoption of P.L. 105-17, the 1997 Amendments to IDEA (Individuals with Disabilities Education Act Amendments, 1997). No longer a perfunctory activity, the Amendments and subsequent regulations (Individuals with Disabilities Education Act Regulations, 1999) provide a more functional role for both initial assessments and reevaluations that emphasizes program effectiveness over classification and eligibility. The Individualized Education Program (IEP) and its link to the general education curriculum take center stage in the revised law: "Initial evaluations will need to be focused on IEP goals and the general curriculum as well as eligibility, whereas reevaluations will require less formal assessment and greater evaluation of services" (Dwyer, 1997, p.4).

School psychologists and other team members have been advocating for such a common-sense approach to the reevaluation for two decades (e.g., Elliott, Piersel, & Galvin, 1983; Hartshorne & Hoyt, 1985; Kovaleski, Lowery & Glickling, 1995; Ross-Reynolds, 1990). This chapter (a) summarizes relevant regulatory changes in the purpose and implementation of special education reevaluations; (b) presents considerations for the IEP team in determining the need for and design of a functional reevaluation; (c) outlines best practice strategies with specific suggestions for reevaluations of young children, older students facing post-secondary planning, and English Language Learners; (d) and discusses implications for staff development and systemic service delivery.

CONSIDERATIONS FOR SCHOOL-BASED TEAMS: IMPLEMENTING REEVALUATION REQUIREMENTS

The most significant changes in IDEA 97 regarding triennial reevaluations include the determination of the need for any new assessment at all and the inclusion of more functional questions to answer in collecting new information, if needed:

IDEA 97 provides a new and heightened emphasis on improving educational results for children with disabilities, including provisions which ensure that these children have meaningful access to the general curriculum through improvements to the IEP, and are included in general education reform efforts related to accountability and high expectations, and that focus on improved teaching and learning (Individuals with Disabilities Education Act Regulations, 1999).

The major requirements of the law and regulations addressing the sequence of reevaluation implementation are presented in the following section; the referenced regulations can be found in the Appendix.

Composition of the Reevaluation Team

IDEA 97 Regulations require that existing evaluation data be reviewed by the IEP Team "and other qualified professionals, as appropriate...." (Individuals with Disabilities Education Act Regulations, 1999). The IEP Team must include the following individuals: (a) the parents of the child; (b) at least one general education teacher (if the child is or may be participating in general education); (c) at least one special education teacher or special education provider; (d) a school district representative (who is qualified to provide or supervise specially designed instruction, is knowledgeable about the general curriculum and about the availability of district resources); (e) someone who can interpret instructional implications of evaluation results; (f) as invited by parents or the district, others who have knowledge or special expertise regarding the child (including relevant related services personnel); and (g) the child, if appropriate. For older students involved in transition planning, there are additional requirements to ensure the student's participation as a member of the IEP Team (see later discussion of Post Secondary Planning).

These requirements indicate that few specific special educators or related services personnel are mandated to be part of the IEP Team and the group reviewing data to determine the need for reevaluation. Further, a single individual may serve in several roles defined previously. For example, the special education teacher could meet the requirements for the special education teacher, the district representative, and the person who can interpret evaluation results. It is conceivable that the IEP team reviewing the need for reevaluation could be limited to one general education teacher, one special education teacher, and the child's parents. It would be best practice, however, to include "other qualified professionals" with expertise in areas relevant to the child's IEP and current areas of concern. Including such individuals has been noted as one means of improving the IEP process (McKellar, 1995). The term "qualified personnel" is defined to include individuals credentialed by the state to provide special education and related services. Thus it would be both appropriate and advisable to include, as relevant to the individual student, such professionals as credentialed school psychologists, social workers, speech clinicians, and occupational therapists as members of the IEP team for the purpose of reviewing information and determining the need for reevaluation. Certainly all professionals who provide service through the IEP should be involved in determining reevaluation needs because they are particularly knowledgeable about the student's progress toward goals in their respective areas.

Additionally, during discussions of student progress and evaluation needs, the involvement of broadly trained professionals such as the school psychologist is recommended. Although often not providing direct services on the IEP, their training in problem solving, psychometric concepts and child development makes school psychologists uniquely qualified to consider a student's current functioning in the context of previous assessments, to comment on the validity and reliability of past assessments and diagnostic decisions, and to assist the team in determining how to best evaluate instructional and program needs (e.g., Deno, 1995; Reschly & Ysseldyke, 1995).

Reevaluation Planning: Are New Data Needed?

Review of Existing Evaluation Data

The team as described previously is charged with determining if there is need for additional data or if existing data are sufficient to determine (a) whether the child continues to have a disability, (b) the child's present levels of performance and educational needs, (c) whether the child continues to need special education and related services, and (d) whether modifications or additional services are needed to "enable the child to meet the measurable goals set out in the IEP... and to participate if appropriate in the general curriculum" (Individuals with Disabilities Education Act Regulations, 1999). Existing data include assessment data and other information provided by parents, current classroom-based assessments, and classroom observations by teachers and related services personnel. Although not explicitly stated, prior assessments, including the initial evaluation, are assumed to be included in "existing evaluation data."

These regulations have significant implications for school personnel: First, it is clear that documentation of ongoing data collection, such as performance monitoring, standards testing, review of annual IEP goals, and classroom performance data, can significantly reduce, if not entirely eliminate, the need for additional assessment. The use of such strategies may "reduce unnecessary testing and therefore reduce costs" (Individuals with Disabilities Education Act Amendments, 1997). It is imperative that team members be able to integrate a wide array of information into a coherent summary of the student's current levels of performance relative to the goals of the IEP in order to answer the question, Is this child's current level of service adequate to meet IEP goals and to progress in the general curriculum? As will be discussed in the "best practices" section, the review of "existing data" should include a careful analysis of the appropriateness and accuracy of the initial (and any subsequent) evaluation and determination of eligibility if the team is to answer a key question, Is this a child who continues to have a disability and to require special education support? The use of a problem solving approach to planning the reevaluation—defining concerns, reviewing existing data in the context of the IEP, identifying missing elements (if any) that are needed to move toward goals, and then identifying strategies to gather that information—is recommended as an empirically supported means to meet the intent of these mandates (e.g., Deno, 1995; Kovaleski et al., 1995; Tilly, Reschly & Grimes, 1999).

If Additional Data Are Not Needed

One of the critical changes in IDEA 97 is the provision for the IEP team to conclude that "no additional data are needed" to determine that the child still has a disability requiring special education and that the school therefore does not need to conduct a formal reevaluation unless so requested by the parents. However, information from the parents is required in reviewing data to determine need for reevaluation. Further, the parents must be notified of their right to request the reevaluation if the IEP team determines that no additional data are needed. In many situations, the formal and systematic review of "existing data" described earlier may be sufficient to comprise a reevaluation if parents agree. However, teams are advised to document a comprehensive review of existing information to justify the decision that no additional data are needed.

Need for Additional Data

If the need for additional data is identified, then the team must proceed to conduct the reevaluation by following all of the technical and procedural safeguards in law and regulation. The team must assure that (a) the review of the IEP follows procedures set in the regulations and that (b) the reevaluation is conducted if warranted, or if requested by parents or teachers, but at least once every 3 years. Thus the team, teacher, or parent might request the reevaluation after only 1 or 2 years.

Each member of the team who is knowledgeable about the child—either through prior data collection or direct service—contributes essential information by summarizing relevant past assessments, current observations and data documenting progress toward IEP goals, and performance in the general education curriculum, if relevant. Parents as well as school personnel can provide invaluable information at this stage. Such information may include assessment data from community sources, observations of relevant behavior and performance in the home setting, expectations, and changes in the child's skills since the last review.

All involved should note areas of concern—new or ongoing—including perceptions and data regarding discrepancy between goals and current performance.

Evaluation Procedures

The procedural requirements for any special education evaluation apply to reevaluations. Further, IDEA 97 specifies that procedures must address the purpose of the assessment; that is, determining if the child has (or continues to have) a disability and identifying the content of the IEP (Individuals with Disabilities Education Act Amendments, 1997; Individuals with Disabilities Education Act Regulations, 1999). In other words, reevaluations are held to the *same standards* of technical adequacy, fairness, scope, and relevance as are initial evaluations, even if the initial procedures are not repeated. Reschly (this volume) summarizes these standards to broadly require that assessments are "reliable, valid, and useful." Although such standards were explicit or implicit in earlier regulations, IDEA 97 breaks new ground with its emphasis on the gathering of functional and developmental information from a variety of sources, including the parent. Reschly (this volume) notes the importance of gathering data from the student's natural environment, to be linked to intervention strategies and to the student's progress in the general education curriculum. Thus the reevaluation is to be implemented in the *context* of the educational plan, promoting selection of procedures that are linked to instruction, and specifically to the *individual* student's instruction. More specifically, the reevaluation procedures should take into account the factors described in the following section.

Technical Adequacy

Reevaluations must address standards of technical adequacy in several contexts:

Standardized tests. The measures selected must be validated for the purpose used and administered by trained personnel. This is not only required by statute and regulation, but also by standards of ethical and professional practice (National Association of School Psychologists, 1997a, 1997b). It is critical that special educators consider the purpose for using standardized measures when planning reevaluation, because the same measure that appropriately addresses a diagnostic question (Does the child have or continue to have a disability?) may not appropriately address questions of response to instruction (What progress has the student made over time? What intervention strategies are most effective?). The Woodcock-Johnson Achievement Battery (Woodcock & Johnson, 1989) is well suited for the former purpose but not adequate for the latter, which might be better addressed by locally normed Curriculum Based Measurement (CBM) probes (see Shinn & Shinn, this volume). "Trained personnel" are not merely individuals who possess recognized credentials, but those who are properly trained to administer the specific measures used. This includes new editions of familiar tests, particularly when those tests undergo significant changes in content, theoretical foundation, and/or administration procedures, such as the Stanford Binet 4th Edition (Thorndike, Hagin, & Sattler, 1986), which marked a radical departure from the earlier Binet Scales.

Nonstandard conditions. "If an assessment is not conducted under standard conditions, a description of the extent to which it varied from standard conditions ... must be included in the evaluation report" (Individuals with Disabilities Education Act Regulations, 1999). Thus, for example, if the test administration were interrupted by a fire drill; if a particular subtest were omitted due to some unforeseen circumstance (a missing puzzle piece); or if a sign language or other language interpreter were present and used during the administration, these deviations from standardized practice must be noted and incorporated into the interpretation of the results.

Technically adequate measures of cognition and behavior. IDEA 97 specifically calls for the inclusion of technically adequate procedures to "assess the relative contributions of cognitive and behavioral factors" (Individuals with Disabilities Education Act Regulations, 1999). Presumedly, the rationale for this specification is the proliferation of new (and often unproven) measures, particularly checklists and rating scales, that could be used *in place of* empirically based procedures. Standards for technical adequacy are not provided in law, and absolute statistical criteria are not prescribed by existing professional standards (Jacob-Timm & Hartshorne, 1998). Nevertheless, professionals are required to "maintain the highest standard for educational and psychological assessment" (National Association of School Psychologists, 1997a, p.11) and selecting "techniques that are consistent with responsible, research-based practice" (Jacob-Timm & Hartshorne, 1998, p.77).

Best practice standards dictate that the determination of technical adequacy is based on the evidence for test reliability, validity, and adequacy of standardization norms (Jacob-Timm & Harsthorne, 1998; National Association of School Psychologists, 1997b; Salvia & Ysseldyke, 1998). These characteristics, therefore, should be applied by team members when making decisions about the selection of cognitive and behavioral measures at the time of reevaluation and in the context of the assessment purpose. If new data are needed to identify the degree of mental impairment, for example, then a recognized, technically adequate measure of intellectual ability such as the Wechsler Intelligence Scale for Children, 3rd Edition (Wechsler, 1991) or the Woodcock-Johnson Test of Cognitive Ability (Woodcock & Johnson, 1989) would be appropriate. If new data are needed to reaffirm the initial diagnosis of an Emotional and Behavioral Disorder, then a reliable, valid, and well-normed measure such as the Behavior Assessment System for Children (Reynolds & Kamphaus, 1992) might be selected. This does not preclude using informal and nonstandardized measures, because such tools may help address other purposes of the reassessment, such as obtaining parent input regarding the student's progress (through a semi-structured interview) or determining frequency of a target behavior following intervention (through a series of structured observations or CBM probes).

Fairness

IDEA 97 calls for assessments and reassessments that fairly address disability, culture, and linguistic factors.

Confounding effects of a disability. Students with disabilities, particularly those with "impaired sensory, manual or speaking skills" (Individuals with Disabilities Education Act Regulations, 1999), are often penalized by strict adherence to standardized procedures and by a limited selection of assessment methods. While requiring team members to report and interpret any deviations for standard administration, the new IDEA 97 also directs team members to take into account the impact of the student's disability on the results of the assessment. Any modifications to minimize the impact of motor disabilities, use of modified materials, or elimination of specific subtests or scales must be considered, as well as the inclusion (or exclusion) of students with similar disabilities in the standardization samples. For example, for a student with hearing impairment, the evaluator may choose to eliminate all verbally administered tasks or use a sign language interpreter; for a student with a vision impairment, the evaluator may select verbally administered tasks only or use measures specifically designed for individuals with visual impairments. Modifications are certainly desirable in order to obtain estimates of optimal performance, and are encouraged by IDEA 97 as long as the impact of these modifications is taken into account and reported (Individuals with Disabilities Education Act Regulations, 1999).

Nondiscrimination. IDEA 97 requires that assessments do not discriminate on the basis of race, culture, or native language. Given the limited representation of nonwhite and non-English speaking students in the standardization samples of most commonly used and available procedures (E. Lopez, 1995; Salvia & Ysseldyke, 1998), this requirement can pose a significant challenge to the evaluation team. However, although specific tools might not fairly represent all individuals, the overall assessment/reassessment plan can be designed to minimize the impact of cultural, economic, and linguistic factors, leading to a fair assessment outcome (e.g., American Psychological Association, 1993; E. Lopez, 1995; Minnesota Department of Children, Families and Learning, 1998). In general, these best practices call for the use of multiple assessment procedures, using multiple sources of information, involving cultural representatives from the school or larger community, expanding the role of the parent in the assessment, and using culturally fair procedures to the extent available. For students with a native language other than English, IDEA 97 reiterates the need for assessment in the student's native language to ensure that the results reflect the student's instructional skills and needs, and not their English language proficiency (Individuals with Disabilities Education Act Regulations, 1999; R. Lopez, 1999b).

Scope

As noted by R. Lopez (1999b), the IDEA 97 and regulations sought to address the overreliance on single measure and metrics (such as an IQ score or simple discrepancy score) by preventing the use of a single procedure as the sole criterion for the identification of a disability or determination of special education placement. Concerns about students' instructional needs in all areas of disability (or suspected disability), not just the broad notion of continuing eligibility, need to be addressed through multiple methods, such as tests, observations, interviews, and reviews of records (Individuals with Disabilities Education Act Regulations, 1999). A broad range of procedures will help ensure that the reevaluation addresses the *content* of the IEP and not just the continuing *need* for the IEP.

Relevance

The IDEA 97 and its regulations require that assessments and reassessments use procedures that are directly relevant to the determination of students' instructional needs (Individuals with Disabilities Education Act Regulations, 1999). As R. Lopez (1999b, p. 35) notes, "the most outstanding refinement in the philosophy of IDEA for assessment and all special education practices is an effort to move toward increasing attention to student progress...," a refinement strongly reflected in this assurance that the reevaluation is considered by the IEP team in conjunction with the review of the IEP and that the reevaluation data are considered in the review and any revision of the IEP.

Teams are thus prompted to plan the reevaluation within the *context* of the IEP and not as a separate activity. In following the intent of this provision, teams will regard the reevaluation as a proactive opportunity to evaluate student and program progress in a functional manner, rather than as a perfunctory activity to assure due process. Questions to be asked of the reevaluation should be individually linked to the goals and objectives of the IEP.

Parental Consent

The new Amendments (IDEA 97) require that informed parent consent is obtained before conducting *either* an initial evaluation or reevaluation. This represents a change from previous regulations that allowed districts to proceed with the reevaluation without consent. However, the regulations (Individuals with Disabilities Education Act Regulations, 1999) do permit a reevaluation to proceed without informed parental consent if the district can demonstrate reasonable effort to obtain parent consent, with no response. What are "reasonable measures" to obtain such consent? Regulations regarding parent participation in an IEP meeting specify that the district must document efforts to "arrange a mutually agreed upon time and place" through records of telephone calls, correspondence, or home/worksite visits (Individuals with Disabilities Education Act Regulations, 1999). This same standard of "reasonable" effort should be applied to reevaluations (Huefner, 2000). Certainly a single mailing of a first class notice to parents would not meet an honest criterion of "reasonableness," nor would leaving a telephone message with a young child. States and local districts may more specifically define options and documentation of effort. In the Minneapolis Public Schools, for example, at least three different modes of communication are required to document effort to obtain parent response (e.g., by mail, by phone, by attempted home visit) (Minneapolis Public Schools, 1998).

The definition of "informed consent" also is open to wide interpretation in the context of reevaluation. Jacob-Timm and Hartshorne (1998) note that informed consent requires three elements: (a) *knowing*, (b) *competent*, and (c) *voluntary*. The individual granting consent, in this case the parent, must understand what he or she is being asked to permit. Thus the team (or team member) must provide sufficient information about the reevaluation procedures and their subsequent application to the child's educational program so that the parent can make an "informed choice." This information should provide, in language that is easily understood, the purpose of the reevaluation (how the information will be used to benefit the child), a description of the assessment tools to be used, and identification of the professionals involved in conducting the assessment. The limits of confidentiality of the information gathered also should be explained when seeking consent. Competence on the part of the parent is generally assumed, unless otherwise documented, although for legal purposes minor children are assumed incompetent. Thus, teams seek informed consent from parents (or guardians) for children and from the student directly if legally an adult. Finally, although teams are legally required to seek parent consent for special education evaluations/reevaluations, parents must provide consent voluntarily, without any coercion or misrepresentation of their rights or of the procedures in question (Jacob-Timm & Hartshorne, 1998).

Special educators and support personnel should note that neither "notice" of services nor "blanket permission" (such as requesting consent to services "as needed") meet the requirements of informed consent (Jacob-Timm & Hartshorne, 1998). Informed consent requires "affirmative permission" (Bersoff & Hofer, 1990), a full description of services with the opportunity for clarification and denial of consent.

If a reevaluation were to include procedures or personnel not included in the initial assessment, then is it appropriate for the team to proceed with the assessment if the parent fails to respond? Is the process in fact a "reevaluation" if the plan were to include assessment of areas not considered previously, such as a child with an IEP and previous assessment addressing only speech articulation, but for whom the team now feels behavioral and cognitive data should be obtained? These questions are not specifically addressed in IDEA 97. However, standards of ethics, as well as best professional practice, require that parents are involved in decision making about the nature of the reevaluation (e.g., Jacob-Timm & Hartshorne, 1998; National Association of School Psychologists, 1997a, 1997b). Although teams may proceed with a "reevaluation" if they can document effort to obtain affirmative consent, it cannot be assumed that the parent understands a request to consent to assessment of a new area if informed consent was not obtained previously. Whenever the team proposes assessing a domain not addressed initially, true informed consent should be obtained before proceeding to assess in the new area.

The review of existing data does not require parent consent, although given that the review should be conducted by the IEP team, which includes the parent, such a review should involve parental participation to the extent feasible. Therefore, when the team determines that "no additional data" are needed to conduct a reevaluation, there is no requirement for parent consent; however, the team must nevertheless inform the parent of the decision that existing data are sufficient, and allow them the opportunity to request reevaluation (Individuals with Disabilities Education Act Regulations, 1999).

Continuing Eligibility and Exit Decisions

Too often, the only consideration at reevaluation is the documentation of an ongoing disability. In better situations, the reevaluation also addresses the rewriting of IEP goals and objectives. What is often missing is a careful consideration of the need to continue special education services at all. Despite improvements in IDEA 97 toward a more functional approach to assessment and the development of the IEP, the new law and regulations remain focused on procedural issues, rather than recognizing "that the efficacy of the curriculum and instruction, not more or less assessment, is the essential source of educational results" (R. Lopez, 1999a, p.9).

Continuing a student's special education status under the new IDEA requires that the team not only reaffirms the presence of a disability but that it determines that the student's needs cannot be met within general education by using appropriate instructional strategies. For example, the provisions of IDEA's regulations (Individuals with Disabilities Education Act Regulations, 1999) indicate that students can display severe discrepancies between ability and achievement, but if these discrepancies can be ameliorated without special education, then the student does not qualify for services under the category of learning disabilities (Kovaleski & Prasse, 1999). Similarly, if appropriate instruction is available within general education to meet the student's current needs, then the team may find at the time of reevaluation that the student should exit special education services.

Although it may seem that existing data are sufficient to determine that a student is ready to exit from special education services, IDEA requires that the IEP team conduct an evaluation prior to determining that a student no longer has a disability. Thus reevaluation—not merely a review—is required prior to terminating a student's special education services, except in the case of graduation or surpassing the age of eligibility for FAPE as defined by the state (Individuals with Disabilities Education Act Regulations, 1999).

Exit Decisions

Although IDEA 97 assures that student progress is reviewed annually and that needs are assessed at least every 3 years and prior to termination of services, little guidance is provided to help teams determine what program modifications might enable a student to participate fully in the regular education program. Allen (1989) proposed that such little attention has been paid to exiting special education because it occurs infrequently and because there are few reliable means of measuring readiness for exit. Logically, the absence of reliable measures to predict mainstream success would likely discourage the practice of terminating services!

Schendel and Ullman (1995) propose that the very philosophy of "disability" may preclude serious consideration of exit decisions for many students; that is, if a true disability exists, would it not be a life-long condition requiring long-term support? They note the following reasons for continuing students in special education despite good progress toward goals: (a) lack of reliable data to determine educational needs (e.g., Allen, 1989), (b) poor communication between special and general education regarding the supports needed and available in the general education classroom, (c) upcoming transition (the reluctance to move a student out of special education at the time of transition to junior high or high school or at the time of a staffing change), (d) lack of clear goals for success, (e) over protectiveness of special educators toward students with disabilities, (f) funding that encourages maintaining students in special education programs, (g) disincentive to exit the most successful students (who are reinforcing to teach), (h) lack of knowledge of expectations in general education, and (i) parent request to maintain child in special education.

Teams planning reevaluations should pay serious attention to the question, Does this child continue to have a disability *and* to need special education? and be able to justify an affirmative answer. Thus, the reevaluation should routinely include gathering information about the student's current or anticipated performance in general education and the degree and nature of support that would be necessary for the student to succeed outside of special education. Schendel and Ullman's list of factors must be considered in interpreting the results of those evaluation components to assure that a student's readiness for program exit is not overlooked or hastily ruled out.

Best Practice Strategies in Implementing Reevaluations

Developing the Reevaluation Plan: Key Considerations

The National Association of School Psychologists (1999) has proposed that the reevaluation be designed to address questions in three key areas:

1. Qualification: Does this child continue to have a disability requiring special education? Formal collection of new data to verify continuing eligibility is not required unless the validity of the initial assessment is questionable, if a change in disability classification is considered, or if parents so request.

2. Accountability: Are the student's current IEP and special education program effective? Has the student made expected progress?

3. Planning: What (if any) changes in instruction or placement are needed to help the child attain appropriate goals and participate as appropriate in general education?

In addressing these areas using a problem-solving model (e.g., Deno, 1995), the team must first develop a plan that will answer these three basic questions: (a) Does the student continue to have a disability? (b) Is the current instructional plan effective (relative to IEP goals and to the general education curriculum)? (c) What changes in the instructional plan—of any—are needed? If the review of existing information indicates that the current program is not meeting the student's needs, then the team must identify and define the nature of the problem, such as slow progress toward attaining calculation or decoding skills, suspected inaccuracy of initial evaluation, or apparent need for a change in placement or instruction.

Once problems are identified and defined, the team can proceed to describe the types of data and (if additional data are needed) the data collection strategies that will best help find solutions. Broadly, the reevaluation must collect or review data that document current functioning, adequacy of implementation of the IEP, expectations for performance in relevant settings (both current and future), and any discrepancy between those expectations and current level of performance. Additionally, if discrepancies are identified, the reevaluation also should address those factors that may contribute to the discrepancy and that will lead the team to generate possible interventions to enhance student success (Deno, 1995). In short, the reevaluation should be designed to evaluate the effectiveness of the student's educational program and the need to continue, modify, or terminate special education services. For the reevaluation to be functional rather than perfunctory, it must also provide information that helps educators make appropriate modifications in instruction or placement.

In the following sections, specific strategies to address these three areas of concern— qualification, accountability, and planning—are presented, including suggestions for determining need for more information.

Qualification: Validating the Disability and Need for Special Education

IDEA 97 does not require traditional retesting to requalify for special education at the time of the triennial reevaluation. "Automatic retesting was eliminated because much of the retesting was perfunctory, costly, and sometimes unrelated to important decisions about IEPs and other programming decisions" (Reschly, this volume). However, IDEA 97 does require an evaluation to determine that a student *no longer* has a disability. There is also an inherent assumption that the initial determination of eligibility was valid and based on reliable data. Although gathering new assessment data to reconfirm the earlier evaluation often is not necessary, the team minimally should review the previous assessment(s) and be able to respond affirmatively to the following set of questions.

Were the Assessment Procedures Used to Determine Eligibility Appropriate for the Student's Age, Language and Culture?

The team should review the procedures used relative to the student's age at the time of the initial assessment to determine if appropriate materials and norms were used. For example, if the student fell at the extreme end of the age norms, then the team should consider the possibility that reliable results were not obtained. For students whose first language is not English, the team should determine if appropriate accommodations were provided to assure a fair assessment, such as interpreters and nonverbal procedures. For all students, the team should verify the use of nondiscriminatory procedures.

Were Any Relevant Accommodations Provided to Assure Accurate and Fair Assessment?

Specific disabilities may interfere with an accurate and fair assessment when traditional procedures are used. For example, for a student with hearing impairment, the team should note if the earlier assessment used sign language, sign language interpreters, or nonverbal procedures. Students with physical impairments may be unduly penalized by tasks requiring manual dexterity when the purpose of the assessment is *not* to measure degree of physical impairment.

Did the Team Take Into Account Any Relevant Factors That Might Have Compromised the Validity or Reliability of Results?

Traditional assessment approaches with very young children are less reliable, valid, and functional than with older children (e.g., Bagnato & Niesworth, 1991; Preator & McAllister, 1995). A child with a significant speech or hearing impairment may exhibit apparent deficits in other areas, including socialization (e.g., Vess & Douglas, 1995). A chronic health condition such as asthma or traumatic brain injury might compromise attention, energy, and motivation during traditional assessment and classroom activities (Bender, 1999; Clark, Russman, & Orme, 1999), or require repeated assessment to detect cognitive or behavioral changes over time (e.g., Armstrong, Blumberg, & Toledano, 1999), or require functional assessment of the child in his or her environment to develop appropriate interventions and IEP goals (Power, Heathfield, McGoey, & Blum, 1999). For many children, concurrent family stress might affect both the child's behavior during assessment and the responses of parents to interview questions or rating scales.

Can the Team Rule Out Any Changes in Circumstances Since the Initial Assessment That Might Negate the Qualification for Special Education?

Particularly with physical or medically based conditions, changes in health status or the impact of intervention must be considered at the time of reevaluation. For example, if a student were found to have a hearing impairment following the initial assessment, and is now using a hearing aid, the team must determine if the student continues to have a disability requiring special education services, and if the nature of needed services has changed. A student who sustained a traumatic brain injury a few months prior to the initial assessment may demonstrate increased learning and behavioral difficulties 3 years later or the student's condition may have resolved to the degree that fewer, if any, services are now needed (Clark et al., 1999).

If the team were to determine that the initial assessment was of questionable validity, or that circumstances have changed that might contribute new data about the student's performance and functioning, then a new assessment to determine eligibility may be warranted. In this case, the new assessment should include a review of all current information about student performance relative to general education expectations, as well as relevant procedures appropriate to determining eligibility for special education. There must be sufficient data to justify continuing special education services and to identify the least restrictive environment for this student.

Exiting Special Education

The question of readiness to exit special education should always be a consideration at the time of reevaluation. If the team or parent questions the student's readiness to exit special education, the assessment must address *exit criteria*, not *entrance criteria*, including a "functional assessment of the student's performance in the special program/placement" (National Association of School Psychologists, 1999). The critical question to answer is, Can this student's needs be met within the resources of general education? In addition to a review of existing data regarding current performance relative to IEP goals, this assessment must include (a) a comparison of current performance with the expectations of general education and (b) a determination of the adequacy of resources within general education needed to accommodate the student. This assessment would not necessarily include the same procedures used to determine initial eligibility; in fact, such procedures would likely be of little use in determining readiness to exit services, as the traditional, norm-referenced approach to eligibility determination does not typically provide data regarding response to instruction or progress over time (Allen, 1989; Gresham & Noell, 1999). CBM procedures can be particularly useful in addressing the question of readiness for exiting service and have been validated as a component of "responsible reintegration" into general education (Shinn, Powell-Smith, & Good, 1996).

The exit evaluation should rely heavily on such sources as (a) observations of the student's actual performance in both general and special education settings; (b) comparisons of the level of supports available across settings and the student's response to these supports; (c) the discrepancy, if any, between the student's skills and those of students who are accommodated within general education; and (d) the identification of instructional supports needed to assure continued progress within general education (Kovaleski et al., 1995; Schendel & Ullman, 1995). In addition to observation, the team should include interviews with staff regarding classroom expectations and goals; with parents regarding their expectations and goals for their child, short- term and long-term; and with students (when appropriate) to determine their goals and perceived needs for support. The general education and special education curricula should be reviewed and compared, as well as the range of student performance found within general education in relevant subject areas. It is not appropriate to compare the student undergoing reevaluation to the *typical* (average) general education peer, but to peers whose skills are within the range of general education instruction; that is, those whose skills are below average but appropriately accommodated in order to progress in the general education curriculum (Allen, 1989; Schendel & Ullman, 1995). For an example of this process, see Table 1.

TABLE 1: Case Study: Reevaluation to Exit Special Education

Reevaluation Component	Description of Procedures and Decision Making
Referral concerns	Triennial reevaluation of sixth grader classified as having a Specific Learning Disability; termination of special education services to be considered.
Plan assessment	Questions to be addressed: Does the student have a disability requiring special education (Is student ready to exit services)? What progress has the student made toward his or her IEP goals and toward returning to general education? What modifications in instruction or accommodations are needed to assure continued progress? Identify procedures and obtain parent consent.
Review of records	Case manager and school psychologist review records of initial and any subsequent special education evaluations, district assessments, progress monitoring data and health records.
Evaluation of current performance in classroom settings	School psychologist observes student in the special education resource room and during similar content (reading) instruction in the sixth grade classroom. Variables observed include time on-task and teacher-student interactions, including requests for assistance; school social worker interviews teacher regarding student's typical classroom performance.
Evaluation of current academic skills relative to IEP goals and general education peers	SLD teacher (case manager) uses locally normed CBM probes to measure reading fluency and comprehension; recent progress monitoring data collected while student participated in general education reading group is reviewed and compared to general education students in the same group.

Table 1 continued on p. 122

Table 1 continued

Input from family	School social worker interviews parents regarding student's strengths, general behavior, motivation, and academic progress as observed at home.
Input from student	School social worker or psychologist interviews student regarding his perception of progress and need for assistance.
Review of results of current evaluation	Team summary of reevaluation data: Student is on-task in the general education classroom 75% of the time versus 83% for peers; interactions between student and teacher are comparable across special and general education settings; student requests for assistance are similar to rate for general education peers (level of support needed is similar across settings). Student's reading fluency in grade level materials (CBM) is at the 28th percentile (general education classroom range is 25th percentile and above); his comprehension skills are higher than fluency rate. Progress monitoring data indicates student's progress is comparable to peers in the general education classroom's low reading group. Parent reports that student is more willing to complete reading homework, to read library books independently, and appears more confident in his reading skills. Student reports that he enjoys reading and feels he is doing well in the general education reading group. General education teacher reports that student is appropriately placed in the low reading group and benefits from direct instruction strategies used with this group.
Team decision	Based on review of all reevaluation components, the team agrees that the student has met IEP goals, that the student benefits from direct instructional approaches and from frequent opportunities to ask questions and receive feedback from the general education teacher or reading specialist. Further, the team agrees that these needs can be addressed with the level of support currently available in the general education classroom. Special education services will therefore be terminated.

Accountability: Evaluating Student Progress and IEP Implementation

Applying IDEA 97's focus on "improving results, changes in reevaluations should mean *more* attention to a student's educational progress resulting from the special education program. Whatever or whoever the source of information ... must provide evidence that the student's special education program is resulting in educational progress. In addition to satisfying basic scientific standards, such as reliability and validity, the assessment practices of reevaluations should focus on critical educational outcomes, most importantly academic achievement" (R. Lopez, 1999a, p. 9).

The ongoing need for special education cannot be determined without data regarding the actual implementation of the IEP and the student's response to this special instruction. Critical questions include, Was the plan implemented as intended? Was the plan effective in helping the student meet IEP goals? To answer these questions, the team must consider data regarding the student's previous and current performance, both in the special education placement and, if relevant, within general education. Ideally, adequate information will exist due to ongoing measurement of progress and continuous revision of instructional objectives (Fuchs & Deno, 1991; Schendel & Ullman, 1995). The team should first review all sources of data regarding past and current skills. Examples of these sources include specific repeated measures such as CBM data; daily, weekly, or other periodic assessments used in both special and general education settings, such as end-of-unit tests, teacher-constructed rubrics, or checklists; homework records; annual standardized tests if appropriate; documented observations; and behavior and performance charts. These data should be reviewed in comparison to the current goals and objectives of the IEP and in comparison to levels of performance over time. For example, if third grader Emily's IEP indicates that her annual goal in reading fluency is to read random passages from the third grade basal reader at a rate of 85 words per minute, the team should review both her previous performance records as well as a variety of current measures of reading fluency to determine if this goal has been met. Emily's reading rate at the time of the last IEP was 41 words per minute in passages from the third grade basal reader. One year later, she is reading at a rate of 74 words per minute from similar passages. Additionally, her case manager has charted weekly results of CBM probes that illustrate slow but steady gains in reading fluency during the first 10 weeks of the instructional period, a leveling off of fluency rates during a 6-week instructional change involving peer tutoring, and finally a more rapid gain in fluency during a 10-week change to direct instruction strategies. Emily's teacher has tracked her homework completion and mastery of in-class assignments. The records indicate that Emily has improved in reading homework completion from 25% complete to 80% complete over the past school year, and that her performance on third grade basal reading series mastery tests has shown slow improvement, from 15% mastery to 45% mastery over the school year. Although Emily has not met her IEP goal in reading fluency, the documentation of progress in response to instruction will assist the team in determining if the goal should be changed, if instruction should be changed, or if additional information (such as error analysis) about Emily's strengths and deficits is needed.

If information about current performance is not adequate for determining progress over time, then new performance data should be included in the reevaluation plan. Traditional standardized measures of achievement, ability, or special areas of skills are of limited use in determining student progress because they are not designed to be sensitive to small increments of growth (Allen, 1989; Deno, 1986). Rather, CBM, criterion-referenced measures of specific relevant skills, and direct observation will be more useful sources of current performance data (Marston & Tindal, 1995; Shapiro, 1996; Shinn, 1989).

The student's need for special education supports is not the only focus of the reevaluation; it also should consider the implementation of the IEP. What instruction and supports were provided relative to what was intended? The determination of treatment fidelity or treatment integrity (implementing an intervention as designed) requires a careful review of the IEP, review of documentation of instruction provided, and, when feasible, direct observation of instruction provided to the student (e.g., Elliot, Witt, & Kratochwill, 1991; Telzrow, 1995). It is essential that any analysis of student progress be considered in the context of the instruction and supports actually provided, and that modifications in the implementation of the IEP be considered before determining that the plan itself is ineffective. Further, it is important to determine why certain aspects of the IEP were not implemented. Were specific services not available? Did staff lack knowledge or experience to implement the plan? Was the plan unrealistic in terms of time, materials needed, staff availability, student motivation? Was this part of the plan unnecessary in the context of other services? IDEA 97 places considerable emphasis on the development of quality interventions. Yet there is evidence that the quality of an instructional *plan* does not relate to the actual *delivery* of a quality intervention (Lynch & Beare, 1990; Rodger, 1995). Considering the questions posed will help the team determine if a more realistic plan should be designed or if different strategies are needed to assure that the plan is implemented as designed.

Planning: Linking Assessment to Modifications in Instruction and Placement

The purpose of the reevaluation goes beyond documenting current levels of performance, response to past instruction, and ongoing need for special education and extends to developing plans that will better serve the student's needs in the future. A problem-solving approach to the reevaluation is recommended as an empirically based means of linking assessment procedures to the ultimate goal of the reevaluation; that is, improved student outcomes (e.g., Batsche & Knoff, 1995;

Deno, 1989; 1995; Graden, Casey, & Bonstrom, 1985). Such models have been successfully implemented in many states and districts, including Florida (Knoff & Batsche, 1995), Illinois (Ysseldyke & Marston, 1999), Iowa (Reschly & Ysseldyke, 1995; Ysseldyke & Marston, 1999), Kansas (Kansas State Education Agency, 1996), Minnesota (Canter & Marston, 1994; Self, Benning, Marston, & Magnusson, 1991; Ysseldyke & Marston, 1999), Ohio (Telzrow, McNamara & Hollinger, 2000), and Pennsylvania (Kovaleski et al., 1995). Approaching reevaluation from the problem-solving perspective, the team must first identify and define areas of concern ("problems"); gather data regarding discrepancies between current performance and expectations of staff and parents; evaluate the effectiveness of current and past interventions; and develop alternative interventions ("solutions"). Further, a functional analysis of student needs—assessing the relationship between ecological and instructional variables and student performance—will help the team to identify factors that limit or enhance progress, identify effective strategies for instruction and behavioral support, set realistic goals, and allow comparison of placement options (e.g., Shapiro, 1996).

Planful review of the data collected in the steps above may be sufficient for the purpose of reevaluation, depending on the nature of the student's program and concerns of parents and staff. The student's response to instruction/intervention is critical for determining ongoing special education needs and requires the collection and interpretation of ecological and historical data. In particular, observations and progress monitoring data will help the team answer questions (i.e., generate alternative solutions) leading to the most appropriate IEP. Such questions include (a) What instructional strategies and program modifications are most related to student success? (b) When, where, and with what supports is the student most successful? (c) Do current goals reflect realistic expectations for the student's progress in the coming year? (d) To the extent feasible, do the current placement and IEP provide opportunities for the student to progress within the general education curriculum? (e) Do the current placement and program match the student's current needs in terms of expectations, instructional strategies, and least restrictive environment?

The final question requires that the team consider not only the characteristics of the current special setting, but the resources and characteristics of alternative special and general education placements. If the student were to respond best to direct instruction strategies in reading, then what options are available for participation in such instruction? Is individual tutoring with a special education teacher necessary to maintain progress, or would the same strategy be effective in a small general education reading group with consultation from special education staff? In what instructional settings is this strategy available? For this student, what are the advantages and disadvantages of alternative settings? The specific strategy of "template matching" (e.g., Hoier, McConnell, & Pallay, 1987; Shapiro, 1996) might be used as part of reevaluation methodology when a change of placement or exit from services is contemplated. In this approach, characteristics of a proposed setting and of individuals who are successful in that setting are compared to the characteristics of the referred student and his or her current setting.

By using the problem-solving approach, the reevaluation provides an opportunity to consider modifications (alternative solutions) in instruction where progress has been limited. On the basis of current performance data, hypotheses about more successful instructional or behavioral strategies can be generated and then implemented and evaluated as part of the assessment. Ongoing, repeated measurements during the reevaluation period can provide essential data to determine the effectiveness of the modifications and the appropriateness of incorporating these changes into the new IEP. The needed modifications must be considered in the context of the current placement; that is, are these modifications realistic given the current placement and services, or are alternative settings and services needed? For students with significant challenging behaviors, functional behavior assessment strategies are useful sources of such information and are proactive relative to the often limited, perfunctory implementation of such procedures in response to disciplinary actions, such as the manifestation determination following suspension (O'Neill et al., 1997; Skiba, Waldron, Bahamonde, & Michalek, 1998; Tilly, Knoster, & Ikeda, this volume).

Special Considerations for Special Populations

Students Who are English Language Learners

The assessment of students who are bilingual or who have limited proficiency in English is complex and problematic, requires considerable time and even creativity to assure reliable and valid results, and generally yields only tentative conclusions about the student's level of functioning and need for services (e.g., E. Lopez, 1995). Given the over representation of English Language Learners (ELL) in special education (E. Lopez & Gopaul-McNichol, 1997), the need for modifications and alternatives to standardized procedures during initial assessments of these students is no less essential at the time of reassessment.

Even where best practices have been followed in the initial assessment [e.g., use of interpreters or assessment in the student's first language; use of dynamic assessment and other alternatives to standardized procedures; extensive collaboration between team and family/community members (E. Lopez, 1995)], there are many factors that may preclude the assumption that the initial assessment is valid 3 years later. These include (a) changes in language proficiency of both student and family members, including the development of Basic Interpersonal Communicative Skills (BICS) and later the development of Cognitive, Academic Language Proficiency Skills (CALPS) (Cummins, 1984); (b) adaptation to American culture and accompanying degrees of "culture shock" and cross-cultural conflicts within the family (E. Lopez & Gopaul-McNichol, 1997); (c) quality of instruction at the time of the earlier assessment (Yates & Ortiz, 1991); (d) changes in health status; (e) impact of time spent in formal education; (f) changes in family social or economic status; (g) changes in cultural sensitivity/awareness of school personnel; and (h) changes in the amount and quality of ELL and bilingual support services.

The team should give serious consideration to the need to redetermine the presence and nature of a disability requiring special education support, particularly at the time of the first reevaluation. Certain factors that may be considered red flags, automatically prompting a new comprehensive assessment, include (a) that the initial assessment was conducted without an interpreter or team members fluent in the child's native language; (b) that the initial assessment consisted primarily of standardized procedures; (c) that the initial assessment was heavily loaded with verbal measures; (d) that decision making was based on standard norms and, particularly, there was no documentation of comparison between this student and his or her peers from similar cultural and educational backgrounds; (e) that there is no documentation that data were gathered from family members or that an interpreter was used in contacts with the family; (f) that the initial assessment was conducted within 1 year of the student's first enrollment in an American school; (g) that significant health or attendance problems were noted at the time of the initial assessment; and (h) that there are any other factors that might interfere with the validity of an initial assessment for *any* student, as noted above.

Whether a reconsideration of eligibility or a reevaluation focusing on current and future needs, procedures used with bilingual and ELL should emphasize observation across settings, interviews with staff and family members who know the student well, response to appropriate instruction (including "test-teach-test" strategies), nonverbal problem solving tasks, current language proficiency in both social and academic settings, direct and repeated measures of academic skills (such as CBM), student products such as portfolios, assessment of social skills, and ecological procedures regarding the instructional environment and classroom interactions (E. Lopez, 1995).

Students in Early Childhood Special Education

Children may have been identified for early childhood services by meeting a preschool-specific classification, the eligibility criteria for the disability categories identified under Part B (CFR 300.7), or a combination of the two (Danaher, 1996). Under IDEA 97, states may use a "developmental delay" category for ages 3–9 years for children experiencing delays (as defined by the state) in one or more of the following areas: physical, cognitive, communication, social/emotional, or adaptive development. For students receiving Early Childhood Special Education (ECSE) services, the reevaluation may be part of the required triennial evaluation of the child's progress in special education, or it may be precipitated by the child's pending birthday that will result in loss of eligibility for early childhood services. Because some children may have been initially identified for early childhood services shortly after birth, an ECSE reevaluation may involve a child as young as 3 or as old as 8 (if the new developmental delay category has been adopted), and any age in-between. These reevaluations may look quite different owing to the age range involved (Bagnato & Neisworth, 1991), but will still need to answer the questions regarding qualification, accountability, and planning discussed previously (Meisels, 1991).

Functional developmental approach. Personnel working in early childhood settings practice one or more of six approaches consistent with early intervention services: (a) an interdisciplinary orientation to build consensus and coordinate decision making among all individuals working with the child; (b) a developmental-behavioral perspective that uses developmental principles to guide intervention and behavioral methods to build competencies; (c) a functional, disability-sensitive approach that links assessment to intervention, identifies strengths, and develops adaptive strategies; (d) a family focused approach that includes families' strengths/needs in developing intervention plans; (e) a treatment-based practices approach that links child progress and program evaluation with an underlying developmental focus; and (f) an ecological perspective that takes into account the role of social and physical contexts in child development, and develops programs and interventions appropriate to a child's needs (Bagnato & Neisworth, 1991). These approaches are interrelated, yielding a functional developmental perspective that provides a framework for working with children from birth through 8 years as well as a way to gauge the intensity of services needed for intervention.

Review of eligibility. When conducting a reevaluation of a child who has been receiving ECSE services, one should begin with a thorough review of the initial eligibility determination (Bagnato & Neisworth, 1991). Identification of disability has far-reaching impact on a child's life, so this first review is critical, particularly because the child was very young at the time of the initial assessment (Preator & McAllister, 1995). Eligibility may have been determined on the basis of a medical condition or genetic diagnosis (e.g., cerebral palsy or Down Syndrome), or it may have been based on convergent sources of information. Identification of specific disability categories for preschoolers is often difficult due to the interrelated nature of some developmental domains, such as cognition and language (Bloom, 1993). Were appropriate measures and methods used to make the eligibility decision? Is there medical information in the file that has implications for the child's development and behavior? Are there home/family circumstances that might negatively affect the child's development, but may rule out the presence of a disability? Is there information about previous, educationally relevant experiences? Were previous testing conditions adequate for obtaining reliable and valid results? (Bagnato & Neisworth, 1991).

Initial eligibility assessments should have used multiple sources of information, including observation across settings, parent and caregiver interviews, curriculum- and norm-based measures, and ecological assessment (Bagnato & Neisworth, 1991; National Association for the Education of Young Children, 1998). Any eligibility decision based solely on a normative measure should be considered suspect and indicate a need for a comprehensive assessment at the time of reevaluation. This critical review of the initial eligibility determination is a minimal safeguard against inaccurate labeling (Lopez, 1999a).

Reviewing student progress. IDEA 97 focuses on the progress of the child in special education and what is needed to help him or her participate in the general curriculum. As with the older child, the purpose of reevaluation is not to conduct a perfunctory repetition of the initial assessment, but to provide information to guide future program planning. The program should maintain records of the child's progress, indicating goals and objectives attained and those not yet mastered. Curriculum-based measures are one way of tracking student progress and are more sensitive to student growth than normative measures, even for preschool-age children. For example, researchers at the University of Minnesota, University of Kansas, and University of Oregon are currently developing measurement systems for children birth to 8 years that includes Individual Growth and Development Indicators (IGDIs) for monitoring progress toward several general growth outcomes (McConnell et al., 1998) and Dynamic Indicators of Basic Early Literacy Skills (DIBELS) (Good & Kaminski, 1996; Good, Simmons & Smith, 1998; Kaminski & Good, 1998).

Reviewing medical information. Many children receiving early childhood services have extensive medical histories. Whenever possible, the reevaluation should include a review of medical records to determine the effects of medical conditions on present level of performance and implications for child development and behavior (Blackman, 1990; Preator & McAllister, 1995; Wolery, 1994). Practitioners need to develop skills in communicating with health care professionals and become familiar with medical risk factors and behaviors associated with medical conditions because they are often required to integrate information from transdisciplinary assessments and act as consultants to educators working with children with complex medical conditions (Preator & McAllister, 1995).

Observing and sampling behavior. Due to the interrelatedness of developmental domains, observation of the child at play and in social interactions will often provide more information on current level of functioning than a normative measure of cognitive skills. There are several observation models available to practitioners. For example, Linder (1993) provides a model for transdisciplinary play-based assessment and observation guidelines for development of children through age 6 in the following areas: cognitive, social-emotional, communication and language, and sensorimotor. Others have described a list of developmental skills that can be used to guide systematic sampling of behavior in various domains (Bagnato & Neisworth, 1991; LeVan, 1990). Dynamic assessment, an approach that "focuses on learner modifiability and on producing suggestions for interventions that appear successful in facilitating improved learner performance ... provides information regarding functional and dysfunctional metacognitive processes, as well as regarding intensity of intervention involved in producing change" (Lidz, 1991, p.6).

Parent interview. Parents are an integral part of the reevaluation team, and can provide valuable information regarding their child's progress and current functioning in the home environment. They can provide information regarding the generalization of skills that the child demonstrates in the school setting. Their description of the child's performance may validate or disconfirm results obtained through other means during the reevaluation process, prompting goals to be addressed in the IEP. Parents may also provide information on assessments conducted through community agencies. Thus, parent interviews should be considered a critical piece of information to be gathered in the reevaluation process.

Exiting ECSE services. For a child transitioning from ECSE services because of an upcoming birthday (e.g., age 7), the purpose of the reevaluation is twofold: to determine whether the child should be exited from special education services and, if not, to determine eligibility for school-age services under one of the IDEA Part B categories: mental retardation, hearing impairment including deafness, speech or language impairment, visual impairment including blindness, serious emotional disturbance, orthopedic impairment, autism, traumatic brain injury, other health impairment, specific learning disability, deaf-blindness, or multiple disability (CFR 300.7). The team must answer the questions noted earlier in the section on exiting special education to determine if the child's needs could be met with resources available within general education. If this is not possible, an initial, multi-factored evaluation requiring informed parental consent is necessary, because categorical eligibility criteria must be thoroughly addressed and will often involve evaluation in several areas not previously assessed. For example, although many toddlers and young children are served through Early Childhood Special Education due to delays in speech and language, they may exhibit additional delays in acquiring reading readiness skills when they enter kindergarten or first grade, areas that may not have been addressed in the initial eligibility evaluation. When assessed again for eligibility under categorical criteria, it may be appropriate to address cognitive ability and academic achievement. As with any initial assessment, the new evaluation will require multiple sources and multiple methods of gathering information, including observations across settings, curriculum- and norm-based measures, judgment-based measures (e.g., subjective ratings or observations), and ecological (environmental) assessment to determine the appropriate level of support and instruction for the student.

Students Facing Post-Secondary Planning

The reassessment of students planning for post-secondary life requires distinctive shifts in roles, attitudes, and foci for professionals, parents, and students. Beginning at age 14, when transition issues and needs begin to be addressed, and continuing through age 22, the process of reassessment and the development and implementation of the IEP should include an ever-widening and leadership role for students. IDEA 97 is explicit about the central role of the student in the IEP process. The law states that if a meeting is to be held concerning transition services for the student, the student must be invited, and, if he or she cannot attend, steps must be taken to ensure that the student's preferences and interests are considered. The student's role will necessarily be defined by individual needs, abilities, and preferences but at a minimum should allow for the development of IEP goals and objectives that are truly student driven. At the same time, family members, educators, and other professionals need to continue providing the resources and supports necessary for helping the student move forward toward his or her goals.

The role of families in the reassessment process for older students is often minimized despite the fact that parents repeatedly express their desire to communicate more with school staff, be more involved in school, and have more information about their children's education (e.g., Connors & Epstein, 1994; Epstein, 1990; Hudley & Barnes, 1993). In addition, post-secondary employment and community living for youth and adults with disabilities is consistently predicted by family support and involvement in education (e.g., Kernan & Koegel, 1980; Schalock et al., 1986). Beyond the legal requirements of IDEA 97, active family participation in the reassessment and IEP processes helps prepare families for their changing roles (Levinson, 1995b; Salembier & Furney, 1997). For some parents, preparing for post-secondary living may involve assuming some of the responsibilities previously provided by the student's case manager such as connecting the student with appropriate services in the community and acting as an advocate for the student in settings other than special education (e.g., Thorin & Irvin, 1992). For other families, preparations might include taking a less active role and providing more opportunities for the student to make decisions and direct the course of action. No matter where on the continuum families fall, the transition to adulthood is likely to be somewhat stressful and unsettling (Salembier & Furney, 1997; Szymanski, 1994). Ensuring family participation in the reassessment process is one way that schools can support students and families through this time of passage.

Educators and other school staff must also shift their roles and levels of involvement when reassessments are focused on older students. Whereas role changes will differ based on the needs and abilities of the student (e.g., the needs of a student with a mild learning disability are likely to be somewhat different from a student with autism), the transition to post-secondary living for school staff typically requires a reduction of some of the active direction setting and taking on the job of supporting and promoting the student's and family's exploration and development of the skills and tools necessary for success. For other students, educator role changes may include designing and implementing curricula and programs focused more on employment and life skills than on traditional academic content, particularly for students with more severe disabilities who may remain at their high school until they are 21. This does not mean that school staff take a hands-off approach or place all of the responsibility for transition planning on the student's shoulders (e.g., requiring the student to find employment or learn about post-secondary options independently). For reassessments, this changing role requires flexibility, creativity, openness, and the ability to start where a student is and move forward from that point.

Notwithstanding the obvious need for assessment measures that are technically adequate and culturally representative, the specific tools used to assess older students facing post-secondary planning are not as critical as the mindset and role expectations each team member brings to the table. The following considerations are intended to help school staff examine their own reassessment policies and procedures for older students.

Incorporate information about reassessment and IEP development into existing life skills, social skills, or independent living skills curricula. As part of an established school curriculum, students can receive direct instruction about reassessments, how they relate to IEPs, and most importantly, what implications the process has for daily life and their goals for the future. Although this might seem obvious, many older students who have received special education services for a number of years do not have a thorough understanding of special education, what having a disability means for them, or even what an IEP is. Through such direct instruction, students can gain important information and begin developing self-determination skills critical for future success. For some students, this could mean learning to lead their own IEP meeting, while for others developing self-determination skills might include learning to make their own appointments, securing a part time job, or beginning a conversation with a parent or guardian about gaining more independence in the community (e.g., Abery, 1999; Martin, Marshall, & Maxson, 1993). Determining where a student falls on the continuum of such skills is an important component of the reassessment process.

Utilize a transdisciplinary reassessment team. Levinson (1995a, 1995b) uses the term "transdisciplinary" rather than "multidisciplinary" to describe the involvement of professionals from across disciplines and outside of schools in school-based vocational assessment. Such a team is useful for any reassessment focusing on post-secondary planning. Data from outside sources such as community agencies or work sites provide invaluable information about student functioning and often bring to light other facets of a student's abilities that may not be revealed by traditional high school courses. Working across disciplines and school boundaries also assists in the reassessment process by allowing team members to gather more information about outside resources and potential entrance requirements for post-secondary programs. For example, having a relationship with the coordinator of services for students with disabilities at the local community college may allow the team to conclude that a standard intellectual assessment is unnecessary because they know that the community college is most interested in a thorough description of the student's academic, adaptive, and study skills. On the other hand, knowing that the local university requires standardized intellectual scores that are less than 3 years old is also important for making decisions about areas of reassessment for more advanced high school students.

If the assessment team decides that additional information is needed, then the reassessment should minimally include student and family interviews, observations, and data from teachers and any relevant community service provider and should address all of the transition areas. There are a number of student and family interview tools that may be used to gather this information. One example is the Transition Information Planning System (TIPS) (Institute on Community Integration, University of Minnesota and Minneapolis Public Schools, 1993). Divided into five transition areas (Employment, Post-Secondary Education and Training, Community Participation, Recreation/Leisure, Home Living/Daily Living), the TIPS is a semi-structured interview used to help students articulate their future goals. Three questions are asked of the student or family member in each area: What are your future goals for _____ (e.g., a career or job)? What are you currently doing to help you toward your goal in _____ (jobs/career training)? What do you need to do or learn in the next year to help you move toward your goal in _____ (jobs/career training)? Follow up questions and prompts are made in each area to help the student broaden his or her thinking. Typically utilized by the student's special education teacher, the TIPS may also be helpful for school psychologists and other team members wanting to formalize or structure their interviews with older students.

Structured planning processes such as the McGill Action Planning System (Forest & Pierpoint, 1992) or Personal Futures Planning (Mount, 1987) also may be useful in the reassessment process. Designed to promote inclusive education for students with disabilities, these planning processes typically involve bringing together a team, including the student, his or her family members, friends, teachers, and anyone else the student feels is important. Group facilitators lead the team through a series of key questions focused on identifying the student's strengths, abilities, and needs as well as the participants' hopes and fears for the future. The goals of these processes are to gather a holistic picture of the student and then match supports to the student's needs. An added benefit is that everyone involved with the student has an equal voice in the discussion and planning.

Attend to the relevance of the reassessment for the student and his or her family. Some high school and post-secondary students may have voiced that they do not want to attend their IEP meetings because "all we talk about is how bad my reading and math skills are." Reassessments that have relevance for the student will be explicit about the link between assessment results, interventions, and IEP goals, and should be clearly understood by all team members, most notably the student and his or her family. This includes the identification of IEP goals and objectives that will help the student progress toward his or her own goals and may require a broader view of the typical reassessment domains. For example, rather than a traditional academic achievement test that provides somewhat limited information about a student's abilities, consider using a curriculum-based vocational achievement assessment which can provide more specific information related to the world of work (Anderson & Hohenshil, 1990).

Similarly, in the social-emotional domain, assessing areas such as communication skills, reactions to supervision, interpersonal skills, and self-awareness can help school staff focus on what other post-secondary survival skills may need further development. For example, a relevant assessment for a 19-year-old interested in a career in the music industry might not focus heavily on her ability to read and write in academic content areas, but could focus on her ability to read music magazines to gain information as well as her ability to talk with many different kinds of people, negotiate, and resolve conflicts. This information could be gathered through interviews with the student, her parents, and supervisor at work as well as observations in relevant settings such as the work place (Levinson, 1995a, 1995b).

Whenever possible, it is helpful to meet with the student before the assessment team summary meeting to discuss results and answer any questions the student may have. By the time they reach middle and high school (i.e., grades 6–12), many students have a long history of being only marginally included in their own assessments and IEP development. Their experiences may have caused them to feel embarrassed or uncomfortable. Meeting individually with students before the full team meeting allows them time and space to hear results and ask questions that they may not be comfortable asking in a large group. This time can also be used to prepare for the upcoming meeting and possibly role-play or talk through situations that cause the student to be nervous or unsure. Individual meetings are particularly important when students are first developing self-determination and other post-secondary survival skills. Not only do such conferences send a message to the student that he or she is important and mature enough to meet and discuss assessment results, but they also provide opportunities for students to practice and build on their emerging skills.

PROFESSIONAL DEVELOPMENT IMPLICATIONS FOR EDUCATORS AND SYSTEMS

A number of the provisions of IDEA 97, including the sections on reevaluation, represent a significant change over the requirements of previous regulations, posing a potential gap between training and best practice. Obviously, special education personnel need to be familiar with the major components of IDEA 97 and its accompanying regulations. Often, such training is available through state departments of education and occurs in the context of workshops about state regulations for implementing IDEA.

Beyond education about the law, there are many issues that may require new or updated professional development. For the most part these issues are germane to the initial as well as reassessment (see Table 2). Although this list looks imposing, many of these topics are interrelated and fall under the general rubric of "problem solving." These strategies are consistent with an integrated, data-driven approach to serving students with special needs, an approach that melds multidisciplinary assessment, collaborative consultation, and team decision making (Batsche & Knoff, 1995). Additionally, a comprehensive professional development plan should help to ensure that reevaluation standards are not addressed in isolation from other legal requirements (e.g., standards for assessment and IEP development) or apart from consideration of instructional supports (e.g., curriculum, teaching strategies and progress monitoring).

TABLE 2: Professional Development Topics: Strategies for Effective Reevaluations

- Team collaboration for effective decision making
- Developing and implementing exit criteria
- Nondiscriminatory assessment procedures in all domains
- Collaboration and communication with diverse families
- Strategies for linking assessment with instruction, and assessment with IEP goals
- Implementing problem-solving models
- Instructional modifications
- Program evaluation
- Progress monitoring
- Alternative assessment procedures in all domains
- Functional behavior assessment
- Approaches to assessing ELL and bilingual students, including working with interpreters
- Approaches to assessing toddlers and young children
- Approaches to assessing transition and post-secondary needs
- Inter-agency collaboration

In-service training regarding the legal requirements and best practice standards for reevaluations should not be limited to case managers or school psychologists, but to all who play a role in this triennial reevaluation process. This would include all special education personnel as well as school administrators who ultimately enforce regulations. In addition to special educators and their supervisors, general education teachers need to be familiar with the purpose and general direction of the reevaluation, for they represent a crucial source of information about students with disabilities. Similarly, in order for parents to be informed participants in gathering information about current performance, expectations, and the IEP's effectiveness, they will require orientation and information concerning their rights and the procedures for reevaluation. For older students facing transition or post-secondary services, training in self-determination skills as well their rights is essential if they are to effectively participate in decisions about their program. Finally, the school district needs to assure that its community partners (e.g., agencies, advocates, related professionals) are well informed about the provisions of the law and the concomitant opportunities for cross-agency collaboration. Although such collaboration perhaps occurs most readily for the youngest and oldest students, the coordination of services, and the periodic review of those services, is essential to creating a functional, goal-oriented IEP for students at all ages.

SUMMARY

The Individuals with Disabilities Act Amendments of 1997 mark a significant change in the purpose of special education regulations, moving from the earlier emphasis on eligibility and entitlement to a new emphasis on planning for optimal student outcomes. The new requirements place a very different burden on the IEP/Assessment Team; that is, to document student progress and treatment integrity rather than focus on continuing eligibility, to develop high, attainable goals, and to specify the instructional strategies to meet those goals rather than merely document current levels of functioning. To meet both the words and the spirit of IDEA 97, teams conducting reevaluations (including parents and older students) must address not only qualification, but accountability and program planning issues.

The ultimate value of the reevaluation rests on its influence on the student's instruction. It is not sufficient to report that the student has a disability requiring continued special education support, or to verify that the IEP has been faithfully followed, or to document student performance since the last evaluation. In addition, the reevaluation should provide a blueprint for the next 3 years of special education services, a map leading from the current levels of performance to a new set of "high level yet reachable outcomes" (Cobb, 1995) that will enhance the student's overall functioning.

REFERENCES

Abery, B. (1999). Supporting self-determination for youth and young adults with deafblindness. *Impact, 1* (2), University of Minnesota: Institute on Community Integration, Minneapolis.

Allen, D. (1989). Periodic and annual review and decisions to terminate special education services. In M. Shinn (Ed.), *Curriculum-based measurement: Assessing special children* (pp. 182- 201). New York: Guilford Press.

American Psychological Association (1993). Guidelines for providers of psychological services to ethnic, linguistic, and culturally diverse populations. *American Psychologist, 48,* 45–48.

Anderson, W. T., & Hohenshil, T. H. (1990). Vocational assessment in the USA. *School Psychology International, 11,* 91–97.

Armstrong, F.D., Blumberg, M. J., & Toledano, S. R. (1999). Neurobehavioral issues in childhood cancer. *School Psychology Review, 28,* 194–203.

Bagnato, S. J., & Neisworth, J. T. (1991). *Assessment for early intervention: Best practices for professionals.* New York: Guilford.

Batsche, G. M., & Knoff, H. M. (1995). Best practices in linking assessment to intervention. In A. Thomas & J. Grimes (Eds.), *Best practices in school psychology III* (pp.569– 585). Washington, DC: National Association of School Psychologists.

Bender, B. G. (1999). Learning disorders associated with asthma and allergies. *School Psychology Review, 28,* 204–214.

Bersoff, D., & Hofer, P. (1990). The legal regulation of school psychology. In C. Reynolds & T. Gutkin (Eds.), *Handbook of school psychology* (2nd ed.) (pp. 937–961). New York: John Wiley.

Blackman, J. A. (1990). *Medical aspects of developmental disabilities in children birth to three* (2nd ed.). Rockville, MD: Aspen.

Bloom, L. (1993). *The transition from infancy to language: Acquiring the power of expression.* New York: Cambridge University Press.

Canter, A., & Marston, D. (1994). From CBM to discrepancy formulae to problem solving: One step in the evolution of noncategorical special education services. *Communiqué, 22* (6), 14, 16–17.

Clark, E., Russman, S., & Orme, S. (1999). Traumatic brain injury: Effects on school functioning and intervention strategies. *School Psychology Review, 28,* 242–250.

Cobb, C. (1995). Defining, implementing and evaluating educational outcomes. In A. Thomas & J. Grimes (Eds.), *Best practices in school psychology III* (pp.325– 336). Washington, DC: National Association of School Psychologists.

Connors, L. J., & Epstein, J. L. (1994). *Taking stock: The views of teachers, parents, and students on school, family, and community partnerships in high schools.* (Center on Families, Communities, Schools, and Children's Learning No. 25). Baltimore, MD: Johns Hopkins University Press.

Council for Exceptional Children (1998). *Comments on the Proposed IDEA Regulations*. Reston, VA: Author.

Cummins, J. (1984). *Bilingualism and special education: Issues in assessment and pedagogy*. San Diego, CA: College-Hill.

Curtis, M., Hunley, S., Walker, K., & Baker, A. (1999). Demographic characteristics and professional practices in school psychology. *School Psychology Review, 28*, 104–116.

Danaher, J. (1996). Preschool special education eligibility classifications and criteria. *Communiqué, 24* (6), Insert.

Deno, S. L. (1986). Formative evaluation of individual student programs: A new role for school psychologists. *School Psychology Review, 15*, 358–374.

Deno, S. L. (1989). Curriculum-based measurement and alternative special education services: A fundamental and direct relationship. In M. R. Shinn (Ed.), *Curriculum-based measurement: Assessing special children* (pp. 1–17). New York: Guilford.

Deno, S. L. (1995). School psychologist as problem solver. In A. Thomas & J. Grimes (Eds.), *Best practices in school psychology III* (pp. 471–484). Washington, DC: National Association of School Psychologists.

Dwyer, K. (1996). Proposed amendments impact school psychologists' role. *Communiqué, 24* (6), 1, 3.

Dwyer, K. (1997). IDEA Amendments become law. *Communiqué, 25* (8), 1, 4–5.

Elliott, S. N., Piersel, W. C., & Galvin, G. A. (1983). Psychological reevaluations: A survey of practices and perceptions of school psychologists. *Journal of School Psychology, 21*, 99–105.

Elliot, S. N., Witt, J. C., & Kratochwill, T. R. (1991). Selecting, implementing and evaluating classroom interventions. In G. Stoner, M.R. Shinn, & H. M. Walker (Eds.), *Interventions for achievement and behavior problems* (pp. 99–135). Silver Spring, MD: National Association of School Psychologists.

Epstein, J. L. (1990). School and family connections: Theory, research, and implications for integrating sociologies of education and family. In D. Unger & M. Sussman (Eds.), *Families in community settings: Interdisciplinary perspectives* (pp. 99–126). New York: Hayworth Press.

Forest, M., & Pierpoint, J. (1992). Common sense tools: MAPS and Circles. In J. Pierpoint, M. Forest, & J. Snow (Eds.), *The inclusion papers: Strategies to make inclusion work* (pp. 40–56). Toronto, ON: Inclusion Press.

Fuchs, L. S., & Deno, S. L. (1991). Paradigmatic distinctions between instructionally-relevant measurement models. *Exceptional Children, 57*, 488–500.

Good, R. H., & Kaminski, R. A. (1996). Assessment for instructional decisions: Toward a proactive/prevention model of decision making for early literacy skills. *School Psychology Quarterly, 11*, 326–336.

Good, R. H., Simmons, D. C., & Smith, S. B. (1998). Effective academic interventions in the United States: Evaluating and enhancing the acquisition of early reading skills. *School Psychology Review, 27,* 45–56.

Graden, J. L., Casey, A., & Bonstrom, O. (1985). Implementing a prereferral intervention system: Part II. The data. *Exceptional Children, 51,* 487–496.

Gresham, F. M., & Noell, G. H. (1999). Functional analysis assessment as a cornerstone for noncategorical special education. In D.J. Reschly, W.D. Tilly III, & J.P. Grimes (Eds.), *Special education in transition: Functional assessment and noncategorical programming* (pp.49–80). Longmont, CO: Sopris West.

Hartshorne, T. S., & Hoyt, E. B. (1985). Best practices in conducting reevaluations. In J. Grimes & A. Thomas (Eds.), *Best practices in school psychology* (pp.207–215). Kent, OH: National Association of School Psychologists.

Hoier, T. S., McConnell, S., & Pallay, A. G. (1987). Observational assessment for planning and evaluating educational transitions: An initial analysis of template matching. *Behavioral Assessment, 9,* 6–20.

Hudley, C., & Barnes, R. (1993, April). Home-school partnerships through the eyes of parents. Paper presented at the Annual Meeting of the American Educational Research Association, New Orleans, LA.

Huefner, D. S. (2000). *Getting comfortable with special education law: A framework for working with children with disabilities.* Norwood, MA: Christopher Gordon.

Individuals with Disabilities Education Act Amendments of 1997, 20 U.S.C. § 1400 *et seq.* (West 1997).

Individuals with Disabilities Education Act Regulations, 34 C.F.R. § 300 and 303. (1999).

Institute on Community Integration, University of Minnesota (1993). *The Transition Information Planning System: A transition planning guide.* Institute on Community Integration, College of Education and Human Development, University of Minnesota.

Jacob-Timm, S., & Hartshorne, T. S. (1998). *Ethics and law for school psychologists* (3rd ed.). New York: John Wiley.

Kaminski, R. A., & Good, R. H. (1996). Toward a technology for assessing early literacy skills. *School Psychology Review, 25,* 215–227.

Kaminski, R. A., & Good, R. H. (1998). Assessing early literacy skills in a problem-solving model: Dynamic Indicators of Basic Early Literacy Skills. In M.R. Shinn (Ed.), *Advanced applications of curriculum-based measurement* (pp.113–142). New York: Guilford.

Kansas State Education Agency (1996). *Management and organization plan: Student support services.* Topeka, KS: Author.

Kernan, K., & Koegel, R. (1980). *Employment experiences of community-based mildly retarded adults* (Working paper No. 14). Los Angeles: University of California, Mental Retardation Research Center, School of Medicine, Socio-Behavioral Group.

Knoff, H. M., & Batsche, G. M. (1995). Project ACHIEVE: Analyzing a school reform process for at-risk and underachieving students. *School Psychology Review, 24,* 579–602.

Kovaleski, J., Lowery, P., & Gickling, E. (1995). School reform through instructional support: Instructional evaluation (The Pennsylvania initiative, part two). *Communiqué, 24* (2), 14–17.

Kovaleski, J., & Prasse, D. (1999). Assessing lack of instruction. *Communiqué, 28* (4), 24–25.

LeVan, R. (1990). Clinical sampling in the assessment of young, handicapped children: Shopping for skills. *Topics in Early Childhood Special Education, 10* (3), 65–79.

Levinson, E. M. (1995a). Best practices in transition services. In A. Thomas & J. Grimes (Eds.), *Best practices in school psychology III* (pp.909–915). Washington, DC: National Association of School Psychologists.

Levinson, E. M. (1995b). Best practices in vocational assessment in the schools. In A. Thomas & J. Grimes (Eds.), *Best practices in school psychology III* (pp.741–751). Washington, DC: National Association of School Psychologists.

Lidz, C. S. (1991). *Practitioner's guide to dynamic assessment.* New York: Guilford.

Linder, T.W. (1993). *Transdisciplinary play-based assessment: A functional approach to working with young children.* Baltimore, MD: Paul H. Brookes.

Lopez, E. (1995). Best practices in working with bilingual children. In A. Thomas & J. Grimes (Eds.), *Best practices in school psychology III* (pp. 1111–1121). Washington, DC: National Association of School Psychologists.

Lopez, E. & Gopaul-McNichol, S. (1997). English as a second language. In G. Bear, K. Minke, & A. Thomas (Eds.), *Children's needs II: Development, problems, and alternatives* (pp. 523–532). Washington, DC: National Association of School Psychologists.

Lopez, R. (1999a, Spring). Reevaluations and IDEA 97: Less and more. *CASP Today,* 7–9.

Lopez, R. (1999b). Assessment and IDEA 97. *Communiqué, 28* (4), 34–35.

Lynch, E. C., & Beare, P. L. (1990). The quality of IEP objectives and their relevance to instruction for students with mental retardation and behavioral disorders. *Remedial and Special Education, 11* (2), 48–55.

Marston, D., & Tindal, G. (1995). Best practices in progress monitoring. In A. Thomas & J. Grimes (Eds.), *Best practices in school psychology III* (pp. 597–607). Washington, DC: National Association of School Psychologists.

Martin, J.E., Marshall, L.H., & Maxson, L.L. (1993). Transition policy: Infusing self-determination and self-advocacy into transition programs. *Career Development for Exceptional Individuals, 16,* 53–61.

McConnell, S., McEvoy, M., Carta, J.J., Greenwood, C.R., Kaminski, R.A., Good, R.H., & Shinn, M.R. (1998). *Selection of general growth outcomes for children between birth and age eight.* (Technical Report No.2). Minneapolis, MN: University of Minnesota, Early Childhood Research Institute for Measuring Growth and Development.

McKellar, N. (1995). Best practices in individualized education programs. In A. Thomas & J. Grimes (Eds.), *Best practices in school psychology III* (pp. 661–666). Washington, DC: National Association of School Psychologists.

Meisels, S. (1991). Dimensions of early identification. *Journal of Early Intervention, 15,* 26–28.

Minneapolis Public Schools (1998). *Due process manual.* Minneapolis: Author.

Minnesota Department of Children, Families and Learning (1998). *A vision for a better education: Reducing bias in special education assessment for American Indian and African American students.* St. Paul, MN: Author.

Mount, B. (1987). *Personal futures planning: Finding directions for change.* Unpublished doctoral dissertation, University of Georgia. Ann Arbor, MI: UMI Dissertation Information Service.

National Association for the Education of Young Children (1998). Position statement on standardized testing of young children 3 through 8 years of age. *Young Children, 46,* 21–38.

National Association of School Psychologists (1997a). *Principles for professional ethics* (revised). Bethesda, MD: Author.

National Association of School Psychologists (1997b). *Standards for the provision of school psychological services* (revised). Bethesda, MD: Author.

National Association of School Psychologists (1999). *Position statement: Three-year reevaluations.* Bethesda, MD: Author.

O'Neill, R.E., Horner, R.H., Albin, R.W., Sprague, J.R., Storey, K., & Newton, J.S. (1997). *Functional assessment and program development for problem behavior: A practical handbook* (2nd ed.). Pacific Grove, CA: Brookes/Cole.

Power, T. J., Heathfield, L.T., McGoey, K. E., & Blum, N. J. (1999). Managing and preventing chronic health problems in children and youth: School psychology's expanded mission. *School Psychology Review, 28,* 251–263.

Preator, K. K., & McAllister, J. R. (1995). Best practices assessing infants and toddlers. In A. Thomas & J. Grimes (Eds.), *Best practices in school psychology III* (pp. 775–788). Washington, DC: National Association of School Psychologists.

Reschly, D., & Grimes, J. (1995). Intellectual assessment. In A. Thomas & J. Grimes (Eds.), *Best practices in school psychology III* (pp. 763–774). Washington, DC: National Association of School Psychologists.

Reschly, D., & Ysseldyke, J. (1995). School psychology paradigm shift. In A. Thomas & J. Grimes (Eds.), *Best practices in school psychology III* (pp. 17–32). Washington, DC: National Association of School Psychologists.

Reynolds, C. R., & Kamphaus, R. W. (1992). *Behavior Assessment System for Children (BASC).* Circle Pines, MN: American Guidance Service.

Rodger, S. (1995). Individual education plans revisited: A review of the literature. *International Journal of Disability, Development and Education, 42,* 221–239.

Ross-Reynolds, J. (1990). Best practices in conducting reevaluations. In A. Thomas & J. Grimes (Eds.), *Best practices in school psychology II* (pp. 195–206). Washington, DC: National Association of School Psychologists.

Salembier, G., & Furney, K.S. (1997). Facilitating participation: Parents' perceptions of their involvement in the IEP/transition planning process. *Career Development for Exceptional Individuals, 20* (1), 29–42.

Salvia, J., & Ysseldyke, J. (1998). *Assessment.* Boston: Houghton-Mifflin.

Schalock, R., Wolzen, B., Ross, I., Elliott, B., Werbel, G., & Peterson, K. (1986). Postsecondary community placement of handicapped students: A five-year follow up. *Learning Disabilities Quarterly, 9,* 295–303.

Schendel, J., & Ullman, J. (1995). Program modification and exit decisions. In A. Thomas & J. Grimes (Eds.), *Best practices in school psychology III* (pp. 511–518). Washington, DC: National Association of School Psychologists.

Self, H., Benning, A., Marston, D., & Magnusson, D. (1991). Cooperative teacher project: A model for students at risk. *Exceptional Children, 38,* 26–35.

Shapiro, E. (1996). *Academic skills problems: Direct assessment and intervention* (2nd ed.). New York: Guilford.

Shinn, M.R. (Ed.). (1989). *Curriculum-based measurement: Assessing special children.* New York: Guilford.

Shinn, M.R., Powell-Smith, K.A., & Good, R.H. (1996). Evaluating the effects of responsible reintegration into general education for students with mild disabilities on a case by case basis. *School Psychology Review, 25,* 519–539.

Skiba, R., Waldron, N., Bahamonde, C., & Michalek, D. (1998). A four-step model for functional behavior assessment. *Communiqué, 26* (7), 24–26.

Szymanski, E.M. (1994). Transition: Life-span and life-space considerations for empowerment. *Exceptional Children, 60,* 402–410.

Telzrow, C. F. (1995). Best practices in facilitating intervention adherence. In A. Thomas & J. Grimes (Eds.), *Best practices in school psychology III* (pp. 501–510). Washington, DC: National Association of School Psychologists.

Telzrow, C. F., McNamara, K., & Hollinger, C. L. (2000). Fidelity of problem solving implementation and relationship to student performance. *School Psychology Review, 29,* 443-461.

Thomas, A. & Grimes, J. (1995). *Best practices in school psychology III.* Washington, DC: National Association of School Psychologists.

Thorin, E.J., & Irvin, L.K. (1992). Family stress associated with transition to adulthood of young people with severe disabilities. *Journal of the Association for Persons with Severe Handicaps, 17,* 31–39.

Thorndike, R. I., Hagen, E. P., & Sattler, J. (1986). *Manual for the Stanford-Binet* (4th ed.). Chicago: Riverside.

Tilly, W.D., III, Reschly, D.J., & Grimes, J.P. (1999). Disability determination in problem solving systems: Conceptual foundations and critical components. In D.J. Reschly, W.D. Tilly III, & J.P. Grimes (Eds.), *Special education in transition: Functional assessment and noncategorical programming* (pp. 285–321). Longmont, CO: Sopris West.

U.S. Department of Education (1977). *1977 Code of Federal Regulations.* Washington, DC: Author.

Vess, S., & Douglas, L. (1995). Program planning for children who are deaf or severely hard of hearing. In A. Thomas & J. Grimes (Eds.), *Best practices in school psychology III* (pp. 1123–1132). Washington, DC: National Association of School Psychologists.

Wechsler, D. (1991). *Manual for the Wechsler Intelligence Scale for Children* (3rd ed.). San Antonio: Psychological Corporation.

Wolery, M. (1994). Assessing children with special needs. In M. Wolery & J.S. Wilbers (Eds.), *Including children with special needs in early childhood programs* (pp.71–96). Washington, DC: National Association for the Education of Young Children.

Woodcock, R. W., & Johnson, M. B. (1989). *Woodcock-Johnson Psycho-educational Battery* (revised). Allen, TX: DLM Teaching Resources.

Yates, J., & Ortiz, A. (1991). Professional development needs of teachers who serve exceptional language minorities in today's schools. *Teacher Education and Special Education, 14* (1), 89–98.

Ysseldyke, J., Dawson, P., Lehr, C., Reschly, D., Reynolds, M., & Telzrow, C. (1997). *School psychology: A blueprint for training and practice II.* Washington, DC: National Association of School Psychologists.

Ysseldyke, J., & Marston, D. (1999). Origins of categorical special education services in schools and a rationale for changing them. In D.J. Reschly, W.D. Tilly III, & J.P. Grimes (Eds.), *Special education in transition: Functional assessment and noncategorical programming.* Longmont, CO: Sopris West.

ANNOTATED BIBLIOGRAPHY

Bagnato, S. J., & Neisworth, J. T. (1991). *Assessment for early intervention: Best practices for professionals.* New York: Guilford.

IDEA 97 has a strong emphasis on parents as partners in the decision-making process. This book provides an excellent reference for planning and delivering early childhood intervention that is team based and focused on family needs. Decision making is described as a collaborative process that takes multiple perspectives into account and relies on convergent information. Informal and formal methods of assessment for children ages birth through 5 are discussed, as are ecological assessment and curriculum-based developmental assessment.

Reschly, D.J., Tilly, W.D., III, & Grimes, J.P. (Eds.) (1999). *Special education in transition: Functional assessment and noncategorical programming.* Longmont, CO: Sopris West.

Historical and theoretical background as well as practical strategies are presented to support the application of problem-solving models of assessment and intervention in special education. Ysseldyke and Marston provide a rationale for nontraditional approaches to addressing disabilities, as well as several examples of implementation nationwide; Gresham and Noell address functional assessment strategies; and Tilly, Reschly, and Grimes consider the identification of disability in the context of a problem solving system. Other chapters address early childhood, transition, severe learning and behavior problems, and curriculum-based assessment. Although reevaluation is not specifically addressed, this entire volume has immediate applications to reassessment planning and decision making.

Ross-Reynolds, J. (1990). Best practices in conducting reevaluations. In A. Thomas & J. Grimes (Eds.), *Best practices in school psychology II.* Washington, DC: National Association of School Psychologists.

This chapter is one of a very few references specifically addressing reevaluation. Although it predates IDEA 97, it nevertheless offers "best practice" guidelines that are still valid a decade later.

Shapiro, E. (1996). *Academic skills problems: Direct assessment and intervention* (2nd ed.). New York: Guilford.

Shapiro provides an overview of assessment approaches applicable to both initial and reassessments as well as to ongoing progress monitoring and intervention evaluation. Of particular relevance to reevaluation are discussions of assessment of progress in the general education curriculum.

Thomas, A., & Grimes, J. (Eds.). (1995). *Best practices in school psychology III* . Washington, DC: National Association of School Psychologists.

This edited volume includes numerous chapters relevant to conducting reevaluations, without offering a chapter specific to the topic. Of particular note are chapters by Schendel and Ullmann on exit decisions, Reschly and Grimes on intellectual assessment, Deno on problem-solving models, Lopez on assessing bilingual and ESL students, Levinson on transition services and vocational assessment, Preator and McAllister on assessment of infants and toddlers, Marston and Tindal on progress monitoring, and Telzrow on intervention adherence.

http://www.ideapractices.org

One of the best sources of information about reevaluation is the law itself, and this particular website is very user-friendly and comprehensive. The law and regulations can be downloaded and searched. The site offers internal and external links to a wide range of resources regarding IDEA 97 implementation.

Appendix

IDEA Regulations Relevant to Reevaluation (Individuals with Disabilities Education Act Regulations, 1999)

§300. 344 IEP team

a. General. The public agency shall ensure that the IEP team for each child with a disability includes—
    1. The parents of the child;
    2. At least one regular education teacher of the child (if the child is, or may be, participating in the regular education environment);
    3. At least one special education teacher of the child, or if appropriate, at least one special education provider of the child;
    4. A representative of the public agency who—
        (i)   Is qualified to provide, or supervise the provision of, specialty designed instruction to meet the unique needs of children with disabilities;
        (ii) Is knowledgeable about the general curriculum; and
        (iii) Is knowledgeable about the availability of resources of the public agency;
    5. An individual who can interpret the instructional implications of evaluation results, who may be a member of the team described in paragraphs (a)(2) through (6) of this section;
    6. At the discretion of the parent or the agency, other individuals who have knowledge or special expertise regarding the child, including related services personnel as appropriate; and
    7. If appropriate, the child.
b. Transition services participants.
    1. Under paragraph (a)(7) of this section, the public agency shall invite a student with a disability of any age to attend his or her IEP meeting if a purpose of the meeting will be the consideration of—
        (i)   The student's transition services needs under §300.347(b)(1); or
        (ii) The needed transition services for the student under §300.347(b)(2); or
        (iii) Both.

Appendix continued on p. 146

Appendix continued

2. If the student does not attend the IEP meeting, the public agency shall take other steps to ensure that the student's preferences and interests are considered. [Authority 20 U.S.C. 1410 (30), 1414(d)(1)(A)(7)(B)]

§300.533 Determination of needed evaluation data

a. Review of existing evaluation data. As part of an initial evaluation (if appropriate) and as part of any reevaluation under Part B of the Act, a group that includes the individuals described in §300.344, and other qualified professionals, as appropriate, shall—
   1. Review existing evaluation data on the child, including—
      (i) Evaluations and information provided by the parents of the child;
      (ii) Current classroom-based assessments and observations; and
      (iii) Observations by teachers and related services providers; and
   2. On the basis of that review, and input from the child's parents, identify what additional data, if any, are needed to determine—
      (i) Whether the child has a particular category of disability, as described in §300.7, or, in case of a reevaluation of a child, whether the child continues to have such a disability;
      (ii) The present levels of performance and educational needs of the child;
      (iii) Whether the child needs special education and related services, or in the case of a reevaluation of a child, whether the child continues to need special education and related services; and
      (iv) Whether any additions or modifications to the special education and related services are needed to enable the child to meet the measurable annual goals set out in the IEP of the child and to participate, as appropriate, in the general curriculum.
b. Conduct of review. The group described in paragraph (a) of this section may conduct its review without a meeting.
c. Need for additional data. The public agency shall administer tests and other evaluation materials as may be needed to produce the data identified under paragraph (a) of this section.
d. Requirements if additional data are not needed.
   1. If the determination under paragraph (a) of this section is that no additional data are needed to determine whether the child continues to be a child with a disability, the public agency shall notify the child's parents—
      (i) Of that determination and the reasons for it; and
      (ii) Of the right of the parents to request an assessment to determine whether, for purposes of services under this part, the child continues to be a child with a disability.

2. The public agency is not required to conduct the assessment described in paragraph (d)(1)(ii) of this section unless requested to do so by the child's parents. [Authority: 20 U.S.C. 1414(c)(1), (2) and (4)]

§300.532 Evaluation procedures

Each public agency shall ensure, at a minimum, that the following requirements are met:

a. 1. Tests and other evaluation materials used to assess a child under Part B of the Act–
   (i) Are selected and administered so as not to be discriminatory on a racial, or cultural basis; and
   (ii) Are provided and administered in the child's native language or other mode of communication, unless it is clearly not feasible to do so; and
2. Materials and procedures used to assess a child with limited English proficiency are selected and administered to ensure that they measure the extent to which the child has a disability and needs special education, rather than measuring the child's English language skills.

b. A variety of assessment tools and strategies are used to gather relevant functional and developmental information about the child, including information provided by the parent, and information related to enabling the child to be involved in and progress in the general curriculum (or for a preschool child, to participate in appropriate activities), that may assist in determining—
1. Whether the child is a child with a disability under §300.7; and
2. The content of the child's IEP.

c. 1. Any standardized tests that are given to a child—
   (i) Have been validated for the specific purpose for which they are used; and
   (ii) Are administered by trained and knowledgeable personnel in accordance with any instructions provided by the producer of the tests.
2. If an assessment is not conducted under standard conditions, a description of the extent to which it varied from standard conditions (e.g., the qualifications of the person administering the test, or the method of test administration) must be included in the evaluation report.

d. Tests and other evaluation materials include those tailored to assess specific areas of educational need and not merely those that are designed to provide a single general intelligence quotient.

e. Tests are selected and administered so as best to ensure that if a test is administered to a child with impaired sensory, manual, or speaking skills, the test results accurately reflect the child's aptitude or achievement level or whatever other factors the test purports to measure, rather than reflecting the child's

Appendix continued on p. 148

impaired sensory, manual, or speaking skills (unless those skills are the factors that the test purports to measure).

f. No single procedure is used as the sole criterion for determining whether a child is a child with a disability and for determining an appropriate educational program for the child.

g. The child is assessed in all areas related to the suspected disability, including, if appropriate—health, vision, hearing, social and emotional status, general intelligence, academic performance, communicative status, and motor abilities.

h. In evaluating each child with a disability under §§300.531-300.536, the evaluation is sufficiently comprehensive to identify all of the child's special education and related services needs, whether or not commonly linked to the disability category in which the child has been classified.

i. The public agency uses technically sound instruments that may assess the relative contribution of cognitive and behavioral factors, in addition to physical or developmental factors.

j. The public agency uses assessment tools and strategies that provide relevant information that directly assists persons in determining the educational needs of the child.

[Authority: 20 U.S. C. 1412(a)(6)(B), 1414(b)(2) and (3)]

§300.505 Parental consent

a. General.
    1. Subject to paragraphs (a)(3), (b) and (c) of this section, informed parent consent must be obtained before—
        (i) Conducting an initial evaluation or reevaluation; and
        (ii) Initial provision of special education and related services to a child with a disability.
    2. Consent for initial evaluation may not be construed as consent for initial placement described in paragraph (a)(1)(ii) of this section.
    3. Parental consent is not required before—
        (i) Reviewing existing data as part of an evaluation or a reevaluation; or
        (ii) Administering a test or other evaluation that is administered to all children unless, before administration of that test or evaluation, consent is required of parents of all children.

b. Refusal. If the parents of a child with a disability refuse consent for initial evaluation or a reevaluation, the agency may continue to pursue those evaluations by using the due process procedures under §§300.507-300.509, or the mediation procedures under §300.506 if appropriate, except to the extent inconsistent with State law relating to parental consent.

c. Failure to respond to request for reevaluation.
    1. Informed parental consent need not be obtained for reevaluation if the public agency can demonstrate that it has taken reasonable measures to obtain that consent, and the child's parent has failed to respond.
    2. To meet the reasonable measures requirement in paragraph (c)(1) of this section, the public agency must use procedures consistent with those in §300.345(d).
d. Additional State consent requirements. In addition to the parental consent requirements described in paragraph (a) of this section, a State may require parental consent for other services and activities under this part if it ensures that each public agency in the State establishes and implements effective procedures to ensure that a parent's refusal to consent does not result in a failure to provide the child with FAPE.
e. Limitation. A public agency may not use a parent's refusal to consent to one service or activity under paragraphs (a) and (d) of this section to deny the parent or child any other service, benefit, or activity of the public agency, except as required by this part.
    [Authority: 20 U.S.C. 1415(a)(1)(C) and (c)(3)]

§300.534 Determination of eligibility
a. Upon completing the administration of tests and other evaluation materials—
    1. A group of qualified professionals and the parent of the child must determine whether the child is a child with a disability, as defined in §300.7; and
    2. The public agency must provide a copy of the evaluation report and the documentation of determination of eligibility to the parent.
b. A child may not be determined to be eligible under this part if—
    1. The determinant factor for that eligibility determination is—
        (i)   Lack of instruction in reading or math; or
        (ii) Limited English proficiency; and
    2. The child does not otherwise meet the eligibility criteria under §300.7(a).
c. 1. A public agency must evaluate a child with a disability in accordance with §§300.532 and 300.533 before determining that the child is no longer a child with a disability.
    2. The evaluation described in paragraph (c)(1) of this section is not required before the termination of a student's eligibility under Part B of the Act due to graduation with a regular high school diploma, or exceeding the age eligibility for FAPE under State law.
    [Authority: 20 U.S.C.1414(b)(4) and (5), (c)(5)]

Appendix continued on p. 150

Appendix continued

§300.535 Procedures for determining eligibility and placement.
a. In interpreting evaluation data for the purpose of determining if a child is a child with a disability under §300.7, and the educational needs of the child, each public agency shall—
1. Draw upon information from a variety of sources, including aptitude and achievement tests, parent input, teacher recommendations, physical condition, social or cultural background, and adaptive behavior, and
2. Ensure that information obtained from all of these sources is documented and carefully considered.
b. If a determination is made that a child has a disability and needs special education and related services, an IEP must be developed for the child in accordance with §§300.340-300.350.
[Authority: 20 U. S.C. 1412(a)(6), 1414(b)(4)]

§300.536 Reevaluation
Each public agency shall ensure—
a. That the IEP of each child with a disability is reviewed in accordance with §§300.340-300.350; and
b. That a reevaluation of each child, in accordance with §§300.532-300.535, is conducted if conditions warrant a reevaluation, or if the child's parent or teacher requests a reevaluation, but at least once every three years.
[Authority: 20 U.S.C. 1414(a)(2)]

Authors' note: We particularly acknowledge the assistance of our colleagues, Dr. Christina Sheran, Dr. Matthew Lau, Dr. Julie Hirsch, Allison House, and Vern Davis-Showell, for their critique and suggestions.

CHAPTER 5

Functional Behavioral Assessment:
Strategies for Positive Behavior Support

W. David Tilly III
Heartland Area Education Agency 11
Johnston, Iowa

Timothy P. Knoster
Instructional Support Systems of Pennsylvania
Lewisburg, Pennsylvania

Martin J. Ikeda
Heartland Area Education Agency 11
Johnston, Iowa

BACKGROUND/PURPOSE OF THE FUNCTIONAL BEHAVIORAL ASSESSMENT PROVISIONS IN IDEA 97

On June 4, 1997, President Bill Clinton signed into law P.L. 105-17, the amended Individuals with Disabilities Education Act (IDEA 97) (Individuals With Disabilities Education Act Amendments, 1997). This law embodies the largest set of changes in special education policy since passage of the Education of the Handicapped Act (P.L. 94-142) in 1975. Perhaps the most controversial provisions in the new law address disciplining students with disabilities . Included in these provisions are requirements for implementing functional behavioral assessments (FBA) and behavioral intervention planning (see Tankersley, Landrum, Cook, and Balan, this volume). Neither the process of FBA nor the persons who will conduct them are specified in the law. This chapter addresses four related sets of issues. First, the IDEA 97 legal foundations related to FBA are reviewed and an analysis of practice implications is provided. Second, the literature base underlying FBA procedures is reviewed. Third, a protocol for implementing an "informants method" FBA in practice is presented. Finally, professional development implications for school psychologists and other educational specialists are discussed.

Context and Legal Foundations of FBA

Given the trajectory of special education policy and practice throughout the past three decades, it is not surprising that Congress included a number of empirically validated, results-focused improvements in IDEA 97. Since passage of the original law, special education has evolved through a series of logical and important developmental phases that lead directly to the focus on educational outcomes. The decade of the 1970s substantially focused on the issue of child find. At the time of passage of the Education of the Handicapped Act (P.L. 94-142; the IDEA predecessor), a million children with disabilities were excluded from the public school system and did not go through the educational system with their peers (Individuals With Disabilities Education Act Amendments, 1997). Indeed, many of these children were excluded from the education system altogether. Thus, locating these children and providing them with a free appropriate public education was both a social policy and political issue. By the late 1970s, most previously unserved children were identified and provided an education. The decade of the 1980s provided the opportunity to improve services for children with disabilities through the expansion of programs and services. Child find remained a priority, but the overriding issues now centered on ensuring that children with disabilities received the comprehensive services to which they were entitled. Case law and administrative interpretations of the law expanded during this time, and the number of specific actions and procedures required of educators to comply with IDEA increased significantly. Moreover, as special education became more complex, an overriding priority for practitioners became making the required processes as efficient as possible.

The decade of the 1990s has fundamentally shifted education's focus from inputs to outputs. Finn (1990) commented on this change by stating that "Under the old conception, education was thought of as process and system, effort and intention, investment and hope…. Under the new definition, now struggling to be born, education is the result achieved, the learning that takes root when the process has been effective" (p. 586). There are myriad reasons motivating this shift. For example, after publication of *A Nation at Risk* (National Commission on Excellence in Education, 1983), professionals and the public began asking critical questions about the results of public schooling. What exactly are we getting from our public schools? Scholars began examining implications of educational excellence for financial security and economic competitiveness at a national and international level. And, as a result of this questioning, a large number of initiatives to define educational learning standards (desired learning outcomes) ensued throughout nearly two decades (Marzano & Kendall, 1996).

Students with disabilities have not been left out of this discussion. Indeed, the 1997 amendments to IDEA are extremely clear in their expectations that children with disabilities are to be full participants in and beneficiaries of the educational outcomes movement. Examples include connecting individual education program goals to the general curriculum, making these goals measurable, reporting to parents more frequently on individualized education programs (IEP) goal progress, and including students with disabilities in large-scale state and district assessments.

When is an FBA Required?

The FBA requirements in IDEA 97 are another example where Congress intended student outcomes to improve through the use of research-based proven practices. Literally speaking, FBA is *required* only when a student with a disability becomes the subject of school discipline proceedings. The new Regulations (Individuals With Disabilities Education Act Regulations, 1999) state:

> Either before or not later than 10 business days after either first removing the child for more than 10 school days in a school year or commencing removal that constitutes a change of placement under §300.519 .... If the LEA did not conduct a functional behavioral assessment and implement a behavioral intervention plan that resulted in the suspension described in subparagraph (a), the agency shall convene an IEP meeting to develop an assessment plan.

Hence, in a strict sense, FBAs could be conducted only in these narrow circumstances. This point of view is probably the simplest answer to the question of when FBA is needed. Given a narrow reading of the Statute (Individuals with Disabilities Education Act Amendments, 1997) and Regulations (Individuals With Disabilities Education Act Regulations, 1999), it could, in some limited circumstances, meet the procedural letter of the law. This position, however, has a series of liabilities that could become problematic for assessment teams and for districts, depending on how the law is interpreted by states and by the courts.

A rationale can be built for implementing FBAs as appropriate throughout the special education decision-making process. There are a series of interactions between related sections of the IDEA 97 Regulations that support this position. First, IDEA states that when conducting full and individual evaluations for any student suspected of having a disability, "Each public agency shall ensure, at a minimum, that... A variety of assessment tools and strategies are used to gather relevant *functional* and developmental information about the child" (emphasis added). The term "functional" in this sentence modifies the word "information." However, it is not clear how functional information could be collected as part of a full and individual evaluation outside the context of an assessment. In addition, IDEA 97 also requires that "The public agency use(s) assessment tools and strategies that provide relevant information that directly assist persons in determining the educational needs of the child" and that "Tests and other evaluation materials include those tailored to assess specific areas of educational need...." Therefore, regardless of what information is collected to identify specific disabilities, assessment teams also must collect information concerning specific educational need in all relevant domains.

By combining the various assessment requirements contained in IDEA 97 the following implications are apparent. If a student with a disability experiences sensory concerns, regardless of specific disability, then a developmental and functional sensory assessment would provide information regarding sensory needs. If mathematics performance is a concern, then a developmental and functional math assessment would provide the needed information. And, if behavioral issues are of concern, regardless of specific disability, then a developmental and *functional behavioral assessment* would contribute important information as part of the full and individual evaluation. In sum, for all students with disabilities who have behavioral needs, applying the FBA thought processes to students' evaluations appears prudent.

To support this interpretation further, the IEP section of the Regulations states clear expectations that positive behavioral programming should be available for all students with disabilities who need it. Specifically, these state that "in the case of a child whose behavior impedes his or her learning or that of others, consider, if appropriate, strategies, including *positive behavioral interventions, strategies and supports* to address the behavior" (emphasis added). The process for developing or implementing these supports is not described in the law. However, positive behavioral interventions, strategies, and supports are fundamentally the purpose for which FBA was developed as indicated by O'Neill et al. (1997).

> The heart of a behavior support plan lies in the extent to which the plan is (a) based on functional assessment results, (b) consistent with fundamental principles of behavior, and (c) a good contextual "fit" with the values, resources, and skills of all people in the setting (p. 85).

Again in this interpretation, the law supports professional and ethical practice by suggesting that for students with disabilities whose behaviors impede their learning or the learning of others, FBA would be used as part of positive behavioral intervention development.

The final reference in the Regulations implying the use of FBA in situations beyond the discipline section comes from the discipline section itself: "If the LEA *did not* conduct a functional behavioral assessment and implement a behavioral intervention plan..." (emphasis added). By constructing the law and Regulations with this language, Congress and the Federal Office of Special Education Programs clearly implied that FBA would have application beyond its use in discipline situations.

The short answer, then, to the question, When should an FBA be conducted? appears to be whenever student behavior warrants an assessment that will lead directly to intervention. To accomplish FBAs in these varied situations, it is important to keep in mind that FBA is a way of structured thinking, not a tool nor an instrument. Indeed, it would be imprudent to define FBA from a policy perspective with specific instruments or procedures (Tilly et al., 1998). FBA is a problem-solving framework that leads to logical, plausible, and defensible interventions. As will be detailed later, it is the application of this thought process with integrity that constitutes an FBA, not specific procedures or protocols.

What Does "Functional" Add to Behavioral Assessment?

The Federal Law and Regulations are generally clear about *when* FBAs need to be done, but how are these behavioral assessments different from behavioral assessments of the past? Behavioral assessment procedures are not new to school psychology (Dwyer, 1998). Indeed, behavioral assessments have been a part of comprehensive assessments since inception of P.L. 94-142, and school psychology has a rich literature and practice base surrounding behavioral assessment (Alessi & Kaye, 1983; Bergan, 1977; Bergan, 1990; Bergan & Kratochwill, 1990; Dwyer, 1998; Elliott, Witt, & Kratochwill, 1991; Gresham, 1985; Kratochwill & Bergan, 1990; Power & Franks, 1988; Shapiro, 1987; Shapiro & Kratochwill, 1988; Stoner, Shinn, & Walker, 1991; Wacker et al., 1990).

So what exactly does the word "functional" add to the requirements? Part of the confusion in answering this question stems from the various uses of the term "functional" in the law and in professional practice. As in many parts of the law, the statute does not provide interpretive guidance, though the word "functional" is used five times, the majority of which refer to assessments or evaluations. Thus, the term needs to be clarified based on dictionary definitions and on generally accepted professional uses of the term. The *Random House Unabridged Dictionary* (1993) contains nine different meanings of the word "function" and eight different meanings of the word "functional," a few of which are used commonly by professionals to modify "assessment." Table 1 presents some of the plausible professional meanings of "functional assessment."

TABLE 1: Meanings/Applications of "Functional Assessment"

Term	Definition (*Random House*)	How it applies to assessment
1. Functional	Of or pertaining to a function or functions	Functional assessment here could mean "an assessment of how well the individual meets environmental expectations (as in school)." A synonym for this meaning might be "adaptive."

Table 1 continued on p. 156

Table 1 continued

2. Functional	Capable of operating or functioning	Functional assessment here could mean "an assessment of how well a person's intact physical or psychological processes are working (e.g., memory, reading skills, musculoskeletal system)."
3. Functional	Having or serving a utilitarian purpose; capable of serving the purpose for which it was designed	Functional assessment here could mean "assessing to determine the function of a student's impeding behavior," "assessments that are practical or pragmatic," or "assessments that measure what they purport to measure" (this is one older definition of validity).
4. Functional	Medical: without a known organic cause or structural change	Functional assessment here could mean "assessments that measure problems without known organic causes" (e.g., specific learning disabilities, emotional disturbance, mild mental retardation).
5. Function	A factor related to or dependent upon other factors	Functional assessment here could mean "assessments that measure how one factor (e.g., student behavior problem, student academic achievement problem) is related to or dependent on other factors (e.g., environmental variables and situations, opportunities to learn)."

Although many of these usages may be applied to assessment procedures used by school psychologists and other educational personnel, what follows are four frequent uses of the term "functional assessment":

• To describe how well an individual is "functioning" in an environment or area of performance. In the context of IDEA 97 this type of assessment is focused on describing an individual's "functional needs." That is, it answers the question, What does an individual need in order to function educationally? The resulting information can be used to address the "need for special education" test of the two-pronged eligibility test for special education. Additionally, this information can be used directly in planning IEPs.

- To describe the status of some intact characteristic of the individual. This type of assessment is used to describe within-person characteristics or to diagnose a problem. In relation to IDEA 97, this type of assessment typically assists in determining the nature of an individual's disability; that is, the "disability" component of the two-prong eligibility test. Examples might include a physical therapist's assessment of a student's strength to determine the severity of a physical disability, a school psychologist's assessment of an individual's "processing deficits" to identify presence of a specific learning disability, or a school psychologists' assessment of cognitive abilities and adaptive behavior in order to identify the presence of mental retardation. This type of assessment typically provides information that is helpful for diagnosis. Often, however, these results are less directly related to intervention planning for individual students (Heller, Holtzman, & Messick, 1982; Howell, Fox, & Morehead, 1993; Jenkins, Pious, & Peterson, 1988; National Association of State Directors of Special Education, 1994; Reschly & Tilly, 1993; Reynolds, Wang, & Walberg, 1987).

- To describe the relationship between a skill or performance problem and variables that contribute to its occurrence. In the context of IDEA 97, this type of assessment is designed to help determine what variables are related to the occurrence and nonoccurrence of a problem so that effective educational programs can be designed. Examples might include (a) examining curricular, instructional, and motivational variables related to the occurrence of a reading problem or (b) examining classroom arrangements, persons present, instructional subject, and work demands as they relate to disruptive behavior in a classroom.

- To determine the function of a student's impeding behavior. This description answers the question, What purpose does the student's behavior serve? This type of definition assumes that the student's behavior, though considered inappropriate, is a reasonable and logical response to the environment. Functional assessment in this context is a search for that logic. The information derived from this analysis provides hypotheses about what the problematic behavior means for the individual, and gives assessors a logical and reasonable justification for selecting specific interventions and supports to promote optimal student functioning.

CONSIDERATIONS FOR SCHOOL-BASED TEAMS IN IMPLEMENTING THE FBA PROVISIONS

What is a Functional Behavioral Assessment?

The process of coming to an understanding about why a student engages in challenging behavior and how student behavior relates to the environment is referred to as functional behavioral assessment (Tilly et al., 1998). The purpose of an

FBA is to gather broad and specific information to understand better the reasons for the student's problem behavior. In particular, FBA can provide a team with insight about (a) why a given student engages in behavior that impedes learning, (b) when the student is most likely to engage in the behavior of concern, and (c) under what conditions the student is more likely to be successful. The student's educational team develops hypothesis statements as a result of the assessment process. Hypotheses serve a number of purposes including (a) to summarize assessment results, (b) to offer explanations for the student's problem behavior, and (c) to guide the development of a behavior intervention plan. Behavioral intervention plans (see Tankersley Landrum, Cook, and Balan, this volume) that are derived from functional behavioral assessments have the intent of teaching a student appropriate behaviors, and increasing the student's access to the general curriculum by keeping the student in school.

Completing an FBA requires going beyond describing the form or shape of behavior. One illustration of behavioral form would be to state that the man is running. Often, behavioral assessment in schools has been concerned with the form of or some dimension of the behavior itself, as in determining on-task rates or frequencies of aggression. This is important information, but not sufficient in and of itself to assist with intervention planning. Functional behavioral assessment is concerned with both how the man is running (e.g., rate, gait) as well as *why* the man is running. Running to get away from a lion may look the same as but serve a different function than running to catch a train. And the intervention for running will be different not based on how fast the man is running, but why. The point is that two instances of the same behavior can look identical, but serve different purposes in different contexts for the same individual and it is the purpose that is critical to identify in order to design plausible interventions with a high likelihood of success.

Background of FBA Research

Before summarizing relevant research concerning functional behavioral assessment, it is important to clarify the distinction between FBA and functional analysis (FA). FBA is a problem-solving framework, and a set of procedures, used to define behaviors, establish the magnitude of problems, and generate hypotheses about the function that a behavior serves for an individual . The outcomes of a thorough FBA are (a) a description of the problem behavior, (b) identification of the events that predict occurrence and nonoccurrence of the behavior, (c) identification of the functions that the behavior serves for that individual (like attention from peers or escape from a demanding task), (d) generating hypotheses about what would happen to the behavior if events prior to or after the behavior were changed, and (e) data from systematic, direct observations in the context in which the behavior occurs (O'Neill et al., 1997).

Functional analysis is a specific experimental procedure in which variables related to behavior function are manipulated, the effects of the manipulations on the behavior are assessed, and an intervention is implemented and monitored as a direct result of the experimental manipulations . Functional analyses of behavior require more precision in manipulation of conditions and in monitoring effects on behavior, and are difficult to implement in practice (Steege & Northrup, 1998). Fundamentally, however, the same logic set underlies both FBA and FA; that is, assessing the function that a behavior serves for an individual so that an acceptable replacement behavior that accesses that function can be taught.

FBA as described in this chapter has evolved from the functional analysis literature and is predicated on a series of fundamental assumptions (Bambara & Knoster, 1998; O'Neill et al., 1997). It is imperative that practitioners who will implement FBAs are aware of these assumptions and examine carefully how these assumptions match their perspectives on human behavior. First, FBA and the resulting behavioral support planning is a process carried out with deep respect for the values, preferences, and dignity of the persons being served. Second, it is assumed that behavior is lawful and is related in predictable ways to the individual's context. Context in this case refers to the broad range of both internal (organic and situational) and external (e.g., environmental, temporal, structural) factors that may influence the way that an individual behaves. Moreover, it means that behavior should be viewed as a constantly changing and evolving entity, rather than as representative of static individual traits or symptoms of disability. Third, it is assumed that challenging behaviors serve a function or purpose for the individual. Though a behavior or behaviors may be perceived as inappropriate or problematic by some, they serve a useful purpose for the person doing the behaviors, which is precisely why they continue to occur. Indeed, Carr, Langdon, and Yarbrough (1999) state that problem behavior is not maladaptive. Maladaptive behaviors are those that do not confer any advantages for their users. In most cases, maladaptive behaviors, when used consistently, provide consistent advantages for their users. Functional assessment is an attempt to look beyond the behavior itself and to understand the logic and the purpose of the behavior. Fourth, it is assumed that the purpose of FBA is to develop and provide supports that maximize human functioning. Rather than attempting to reduce or diminish behaviors perceived to be problematic, FBA focuses on promoting, supporting, and teaching effective alternatives. Finally, it is assumed that the best outcome is the one that produces the best results for the person receiving services (Reschly & Tilly, 1993). Rather than focusing on the amount and the technical quality or quantity of data or the "level of understanding" produced by assessments, this "outcomes criterion" forces examination of our assessment processes based on bottom line student results.

The following summaries of research examine the application of functional assessment across a variety of problem behaviors and disabilities (severe to mild), and in a range of settings (clinic, self-contained classroom, regular education classroom). Although representing only a small sample of the available research, these data provide a foundation regarding the types of research available and the technical adequacy of functional assessment procedures.

Three representative studies are presented in this section. First, a seminal study by Iwata, Dorsey, Silfer, Bauman, and Richman (1982) will be summarized. Next, an application study in which Umbreit (1995) demonstrates use of functional assessment strategies for a student with attention deficit hyperactivity disorder will be reviewed. Third, a study by Dunlap et al. (1993) is used to describe a line of research demonstrating application of functional assessment, including curricular modifications, for students receiving special education under the category "emotionally behaviorally disturbed."

Iwata et al. (1982) examined the impact of social and physical environments on behavior. Nine children and youth between the ages of 1 and 17 were treated. All subjects had developmental delays and exhibited self-injurious behavior. Each child was observed under four conditions: (a) social disapproval, (b) academic demand, (c) unstructured play, and (d) alone. In the social disapproval condition, attention was given to the child when self-injury occurred. Under the academic demand condition, an educational task was removed from the child when self-injury occurred. In the unstructured play condition, attention was given to each child when the child was engaged in appropriate behavior (thus could not be engaged in self-injury). In the alone condition, each child was in the room alone, with access to toys. The results of the study suggested that the self-injurious behavior of each child was not random but differed depending on the conditions under which the child was observed. The authors concluded that knowledge of what was maintaining self-injurious behavior was important for developing effective interventions.

There are numerous applications of functional assessment with students with severe disabilities in the professional literature. It is important to emphasize that functional assessment has also been applied successfully to students with less severe disabilities. For example, Umbreit (1995) reported on an 8-year-old boy diagnosed with attention deficit hyperactivity disorder, for whom functional assessment was used to develop an intervention to supplement medication treatment. By observing the child's disruptive and appropriate behavior under several conditions, hypotheses about the maintaining variables were made. Initial observations suggested that escape from task demands was maintaining the disruptive behavior. Umbreit then observed the child working under different conditions in the classroom, seated near or away from peers in independent and cooperative activities. The resulting data suggested higher rates of appropriate behavior when seated away from peers. The assessment data were used to develop an intervention in which the student worked away from peers or outside of the student's regular group of friends, the student was taught to request breaks as he needed them, and the teaching staff ignored disruptive behavior. The intervention resulted in near 100% of intervals observed being engaged in appropriate behavior across three settings using a multiple baseline design. The intervention also had high treatment acceptability by teachers. This study is important because it demonstrates that functional assessment in general education settings can be applied to students with mild disabilities. This research is also important because it extended on other work that examined the contribution of curricular factors in the child's behavior.

Dunlap and Kern have conducted some of the foundational work examining curricular variables as they relate to behavior. Their work is also important because they have applied functional assessment to students identified as emotionally or behaviorally disordered. In one study, Dunlap et al. (1993) developed interventions for five students with average to low average cognitive ability who were served in a self-contained classroom in a public school setting. Interviews, records reviews, and direct observations of students were conducted to generate hypotheses about the variables that preceded and followed each student's defined problem behavior. The results suggested very individualized variables that predicted and maintained behaviors, and that functional assessment could be successfully used in the context of a public school setting with children with emotional or behavior disorders.

The studies summarized represent a cross section of the research on application of functional assessment in school settings. There are five broad conclusions that can be drawn from the research base on functional assessment. First, functional assessment attempts to match the intervention to the function of the behavior (O'Neill et al., 1997). Second, functional assessment has evolved out of the applied behavior analytic research and focuses on identifying factors that contribute to, predict, or maintain problem behaviors. In this sense, intervention efforts focus not only on how teachers and support staff respond to behavior, but what teachers and support staff do to promote the desired behavior and to not promote the undesired behavior (Kern & Dunlap, 1998). Third, there are data-based examples of successful applications of functional assessment to suggest that functional assessment helps develop interventions that address problems being experienced by students with severe and mild disabilities (Dunlap et al., 1993; Umbreit, 1995). Fourth, to adequately implement functional assessment to prevent behaviors will take a team-based approach (Sugai, Horner, & Sprague, 1999). Finally, although functional assessment methods are not new, there is little evidence to suggest that sufficient pre-service training occurs for teachers and itinerant staff to successfully integrate functional behavioral assessment in their practice (Scott & Nelson, 1999).

BEST PRACTICE STRATEGIES FOR CONDUCTING FUNCTIONAL BEHAVIORAL ASSESSMENTS

For any assessment to be functional, it must lead to the design of an intervention that has a high probability of success. There are three common approaches to collecting functional assessment information in school based programs (O'Neill et al., 1997). The first approach is known as "informant methods," and involves talking with the student who presents the problem behavior and to those people who have direct contact with, and knowledge about, the student. The second approach is "direct observation," which requires systematic observation of the student within typical routines across settings. Typically, teams that employ either or a combination of these approaches will derive adequate information from which to formulate hypotheses. In addition to these two approaches, there is a third less frequently used method known as "experimental analysis" (also referred to as functional analysis) in which specific variables that are hypothesized as being related to the occurrence or non-occurrence of the student's problem behavior are systematically manipulated to test the team's hypotheses.

FBA as a General Approach

The process of conducting FBAs can best be understood as a continuum of integrated assessment procedures that may involve a broad array of data collection tools and procedures. Determining the amount of resources and precision of behavioral assessment to apply should be made, on a case-by-case basis, in relation to the degree of need (e.g., persistence/severity/durability of problem behavior) as depicted in Figure 1. In essence, FBA is neither a tool nor an instrument. Rather, it is a problem-solving framework that leads to intervention. What is critical to note when matching assessment rigor to problems, is that no matter which specific procedures are used, the same thought processes undergird the FBA. The thinking structure does not vary, though the level of precision needed in one's data does.

FIGURE 1: Conceptual Relationship Between Degree of Behavioral Problem and Amount of Behavioral Assessment Resources Needed

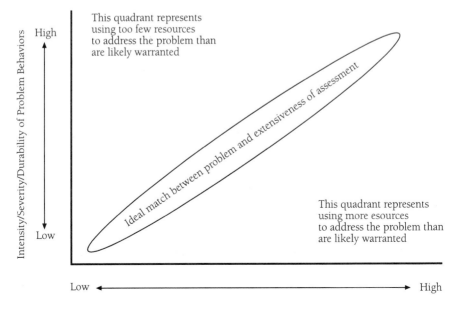

CHAPTER 5
Functional Behavioral Assessment |

It may be helpful to illustrate the concept of FBA as both a continuum and array of assessment methods through analogy with assessment practices in the medical profession. Most of us at some point in time experience headaches. On the basis of some simple low-technology interventions premised on intuitive decision making, typical headaches often subside within a reasonable time frame (e.g., rest, fluids, and aspirin used until the headache subsides). At some juncture if our headache persists despite our interventions we would likely seek advice from others including possibly our doctor.

During an appointment with a physician it is unlikely that he or she would refer us initially to further specialists or order extensive (intrusive and costly) procedures (this is particularly true in today's world with managed care). Rather, it is more likely that our doctor would provide guidance and, based on circumstances, prescriptions to help us in addressing both pain management and what our doctor believes is the underlying cause of our headache. Only in the absence of positive outcomes would our doctor likely move us further down the continuum of intrusiveness and cost in terms of medical assessment. In other words, our doctor would look to create the ideal match between (a) intensity/severity/durability of the problem (e.g., headache), and (b) resources and precision of the assessment procedures (e.g., informant methods up through more comprehensive/invasive/costly medical tests).

The use of FBA in schools closely parallels the use of medical technology to assess physical illness. Student-centered school-based teams will enter into the FBA continuum at different points based on the nature of the concerns. As a result, teams will use an array of tools and procedures under different circumstances and varied degrees of need. For example, one team may be working with a student in general education who presents a high frequency of what might be considered mild behavioral concerns such as out-of-seat behavior. Another team may struggle to provide an IEP for a student who engages in high intensity problem behavior of crisis proportion in the form of self injury.

Salvia and Ysseldyke (1988) provided a framework for special education decision making that is relevant to FBA and has direct utility in schools. Table 2 on page 164 provides a decision-making framework that is based on Salvia and Ysseldyke's original formulation that has been increasingly accepted and used by school practitioners. Although the IEP serves as the centerpiece of the special education decision-making process, teams educating students who exhibit problem behavior may systematically commence an FBA at any point in time in the noted decision making framework. Examples include (a) a first-grade student whose off task behavior has become increasingly problematic over the past 5 months during general academic instruction and concern is noted by the teacher, (b) a third-grade student's persistent tantrums and hitting of his peers as a way of resolving conflicts have prompted a full and individual evaluation for consideration of eligibility and need for special education, (c) a sixth-grade student with an IEP who previously has not required a behavior intervention plan but who increasingly displays problem behavior that impedes his learning or the learning of others, and (d) an eighth-grade student with an IEP for whom, as a result of a manifestation determination, the IEP team is systematically initiating a comprehensive FBA.

TABLE 2: Special Education Decisions

Decision-Making Framework for Special Education

Initial indication of concern

Screening and intervention in general education

Referral for a full and individual evaluation

The full and individual evaluation

Instructional planning (including IEP)

IEP progress monitoring and program modification

Given the range of possible implementations of FBA, educational teams need to have the capacity to determine where on the continuum they are with regard to a given student and how to use an array of tools and procedures to gather information throughout a functional behavioral assessment. Table 3 depicts examples of effective tools and procedures that are often used along the continuum of FBA implementation.

Specific FBA Components

Gathering Broad Information

Once a team decides to systematically move beyond intuitive decision making, the first step in the FBA is to gather broad contextual information about the student: skills and abilities, preferences and interests, and general health and quality of life. This information is vital not only to increase understanding about why an individual engages in problem behavior, but also to develop effective intervention plans that are tailored to the student's preferences, needs, and life circumstances.

When gathering broad information, teams should build on current strengths in each area assessed. Conversely, consideration should be given to negative influences or the absence of positive factors that may be contributing to the problem behavior. For example, teams may consider how specific deficits in communication and social skills, such as the student's having a limited system of communication, may be contributing to problem behavior. Teams may also ask, How does the

TABLE 3: **Continuum and Array of FBA**

Level of Rigor on Continuum	Examples of Array of Tools/Procedures
Intuitive decision making	• Teacher extemporaneous decision making in the ebb and flow of daily routines • Teacher reflection devoid of a systematic process • Teacher discussions devoid of a framework/protocol
Informant methods	• Person Centered Assessment • Functional Assessment Interview • Social Network Analysis • The Motivation Assessment Scale • Quality of Life Cue Questions • Positive Environment Checklist • Interaction Observation Form • Curriculum Activity Profile • Communication Interview Format • Initial Line of Inquiry
Direct observation	• A-B-C (S-R-C) Analysis • Scatterplots • Functional Analysis Observation Form • Anecdotal records • Behavior Maps • Communicative Functions Analysis

student communicate currently, and how might these skills be improved to ameliorate problem behaviors?

When assessing routines and preferences, team members should examine what the student enjoys and consider whether daily school and home routines provide sufficient opportunities for the student to pursue his or her interests and participate in preferred activities. Conversely, whether the student's day is filled with events that are disliked, problematic, or particularly stressful should be evaluated.

In addition, teams should examine whether problem behaviors are related to illness or pain (e.g., a cold, menstrual cramps, fatigue) sensory problems, poor dietary or sleep habits, or mental health issues (e.g., depression). Ultimately, the team will need to identify interventions that will either address health concerns directly (e.g., seek medical assistance) or indirectly (e.g., lessen classroom demands on days when the student does not feel well).

Finally, when conducting a comprehensive FBA, it is important to gather information about the student's overall lifestyle. Relevant questions include (a) what is the quality of the student's relationship with peers and family members, (b) does the student seem happy or content, (c) does the student have opportunities for choice and control within daily routines, (d) does the student have sufficient access to preferred activities, and (e) is the student included in typical school and community activities? Answers to such questions provide not only important clues for understanding what factors appear to be contributing to the student's problem behavior but also help the team in partnership with the student identify relevant goals for the student's support plan of intervention.

Gathering Specific Information

In the second stage of the FBA, the team gathers specific information that will (a) pinpoint the conditions that are regularly associated with the problem behavior and (b) identify the function or purpose of the individual's behavior. Specifically, the team should ask the following series of questions: (a) *When is the student most likely to engage in problem behavior?* In answering this question the team seeks to identify specific time periods, activities, or daily routines most associated with the occurrence of the problem behavior. (b) *What specific events appear to be contributing to the problem situation?* Here the team analyzes problematic activities to identify discrete antecedent and setting events that immediately trigger the problem. (c) *What function does the problem behavior serve for the individual?* Functions served by the behavior are determined by observing what happens after a problem behavior occurs (e.g., what the student gets, how people respond), but may also be inferred from the antecedent conditions. Table 4 provides examples of common functions of problem behavior.

TABLE 4: Common Functions and Communicative Intent of Problem Behavior

Function	Possible Message
To gain access to social interaction	"Play with me."
	"Watch what I'm doing."
	"Did I do good work?"
	"Spend time with me."
	"Let's do this together."
	"Can I have a turn, too?"
	"I want to be one of the gang."

To gain access to activities, objects	"I want to play outside."
	"Can I have what she has?"
	"I want to listen to more music."
	"I don't want to stop; I'm enjoying this."
	"I'm hungry."
To terminate or avoid unwanted situations	"Leave me alone."
	"This is too hard. I need help."
	"I don't want to do this."
	"Don't tell me what to do."
	"I don't like to be teased."
	"I'm bored."
	"I'm not feeling well."
	"I need a break."
To gain access to stimulating events	"I like doing this."

Generating Hypothesis Statements

Once the FBA process is completed and predictable patterns emerge that explain when and why the student engages in problem behavior, the team is ready to develop hypothesis statements. Hypothesis statements summarize assessment results by offering a logical explanation for problem behavior and guide the development of intervention plans. Interventions developed without FBA-based hypotheses are likely to be unsuccessful, because they ignore the conditions contributing to the problem behavior (Carr, 1999). More importantly, non-FBA–based hypotheses ignore the reason for the problem behavior from the student's perspective. For example, imagine the frustration of being redirected back to an academic task when attempting to communicate that you feel ill.

Bambara and Knoster (1995, 1998) recommend formulating two types of hypotheses to guide intervention efforts: specific and global. Specific and global hypotheses work in tandem to guide the student's educational team to design the behavior intervention plan.

A specific hypothesis synthesizes the specific information gathered during the functional assessment process. Specific hypotheses explain why a problem behavior occurs by (a) describing antecedent and setting events regularly associated with it and (b) identifying its possible function. Specific hypotheses consist of three component statements (see Table 5 on page 168).

Specific hypotheses are essential for building effective intervention plans, but they alone cannot provide a comprehensive understanding of the complexity of

TABLE 5: Format for Writing Specific Hypotheses

When this happens: (a description of specific antecedent and setting events associated with the problem behavior),

the student does this: (a description of the problem behavior),

in order to: (a description of the possible function of the problem behavior).

---

conditions that might be adversely influencing behaviors. Therefore, the team should also formulate a global hypothesis summarizing relevant contextual information gathered during the functional assessment process. A global hypothesis addresses broad influences related to an individual's skills, health, preferences, daily routines, and overall quality of life. In effect, a global hypothesis provides a contextual explanation for why the events identified in the specific hypothesis are problematic for the student. It is important to formulate both types of hypotheses in preparation for the decision-making phase of the behavior intervention plan.

A Practical Place to Start

The challenge of translating FBA's critical components into practice falls to the educational team. To realize the potential of FBA, teams need a practical place to start the assessment process that practitioners will find acceptable and useful (Lohrmann, Knoster, & Llewellyn, 1997). The logistical constraints (e.g., time, immediacy of need) and the comprehensive nature of FBA can appear overwhelming to team members who are just learning about the process. However, a series of structures and strategies have been developed to aid professionals in their FBA implementation.

Screening for Understanding

To give educational teams—including IEP teams—a concrete starting point, Knoster and Llewellyn (1998) developed *Screening for Understanding of Student Problem Behavior: An Initial Line of Inquiry* to serve as a user-friendly starting point for conducting an initial systematic assessment of a student's challenging behavior. The authors designed this line of inquiry for use within the context of a team planning process, making it a good fit within the existing IEP structure delineated in IDEA 97. A copy of this document is contained in Appendix A of this chapter and will serve as an initial training structure to assist practitioners in implementing FBAs.

The Initial Line of Inquiry serves as an initial screening tool for identifying patterns of student behavior. A facilitator conducts the Initial Line of Inquiry within the context of a team planning process. The facilitator is either an internal (e.g., school psychologist) or external (e.g., consultant) member of the team. Core team members include those who know the child well and the child himself or herself, whenever appropriate. The IEP team should serve as the nucleus for students receiving special education services and programs. The primary emphasis throughout the assessment process is on facilitating team consensus regarding relevant factors related to the student's behavior. The facilitator's role is to work with the team in six main areas (see Figure 2):

FIGURE 2: **Facilitator's Chart Setup for Informant Method FBA**

Strengths of the Student:				
Slow Triggers (Setting Events)	Fast Triggers (Antecedents)	Problem Behavior	Perceived Function	Actual Consequence

- Student strengths
- Problem behavior
- Slow triggers (setting events)
- Fast triggers (antecedents)
- Actual consequence
- Perceived function (see Table 6 on page 170)

To promote communication among team members, consistent and user-friendly terminology is used in place of more traditional terms with which some team members may not be familiar. For example, the term "fast trigger" refers to antecedents, or those events with a discrete onset and end point that are present immediately before occurrences of behavior. The term "slow trigger" refers to setting events, or those events that may occur before or during the targeted response that cause the student to respond to a "typical" situation in an "atypical" manner. "Perceived function" refers to the team members' initial explanation of why the behavior is occurring.

TABLE 6: Self-Check for Conducting a Functional Assessment

Was a functional assessment conducted before implementing a behavior intervention plan?	Y	N
Were both broad and specific information gathered in an effort to obtain a comprehensive understanding of the possible reasons for the problem behavior?	Y	N
Did the broad assessment contain information on the student's skills and abilities, preferences, general health, and overall quality of life?	Y	N
Did the specific assessment guide the team to identify (a) when the problem behavior is most and least likely to occur, (b) specific events that trigger or set the stage for the problem behavior, and (c) the function of the problem behavior?	Y	N
Were the assessment results summarized in both global and specific hypothesis statements?	Y	N
Did the specific hypothesis include the following three components: (a) when this happens (b) the individual does (c) in order to?		
Is your team prepared to link support strategies back to the hypothesis?	Y	N

By using a flip chart or chalkboard, the facilitator records relevant information for all members to view collectively throughout the process. As team members engage in dialogue, the facilitator serves as a scribe and interpreter of emerging patterns leading to the development of hypotheses regarding behavioral function. The inquiry typically takes between 60 and 90 minutes. At the end of the team meeting, the group will have generated specific and global hypothesis of behavioral function and descriptions of the relevant factors related to the child's challenging behavior. If team members decide that they need a more comprehensive FBA, then the type of information and necessary strategies for obtaining that information (e.g., more in-depth interviews, direct observation) are identified and action plans are developed.

PROFESSIONAL DEVELOPMENT IMPLICATIONS FOR EDUCATORS AND SYSTEMS

Implementing FBA in practice will require additional learning on the part of nearly all educators. The imperative to develop these new skills is heightened because the FBA provisions from IDEA are presently in effect; that is, requiring that FBAs be conducted as needed in extant casework. In many ways, policy has preceded practice and is driving the need for further skill development (Nelson, Roberts, Mathur, & Rutherford, 1999). As a result of this situation, it is incumbent upon school psychologists and other educational professionals to take stock of their current FBA knowledge and skills and to pursue individual professional development activities to develop facility with FBA.

A number of documents describe comprehensive professional development programs and curricula related to FBA (Dunlap et al., in press; Tilly et al., 1998). Practitioners interested in implementing comprehensive FBA staff development programs are directed to these materials for more in-depth coverage. From an individual practitioner perspective, however, the authors' experiences provides some guidance regarding tooling up practicing professionals' FBA skills.

Build Knowledge

Learning to implement FBA in practice occurs most effectively through a combination of knowledge building and case-oriented skill training. Team members should attend to both developing overarching knowledge about FBA as well as developing specific knowledge in particular skill areas. Training activities such as workshops as well as structured reading programs can develop knowledge competencies. FBA workshops abound since passage of IDEA 97 and many of these are excellent. One consideration in selecting individual workshops that may be most useful is to select a workshop leader with extensive experience implementing FBA in practice, preferably in schools. Conceptual overviews serve a purpose, but often FBA concepts can best be described by using case illustrations. Also, workshops that are activity-based typically result in more practical knowledge than do "lecture only" styles. Selecting presentations that meet these criteria increases the probability that applicable learning will result.

Two types of readings should be considered: overview and topic-specific. For overview readings, this chapter provides a good starting point. Next, practitioners may wish to consider adding a more in-depth overview of FBA requirements and practices. The annotated bibliography identifies two specific works (Bambara & Knoster, 1998; O'Neill et al., 1997) that can serve this purpose. To build topic-specific knowledge, Dunlap et al. (in press) argue persuasively that FBA must be viewed as *one part* of the knowledge needed to develop effective behavioral support plans. These authors recommend knowledge and skill development in seven areas including (a) establishing a collective vision and goals for intervention (Horner & Carr, 1997; Kincaid, 1996; Koegel, Koegel, & Dunlap, 1996), (b) collaboration and team building among families and professionals (Dunst, Trivette, & Johanson, 1994; Givner & Haager, 1995), (c) functional assessment, (d) designing hypothesis-driven, individualized, comprehensive behavioral support plans (Albin, Lucyshyn, Horner, & Flannery, 1996; Horner, Albin, & O'Neill, 1990), (e) implementing intervention strategies ENR fu (Bellamy, Newton, LeBaron, & Horner, 1990; Lewis & Sugai, 1993), (f) monitoring and evaluating outcomes (Farlow & Snell, 1996; Meyer & Evans, 1993), and (g) infusing positive behavioral support approaches into broader systems (Colvin, Kameenui, & Sugai, 1993; McEvoy, Davis, & Reichle, 1993). Not all of these areas directly reflect FBA processes and procedures; however, each component adds something important to the overall picture of behavior support planning for students.

Build Skills

As described in this chapter, there are three general sets of strategies for conducting FBAs: informant methods, direct observation, and experimental manipulations (functional analysis). Although these levels are not mutually exclusive, they do vary along a continuum from least intrusive to most intrusive. For practitioners implementing their first FBAs in schools, it makes sense to begin by using informant methods strategies with a series of less intense cases. Informant methods strategies have the advantage of clearly illustrating the FBA thought process and problem solving framework without the extra load of having to learn to use new tools, such as observation codes and rating scales as well.

One resource that has proven exceptionally helpful for initial learning is the *Screening for an Understanding of Student Problem Behavior: An Initial Line of Inquiry* contained in the Appendix of this chapter. This format is scripted and guides both the structure of an FBA-facilitated meeting as well as guiding the FBA thought process from beginning to end. This protocol has been implemented successfully by hundreds of practitioners nationally and has been refined to a point where the authors are confident recommending it.

As practitioners gain experience using the Initial Line of Inquiry to conduct FBAs, cases will be encountered where informant methods data do not provide sufficient precision to develop behavior support plans. Perhaps a behavior support plan was implemented but did not have the intended result or the intensity of a student's problem behaviors warrant data with more precision than can be attained by using informants methods. In these cases, the educators' knowledge of the FBA framework can be used to guide the addition of other direct assessment procedures to the needed FBAs. The underlying framework for assessment (i.e., the assessment questions and assumptions) remains the same, but the types of data that are collected to address the questions differ.

FBAs conducted by using informant methods and direct observation methods provide teams with robust methodologies that are relevant for many, perhaps a majority, of behavior problems encountered in school environments. One caveat, however, is that FBA using informant methods and observations will not be sufficient to address all of the behavior problems encountered in schools. In some cases, where problem behaviors are at the high end of the intensity/durability scale or in cases where the nature of problem behaviors are sufficiently complex as to render informant methods/direct observation hypotheses questionable or in cases where there are other significant concerns (e.g., medical issues, mental health problems), it is always appropriate to consider referral to or collaboration with other professionals. Indeed, there are cases where individual problems require intensive experimental analyses (functional analyses) to derive accurate hypotheses on which behavior support plans can be built. In these cases, it is often prudent to involve colleagues with significant experience conducting functional analyses. The training and experience required to conduct such assessments demands commitment of significant professional time. It requires completion of a formal and rigorous course of study and supervised experience implementing functional analyses in controlled settings. In most cases, such assessments would rarely, if ever, be conducted in school settings.

SUMMARY

This chapter has reviewed the foundations of functional behavioral assessment from both a legal and practical perspective. An initial grounding in the functional assessment literature was provided, and an initial tool for use when learning to conduct functional behavioral assessments was introduced. With investment of reasonable time and energy, educational professionals can become effective facilitators for legally defensible and educationally effective FBAs that lead directly to effective behavioral supports for students.

REFERENCES

Albin, R. W., Horner, R. H., & O'Neill, R. E. (1993). Proactive behavioral support: Structuring and assessing environments. Eugene: Unpublished manuscript, University of Oregon, Specialized Training Program.

Albin, R. W., Lucyshyn, J. M., Horner, R. H., & Flannery, B. K. (1996). Contextual fit for behavioral support plans: A model for "goodness of fit." In L. Koegel, R. Koegel, & G. Dunlap (Eds.), Positive behavioral support: Including people with difficult behavior in the community (pp. 81-98). Baltimore, MD: Brookes.

Alessi, G. K., & Kaye, J. H. (1983). Behavior assessment for school psychologists. Washington, DC: National Association of School Psychologists.

Anderson, J. L., Mesaros, R. A., & Neary, T. (1991). Community references nonaversive behavior management trainers manual: Vol. 1. Washington, DC: National Institute on Disability and Rehabilitation Research.

Bambara, L. M., & Knoster, T. (1995). Guidelines: Effective behavioral support. Harrisburg, PA: Pennsylvania Department of Education, Bureau of Special Education.

Bambara, L. M., & Knoster, T. (1998). Designing positive behavior support plans. Washington, DC: American Association on Mental Retardation.

Bellamy, G. T., Newton, J. S., LeBaron, N., & Horner, R. H. (1990). Quality of life and lifestyle outcomes: A challenge for residential programs. In R. Schalock (Ed.), Quality of life: Perspectives and issues (pp. 127-137). Washington, DC: American Association on Mental Retardation.

Bergan, J. R. (1977). Behavioral consultation. Columbus, OH: Charles E. Merrill.

Bergan, J. R. (1990). Contributions of behavioral psychology to school psychology. In T. B. Gutkin & C. R. Reynolds (Eds.), Handbook of school psychology (2nd ed.) (pp. 126-142). New York: John Wiley.

Bergan, J. R., & Kratochwill, T. R. (1990). Behavioral consultation and therapy. New York: Plenum.

Carr, E.G., Langdon, N. A., & Yarbrough, S. C. (1999). Hypothesis-based intervention services for severe behavior problems. In A. C. Repp & R. H. Horner (Eds.), Functional analysis of problem behavior (pp. 7-31). Belmont, CA: Wadsworth Publishing.

Colvin, G., Kameenui, E. J., & Sugai, G. (1993). Reconceptualizing behavior management and school-wide discipline in general education. Education and treatment of Children, 16, 361–381.

Dunlap, G., Hieneman, M., Knoster, T., Fox, L., Anderson, J., & Albin, R. W. (in press). Inservice training in positive behavior support: Issues and essential elements. Journal of Positive Behavioral Support.

Dunlap, G., Kern, L., dePerczel, M., Clarke, S., Wilson, D., Childs, K. E., White, R., & Falk, G. D. (1993). Functional analysis of classroom variables for students with emotional and behavioral disorders. Behavioral Disorders, 18, 275–291.

Dunst, C. J., Trivette, C. M., & Johanson, C. (1994). Parent-professional collaboration and partnerships. In C. Dunst, C. Trivette, & A. Deal (Eds.), Supporting and strengthening families: Vol.1: Methods, strategies, and practices (pp. 197-211). Cambridge, MA: Brookline Books.

Durand, V. M. (1988). The Motivation Assessment Scale. In M. Hersen & A. S. Bellack (Eds.), Dictionary of behavioral assessment techniques (pp. 309-310). New York: Pergamon.

Dwyer, K. P. (1998). Using functional assessment of behavior. Communiqué, 26(5), 1,4,5.

Elliott, S. N., Witt, J. C., & Kratochwill, T. R. (1991). Selecting, implementing, and evaluating classroom interventions. In G. Stoner, M. R. Shinn, & H. M. Walker (Eds.), Interventions for achievement and behavior problems (pp. 99-135). Silver Spring, MD: National Association of School Psychologists.

Farlow, L. J., & Snell, M. E. (1996). Making the most of student performance data. Washington, DC: American Association on Mental Retardation.

Finn Jr., C. E. (1990). The biggest reform of all. Phi Delta Kappan, 71(8), 584–592.

Foster-Johnson, L., Ferro, J., & Dunlap, G. (1991). Curricular Activity Profile. Tampa, FL: Florida Mental Health Institute, University of South Florida.

Givner, C. C., & Haager, D. (1995). Strategies for effective collaboration. In M. A. Falvey (Ed.), Inclusive and heterogeneous schooling: Assessment, curriculum, and instruction (pp. 93-114). Baltimore, MD: Brookes.

Gresham, F. M. (1985). Behavior disorder assessment: Conceptual, definitional, and practical considerations. School Psychology Review, 14, 495–509.

Heller, K. A., Holtzman, W., & Messick, S. (1982). Placing children in special education: A strategy for equity. Washington, DC: National Academy Press.

Horner, R. H., Albin, R. W., & O'Neill, R. E. (1990). Supporting students with severe intellectual disabilities and severe challenging behaviors. In G. Stoner, M. Shinn, & H. Walker (Eds.), Interventions for achievement and behavior problems (pp. 269–287). Silver Spring, MD: National Association of School Psychologists.

Horner, R. H., & Carr, E. G. (1997). Behavioral support for students with severe disabilities: Functional assessment and comprehensive intervention. Journal of Special Education, 31, 84–104.

Howell, K. W., Fox, S. L., & Morehead, M. K. (1993). Curriculum-based evaluation: Teaching and decision making (2nd ed.). Pacific Grove, CA: Brooks/Cole.

Individuals with Disabilities Education Act Amendments of 1997, 20 U.S.C. § 1400 et seq. (West 1997).

Individuals with Disabilities Education Act Regulations, 34 C.F.R. § 300 and 303. (1999).

Ittelson, W. H., Rivlin, L. G., & Proschansky, H. M. (1976). The use of behavioral maps in environmental psychology. In H. M. Proschansky, W. H. Ittelson, & L. G. Rivlin (Eds.), Environmental psychology: People and their physical setting (pp. 265-282). New York: Holt, Rinehart & Winston.

Iwata, B. A., Dorsey, M., Silfer, K., Bauman, K., & Richman, G. (1982). Toward a functional analysis of self-injury. Analysis and Intervention in Developmental Disabilities, 2, 3–20.

Jenkins, J. R., Pious, C. G., & Peterson, D. L. (1988). Categorical programs for remedial and handicapped students: Issues of validity. Exceptional Children, 55, 147–158.

Kanfer, F. H., & Saslow, G. (1969). Behavioral diagnosis. In C. M. Franks (Ed.), Behavior therapy: Appraisal and status (pp. 417–444). New York: McGraw-Hill.

Kennedy, C. H., Horner, R. H., & Newton, J. S. (1990). The social networks and activity patterns of adults with severe disabilities: A correctional analysis. Journal of The Association of Persons with Severe Handicaps, 15, 86–90.

Kern, L., & Dunlap, G. (1998). Developing effective program plans for students with disabilities. In D. J. Reschly, W. D. Tilly, & J. P. Grimes (Eds.), Functional and noncategorical identification and intervention in special education (pp. 165–180). Des Moines, IA: Iowa Department of Education.

Kincaid, D. (1996). Person centered planning. In L. K. Koegel, R. L. Koegel, & G. Dunlap (Eds.), Positive behavioral support: Including people with difficult behavior in the community (pp. 439-465). Baltimore, MD: Brookes.

Knoster, T., & Llewellyn, G. (1997). Screening for an understanding of student problem behavior: An initial line of inquiry (2nd ed.). Lewisburgh, PA: Instructional Support System of Pennsylvania: Pennsylvania Department of Education.

Koegel, L. K., Koegel, R. L., & Dunlap, G. (Eds.). (1996). Positive behavioral support: Including people with difficult behavior in the community. Baltimore, MD: Brookes.

Kratochwill, T. R., & Bergan, J. R. (1990). Behavioral consultation in applied settings: An individual guide. New York: Plenum.

Lewis, T. J., & Sugai, G. (1993). Teaching communicative alternatives to socially withdrawn learners: An investigation on maintaining treatment effects. Journal of Behavioral Education, 3, 61–75.

Lohrman, S., Knoster, T., & Llewellyn, G. (1999). Screening for understanding: An initial line of inquiry for school based teams. Journal of Positive Behavior Interventions, 1, 35-42.

Marzano, R. J. & Kendall, J. S. (1996). A comprehensive guide to designing standards-based districts, schools and classrooms. Aurora, CO: Mid-Continent Regional Educational Laboratory.

McEvoy, M., Davis, C., & Reichle, J. (1993). District-wide technical assistance teams: Designing intervention strategies for young children with challenging behaviors. Behavioral Disorders, 19, 27–34.

Meyer, L. H., & Evans, I. M. (1993). Science and practice in behavioral intervention: Meaningful outcomes, research validity, and usable knowledge. Journal of the Association for Persons with Severe Handicaps, 18, 224–234.

Mount, B., & Zernick. (1988). It's never too early. It's never too late: A booklet about personal futures planning. St. Paul, MN: Metropolitan Council.

National Association of State Directors of Special Education. (1994). Assessment and eligibility in special education: An examination of policy and practice with proposals for change. Alexandria, VA: Author.

National Association of State Directors of Special Education. (1998). Interim alternative educational settings for students with disabilities involved in disciplinary actions. Alexandria, VA: Author.

National Commission on Excellence in Education. (1983). A nation at risk: The imperative for educational reform. Washington, DC: U.S. Government Printing Office.

Nelson, J. R., Roberts, M. L., Mathur, S. R., & Rutherford, R. B. (1999). Has public policy exceeded our knowledge base?: A review of the functional behavioral assessment literature. Behavioral Disorders, 24, 169–179.

O'Brien, J., & Lyle, C. (1987). Framework for accomplishment. Decatur, GA: Responsive Systems Associates.

O'Neill, R. E., Horner, R. H., Albin, R. W., Sprague, J. R., Storey, K., & Newton, J. S. (1997). Functional assessment and program development for problem behaviors: A practical handbook. Pacific Grove, CA: Brooks/Cole.

O'Neill, R. E., Horner, R. H., Alvin, R. W., Storey, K., & Sprague, J. R. (1990). Functional analysis of problem behavior: A practical assessment guide. Sycamore, IL: Sycamore Publishing.

Power, M. D., & Franks, C. M. (1988). Behavior therapy and the educative process. In J. C. Witt, S. N. Elliott, & F. Gresham (Eds.), Handbook of behavior therapy in education (pp. 3–36). New York: Plenum.

Random House Unabridged Dictionary (1993) (2nd. ed.). New York: Author.

Reese, E. P., Howard, J. S., & Reese, T. W. (1977). Human behavior: An experimental analysis and its applications. Dubuque, IA: Wm. C. Brown.

Reschly, D. J., & Tilly, W. D. (1993). The why of system reform. Communiqué, 22(1), 1–6.

Reynolds, M. C., Wang, M. C., & Walberg, H. J. (1987). The necessary restructuring of special and regular education. Exceptional Children, 53, 391–398.

Salvia, J., & Ysseldyke, J. E. (1988). Assessment in special and remedial education (4th ed.). Boston: Houghton-Mifflin.

Schuler, A. L., Peck, C. A., Tomilinson, C. D., & Theimer, R. K. (1984). Communication Interview. In C. A. Peck, C. Schuler, R. K. Tomilson, T. Theimer, T. Haring, & M. Semmel (Eds.), The social competence curriculum project: A guide to instructional programming for social and communicative interactions (pp. 43–62). Santa Barbara: University of California - Santa Barbara.

Scott, T. M., & Nelson, C. M. (1999). Functional behavioral assessment: Implications for training and staff development. Behavioral Disorders, 24, 249–252.

Shapiro, E. S. (1987). Behavioral assessment in school psychology. Hillsdale, NJ: Lawrence Erlbaum Associates.

Shapiro, E. S., & Kratochwill, T. R. (1988). Behavioral assessment in schools: Conceptual foundations and practical applications. New York: Guilford.

Shepard, L. (1993). Setting performance standards for student achievement. Stanford, CA: National Academy of Education, Stanford University.

Steege, M. W., & Northrup, J. (1998). Functional analysis of problem behavior: A practical approach for school psychologists. Proven Practice: Prevention & Remediation Solutions for Schools, 1, 4–11.

Stoner, G., Shinn, M. R., & Walker, H. M. (Eds.) (1991). Interventions for achievement and behavior problems. Silver Spring, MD: National Association of School Psychologists.

Sugai, G., Horner, R. H., & Sprague, J. R. (1999). Functional-assessment-based behavior support planning: research to practice to research. Behavioral Disorders, 24, 253–257.

Tilly, W. D., Knoster, T. P., Kovaleski, J., Bambara, L., Dunlap, G., & Kincaid, D. (1998). Functional behavioral assessment: Policy development in light of emerging research and practice. Alexandria, VA: National Association of State Directors of Special Education.

Touchette, P. E., MacDonald, R. F., & Langer, S. N. (1985). A scatter plot for identifying stimulus control of problem behavior. Journal of Applied Behavior Analysis, 18, 343–351.

Umbreit, J. (1995). Functional assessment and intervention in a regular classroom setting for the disruptive behavior of a student with attention deficit hyperactivity disorder. Behavioral Disorders, 20, 267–278.

Vandercook, T., Y., & J. Forest, M. (1989). The McGill Action Planning System (MAPS): A strategy for building the vision. Journal of the Association for Persons with Severe Handicaps, 14, 205–215.

Wacker, D., Steege, M., Northup, J., Reimers, T., Berg, W., & Sasso, G. (1990). The use of functional analysis and acceptability measures to assess and treat severe behavior problems: An outpatient model. In A. C. Repp & N. N. Singh (Eds.), Perspectives on the use of nonaversive and aversive interventions for persons with developmental disabilities (pp. 349–359). Pacific Grove, CA: Brooks/Cole.

ANNOTATED BIBLIOGRAPHY

Repp, A. C., & Horner, R. H. (Eds.). (1999). *Functional analysis of problem behavior*. Belmont, CA: Wadsworth.

Representing the most comprehensive single work on functional assessment to date, this book is essential reading for practitioners interested in up-to-date information on the state of FBA research and application. The authors of the chapters in this edited work represent a "who's who" in functional assessment, including many of the original developers of the technology. Topics covered include conceptual issues (e.g., linking functional assessment to intervention, threats to internal and external validity) and a wide range of applications of functional assessment in schools and community settings. Each chapter includes extensive citations to the primary literature on functional assessment and numerous case examples and illustrations are provided by chapter authors.

O'Neill, R. E., Horner, R. H., Albin, R. W., Sprague, J. R., Storey, K., & Newton, J. S. (1997). *Functional assessment and program development for problem behavior: A practical handbook*. Pacific Grove, CA: Brooks/Cole.

This user-friendly handbook presents an accessible and concise overview of functional assessment processes and procedures. Intended as a guidebook for practitioners who implement functional assessments, this work includes a series of exceptionally useful protocols and formats. A functional assessment semi-structured interview is provided, as is a scatterplot observation protocol and a student-directed functional assessment interview. Additionally, this handbook presents and develops an important conceptual organizer called a competing behavior diagram that assists in behavior support planning. From these tools, the process of developing effective positive behavioral supports is reviewed.

Bambara, L. M., & Knoster, T. (1998). *Designing positive behavior support plans*. Washington, DC: American Association on Mental Retardation.

This short booklet provides a brief overview of functional assessment and its grounding in positive behavioral support planning. Especially useful to practitioners is the use of table formats throughout the document. Ten tables are provided including presentation of "characteristics of positive behavioral support," "common functions and communicative intent of problem behavior," "antecedent and setting event modifications," and "lifestyle interventions." These tables and the supporting text provide a clear and concise tour through FBA and its application in school settings. A case study is presented to illustrate the FBA and behavior support process in action.

APPENDIX

Screening for an Understanding of Student Problem Behavior:
An Initial Line of Inquiry
(Second Edition)
Tim Knoster
Greg Llewellyn

Educators increasingly find themselves challenged by student problem behavior. Most educators generally agree that they can effectively teach students whose behavioral incidents are viewed as minor and infrequent. They speak in a unified voice, however, when they say they lose increasingly large amounts of instructional time managing frequent and/or significant student problem behavior.

Various models of school-based behavioral interventions have been documented in the literature and application of most models allows a moderate degree of systematic individualization in classroom settings; however, they typically do not provide the degree of flexibility nor specificity required when a student displays significant challenging behavior. Functional behavioral assessment provides a viable problem-solving framework in such instances and can serve as a means to provide effective programs for students who present serious problem behavior.

The process of coming to an understanding of why a particular student engages in challenging behavior and how that student's behavior relates to the environment is referred to as functional behavioral assessment (FBA). FBA gathers broad and specific information in order to understand better the specific reasons for the student's problem behavior. In the instance where a student with disabilities presents serious problem behavior, this type of assessment can provide an IEP team with useful insight into: (a) why the student engages in impeding behavior; (b) when the student is most likely to engage in the behavior of concern; and (c) under what conditions the student is less likely to engage in the problem behavior. IEP teams develop hypothesis statements as a result of the assessment process. Hypothesis statements serve a number of purposes including: (a) to summarize assessment results; (b) to offer explanations for the student's problem behavior; and (c) to guide the development of a behavior intervention plan.

There are two common approaches to conducting an FBA in school-based programs. The first relies on "informant methods" which involves talking with the student who presents the impeding behavior and to those people who have direct contact with and knowledge about the student. The second approach is "direct observation" which requires systematic observation of the student within typical daily routines across settings over time. Typically, IEP teams that employ these approaches when conducting an FBA will derive useful information from which to formulate hypotheses.

The first stage of an FBA is to gather broad information about the student's skills, abilities, interests, preferences, general health, and well- being. Such information is essential to designing effective behavior intervention plans. These intervention plans will help the student achieve outcomes that positively influence his or her quality of life, as well as reduce problem behavior. This type of information typically is gathered through review of existing information and evaluation data, IEP team discussions and interviews, use of rating scales, and person-centered planning processes.

In the second stage of an FBA, the IEP team gathers contextual information specifically pinpointing the circumstances/situations regularly associated with the occurrence of problem behavior and the function of the student's problem behavior. Six basic questions asked during this stage are:

1. When is the student most likely to engage in the problem behavior?

2. What specific events or factors appear to be contributing to the student's problem behavior?

3. What function(s) does the problem behavior serve for the student?

4. What might the student be communicating through problem behavior?

5. When is the student most successful, and therefore less likely to engage in the problem behavior?

6. What other factors might be contributing to the student's problem behavior?

One of the primary challenges that school-based teams (e.g., IEP teams) face is translating the critical components of FBA into practice across a variety of school situations. In particular, school-based teams need both a tangible and time-efficient place to start that yields will be useful data upon which to base services and programs.

Acknowledging this reality, the authors in collaboration with the Instructional Support System of Pennsylvania and the Tri-State Consortium on Positive Behavior Support, have developed the second edition of "Screening for an Understanding of Student Problem Behavior: An Initial Line of Inquiry." The Initial Line of Inquiry can serve as a starting place for educational teams to more systematically determine: (a) the function of a given student's problem behavior, and (b) factors associated with occurrence and non-occurrence of the student's impeding behavior. In particular, this tool can help educators formally move beyond intuitive program decision-making to design more comprehensive and effective interventions with students who present persistent problem behavior. The Initial Line of Inquiry relies on informant methodology to initially ascertain both the function of

Appendix continued on p. 182

Appendix continued

a given student's problem behavior and the contributing factors associated with occurrence and non-occurrence of those problem behaviors. It is likely that many educational teams will find that the Initial Line of Inquiry provides sufficient information to design multi-component behavior support plans. However, a comprehensive FBA including direct observations over time as delineated in PDE Guidelines on Effective Behavior Support should be conducted when satisfactory outcomes are not realized by the local team as a result of intervention based on hypotheses generated through the Initial Line of Inquiry. The Initial Line of Inquiry has been demonstrated as useful by teams educating diverse student populations (e.g., students enrolled in general and special education across age levels).

In general, facilitated teams can efficiently work through this screening tool in an hour's time. Within this time frame, the team will systematically link student and teacher behaviors with additional environmental influences on the student's behavior in school settings (e.g., classroom directions and feedback, instructional design, curriculum match). As a result, teams position themselves to more logically link interventions of choice to the particular student's needs and to the specific environmental and lifestyle variables that adversely influence the student's behavior.

The screening tool is formatted for use by a facilitator with student-centered teams. Facilitators can be external consultants or internal resource staff. The left-hand column provides a general script of questions (i.e., Line of Inquiry). The right-hand column outlines general thoughts the facilitator should be cognizant of throughout the facilitation process.

Screening for an Understanding of Student Problem Behavior

An Initial Line of Inquiry

Line of Inquiry	Guiding Thoughts for the Interviewer/Facilitator

Introduction of the Interview Process to the Team

What we are going to do is go through a process that is designed to give you a better understanding of (student's name)'s behavior. The outcome of this process is that you will gain some new insights about his (or her) behavior and you will therefore be in a better position to develop some useful hypotheses about what is influencing his or her behavior. From these hypotheses you can begin to develop strategies that will help you and (student's name) have greater success at school. The process also should identify skill deficits and lifestyle issues to address over the longer term. By the end of the meeting, we should have developed some hypotheses and an initial behavior support plan to achieve some short term reduction in problem behavior. We should also have begun to look at an intermediate time span where we can help the student learn new, socially acceptable alternative skills that he or she needs to learn.

If you are ready to begin, I'll get us started by simply recording what you see as the student's greatest strengths or problem behavior. The next thing we're going to talk about are things that appear to set off the

- The process of the interview will be greatly aided if the interviewer/facilitator uses a flip chart (as opposed to a piece of paper at the table) to record salient information from the team. This helps the team both see and hear emerging patterns of behavior as the student's performance is discussed.

You should set your top page on the flip chart in the following format to parallel the line of inquiry:

Strengths of the Student:				
Slow Triggers (Setting Events)	Fast Triggers (Antecedents)	Problem Behavior	Perceived Function	Actual Consequence

- Wherever possible, the process should include family members, others who know the child well, and the child him/herself (where appropriate) in addition to school staff in the process. Also, where appropriate, other agency staff should be recruited to participate.

- Primary emphasis throughout the process is to facilitate the team to reach consensus on relevant factors

Appendix continued on p. 184

Line of Inquiry	Guiding Thoughts for the Interviewer/Facilitator
student's problem behavior. These are what we call Fast Triggers. Fast Triggers are specific things that are going on as the problem occurs. (Facilitator's Note: We suggest using the metaphor of Fast Triggers when speaking about Antecedent conditions. We encourage you to label that column on the flip chart as such and not as Antecedent. The same holds true for Setting Events being referred to as Slow Triggers.) Next we will talk about Slow Triggers. These are setting events that will adversely influence the student's behavior from a distance in space/time. These are things that directly influence the student's quality of life such as the family situation, lack of opportunity, issues of general health and well-being, and things that tend to reduce the student's coping mechanisms or impede his or her abilities. Next we will talk about what happens to the student when he or she engages in the noted problem behavior. Then we're going to talk about why the student might be acting the way he or she is acting.

Having overviewed the process, what are the student's greatest strengths or what does he or she do that you see as a significant problem? | related to the child's behavior. This is a result of responses/dialogue on focused questions.

• It is important to generally adhere to the line of inquiry as presented as it should help keep the team focused on relevant program issues as opposed to the meeting serving only as an outlet to vent frustration with or at the child. |

Line of Inquiry	Guiding Thoughts for the Interviewer/Facilitator

Identifying Student Strengths:
 	
• Ask: "What does he or she do that is helpful to other students?"
  - "How does he or she show respect?"
  - "What are his or her greatest attributes?"
	• While it is ideal to start by discussing student strengths, it is likely that the team you are facilitating agreed to meet in light of what they feel are problems concerning this particular student's behavior. Therefore, it is prudent to acknowledge the team's current mindset, and to subsequently start by focusing on either strengths or the student's problem behavior based on each team's orientation or predisposition.

Identifying Problem Behaviors:
 	
• Ask: "What does he or she specifically do that is a problem?"
• Ask questions that operationalize the behaviors. For example:
  - "What does he or she do that aggravates other students?"
  - "How does he or she show disrespect?"
  - "What does his or her defiance look like? Sound like?"
	• In instances where a team starts by addressing the student's problem behavior, it is important to help the team identify not only what the problems are, but also what positive attributes of the student can be developed and built upon. (List the positive attributes in the "strengths" section.) Strengths should be documented on an ongoing basis throughout the team process.

Identifying Antecedents and Setting Events: • Ask: "What sets his or her problem behavior off?" • Ask: "What is going on when he or she does these things?" • Ask: "What else is going on when the problem behavior occurs?"	• Try to help the team operationally focus on Fast Triggers at this point in the process. It is not uncommon for the Facilitator to occasionally be assertive and guide the team members back to refocus on Fast Triggers as issues start to emerge through discussion.

Appendix continued on p. 186

Line of Inquiry	Guiding Thoughts for the Interviewer/Facilitator

- Clarifying and re-labeling. For example:
    - Ask questions like: "Does getting started on all assignments create difficulty, or only certain types of assignments?"
    - Follow up by asking questions like: "If written tasks are the primary problem, are they a problem across all subject areas?"
- General Discovery. Specifically:
    - Ask: "Are there problems with transitions?"
    - Ask: "Are there problems with specific kids?"
    - Ask: "Are there problems with specific adults?"
    - Ask: "Are there problems with other general features?"

Interviewer Note: Problem behaviors are added as they are identified throughout the interview process.

- During the interview, we recommend separating Antecedents and Setting Events on the chart paper. Setting Event issues tend to emerge naturally throughout the interview. The facilitator should listen for evidence of life stressors, general health issues, coping skills, (or lack thereof) etc. These should be recorded on the chart as Slow Triggers. In the event that these issues do not emerge, the interviewer/facilitator should make specific inquiries into these areas. Also, some teams may be predisposed to focusing exclusively on Slow Triggers as these tend to be the most removed from the immediacy of influence by teachers (e.g. outside of school factors). While it is important to document such factors, it is essential to also document Fast Triggers as these typically are most within the sphere of immediate influence of teachers (e.g., curriculum and instructional design).

Predictably, you have many examples of what will likely be described as different kinds of work refusal or defiance. While it was useful in the previous step (Problem Identification) to operationalize problem behavior, it is more useful at this stage to use generalities at this stage in this section. Thus, in the above example, we recommend

Line of Inquiry	Guiding Thoughts for the Interviewer/Facilitator
	that you initially summarize the work refusal and defiance as simply "whenever a demand or a request is made." Similarly, problems in halls, cafeteria and recess initially can be summarized broadly as "transitions". This can have the effect of simplifying the issue for the team at this point, though it should be used judiciously.

Identifying Consequences of Problem Behaviors:
 	
 • Ask: "What do you do when the problem behavior occurs?"
 • Ask: "What happens immediately after the problem behavior occurs?"
 • Ask questions that will elicit both imposed (structural) consequences (e.g., loss of points) as well as more naturally occurring environmental (functional) consequences (e.g., reactions of other children). For example, ask:
   - "What do you do immediately when he or she engages in the problem behavior?"
   - "What do the other students do immediately when he or she engages in the problem behavior?"
   - "What happens to the task or assignment at hand when he or she engages in the problem behavior ?"
	• It is important to help the team understand the difference between imposed or structural consequences and natural or functional consequences. In a simple sense, this focuses the team on the differences between the intent of interventions tried thus far and what actually happens as a result of those interventions being used.
	
	 • At this stage of the process some participants will offer strategies to address the problem such as "Praise him for doing his work." This response should be redirected to something like, "But tell me what you actually do after he engages in the problem behavior?"

Appendix continued on p. 188

Appendix continued

Line of Inquiry	Guiding Thoughts for the Interviewer/Facilitator

Identify Perceived Function:
 	
• Ask: "What do you think he or she gets by behaving this way? What actually happens?"
• Ask: "What might he or she get out of or avoid?"
• Ask: "What else does he or she get or access?"
• General Discovery. Specifically:
  - Ask: "Does his or her behavior result in a power struggle?"
  - Ask: "Does his or her behavior help him clarify the parental (family) system?"
 	
Facilitator Note: Most teams will identify one, some, or all of the following perceived functions:
  - Gain access or connection with others
  - Get access to preferences
  - Obtain a sense of power and control
  - Clarify the rules
  - Clarify parental roles
  - Avoid unpleasant circumstances (work, person, place, activity, etc.)
  - Reduce anxiety or release tension
  - Escape feeling of inadequacy
  - Sensory feedback (feels good)
	• Keep in mind that it is not uncommon for a child's particular behavior to serve more than one purpose/function across different settings. Therefore, be sure the team focuses on all relevant settings and clearly seeks to understand the relationship between the child's behavior and its function across settings. While using the time efficiently, (most teams have scheduled time frames within which to meet), try to elicit as much detail from team members as possible concerning the function of the student's problem behavior across various settings.
	
	• If you find that the team thus far has exclusively focused on the student's problem behavior and remains resistant to identifying strengths (i.e., giving no recognition of anything positive that the student does), there are a number of strategies you can use to broaden the team's focus. For instance, it may be helpful to clarify that while the team is trying to find the function for problem behavior, it also is important to acknowledge that there are probably instances of appropriate behavior. It may be useful to ask for a story of what happens when the student engages in appropriate behavior. It is recom-

| Line
of Inquiry | Guiding Thoughts for the
Interviewer/Facilitator |
|---|---|
| | mended that you put that sequence on the chart under the categories of Behavior, Antecedents, Perceived Functions and Actual Consequences. It can be quite powerful for the team to see that the student gets the perceived functions (needs) met by what is perceived as appropriate behavior as well. This can be brought back up when developing strategies and when using the Competing Path Analysis. |
| | • The goal here is to have the team understand that most, if not all, problem behaviors are a response to any given set of antecedent and setting event conditions. Specifically, the presence of the noted antecedent conditions will increase the likelihood of the student using the noted problem behavior. It is unusual at this stage of the assessment process that a specific antecedent will be directly paired with only one specific problem behavior. Rather, the noted antecedents will likely be associated with groups/clusters of problem behaviors. This concept seems to make a great deal of sense to teams. |
| • Summarize Perceived Functions segment. Examples:
- "These are the things he or she is trying to get or avoid" (Verbally list them for added impact). | • When summarizing team members' statements, try to use their language to the greatest extent possible. Be sure to explain your translation of |

Appendix continued on p. 190

Appendix continued

Line of Inquiry	Guiding Thoughts for the Interviewer/Facilitator
- "Most, if not all of these are things that all children need!" (Get agreement from team). - "Most kids get these types of needs met through socially acceptable means." - "The problem is that he or she is getting (perceived function) by doing (problem behavior) at an unacceptable frequency, intensity, duration, or at inappropriate times instead of using more acceptable ways to obtain the same result."	their terms into other words where necessary. This serves many purposes, not least of which is engagement and "buy-in" with the process by team members. • Despite the fact that the Initial Line of Inquiry will serve as an entry point for most teams, it is recommended that the team develop specific hypothesis statements be developed by the team and that the influence of the identified quality of life factors be discussed (i.e., Setting Events).

Specific Hypothesis Formation:
 	
 • Ask/summarize as follows: "Any of these antecedents (verbally list them again for impact/review) appear to set off any of these problem behaviors. Do you agree?"
 • Ask/summarize as follows:
   - "When this occurs "(write a description of the fast and slow triggers associated with the student's problem behavior)
   - "The student does" (write a description of the problem behavior)
   - "In order to "(write a description of possible function)
	• The facilitator/consultant leads the team to the specific hypothesis by selecting any Antecedent and Setting Event and pairing it with any problem behavior, and then inviting the team to supply the function (in order to…). This serves the dual purpose of teaching the structure of writing specific hypothesis statements in the A-B-C format and identifying any idiosyncratic antecedent/problem behavior relationships they will be more than likely identified here. At this point, teams are generally opening up their perspective to new relationships and possibilities and are energized for brainstorming solutions.

Line of Inquiry	Guiding Thoughts for the Interviewer/Facilitator
Examples : When Karen is not engaged with others or activities for 15 minutes or longer (especially during lunch or free time), or when she did not get to sleep before 11 p.m. the previous evening or does not feel well, she screams, slaps her face, and pulls her hair to gain access to teacher attention. When David is presented with academic work in large or small group settings requiring writing, multiple worksheets, or work that he perceives to be too difficult he will mumble derogatory comments about the teacher, refuse to complete his work, destroy his assignment sheet, and/or push/kick his desk or chair over in order to escape academic failure in front of his peers. • Repeat this process until all viable specific hypotheses emerge and are documented. Then verify, weed out redundancies, and cluster with team input as appropriate.	• The facilitator should be analyzing Antecedent Events (Fast Triggers) in order to cluster into categories such as "interactions with others," "school work," or "transitions." Typically, Antecedent Events can be clustered into several groups that are powerful predictors of problem behavior. Likewise, the relevant functions identified by the team during the team meeting can be consolidated. Typically, a team will reduce their initial list to 2 or 3 possibilities. This activity serves to sharpen the team's focus on the specific hypothesis statements. • In generating specific hypotheses it may be helpful to formally introduce the team to the Competing Path Analysis (O'Neill, Horner, Albin, Sprague, Storey, & Newton,1997). If the circumstances at this particular juncture do not lend themselves to a formal introduction you will want to follow up with (at

Appendix continued on p. 192

Appendix continued

Line of Inquiry	Guiding Thoughts for the Interviewer/Facilitator
	a minimum) key team members following the meeting. In either case, you should incorporate your understanding of the Competing Path Analysis into your facilitation of the team.
Global Hypothesis Formation • Ask the team to summarize the bigger information picture that has emerged. In other words, what are the larger contributing factors (i.e., Slow Triggers) that appear to adversely influence (student's name) performance. Specifically, what is the state of the student's: (a) communication skills and systems; (b) relationships with others; (c) opportunities for choice and control; and (d) general health and well being? Examples: **Karen** Karen enjoys interacting with others and keeping busy with activities. She seems happiest when she is interacting one-to-one with an adult (e.g., teacher) or participating in adult-led activities. She will occasionally sit alone for 15 minutes when listening to music of her choice, although she seems to grow bored in such situations. Karen currently has limited means of for-	Identify the "desired behavior" and an "alternative behavior"  • While specific hypotheses are essential to build effective behavior intervention plans, they alone cannot provide a comprehensive understanding of the student nor the complexity of conditions that might negatively influence behavior. Therefore, the IEP team should next develop a global hypothesis statement. A global hypothesis attends to broad influences in the student's life in and outside of school such as the student's skills, health, preferences, daily routines, relationships, and general quality of life. This type of statement provides a description of the IEP team's understanding about the student and his or her quality of life as it relates to the student's problem be-

Line of Inquiry	Guiding Thoughts for the Interviewer/Facilitator
mal communication. While she enjoys interacting with others, she has never been observed to independently initiate appropriate interactions with her teacher or other students. Her independent initiation skills are very limited. Karen has limited access to non-disabled peers during her day at school (e.g., afternoon recess) and has a history of colds and viral infections which, in turn, adversely affect her sleep patterns. Karen's self-injury appears to signal her desire for social interaction, something to do, teacher assistance, or comfort when she is tired and/or not feeling well. Given her current situation, Karen's self-injury appears to be her most viable means to communicate these basic needs.	havior. This type of information positively influences both short and long term prevention strategies developed by the IEP team.
	• The intent here is to facilitate the team to see the "big picture" for the student. Specifically, the goal is for the team to create brief summary statements (usually 1–2 paragraphs) about the relationship between and among the Slow and Fast Triggers and the student's problem behavior.
	• Be sure to use the flip chart with team notes to re-focus the team on an ongoing basis. This should also serve to reinforce the team for their work throughout the process.

David

David is a third grader who receives itinerant emotional support within the regular third grade classroom. He has developed appropriate independent school work habits and is able to keep up with the general curriculum with accommodations. David has established some minimal relationships (acquaintances) with a few classmates at school. His interactions however, typically are limited to peripheral activities such

Appendix continued on p. 194

Appendix continued

Line of Inquiry	Guiding Thoughts for the Interviewer/Facilitator
as brief conversations during group events. For example, David never has been observed to lead a group of peers or to be at the center of a group's related activities. It has been noted that David plays with a few of the other kids from the neighborhood outside school in a similar manner. (None of these kids is in the same third grade classroom as David). David's mumbling of derogatory comments, work refusal, destruction of materials, and or pushing/kicking his desk or chair appear to signal a lack of comfort when placed in group situations where he is expected to achieve outcomes in the presence of his peers. *Developing Interventions:* • Ask the team to: "look at the list of both imposed and actual consequences and decide if the child is meeting his or her needs (function) by engaging in use of the problem behavior (e.g., student is trying to avoid doing a difficult task and the consequence for misbehavior is termination of the task at hand in order to be sent to the office). The first step in planning interventions is to identify different ways for the student to meet his or her needs that are socially acceptable to achieve the same function (i.e., replacement behavior)."	• Where warranted, the team can develop a more complete understanding of antecedent events by doing an instructional assessment and analyzing the Instructional, Curricular and Environmental Variables which affect the student's performance. Manipulation of these variables can provide the basis for powerful preventative interventions. • When formulating interventions be sure to consistently link (through restatements) the relationship between the team's hypotheses and their interventions of choice. Be sure to initially place greatest emphasis on: (a) antecedent/setting event strategies to engineer environments to minimize the likelihood to the greatest extent possible of the student's need to use the problem behavior, and (b) the teaching and subsequent learning of new alternative skills. At this point in the process it is worthwhile to explain that redirection of problem behavior will become a secondary effect once the child learns/uses the socially acceptable alternative skills on a consistent basis. Also, be sure to emphasize the importance of the team reinforcing/honoring the child's use of alternative skills (particularly functional equivalents to the problem behavior) so that the problem behavior becomes ineffective, inefficient, and irrelevant.

Line of Inquiry	Guiding Thoughts for the Interviewer/Facilitator
• Describe how: "(a) we as a team can influence, and in some instances, change antecedent and setting event conditions, (b) that the team can teach new skills to the student in order to help him or her (1) learn a replacement behavior, (2) improve general skills, and (3) improve self control, and (c) that consequence strategies need to stress reinforcement strategies to increase use of alternative behaviors as well as reflect re-direction and de-escalation procedures."	

• In light of the specific and global hypotheses, facilitate the team in structured brainstorming and selection of interventions across each of the following areas by asking the noted questions.
 	
Antecedent/Setting Event Strategies :
   "What can we do to positively change or alter the situations or environmental factors which appear to trigger (student's name) use of (problem behavior)?"
 	
Alternative Skills Instruction:
   "What can we teach (student's name) to use as a replacement behavior that is socially acceptable AND will serve the same function?"
	• The intent is for the team to develop a multi-component support plan for the student. An effective behavior support plan is hypotheses driven and consists of: (a) Antecedent and Setting Event strategies; (b) teaching socially acceptable alternative skills; (c) interventions for both types of consequences; and (d) long-term prevention. In addition, Facilitators will need to help team members to identify and document relevant supports that they need in order to implement the support plan.
	
	• It is recommended that Facilitators first overview in total the multi-component aspect of effective behavior support plans at this point

Appendix continued on p. 196

Appendix continued

Line of Inquiry	Guiding Thoughts for the Interviewer/Facilitator
"What general skills can we emphasize through instruction that will positively influence success with (student's name)?" "What coping, stress reduction, or self management skills do we need to teach (student's name)?" *Instructional Consequence Strategies :* "In light of the alternative skills we will teach, how will we reinforce the acquisition and use of those alternative skills?" *Reduction Oriented Consequence Strategies* "In light of the hypotheses, what would be possible re-direction and de-escalation procedures to use when (student's name) engages in the problem behavior?" *Long Term Prevention* "What long-term support structures or outcomes will likely help (student's name) maintain and generalize newly learned alternative skills?" "Also, how do we help (student's name) maintain and generalize use of these approaches over time and across settings?" *Support for Team Members* "What additional help, training, materials, etc. do staff and family need in order to implement the support plan?"	in the process. This should be followed by taking each strategy area as listed in turn and processing the team as follows: 1. brainstorm possible support strategies; 2. discuss the brainstormed ideas in light of reality, constraints, and other relevant contextual factors; 3. select and document the one, two, or three best fit strategies in the area; 4. identify and document the necessary supports for team members associated with the selected strategies; and 5. review the team's decision and move on to the next component part until all components have been addressed. • Finally, it is recommended that the process of intervention design follow the sequence as noted above (e.g., starting with Antecedent and Setting Event strategies and culminating with the identification of supports team members need).

This screening tool provides specific examples of initial guiding questions for consultants/facilitators to use with local teams in an effort to more systematically decode student problem behavior. It is important that the Line of Inquiry, while useful as an initial screening tool, not be mistaken as a comprehensive functional behavioral assessment for all students who present serious problem behavior. The Initial Line of Inquiry is based exclusively on informant methodology and therefore does not incorporate direct observational procedures. Most teams across student populations will more than likely find that responses to these questions will sufficiently help the team to gain new insights into potentially useful interventions in a time-efficient manner. It is recommended, however, that the team perform a comprehensive functional behavioral assessment when any of these criteria are present after an intervention based on hypotheses generated through the Initial Line of Inquiry has been initiated:

- The child's challenging behavior persists despite consistently implemented support plans that have been based on less comprehensive and less formal methods of assessment.

- The child's behavior places the child or others at risk of (a) harm or injury, and/or (b) exclusion and devaluation.

- The local team is considering more intrusive and restrictive procedures, and/ or a more restrictive placement for the child.

CHAPTER 6

Manifestation Determinations:
Discipline Guidelines for Children with Disabilities

Robert J. Kubick, Jr.
E. M. Bard
Akron Public Schools
Akron, Ohio

Joseph D. Perry
Barry University

BACKGROUND/PURPOSE OF MANIFESTATION DETERMINATIONS

The discipline provisions of the 1997 Amendments to the Individuals with Disabilities Education Act (IDEA 97) (Individuals with Disabilities Education Act Amendments, 1997) have caused controversy and confusion (National Association of State Directors of Special Education, 1998; Zirkel, 1999). Two areas of education that present great challenges for school officials are special education and discipline, and the combination of these two areas in IDEA 97 has often resulted in confusion about best practice. At the very least, a lack of understanding as to what constitutes appropriate policies and procedures with regard to disciplining students with disabilities has challenged school officials at all levels. This is particularly true in light of evolving legal mandates at federal, state, and local levels.

Perhaps no issue creates more confusion regarding appropriate procedure than the manifestation determination mandate. Because of the recency of this new legal mandate, there is relatively little literature about what constitutes best practice in implementing manifestation determination procedures. Although some reviews of the mandate and its implications for school officials have been published (Katsiyannis & Maag, 1998; Osborne, 1998; Telzrow, 1999; Yell & Shriner, 1997;

Zurkowski, Kelly, & Griswold, 1998), more information is needed regarding various best practice procedures for making the manifestation determination a positive and constructive procedure for students and their families.

The purpose of this chapter is to (a) provide a review of the manifestation determination mandate, (b) discuss implications of the mandate for practice, (c) provide best practice guidelines for school-based teams in manifestation determinations, (d) discuss professional development implications, and (e) forecast future trends in this area. In addition, the need for expanded conceptual approaches and empirically based knowledge on this topic is also reviewed.

Conceptual and Empirical Foundations

Heumann (1997) cited four basic themes in disciplining students with disabilities: (a) all children, including children with disabilities, deserve safe, well-disciplined schools and orderly learning environments; (b) teachers and school administrators should have the tools they need to assist them in preventing misconduct and discipline problems and to address these problems, if they arise; (c) there must be a balanced approach to the issue of discipline of children with disabilities that reflects the need for orderly and safe schools and the need to protect the rights of students with disabilities to a free appropriate public education (FAPE); and (d) appropriately developed individualized education programs with well-developed behavior intervention strategies to decrease school discipline problems. It is these themes that should guide educators in the discipline process. Disciplining students with disabilities should be an educational, rather than a punitive, process. The manifestation determination mandate was designed to reduce the tendency of schools to use frequent and punitive removals a primary means of disciplining students with disabilities.

One the most commonly used punitive methods of discipline is suspension, the removal of the student from his/her educational environment. Suspension is an aversive practice designed to reduce misbehavior that involves removing a student from reinforcing stimuli for a certain time (Algozzine, 1985). What is often not considered is that suspension is only effective if the environment *from* which the student is removed is more interesting and reinforcing than the environment *to* which the student is removed (Rutherford, 1978). Suspension may be counterproductive when it provides students with an escape from an environment that they perceive as difficult or unpleasant (Polsgrove, 1991). A recent study demonstrated that suspension resulted in low interest in schoolwork and difficulty with rule compliance (Costenbader & Markson, 1998). Respondents in the study indicated that suspension was not a deterrent to future misbehavior, nor was it a solution to underlying problems that manifested themselves in misbehavior.

Other studies have criticized out-of-school suspensions on the grounds that they (a) displace school problems to the larger community; (b) exacerbate the original problem, (c) reinforce truancy and inappropriate behavior, (d) interfere with educational progress, and (e) fail to address the underlying problem(s) that caused the misbehavior (e.g. Hundley, 1994; Radin, 1988). In-school suspensions have also not been supported as an alternative. Stage (1997), for example, found there were no apparent effects of in-school suspension on classroom disruptive behavior. In fact, the rate of student misbehavior remained rather constant across the four in-school suspension interventions studied. In-school alternatives can be a valuable step toward better meeting students' needs, but they must not be allowed to deter or replace more fundamental education efforts, which will prevent the kinds of behavior to which in-school alternatives are a response (Mizell, 1978). A review of some of these individualized alternatives to suspensions found the students in these alternative programs to have a diverse array of academic and social needs (Morgan-D'Atrio, Northup, LaFleur, & Spera, 1996). Such needs are not addressed when a student is excluded from his or her education environment (e.g., suspension).

The manifestation determination is a legal mandate that seeks to prevent the negative effects of suspensions and other removals from school by prohibiting arbitrary removals. It was case law that led to the emergence of the "manifestation of the disability doctrine" (Osborne, 1998). This doctrine stated that a student with disabilities could not be expelled for misbehavior that was a manifestation of the student's disability, but could be expelled if there was no relationship between the misconduct and disability. The manifestation determination is an individualized review process, based on an individual student analysis. It is intended to investigate causal relationships between a "critical behavior event" and the nature of a student's disability. The manifestation review meeting assesses whether the behavior for which the student is being disciplined is directly and causally related to the student's disability, or due to an inappropriate Individualized Education Programs (IEP) or placement. Although the manifestation review process can be demanding and overwhelming for school officials, a number of practices that can make the process manageable and constructive for all involved parties are described in this chapter. In particular, it is agreed that if a foundation for later comparison of behavior is established initially within the multidisciplinary team process and a preventative orientation is maintained, the determination is often avoided or, at the very least, made much easier.

Legal Mandates

Special education in the United States has been chiefly governed by a few key pieces of federal legislation. The major legal mandates were the Education for All Handicapped Children Act (EHA, U.S. Congress, 1975), the Individuals With Disabilities Education Act (IDEA, U.S. Congress, 1990), and the Individuals with Disabilities Education Act Amendments (IDEA 97; Individuals with Disabilities Education Act Amendments, 1997). These laws were designed to prevent students with disabilities from being arbitrarily denied their right to receive FAPE in the least restrictive environment (LRE). IDEA 97, in particular, was designed to (a) increase communication between the school and the home, (b) provide safe and secure learning environments, and (c) ensure that all students were educated in a manner consistent with their IEPs. At present, methods of implementing the federal regulations at state and local levels continue to evolve. Consequently, many local school officials have limited insight as to how these federal guidelines will be followed in their respective school districts.

There is nothing specifically stated in IDEA 97 that disallows schools from appropriately disciplining students with disabilities. With few exceptions, such students are generally subject to the same types of disciplinary procedures as their typical peers. However, the 1988 Supreme Court case of *Honig v. Doe* (484 U.S., 98 L.Ed.2d 686, 108 S.Ct. 592) established that exclusion from school for more than 10 consecutive days amounted to a change in placement that could not be permitted, even for dangerous behavior. This landmark ruling was intended to "strip schools of the unilateral authority they had enjoyed to exclude disabled students, particularly emotionally disturbed students, from school" (484 U.S. 323, 108 S.Ct. at 604). Osborne (1988) stated that, "although the due process requirements established for handicapped students are more stringent than those provided to non-handicapped students, this is necessary in order to prevent a recurrence of past wrongs against this population" (p. 1111). As a result, before a school can contemplate disciplinary decisions that may result in a change in placement, a number of procedural safeguards must be followed.

In general, manifestation determinations should be conducted at any time when removal of a student with a disability from an educational program beyond the tenth day is being considered. Emergency options that involve the removal of a child from the educational setting might be interpreted as a change in placement. Factors that may influence the decision about whether a given removal option is considered a change in placement (and probably inconsistent with a student's IEP) could include (but are not limited to) the length of the suspension, the total amount of time the student is removed from the school setting, and the proximity of the suspensions to each other. For these reasons, it may be necessary to either implement alternatives to these removals or develop a new IEP that allows for these changes in placement. Because many parents may understandably be reluctant to consent to a new IEP that allows their child to be removed from a school-based placement, school officials should have a range of alternative disciplinary measures prepared for students in advance. Although there may be considerable financial and human resources needed to provide these alternative settings, developing such alternatives is often far less expensive than the costs of litigation (Osborne, 1998).

To comply with the *Honig* safeguards, schools are obligated to take specific steps to ensure that the rights of students with disabilities are protected. Unfortunately, these steps have led some educators to believe that students with disabilities are either "above the law" or are subject to a different set of expectations and standards for behavior, a so-called "dual discipline system" (Council of Administrators of Special Education, 1996). Rather than seeking the creation of two systems of discipline in the schools, legislators have, instead, sought to ensure that the individual concerns and diverse needs of students with disabilities are fully considered before they are simply excluded from the educational setting. Schools must demonstrate that they have made reasonable efforts to meet the unique needs of students with disabilities before removing them from the learning environment. The challenge for the educational institution is to balance the rights of students with disabilities with the responsibility for maintaining a safe environment that is conducive to student learning. Zurkowski et al. (1998) have indicated that because IDEA 97 is new education law, its final meaning will be revealed only through implementation in the schools and interpretation by the courts. They state, "Legislators write the law, but it is the courts that interpret it. Until the courts have construed the provisions of IDEA 1997, school districts should approach matters of discipline involving students with disabilities with a conservative eye and with 'best practices' in mind" (p. 9).

ISSUES AND CONSIDERATIONS IN CONDUCTING MANIFESTATION DETERMINATIONS

Before holding an actual manifestation hearing or disciplining a student, school personnel should consider a number of factors that may influence team conclusions. Such factors include (a) the range of alternative programs available to the school district to intervene with behavioral concerns, (b) what steps must be taken for general education students suspected of having a disability, (c) what options are available when a student has already been suspended for 10 school days (or is nearing that limit), (d) what exceptions exist for the "10-day limit," and (e) the right of all students with disabilities to a FAPE.

Use of Alternative Programming to Remedy Behavioral Concerns

The use of long-term suspension or expulsion as well as similar removals should be viewed as "last resort" procedures. Instead, more positive interventions for school officials to address misbehavior should be emphasized (Mizell, 1978). These interventions include appropriate instructional strategies, conflict management/behavior management plans (using empirically validated behavioral methods such as reinforcement and extinction), related special education services, student and teacher training, level systems, contingency contracting, and alternative programs (Wright & Gurman, 1998). Many of these positive alternative options, used either in isolation or in some combination, might be effective in promoting successful student deportment (see Telzrow and Naidu, this volume). In addition, these interventions might also save schools from the financial and human resources that are often necessary to conduct manifestation determinations. More importantly, these options are more responsive to addressing the needs of students with disabilities. It should be noted that any implementation of these options must be consistent with the student's current IEP. Any change in placement or use of an option that conflicts with a student's IEP necessitates a meeting to develop a new IEP.

Developing prompt and appropriate behavior assessments and interventions can significantly reduce the amount of time a student is removed from the school setting. Indeed, if the school can determine the cause of a given incident of misbehavior and develop an appropriate plan for intervention, the student could be returned to the school setting as soon as it is feasible. In situations involving drugs and/or weapons, if the student's parents request a due process hearing, the student remains in an interim placement (as opposed to their current placement) until the proceedings are resolved or an agreement about placement is made. However, the length of time that a student is placed in an interim placement is not to exceed 45 days. In addition, if it is determined that the student is not disabled under IDEA 97, then he or she may be subjected to disciplinary procedures of nondisabled students.

Eligibility of Students With Suspected Disabilities

It is imperative that school officials be aware that many of the IDEA 97 protections for students with disabilities also apply to those students who are *suspected* of having a disability. Prior to 1997, IDEA legislation maintained that students were considered "suspected handicapped" when the school "had knowledge" that the student might have a disability. One of the ways that the school could be deemed to have knowledge included only some form of expressed concerns from one school employee to another. IDEA 97 sought to depart from these prior bases of knowledge that could be derived from simple and informal conversations between school personnel.

At the time of this writing, for legal protections to be provided to a student suspected of a disabling condition, the school must have been placed "on notice." The IDEA 97 regulations stated that the school is placed on notice if the teacher of the child, or other personnel of the local educational agency, has expressed concern about the behavior or the performance of the child to the director of special education of the agency or to other personnel in accordance with the agency's child find or special education referral system. Once a school has been provided with this notice, the student who is suspected of having a disability under IDEA 97 is entitled to many of the procedural safeguards that protect students already identified as having a disability. According to the reauthorization, a student suspected of having a disability could be subject to a removal from their current educational program, but would require an expedited evaluation to determine eligibility. The determination of disability (i.e., a multifactored evaluation) may conclude that the student does not have a disability under IDEA 97 and may therefore be disciplined like his or her peers who do not have a disability. In the event that the student is determined to have a disability under IDEA 97, the student has all of the rights provided for students with disabilities under the law.

Options for Suspensions: The "10-Day-Limit"

Students with disabilities may be subject to school suspensions for no more than 10 consecutive (or cumulative, if it could be interpreted as a change in placement) days (Hartwig, 1999). For such suspensions, there is no burden on school districts to ascertain whether the child's behavior problems were a manifestation of his or her disability. However, school officials should conduct a functional behavior assessment (see Tilly, Knoster, and Ikeda, this volume) once student behavior rises to the level where significant removal is being considered, because a pattern of excluding a student with a disability (e.g., a series of suspensions) could be interpreted as a change in placement.

If it appears that a student with a disability has a history of removals that could be interpreted as a change in placement, then he or she should receive a functional behavior assessment and a manifestation determination by the school *before* additional removals are made. If schools are considering suspension beyond 10 days or prolonged removal (e.g., expulsion), then the change in placement becomes a pivotal issue, and a manifestation determination is mandated. The manifestation determination must be made immediately, if possible, but must occur no later than 10 days after the decision to take disciplinary action is made.

Costenbader and Buntaine (1999) suggested that prolonged absences from school might have significant negative consequences on students with disabilities. Research has illustrated that students who are suspended show delays in academic skills, disturbances in social/emotional adjustment, higher rates of delinquency, and distrust and rejection experiences in the larger community (Mendez & Sanders, 1981). Other studies correlate suspension with drug use (Swadi, 1992), poor academic achievement (Yelsma, Yelsma, & Hovestadt, 1991), grade retention (Safer, 1986), and higher rates of school dropout (Johnston, 1989). There is further evidence that, without effective behavioral support, students who demonstrate behavioral problems are often prone to medical risks, exposed to highly intrusive forms of control and treatment, and isolated in their education, community, vocation, and socialization (National Institutes of Health, 1989).

Exceptions to the "10-Day-Rule"

A school district has the right to seek an order from a hearing officer to remove a student with a disability from school if the school can show (by substantial evidence) that *all* of the following are true: (a) a student's continuation in the current school program is substantially likely to cause injury to the student or others, (b) the appropriateness of the current placement has been considered by the hearing officer, (c) the school has made reasonable efforts to minimize the risk of harm in the student's current placement (including the use of supplementary aids and services), and (d) the student is allowed to participate in the general curriculum in a manner consistent with his or her IEP and with the appropriate services and modifications used to address behavioral concerns.

Under IDEA 97 school officials are permitted to make immediate and unilateral changes of placement of up to 45 calendar days for those students who either carry a weapon to school or to a school function or knowingly possess or use illegal drugs or sell or solicit the sale of a controlled substance while at school or at a school function. This act also applies to students with disabilities. However, for these students the provisions of the Gun Free Schools Act must be implemented in a manner consistent with the student's IEP. For example, a student who takes a firearm to school may only be expelled if it is determined by a group of individuals who are knowledgeable about that student that the student's bringing the firearm to school was not related to a disability.

Free and Appropriate Public Education, Regardless of Determination

In all cases, regardless of whether behavior was found to be a manifestation of a disability, the district must ensure that a FAPE is made available to all eligible students with disabilities consistent with the mandated age guidelines. Consequently, to be consistent with FAPE requirements, educational services must be provided for those students removed for more than 10 days from the school setting, even in the case of those whose misconduct was not related to their disability. Educational services must be consistent with the other provisions outlined under IDEA 97, as well as responsive to the individual needs of the student. Dwyer (1997) stated that "it is in no one's interest to terminate FAPE to a child with a disability who is need of special education and related services" (p. 8).

BEST PRACTICES IN CONDUCTING MANIFESTATION DETERMINATIONS

Developing a Preventative Orientation

Perhaps one of the best practices in relation to the manifestation determination is to eliminate the need for conducting them by being proactive in dealing with behavioral concerns of students with disabilities. School officials should begin addressing any misconduct by students with disabilities before the development of serious behavioral patterns. Behavioral interventions should be implemented even in situations where behaviors are perceived as isolated and/or unrelated to a student's disability. These interventions could be accomplished, in part, by identifying behavioral concerns when initial multifactored and triennial re-evaluations are conducted and developing programs in the IEP that respond to these concerns (Hartwig & Ruesch, 1995). Facilitating new IEP meetings and developing positive behavior plans in which ongoing feedback and evaluation are emphasized would be an important means of addressing misconduct before manifestation determinations are considered. Student discipline follows a maxim common to many areas of education: prevention is often the best intervention.

A preventative orientation has obvious positive benefits. Chief among these is that, as opposed to working in a reactionary manner to concerns that have gone unabated, preventing problems from occurring is more congruent with serving the welfare of the child. Another important benefit is that should preventative efforts not realize their full effectiveness and a manifestation determination becomes necessary, there will be baseline data concerning the nature of the interventions and accommodations used as well as the effectiveness of each of these. In addition, involved professionals and parents could establish a "reference system" in advance of any potential manifestation determination (Hartwig & Ruesch, 1995).

The reference system refers to the ongoing collection of relevant baseline data related to the nature of the student's individual behavioral needs (Hartwig & Ruesch, 1995). This would include data regarding the behavioral needs as indicated in the initial multifactored evaluation, subsequent reevaluations, teacher assessments, parent reports, classroom/school observations, student interviews, and other assessment data. It is critical that these assessment procedures focus on frequency, intensity, and duration of the behavior(s) in question. When the reference system assesses specific and objective measures of behavior, it is relatively simple to detect behavioral trends. By consistently using the same benchmarks of a student's progress with each evaluation, the same methods of measurement will allow educators to make comparisons over time. It is thus prudent for local school districts to develop specific guidelines reflecting consistent measures used to address behavioral status during the multifactored evaluation process.

General Considerations for Conducting Manifestation Determination

The manifestation determination minimally involves the following: (a) a comprehensive review of the student's current educational program, (b) consideration of whether a change in placement would be appropriate for addressing the misbehavior, and (c) a determination of the existence of a relation between the critical behavior event and the student's disabling condition (Hartwig & Reusch, 1995). Failure to follow these procedures could provide an outcome that is tantamount to finding that the critical behavioral event was a manifestation of the disability (and consequently prohibiting further removals). Because any burden of proving that there was no manifestation between a critical behavior event and a disability is squarely on the school personnel, they are likewise responsible for ensuring that all relevant guidelines in the process are followed. Therefore, procedural compliance is essential, including immediate notification to the parents of their rights and providing written prior notice of the decision to change the placement.

The manifestation determination meeting should follow the format of a standard IEP meeting. The meeting must be conducted by the members of the IEP team, which include the student's parents if the student is a minor. If the parents do not participate, then there must be documentation of attempts to secure their involvement. The team should be composed of individuals who are qualified to interpret assessment data and use that data appropriately in the decision-making process (e.g. school psychologists, counselors, agency representatives, related service providers). Also present at this meeting should be the student's special education teacher and a general education teacher. The chairperson of the IEP team is responsible for structuring the meeting, working through the required procedural steps, and committing appropriate educational resources.

It is not appropriate to make decisions based on the student's classification or categorical label. For example, determining manifestation solely on the basis of a student having been identified as having an emotional or behavioral disorder is improper. Such a label has no bearing on whether a given behavior is related to a given disability. The decision is made on a case-by-case basis by considering the individual needs of the student and whether his or her educational program was appropriate to meet those needs.

Guidelines for Conducting Manifestation Determinations

No established, or even suggested, standards exist in the IDEA reauthorization that could guide school officials in the manifestation determination process (Hartwig & Reusch, 1995). Guidelines are presented here that address the legal mandates of IDEA 97 as well as best practice. Hartwig and Reusch (1995) identify two central questions that must be answered in the manifestation determination process: (a) Was the IEP appropriate for meeting the student's needs? (b) Was the critical behavior event a manifestation of the student's disability? Examples of manifestation determination forms that serve to both guide the team in making the determination and document the team's conclusions can be found in Figures 1, 2, and 3 on pages 209-217.

The first step involves identifying the specific critical behavioral event that initiated the referral for a manifestation determination (Hartwig & Reusch, 1995). This behavior should be stated in specific terms that are both observable and measurable. If the team is unable to establish a specific critical behavior event for review, then the review should be terminated and the IEP should be revised in order to address any global behavioral concerns.

FIGURE 1: **Manifestation Determination Form–Example 1**

> **Determination of the Relationship
> of the Behavior of Concern to the Student's Disability**

A. Was the IEP appropriate and carried out as specified? _____ Yes _____ No

Reasons/evidence for determination:

B. Was the student provided special education services _____ Yes _____ No
    that were consistent with his or her IEP and placement?

Reasons/evidence for determination:

C. Was the student provided supplementary aids that _____ Yes _____ No
    were consistent with his or her IEP and placement?

Reasons/evidence for determination:

Figure 1 continued on p. 210

Figure 1 continued

D. Was the student provided behavior intervention   _____ Yes _____ No
    strategies that were consistent with his or her
    IEP and placement?

    Reasons/evidence for determination:

E. Is the current placement appropriate?   _____ Yes _____ No

    Reasons/evidence for determination:

If "YES" on ALL of A-E above, then the IEP was appropriate to the student's disability and behavioral needs. Proceed to F and G.

If "NO" on ANY of A-E above, then the IEP needs to be revised to address the student's behavior. Modify and implement the IEP. Discontinue to manifestation review.

1. State the team's remedy of any deficiency found in student's IEP, LRE, design
    or implementation of special education interventions.

2. Date of return to LRE:_____

> ## Determining if the Student's Disability Manifested Itself in the Behavior Subject to Disciplinary Action

F. Because of his or her disability, was the student's _____ Yes _____ No
ability to understand the impact and consequences
of the behavior subject to disciplinary action impaired?
(*If "YES," student's behavior is subject to IDEA 97 disciplinary procedures*)

Reasons/evidence for determination:

G. Because of his/her disability, was the student's ability _____ Yes _____ No
to control the behavior subject to disciplinary action
impaired?
(*If "YES," student's behavior is subject to IDEA 97 disciplinary procedures*)

Reasons/evidence for determination:

If BOTH F-G (above) answered "NO," then the behavior subject to disciplinary action IS NOT a manifestation of the student's disability. Relevant school disciplinary procedures apply.

1. State the disciplinary action taken (include date of onset):

2. State the special education and related services to be provided:

Figure 1 continued on p. 212

Figure 1 continued

```
┌─────────────────────────────────────────┐
│      Manifestation Determination          │
│              Worksheet                    │
└─────────────────────────────────────────┘
```

Student's Name:_____ Date:_____

IEP team members (by name and role):

_____   _____

_____   _____

_____   _____

Nature of the Behavior Subject to Disciplinary Action

Describe in observable, measurable terms the behavior subject to disciplinary action.

Nature of Disability

1. Describe the observable, measurable characteristics of the student's disability (including its behavioral characteristics and specific severity).

2. Describe how the disability affects:
   - the student's academic progress.

   - the student's social skill development.

   - the student's self-care, domestic, and community skills.

   - the student's receptive and expressive language skills.

(Adapted from the Ohio Department of Education – Model Policies and Procedures for the Education of Children with Disabilities)

FIGURE 2: **Manifestation Determination Form–Example 2**

Making a Manifestation Determination

Student's Name_____Date_____

Description of critical behavior event:

STEP ONE: REVIEW OF ASSESSMENT DATA

1. What do assessment results suggest about this student's past, current, and possible behavior patterns? Be sure to integrate information from the initial disability evaluation, reports from specialists, and multi-disciplinary team reports (reevaluations).

2. Based on the information from all assessment results, what are the implications for educational needs with this student?

STEP TWO: REVIEW OF SPECIAL EDUCATION SERVICES

1. In reviewing the student's IEPs (current and past), have behavioral needs been addressed through service delivery, implementation of behavior programs, and addition/modification of behavioral goals and objectives?

2. In looking at the student's current IEP, do the behavioral goals reflect the student's current behavioral needs? Is the student's IEP appropriate at this time?

Figure 2 continued on p. 214

Figure 2 continued

3. What progress has been made toward the mastery of the identified behavioral goals?

STEP THREE: REVIEW OF SCHOOL RECORDS

1. What behaviors have been exhibited and what disciplinary actions have been taken over the last 2 years? (This includes anecdotal notes of student behaviors.)

2. How have the home and school communicated about behavioral issues and/ or concerns?

STEP FOUR: MAKING THE DETERMINATION

When integrating all of the information discussed above, is the student's critical behavior event (the behavior that necessitated this determination) a manifestation of the student's disability?

_____

____ It has been determined that the behavior under discussion is a manifestation of this student's disability.

or

____ It has been determined that the behavior under discussion is NOT a manifestation of this student's disability.

STEP FIVE: DOCUMENTATION OF PARTICIPATION

It has been determined that the behavior of discussion is/is not (circle one) a manifestation of _____'s disability.
(student's name)

Name	Title	agree	disagree	Date
Name	Title	agree	disagree	Date
Name	Title	agree	disagree	Date
Name	Title	agree	disagree	Date

Dissenting opinions should be attached and noted on this page.

FIGURE 3: **Manifestation Determination Form–Example 3**

Removal of Students With Disabilities

(This page must be completed at an IEP when a student is being considered for removal)

Student Name_____ Date_____Disability_____

Identify the behavior for which removal is being considered in terms that are observable and measurable:

1. Has this student been appropriately determined eligible for special education?
    YES   NO   (If no, proceed with expedited evaluation to determine eligibility)

2. Is the student in an appropriate special education program in the least restrictive environment?
    YES   NO   (If no, do not proceed with removal)

3. It is reasonable to believe that the inappropriate behavior *was not* precipitated by the following:

    A. Programs and services   YES   NO   (If no, do not proceed with removal)
    B. Method of delivery   YES   NO   (If no, do not proceed with removal)
    C. Environment where they   YES   NO   (If no, do not proceed with removal)
        were delivered

4. In relationship to the behavior subject to discipline, was the IEP implemented appropriately?
    YES   NO   (If no, do not proceed with removal)

5. Is the misbehavior a manifestation of the student's disability? (IEP committee members who disagree should provide a written rationale and initial it)
    YES   NO   (If yes, do not proceed with removal)

6. Was the student informed of the school's policy regulating the inappropriate behavior?
    YES   NO   (If no, do not proceed with removal)

7. Is it reasonable to believe the student understood the school's policy given his orher disability?

    YES   NO   (If no, do not proceed with removal)

8. Is it reasonable to believe the student could control his/her behavior in the situation?

    YES   NO   (If no, do not proceed with removal)

The second step involves a thorough review of all assessment data collected to that point in time (Hartwig & Reusch, 1995). This review would include any multifactored evaluations that have been conducted, teacher assessments, classroom observations, parent reports, school records, and any relevant information from outside agencies. A student's physical, cognitive, developmental, mental, and social/emotional needs must all be considered. None of these factors should be examined in isolation, because their effects may be interrelated. In addition, the student's parents may supply evaluative data gathered from outside the school district (e.g., private psychological evaluations) that also should be reviewed. There are often times when a student has recently enrolled in the district and records are not available for consideration by the team. In such instances, the school should contact previously attended educational institutions to procure relevant records and to obtain parental consent. If the data cumulatively suggest that the student had impaired understanding of the student code of conduct, impaired understanding of how his or her behavior violated this code, or had impaired ability to control his or her behavior, then the review should be terminated and the IEP should be revised to address these limitations.

The third step in conducting the manifestation determination involves reviewing the student's current IEP and determining its appropriateness (Hartwig & Reusch, 1995). The purpose of this examination is to ensure that the critical behavioral event is not due, directly or in part, to an inappropriate educational environment. The student's history of special education involvement should be examined thoroughly. General progress on the goals and objectives on the IEP (both academic and behavioral) should be assessed. Communication between the home and school regarding the student's progress in his or her educational program is another important aspect of the review. The specific accommodations and interventions used to assist the student with his or her behavior must be documented. As any behavior management plan is part of the student's IEP, that plan (and its effectiveness) should be part of the review process. Considerations such as language needs for students with limited English proficiency, instruction in Braille for students with visual impairments, communication needs for students with auditory disabilities, and assistive technology devices/services, that are required as part of any IEP meeting must also be integrated. A determination by the members that the current IEP is inappropriate should result in a termination of the review. In this case, the IEP must be revised and made appropriate based on the student's present levels of functioning.

The fourth step in the manifestation determination involves reviewing the specific behavioral needs previously identified in the student's multifactored evaluation (MFE) and IEP (Hartwig & Reusch, 1995). The team should conduct a review of the relevant behaviors (and disciplinary actions for each of them) during the current school year and at least two previous school years. In this way, a pattern of behaviors may be examined over time. It is for this reason that it is imperative to gather reliable, specific, and measurable baseline data to provide this historical perspective. The manifestation review should be stopped if it is determined that the student's individual behavioral needs have not been addressed appropriately in his or her IEP. These considerations would need to be included in a revised IEP if not appropriately incorporated in the past.

The fifth and final part of the manifestation determination process involves reviewing the incident under investigation by answering the central question: Is there a relation between the critical behavioral event and the student's disability? This is often referred to as "The Relationship Test," an elusive doctrine embraced by the courts (Hartwig & Ruesch, 1995). IDEA 97 provides no direction about how this relationship test should be conducted. However, the burden of proving that the critical behavior event was not a manifestation of the student's disability is always placed on the school.

A functional behavior assessment (see Tilly, Knoster, and Ikeda, this volume) may include many of the above assessments in addition to systematic observation and ecological analysis (Wright & Gurman, 1998), providing information regarding the frequency, duration, and intensity of the target behavior, as well as the antecedents and consequences of the behavior. Ecological analysis involves evaluating the settings where the behavior occurs (e.g., physical, social, scheduling variables). Data such as these are important because they provide an appropriate context and frame of reference for determining the relationship between a critical behavior event and a student's disability.

It may be nearly impossible to empirically determine that the manifestation of a behavior is entirely attributable, or not at all related to, a student's disability. It seems rare that an instance of misbehavior is explained by a singular factor. Instead, behavior appears more often as the manifestation of a culmination of interrelated variables. Hence, to minimize the need for making these "all or nothing" assertions in a manifestation determination, school officials should emphasize proactive interventions that will succeed in managing a child's behavior. Sorenson (1993) maintained that in the manifestation case, it is probable that a decision about relatedness arrived at by a proper group of individuals, following federal law, will be upheld at higher levels of appeal. However, many school districts may be reluctant to allow these decisions to progress to this onerous level. Consequently, they may prefer to look at alternatives to removals.

Many arguments could be made that there is some relation between a given behavioral event and a child's disability. The key is the strength of that relationship. A significant relationship between the two would mean that it could be determined that the critical behavior event was a manifestation of the disability. This determination cannot be made if the relationship is only tenuous. There should be a significant, direct, and *causal* link between the critical behavior event and the student's disability rather than an attempt to stretch the intent of the law to embrace any number of tenuous relationships between disabilities and behaviors. The IEP team must also consider whether the student's disability limited his or her understanding of the rules that were violated, understanding of the impact and consequences of the misbehavior, or the student's ability to control the behavior. In an interview about the discipline provisions of IDEA 97, Yell contended that the determination is not just a question of whether the student knew right from wrong, but is also a question of the student's ability to understand the potential consequences of his or her actions (Walther-Thomas & Brownell, 1998).

Another factor complicating the relationship test is that manifestation reviews take place after the critical behavior event (Hartwig & Reusch, 1995). This delay necessitates a retroactive comparison of evaluative data gathered from a student's history with a serious behavioral incident that recently occurred. For example, one consideration that may need to be taken into account is the amount of impulsivity related to a student's actions (and whether impulsivity is an aspect of his or her disability). Moreover, the frequency, intensity, and duration of the behavior as well as possible functions of the behavior (which can be derived from a functional behavior assessment) should be reviewed, as well as other issues that may be occurring in a student's life at the time (e.g., stressors).

Reaching Conclusions and Making Decisions

At the conclusion of the manifestation determination, all participants should sign and designate whether they agree or disagree with the decision reached. If the manifestation review committee decided that the student's behavior was a manifestation of his or her disability, then the student may not be expelled or suspended for more than 10 consecutive school days. This determination, however, does not rule out a change in placement. Indeed, it may be determined that a change in placement is appropriate based on information that the team reviews. The decision to make a change in placement (but not additional suspension or expulsion action) would follow the procedures used in a standard IEP meeting. Any determination concluding that a critical behavior event was the result of a student's disability necessitates that a meeting be conducted to revise the student's IEP and that the student be provided with an appropriate special education program and related services.

In contrast, when a team decides that there was no relationship, they must illustrate that the student's disability did not impair his or her ability to control his or her conduct during the critical behavior event (Hartwig & Ruesch, 1995). If the team determines that the critical behavior event did not bear some type of significant, direct, or causal relationship to the student's disability *and* determines that the student's IEP and placement were appropriate, then the student may be subjected to the school's disciplinary procedures that are used with peers who do not have a disability. These procedures must involve due process rights that are afforded to typical students, including (but not limited to) (a) advising the student of the reason(s) for the exclusion from school, (b) providing the student with an opportunity to explain his or her position with regard to the critical behavior event, (c) providing timely notice to the student's parents, and (d) informing the student and his or her parents of their right to appeal the decision.

Guidelines for Leading School-Based Teams

Once the details of the manifestation determination process are understood, school officials often find great utility in a concise model that provides the basic procedures to be used. Such a model of options surrounding the manifestation determination is provided in Figure 4. This figure illustrates two situations when for removal from school may occur. The first option describes more typical removals, such as suspensions, where a student can be removed for up to 10 days. These removals can be extended up to 45 days if the required elements for "dangerousness" (as described on the chart) are judged to have been met by a hearing officer. Under the second option, removals to interim alternative settings for up to 45 days for conduct violations involving weapons or drugs are summarized. In either option, if removals for more than 10 days are being considered, then a functional behavior assessment, behavior management plan, and manifestation determination must be conducted.

Another, more detailed, overview of the sequence of decisions related to disciplining students with disabilities, including the manifestation determination, is provided in Figures 5 and 6 on pages 222-228. Both figures describe a step-by-step approach to disciplinary procedures from publicizing rules through conducting manifestation determination. Figure 5 provides a detailed and narrative description of the process, whereas Figure 6 illustrates this decision-making sequence in graphic form. Areas where a school would be in violation of IDEA 97 on figures 5 and 6 are noted with a "WARNING!" indicator. Such an overview can be a useful tool in guiding school teams through the procedural requirements surrounding special education discipline and facilitating their compliance with relevant regulations.

FIGURE 4: Process for Disciplining Students With Disabilities Under the IDEA Reauthorization

(Reprinted with permission from The School Discipline Advisor. Copyright 1999 by LRP Publications, P.O. Box 980, Horsham, PA, 19044-0980. All rights reserved. For more information on this newsletter or other products published by LRP Publications, please call 1-800-341-7874, ext. 275.)

Disciplining Children With Disabilities

UNDER NEW I.D.E.A. 97 REGS

Child Violates Code of Conduct

Option #1:

Principal can refer student to alternative placement or suspend for a maximum of 10 school days per school year with no educational services. Parents must be immediately notified of the discipline decision and all procedural safeguards. (Options 1 and 2)

Option #2

In case of a dangerous weapon or drugs, principal can place child in interim alternative educational setting for a maximum of 45 calendar days (IEP team determines the setting and child returns to regular placement on the 46th day).

For Both Options:

For removals over 10 school days in a given school year, LEA must, within 10 business days of a decision to impose the discipline, conduct a *functional behavioral assessment* and implement a *behavior intervention plan* as developed by the IEP team AND must conduct a *manifestation determination** with the parents' participation.

OR

LEA can go before a hearing officer to prove that the student is dangerous ("beyond" a preponderance of the evidence) and request an injunction to place student in an alternative setting for no more than 45 calendar days.

Required Elements for "Dangerousness":

1. Substantial likelihood of injury; **and**
2. Reasonable steps to minimize likelihood of harm.
3. Current IEP is appropriate.
4. Interim educational setting **allows child to participate in general curriculum and continue to receive IEP services** and provides services to ensure behavior doesn't recur.

*Manifestation Determination

Must Consider:

1. Evaluation/diagnostic results
2. Observations
3. IEP/placement

AND prior to finding "no manifestation"

Must Determine:

1. IEP/placement were appropriate
2. Supplementary aids and services were provided
3. Behavioral interventions were provided
4. The child understood his or her behavior and could control the behavior

No Manifestation:

Child can be disciplined as nondisabled, *but must continue FAPE* for suspensions/ expulsions over 10 school days in a given school year. (Parents have a right to an expedited hearing.)

Is a Manifestation:

Child's placement can only be changed via IEP team process.

FIGURE 5: A Step-by-Step Approach to Disciplining Students with Disabilities in Narrative Form

(Courtesy of the law firm of Means, Bichimer, Burkholder & Baker Co., L. P. A., Cleveland, Ohio)

Discipline of Students with Disabilities: A "Step-by-Step" Approach

The purpose of the following analysis of the final IDEA regulations is to highlight general rules regarding disciplining children with disabilities for the purpose of discussion only. As always, if the reader has concerns regarding a specific legal requirements, legal counsel should address those concerns.

Step 1:   *Has the board of education adopted disciplinary rules and regulations in accordance with federal, state, and local law?*
(If yes, go to step 2. If no, WARNING!)

Step 2:   *Has the student been given appropriate notice and opportunity to be heard in accordance with federal, state, and local law?*
(If yes, go to step 3. If no, WARNING!)

Step 3:   *Is the student a child with a disability?*
(If yes, then IDEA 97 regulations apply. Go to step 4. If no, then enforce appropriate sanctions, including suspension or expulsion.)

Step 4:   *Has a determination been made that the student is eligible for special education and related services?*
(If yes, go to step 5. If no, go to step 8.)

Step 5:   *Does disciplinary removal constitute a change in placement?* A change of placement occurs if either: (a) the removal is for more than 10 consecutive school days or (b) the child is subjected to a series of removals that constitute a pattern because they accumulate to more than 10 days in a year and because of such factors as the length of each removal, the total amount of time the child is removed, and the proximity of the removals to one another.
(If yes, go to step 6. If no, go to step 10.)

Step 6:   *Was either a weapon or controlled substance involved?*
(If yes, go to step 7. If no, go to step 13.)

Step 7: A school district may order a change in placement of a child with a disability to an appropriate interim alternative educational setting for the same amount of time that a child without a disability would be subject to discipline, but not for more than 45 days, if the child either (a) carries a weapon to school or to a school function under the jurisdiction of a state or a school district or (b) knowingly possesses or uses illegal drugs or sells or solicits the sale of a controlled substance while at school or a school function under the jurisdiction of a state or school district.
(Go to step 13.)

Step 8: *Did the school "have knowledge" that the pupil was a child with a disability before the behavior that precipitated the disciplinary action occurred?* A school district is deemed to have knowledge that a student is a child with a disability if one of the following is true: (a) The parent of the child has expressed concern in writing (or orally if the parent does not know how to write or has a disability that prevents a written statement) to personnel of the school that the child is in need of special education and related services; (b) the behavior or performance of the child demonstrates the need for special education and related services; (c) the parent of the child has requested an evaluation of the child; or (d) the teacher of the child, or other personnel of the district, has expressed concern about the behavior or performance of the child to the director of special education of the school or other personnel in accordance with that district's established child find or special education referral system. An exception to this occurs when either the school conducts an appropriate evaluation and determines that the child did not have a disability or the schools determined that the evaluation was not necessary. In such a case, the school must provide written notice to the child's parents of its determination that either an evaluation was not necessary or the evaluation determined that the child was not a child with a disability.
(If yes, WARNING! If no, go to step 9.)

Step 9: The student may be subjected to the same sanctions as children without disabilities consistent with the following limitations: (a) If a request is made for an evaluation of a child during the time period in which the child is subjected to disciplinary measures, the evaluation must be completed in an expedited manner; (b) until the evaluation is completed, the child remains in the educational placement determined by school authorities, which can include suspension or expulsion without educational services; (c) if the child is determined to be a child with a disability, taking into consideration information from the evaluation conducted by the

Figure 5 continued on p. 224

Figure 5 continued

school and information provided by the parents, the district must provide special education and related services.
(STOP)

Step 10: School districts may order the removal of a child with a disability from the child's current placement for not more than 10 consecutive days for any violation of school rules and additional removals of not more then 10 consecutive days in that same year for separate instances of misconduct. However, after a child with a disability has been removed from his or her current placement for more than 10 days in the same school year, the district must provide services to ensure the child is provided "services to the extent necessary to enable the child to appropriately progress in the general curriculum and appropriately advance toward achieving the goals set out in the child's IEP."
(Go to step 11.)

Step 11: *Has the student been removed for more than 10 school days in a school year?*
(If yes, go to step 12. If no, go to step 17.)

Step 12: With a child with a disability who has a behavioral intervention plan and who has been removed from the child's current educational placement for more than 10 school days in a school year (which does *not* constitute a change in placement), the IEP team members must review the behavioral intervention plan and its implementation to determine if modifications are necessary. If one or more of the IEP team members believe that modifications are needed, then the IEP team must meet to modify the behavioral intervention plan and its implementation to the extent the IEP team determines necessary.
(STOP)

Step 13: *Has a functional behavior assessment been completed and a behavior intervention plan developed?*
(If yes, go to step 14. If no, go to step 15.)

Step 14: The IEP team must meet to review the plan and its implementations and modify the plan and its implementations as necessary to address the behavior either before or not later than 10 business days after either removing the child for more than 10 school days in any school year or commencing a removal that constitutes a change in placement (see also,

step 12, which may not require an IEP meeting if modifications are not deemed necessary).
(Go to step 16.)

Step 15:   The IEP team must meet to develop the plan and its implementation as necessary to address the behavior either before or not later than 10 business days after either removing the child for more than 10 school days in any school year or commencing a removal that constitutes a change in placement.
(Go to step 16.)

Step 16:   Has a determination been made whether or not the behavior was a manifestation of a child's disability?
(If yes, go to step 18. If no, go to step 17.)

Step 17:   Generally: No later than the date on which the decision to take a disciplinary action is made, the parents must be notified of that decision and provided the applicable procedural safeguard notice. Immediately, if possible, but in no case later than 10 school days after the date on which the disciplinary decision is made, a review must be conducted of the relationship between the child's disability and the behavior subject to the disciplinary action. The manifestation determination review must be conducted by the IEP team and other qualified personnel in a meeting. In carrying out the manifestation determination review, the IEP team and other qualified personnel may determine that the behavior of the child was not a manifestation of the child's disability only if the IEP team and other qualified personnel both:

   1.   Consider, in terms of the behavior subject to disciplinary action, all relevant information, including the following: (a) evaluation and diagnostic results, including the results or other relevant information supplied by the parents of the child; (b) observations of the child; and (c) the child's IEP and placement.

   2.   Determine that (a) in relationship to the behavior subject to disciplinary action, the child's IEP and placement were appropriate and the special education services, supplementary aides and services, and behavior intervention strategies were provided consistent with the child's IEP and placement; (b) the child's disability did not impair the ability of the child to understand the impact and conse-

Figure 5 continued on p. 226

Figure 5 continued

quences of the behavior subject to disciplinary action; and (c) the child's disability did not impair the ability of the child to control the behavior subject to disciplinary action.

If the IEP team and other qualified personnel determine that any of the aforementioned standards were not met, then the behavior must be considered a manifestation of the child's disability. The manifestation determination review may be conducted at the IEP meeting that is convened to determine the appropriateness of the child's functional behavior assessment plan. If in the manifestation determination review the district identifies deficiencies in the child's IEP or placement or in their implementation, then the school must take immediate steps to remedy those deficiencies.
(Go to step 18.)

Step 18: If a determination has been made that the behavior was not manifestation of the child's disability, then the relevant disciplinary procedures applicable to children without disabilities may be applied to the child in the same manner in which they would be applied to children without disabilities. However, in the case of a child who has already been removed for more than 10 school days in a school year, the district must provide "services to the extent necessary to enable the child to appropriately progress in the general curriculum and appropriately advance toward achieving the goals set out in the child's IEP." Note that if the school district initiates the disciplinary procedures applicable to all children, then it must ensure that the special education and disciplinary records of the child with a disability are transmitted for consideration by the person or persons making the final determination regarding the disciplinary action.
(Go to step 19.)

Step 19: If the behavior is determined to be a manifestation of the disability, then the district's options becomes severely limited; that is, 10 days in a school year and/or additional removals of less than ten days if the removal does not constitute a change in placement. For significant behavior that is related to the disability, districts are encouraged to convene the IEP team to consider placement options.
(STOP)

FIGURE 6: **A Step-by-Step Approach to Disciplining Students with Disabilities in Graphic Form**

(Courtesy of the law firm of Means, Bichimer, Burkholder & Baker Co., L. P. A., Cleveland, Ohio)

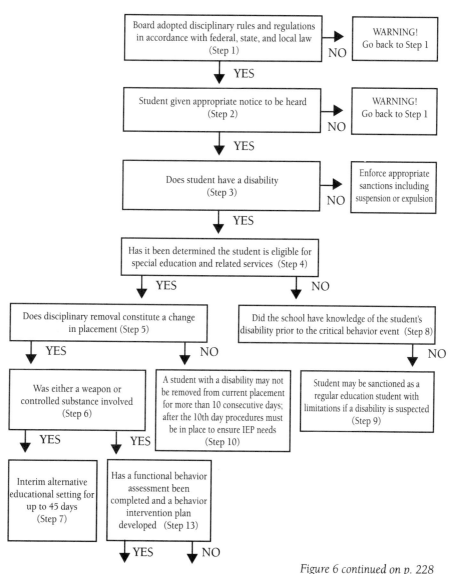

Figure 6 continued on p. 228

Figure 6 continued

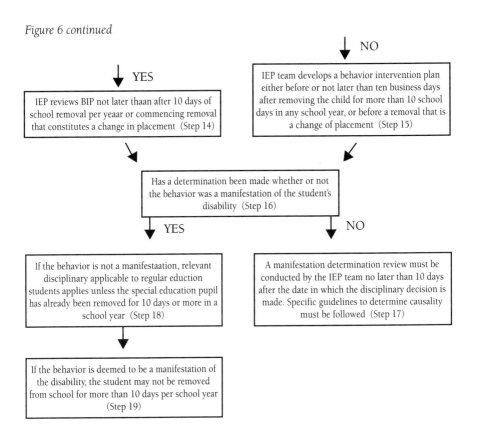

The first step in disciplining students with disabilities involves ensuring that the school district has adopted rules and regulations in accordance with state, federal, and local law and that these have been made available to students and their families. Although it is important for all students to be familiar with the rules, in the case of students with disabilities the staff should ensure that the students comprehend the rules, the rationale of the rules, and the consequences of rule violations. The second step involves providing the student with an opportunity to be heard when he or she is referred for disciplinary action for violating the rules. The third and fourth steps relate to the determination of whether the referred student has a disabling condition under IDEA 97. If the student is not found to have a disability under IDEA 97, then the student can be disciplined in a manner consistent with general education students. However, if a qualifying disability is present, but the school was not put on notice about the disability, then limited sanctions can be imposed until the determination of disability is made (steps 8 and 9). If the school were aware of the disability and the student were on an active IEP at the time of the critical behavior event, then the school needs to determine if a removal would constitute a change in placement (step 5). Interim alternative removals can be considered when conduct violations involve weapons or drugs (step 6).

The tenth step serves as a reminder that the student can be removed for up to 10 days, but will need further intervention if a longer period of removal is being considered. The eleventh step involves determining how many days the student has already been removed during the current school year, because that may limit the extent of removal that is now permissible without conducting a manifestation determination. Step 12 discusses reconvening the IEP to revise a behavior intervention plan. These modifications are often deemed necessary if the plan has not been helpful in addressing the student's inappropriate behavior. Should the violation not permit the immediate removal to an interim alternative educational setting, the school must conduct a functional behavior assessment and develop a behavior management plan (step 13).

Steps 14 and 15 involve reviewing the existing IEP and behavior plan to ensure their appropriateness for the student. Steps 16 and 17 include making the determination as to whether the critical behavior event was a manifestation of the student's disability. Should the decision of the team be that the behavior was not a manifestation (step 18), then relevant disciplinary procedures for general education students may be used. Should it be determined that the behavior was a manifestation (step 19), the student may not be removed for more than 10 days per school year.

Guidelines for Appeals

In conducting manifestation determinations, there may be times when parents disagree with the conclusions reached by the school. If the student's parents were to disagree with these conclusions, then the parent should document their dissent in writing. Should the student's parents challenge the manifestation hearing decision through due process (and the critical behavior event does not involve the student bringing a firearm to school or possessing/selling drugs at school), the student must remain in his or her current educational placement until all of the proceedings have concluded. If the school and parents are able to agree on an interim placement until these proceedings are completed, then this temporary placement may be used for up to 10 days. As in any case where weapons and/or drugs are involved, the school may make a unilateral placement in an interim alternative educational setting for up to 45 days. An interim site might be a juvenile detention center, an alternative school setting, a treatment facility, or another supervised site agreeable to the parents and school.

Alternative settings should "enable the child to continue to participate in the general curriculum, although in another setting, and to continue to receive these services and modifications, including those described in the child's current IEP, that will enable the child to meet the IEP goals." The alternative setting may be the same setting for which students without disabilities are referred for behavioral violations so long as these conditions are present. Also included in the IEP are services and modifications designed to address the behavior that led to the removal (of more than 10 days) *in order that the behavior does not recur.* Although IDEA 97 mandated participation in the general curriculum, there is no entitlement to participation in the general educational setting. However, school officials can anticipate parent challenges with regard to both quality and quantity of services of students transferred to interim alternative educational settings. The school must arrange for an expedited hearing should the parents request due process. The hearing officer then determines if the manifestation determination was consistent with IDEA 97 and may determine an appropriate placement for the student's interim alternative setting.

Methods of Documenting the Manifestation Determination Meeting

Just as IDEA 97 did not provide specific guidelines for conducting the manifestation review, it also did not provide information about methods for documenting the process. As a result, many school districts have been compelled to develop their own methods for documenting manifestation reviews. Specific forms often have great variance in their level of complexity. The amount of detail needed in these forms often is a function of such issues as the volume of cases that a school may need to manage.

Case for Proactive Approaches

Best practice clearly involves adopting a prevention orientation that seeks to address and intervene on ongoing behavioral concerns before they escalate to a point where a manifestation determination becomes necessary (see Tankersley, Landrum, Cook, and Balan, this volume). An important part of this approach involves delineating behavioral expectations and specific consequences for all students. For students with disabilities, an individualized statement should be included on the IEP about the student's ability to follow district behavior codes that can be supported by evidence (i.e., data from recent evaluations). The statement should not take the form of a "blanket statement" about the student's ability to follow the code of behavior, but rather a detailed evaluation of his or her ability to understand and comply with school and classroom rules (Wright & Gurman, 1988). Appropriate steps also should be taken to assist the student in following the behavior code. In addition, by developing dynamic behavior intervention plans and conducting functional behavior assessments that lead to effective interventions, many critical behavior events can be avoided in advance (Wright & Gurman, 1998).

Preventing behaviors from escalating to the point of student removal may be accomplished by identifying specific behaviors of concern that are observable, measurable, and operationally defined. A baseline of behavior for each area of concern should be established to recognize patterns that may occur (Hartwig & Ruesch, 1995). These baseline measurements should analyze the frequency, intensity, and duration of the behaviors targeted. Antecedents that precede behaviors and the consequences that follow the behaviors of concern, as well as the environmental factors and ecological context in which these behaviors occur, should be evaluated. An analysis of the purpose and the effect of the behavior through which team members can develop hypotheses about why the behavior is occurring is a central part of using assessment data for intervention (see Tilly et al., this volume, for a thorough review).

Another aspect of developing a preventative orientation is to conduct multifactored evaluations and functional behavior assessments that lead to interventions. The team can be preventative by looking at the student's present level of functioning with regard to behavior and identify areas of concern. These concerns may then be brought to the IEP team meeting for discussion and intervention. Moreover, multifactored evaluations and functional behavior assessments contribute to baseline data gathering. Use of the same methods of empirical measurement from evaluation to evaluation can contribute to the reliability of assessing the behavior over time. In addition, comprehensive evaluations include data gathering from parents and ongoing communication with the home.

In many instances, the steps just outlined not only succeed in preventing critical behavior events, but also provide the necessary background needed for a manifestation determination should a review be necessary before the actual determination. The clear advantage of diligently documenting all appropriate steps to intervene with troublesome behaviors could be realized when the manifestation team has access to detailed historical data concerning the target behavior(s).

Establishing Home-School Collaboration as a Priority

No student's education occurs entirely within the school environment. Consequently, cooperative ventures between schools and families are of paramount importance. Parents are in a unique position to provide schools with information about standards for behavior that are reasonable, yet ambitious. School officials should never ignore behavioral concerns reported or evaluative data supplied by parents. Parents are an integral part of the entire IEP process, including functional behavior assessments and behavior management plans. The active participation of parents in the process would likely lessen the possibility of future critical behavior events. At the very least, forging these partnerships in advance of problems often significantly reduces tensions that may exist between families and schools when major disciplinary issues are being addressed (see Sheridan, Cowan, and Eagle, this volume).

PROFESSIONAL DEVELOPMENT IMPLICATIONS OF MANIFESTATION DETERMINATIONS

Particularly in light of the evolving nature of the legal mandates surrounding the manifestation determination (and IDEA 97 in general), it has never been more important for school officials to be knowledgeable about federal, state, and local laws that apply to children with disabilities. Information regarding appropriate practice must be shared with any personnel involved in providing special education and related services to students. It is advised that school officials begin such personnel training *before* manifestation determinations need to be made. Because reviews often occur over a relatively short period, preparing teachers and other school personnel fully about their legal responsibilities in advance is strongly recommended. In addition, school staff must fully understand their role in each step of the disciplinary process to write appropriate goals, effectively evaluate progress, and accurately document outcomes for students with disabilities (Hartwig & Ruesch, 1995).

Aside from instruction, the expanding roles of school personnel now also consist of evaluation, consultation, intervention, and prevention. The roles have grown to the point where staff members are often asked to understand and comply with potentially problematic and complicated legislation (Zurkowski et al., 1998). Although school personnel should not position themselves as legal counsel for any reason, knowledge of legal issues could be particularly useful in facilitating a variety of disciplinary procedures.

In addition, school personnel are frequently expected to be knowledgeable about an array of classroom interventions for dealing with challenging behaviors (Hartwig & Ruesch, 1995). School psychologists, counselors, and other school-based mental health providers can be invaluable in understanding the factors that contribute to successful student deportment. Scott and Nelson (1999) maintain that teaming strategies rely on collective brainstorming and input, as opposed to an individual "expert" model. Consequently, they suggest that team-based intervention planning demands shared expertise. In the case of manifestation determinations, school personnel may underestimate the impact a disabling condition may have on a student's behavior. School staff will need to gain more awareness into the nature of a variety of disabling conditions and their impact on behavior. They should continue to improve their knowledge and competencies in these areas through continuing education activities. School officials also need more knowledge about alternative environments for students with disabilities who have behavioral concerns. A menu of disciplinary options should be developed and ready for use in lieu of repeated exclusions (see Telzrow and Naidu, this volume).

An understanding must also be reached among educators that good disciplinary practices seek to teach students positive alternative behaviors (Wright & Gurman, 1998), rather than simply rely on punitive processes. School officials at all levels may need to periodically reevaluate their positions on the function of discipline in the schools. Instead of excluding students for misdeeds, disciplinary actions should serve to educate student on making better decisions, taking more responsibility for their actions, and developing the social skills necessary to be successful long after their school years.

Perhaps even more important than specific skills training is exploring the attitudes of school personnel and addressing attitudes that may prove detrimental to the manifestation determination process. Educators may be antagonistic and resistant to providing services for students whose behavior is unattractive and difficult to manage (Costander & Buntaine, 1999; Forness, 1992; Maag & Howell, 1992). Additionally, there may be reluctance to serve students who present with deviant behaviors, particularly defiant, aggressive, or extremely disruptive behaviors (Costander & Butaine, 1999; Nelson, Rutherford, Center, & Walker, 1991). School officials should also recognize that manifestation determinations often occur in a highly tense atmosphere and there are usually political ramifications that result from reviews. Members of review teams will require intensive training in order that they trust their own judgment, rather than capitulating to outside pressures.

Nelson, Roberts, Mather, and Rutherford (1999) pointed out the critical need for an expanded knowledge base and improved assessments to guide schools in addressing the challenges posed by the manifestation determination mandate (e.g. problem behavior caused by a disability). Although it is typically recommended that results of functional behavior assessments be used as a foundation for the manifestation determination, this approach includes no standard measures but rather is a problem-solving process by using applied behavior analysis. A critical component of functional behavior assessments is developing hypotheses about the "function" of problem behavior (Nelson et al., 1999). This process could be enhanced by applying empirically based assessments and research regarding the nature of problem behavior specific to types of disabilities. Perry, Bard, and Wallbrown (1993) developed an intervention model based on multiaxial assessment of parent and teacher ratings as well as child interviews regarding positive and problem behavior of youth with disabilities. Such an approach could provide empirically based assessments for developing functional hypotheses. In addition, by also identifying positive social behaviors, this approach could provide interventions directed at promoting alternatives to problem behavior as recommended by Wright and Gurman (1998). It is clear that the demands for staff development will significantly increase as public policies continue to shape the delivery of educational services.

SUMMARY

Educators should anticipate that requests for manifestation determinations will increase in the coming years. Prevention and preparation will become far more crucial in order to address the volume of reviews that may result. As the number of reviews that are conducted nationwide continues to increase, case law will begin to provide greater direction in this area of special education. Because the manifestation determination is a relatively new procedure, it has been exposed to little judicial scrutiny to date. Until there is more guidance from the law, gray areas about procedural practices will persist. As a result, educators can anticipate that there will be more challenges from parents to actions taken by school districts.

Osborne (1988) indicates that, because schools would still have to pay for educational services if the student is expelled, going through the entire manifestation determination process (although "technically available") is not a viable remedy as a practical matter due to the financial, legal, and human resource costs that may result. This viewpoint necessitates the development of a prevention orientation that emphasizes staff training in interventions and partnerships with families. Telzrow (1999) contended that, because FAPE must continue regardless of the relationship between the behavior of concern and the disability when removals exceed 10 days, deliberations presumably would be better directed toward problem-solving creative intervention alternatives than toward a "causal analysis of dubious merit" (p. 21). Likewise, Sorenson (1990) stated, "the better and easier approach should relatedness be a relevant issue, would be to assume relatedness unless there is substantial and convincing evidence to the contrary: in that way, attention can be focused on the more important issue of providing an appropriate education" (p. 394).

The current knowledge base applied to the manifestation determination process has been limited to outcomes of litigation (Meloy, 1999) and behavioral theoretical models. Considering the complexity of determining if a disability is "causing" a problem behavior, a broader conceptual knowledge base supported by research would be helpful. For example, Zigler's developmental approach to mental retardation has documented that students with mental retardation typically experience behavioral problems such as positive and negative reaction tendencies as well as outerdirectedness (Hodapp & Zigler, 1995). This approach has recently been expanded to studying behavior problems experienced by youths with other types of disabilities (Hodapp, 1997). Family system theorists have provided evidence that family ecological variables (e.g. emotional climate) influence the behavior of children with disabilities in patterns beyond some of our conventional models (Burr & Klein, 1994). Knowledge from disciplines related to school psychology, such as rehabilitation psychology, may also provide other approaches to assessing the disability and behavior relationship. For example, Cook (1992) has provided a review of the theories and research in rehabilitation regarding adjustment to disabilities. However, this rehabilitation psychology knowledge base is primarily relevant to adults with disabilities.

It is hoped that future research will provide improved empirically based knowledge regarding maladaptive behavior specific to the various disabilities. This knowledge could serve as a foundation for improved assessments to guide the completion of manifestation determinations. For example, it would be helpful to investigate the psychological constructs of the problem behavior for students with various disabilities. Separate narrative data for each type of disability would also be helpful to describe the types of positive behavior lacking and problem behavior typically experienced by students with different difficulties. There is also a need to evaluate stressors, support systems, and diversity issues relevant to understanding the behavior of students with disabilities. Beyond providing a knowledge base with implications for manifestation determinations, this type of information would help document the type of behavioral interventions most appropriate for students with disabilities. Landrum and Tankersley (1999) stated that the need for earlier and better services for young children before they develop emotional and behavior problems is our most critical task because once developed, the behaviors tend to remain stable. Our efforts should seek to prevent the development of such behavior and to lessen their effects (e.g., see Telzrow and Naidu, this volume).

In conclusion, the current state of the art in conducting manifestation determinations is fraught with limitations. The cautions and concerns pointed out by Katsiyannis and Maag (1998) should be considered by practitioners when conducting this task. These include the following: (a) There are presently no valid empirical or theoretical foundations for manifestation determinations, (b) schools should guard against using subjective "naturally occurring student characteristics" (p. 284) such as race or gender in making manifestation determinations, and (c) there may be social and political pressure to use manifestation determinations to avoid providing the appropriate specialized services to meet the behavioral needs of youths with disabilities.

REFERENCES

Algozzine, R. (1985). *Problem behavior management: Educator's resource service.* Rockville, MD: Aspen Systems Corporation.

Burr, W. R., & Klein, S. R. (1994). *Reexamining family stress: A new theory and research.* Thousand Oaks, CA: Sage.

Cook, D. (1992). Psychosocial impact of disability. In R. M. Parker & E. M. Szymanski (Eds.), *Rehabilitation counseling* (2nd ed.) (pp. 233-268). Austin, TX: PRO-ED.

Costenbader, V., & Buntaine, R. (1999). Diagnostic discrimination between social maladjustment and emotional disturbance: An empirical study. *Journal of Emotional and Behavior Disorders, 7* (1), 2–11.

Costenbader, V., & Markson, S. (1998). School suspension: A study with secondary school students. *Journal of School Psychology, 36,* 59–82.

Council of Administrators of Special Education (1996). *Resource guide: Addressing student with disabilities who may exhibit violent, aggressive, and/or dangerous behaviors.* Albuquerque, NM: Council of Administrators of Special Education.

Dwyer, K. P. (1997). IDEA '97: Disciplining students with disabilities, *Communiqué, 26*(2), 1–8.

Forness, S. R. (1992). Broadening the cultural-organizational perspective in exclusion of youth with social maladjustment: First invited reaction to the Maag and Howell paper. *Remedial and Special Education, 13* (1), 55–59.

Hartwig, E. P. (1999). Q & A with Eric Hartwig. *Today's Psychologist, 2*(10), 3.

Hartwig, E. P. & Ruesch, G. M. (1995). How to make a manifestation determination [Video]. Horsham, PA: LRP Publications.

Heumann, J. E. (1997). *Initial disciplinary guidance related to removal of children with disabilities from their current educational placement for ten days or less.* Washington, D.C.: Office of Special Education and Rehabilitation Services (Memo).

Hodapp, R. M. (1997). Developmental approaches to children with disabilities: New perspectives, populations, prospects. In S. S. Luthor, J. A. Burack, P. Cicchetti, & J. R. Weisz (Eds.) *Developmental psychopathology: Perspectives on adjustment, risk, and disorder* (pp. 189–207). New York: Cambridge University Press.

Hodapp, R. M., & Zigler, E. (1995). Past, present, and future issues in the developmental approach to mental retardation and developmental disabilities. In D. Cicchetti & D. J. Cohen (Eds.) *Manual of developmental psychopathology, Vol. 2: Risk, disorder, and adaptations* (pp. 299–331). New York: John Wiley.

Hundley, C. A. (1994). The reduction of childhood aggression using the brainpower program. In M. Furlong & D. Smith (Eds.), *Anger, hostility and aggression: Assessment, prevention and intervention strategies for youth* (pp. 313–344). Brandon, VT: Clinical Psychology.

Individuals with Disabilities Education Act Amendments of 1997, 20 U.S.C. § 1400 *et seq.* (West 1997).

Johnston, J. S. (1989). High school completion of in-school suspension students. *NAASP Bulletin, 73,* 89–95.

Katsiyannis, A., & Maag, J. (1998). Disciplining students with disabilities: Issues and considerations for implementing IDEA '97. *Behavior Disorders, 23,* 276–289.

Landrum, T. J., & Tankersley, M. (1999). Emotional and behavior disorders in the new millennium: The future is now. *Behavior Disorders, 24,* 319–330.

Maag, J. W., & Howell, K. W. (1992). Special education and the exclusion of youth with social maladjustments: A cultural organizational perspective. *Remedial and Special Education, 13,* 47–54.

Meloy, L. L. (1999). Manifestation determination. *Communiqué, 28,* 8–9.

Mendez, R., & Sanders, S. (1981). An examination of in-school suspension: Panacea or pandora's box? *NAASP Bulletin, 65,* 63–73.

Mizell, M. H. (1978). Designing and implementing effective in-school alternatives to suspension. *The Urban Review, 10,* 213–226.

Morgan-D'Atrio, C., Northup, J., LaFleur, L., & Spera, S. (1996). Toward prescriptive alternatives to suspension: A preliminary evaluation. *Behavior Disorders, 21,* 190–200.

National Association of State Directors of Special Education. (1998). *Interim alternative educational settings for students with disabilities involved in disciplinary actions.* Alexandria, VA: Author.

National Institutes of Health (1989). *Treatment of destructive behaviors.* Abstract presented at the National Institutes of Health, Consensus Development Conference, Rockville, MD.

Nelson, C. M., Rutherford, R. B., Center, D. B., & Walker, H. M. (1991). Do public schools have an obligation to serve troubled children and youth? *Exceptional Children, 57,* 406–415.

Nelson, J. R., Roberts, M. L., Mathur, S. R., & Rutherford, R. B. (1999). Has public policy exceeded our knowledge base? A review of the functional behavior assessment literature. *Behavior Disorders, 24,* 169–179.

Osborne, A. G. (1988). Dangerous handicapped students cannot be excluded from the public schools. *West's Education Law Reporter, 46,* 1105–1113.

Osborne, A. G. (1998). Governing discipline under the 1997 IDEA. *School Business Affairs, 64*(8), 21–24.

Perry, J. D., Bard, E. M., & Wallbrown, F. (1993). An intervention model to promote students' coping with disabilities. *Rehabilitation Psychology, 38,* 140–148.

Polsgrove, L. (1991). *Reducing undesirable behaviors.* Reston, VA: The Council for Exceptional Children.

Radin, N. (1988). Alternatives to suspension and corporal punishment. *Urban Education, 22,* 476–495.

Rutherford, R. (1978). Theory and research on the use of aversive procedures in the education of behaviorally disordered and emotionally disturbed children and youth. In F. Wood & K. C. Lankin (Eds.), *Punishment and aversive stimulation in special education* (pp. 41-64). Reston, VA: Council for Exceptional Children.

Safer, D. (1986). Nonpromotion correlates and outcomes at different grade levels. *Journal of Learning Disabilities, 19,* 500–503.

Scott, T. M., & Nelson, C. M. (1999). Functional behavior assessments: Implications for training and staff development. *Behavior Disorders, 24,* 249–252.

Sorenson, G. P. (1990). Special education discipline in the 1990s. *West's Education Law Reporter, 62,* 387–398.

Sorenson, G. P. (1993). Update on legal issues in special education discipline. *West's Education Law Reporter, 81,* 399–410.

Stage, S. A. (1997). A preliminary investigation of the relationship between in-school suspension and the disruptive classroom behavior of students with behavioral disorders. *Behavioral Disorders, 23,* 57–76.

Swadi, H. (1992). Relative risk factors in detecting adolescent drug abuse. *Drug and Alcohol Dependence, 29,* 253–254.

Telzrow, C. F. (1999). IDEA amendments of 1997: Promise or pitfall for special education reform? *Journal of School Psychology, 37,* 7–28.

Walther-Thomas, C., & Brownell, M. T. (1998). An interview with Dr. Mitchell Yell: Changes in IDEA regarding suspension and expulsion. *Intervention in School and Clinic, 34* (1), 46–49.

Wright, O.B., & Gurman, H.B. (1998). *Positive interactions for serious behavior problems.* Sacramento: California Department of Education.

Yell, M. L., & Shriner, J. G. (1997). The IDEA amendments of 1997: Implications for special and general education teachers, administrators, and teacher trainers. *Focus on Exceptional Children, 30,* 1–19.

Yelsma, P., Yelsma, J., & Hovestadt, A. (1991). Autonomy and intimacy of self and externally disciplined students: Families of origin and the implementation of the adult mentor program. *School Counselor, 39,* 20–29.

Zirkel, P. A. (1999). The IDEA's suspension/expulsion requirements: A practical picture. *West's Education Law Reporter, 134,* 19–23.

Zurkowski, J. K., Kelly, P. S., & Griswold, D. E. (1998). Discipline and IDEA 1997: Instituting a new balance. *Intervention in School and Clinic, 34* (1), 3–9.

ANNOTATED BIBLIOGRAPHY

Hartwig, E. P., & Ruesch, G. M. (1995). *How to make a manifestation determination* [Video]. Horsham, PA: LRP Publications.

This videotape provides comprehensive assistance to school personnel who need guidance in conducting the manifestation determination process. General steps are provided to lead teams through effective decision making with respect to ascertaining the appropriateness of an IEP, the appropriateness of a placement, and the relationship test. Simulated meetings are provided to illustrate how a practical meeting might look. The authors discuss several implications for practice.

Hartwig, E. P., & Ruesch, G. M. (1999). *Discipline under the new IDEA* [Video]. Horsham, PA: LRP Publications.

A practical explanation of the discipline measures and procedures school officials are permitted to use for students with disabilities is provided. Overviews on key legislative changes with regard to suspension, expulsion, and placement are included.

Maloney Baird, M. (1999). *The new IDEA regulations: Know your legal responsibilities* [Video]. Horsham, PA: LRP Publications.

This resource compares and contrasts the IDEA reauthorization with the former IDEA regulations. Analyses from experts on topics ranging from evaluations to procedural safeguards are provided. The responsibilities of school officials are discussed in a precise overview of the legal requirements.

Katsayannis, A., & Maag, J. (1998). Disciplining students with disabilities: Issues and considerations for implementing IDEA '97. *Behavior Disorders, 23,* 276–289.

This article provides a comprehensive overview of the IDEA reauthorization as it pertains to a variety of disciplinary issues. The historical overview of the regulations is provided as a basis for discussion. Functional behavior assessments, manifestation determinations, and alternative placements are discussed at length, with numerous suggestions for best practice.

CHAPTER 7

Developing Behavioral Intervention Plans for Students with Disabilities

Melody Tankersley
Kent State University

Timothy J. Landrum
Cleveland State University

Bryan G. Cook
Christine Balan
Kent State University

BACKGROUND/PURPOSE OF BEHAVIORAL INTERVENTION PLAN PROVISIONS IN IDEA 97

By most accounts, the number of students who exhibit challenging classroom behavior in schools is increasing (Walker, Colvin, & Ramsey, 1995). These students place heightened demands not only on teachers' management skills but also on their instructional ability as well. In fact, behavioral problems and poor academic achievement and learning often go hand in hand (e.g., Patterson, Reid, & Dishion, 1992). For example, Tremblay, Masse, LeBlanc, Schwartzman, and Ledingham (1992) found that poor school achievement in the first grade was strongly associated with first-grade disruptive behavior and poor fourth-grade school achievement.

Although academic problems are the most cited reasons for referring children for special education services (Lloyd, Kauffman, Landrum, & Roe, 1991), in many cases teachers may not request assistance unless behavior problems accompany learning problems (Soodak & Podell, 1993; Thurlow, Christenson, & Ysseldyke, 1984). In fact, Carta et al. (1994) reported that challenging behaviors are the number one reason given by teachers for referring young children to special education programs.

241

Moreover, teachers often resist the placement of students who exhibit specific behavior problems in their classrooms (Walker, 1986).

School personnel are currently faced with many considerations concerning student behavior. Today more than ever, all school personnel, not only special educators, are asked to provide classroom instruction, supervision, and discipline to students with disabilities. This has increased the demand to collaborate for addressing not only academic problems, but also behavior problems that may interfere with academic progress. The 1997 amendments to the Individuals with Disabilities Education Act (IDEA 97) (Individuals with Disabilities Education Act Amendments, 1997) address issues related to classroom behavior and the relationship to learning through collaboratively developed individualized education programs (IEPs) that include behavior intervention plans for students with disabilities who have problem behavior.

Given the importance of the relationship between behavior and learning, the 1997 reauthorization of IDEA requires that IEP teams actively consider the impact of a student's behavior on his or her learning as well as on the learning environment. According to IDEA 97, "the IEP team shall, in the case of a child whose behavior impedes his or her learning or that of others, consider, when appropriate, strategies, including positive behavioral interventions, strategies, and supports to address that behavior." This statement acknowledges the link between learning and behavior and mandates that school personnel act upon this relationship by instituting appropriate strategies, interventions, and supports when the behavior of a child interferes with learning. This constitutes the need for behavioral intervention plans to be included in students' IEPs. A behavioral intervention plan is a written document based on assessment outcomes that identifies goals and objectives for addressing students' social, emotional, and behavioral development through positive behavioral interventions and other strategies.

Assessment and intervention planning targeted at problem behavior are not new to IDEA 97, inasmuch as these have been required since the inception of the Act. However, the 1997 amendments are more prescriptive than past mandates for addressing this area. Specifically, IDEA 97 identifies two points at which behavior plans must be developed or reviewed by the IEP team: (a) when, as noted in the previous paragraph, the behavior of the child interferes with his or her learning or the learning of others and (b) in response to disciplinary actions resulting in suspension or expulsion of a student with disabilities. Specifically, the statue states "either before or not later than 10 days after taking a disciplinary action...if the local education agency did not conduct a functional behavioral assessment and implement a behavioral intervention plan for such child before the behavior that resulted in the suspension..., the agency shall convene an IEP meeting to develop an assessment plan to address that behavior; or if the child already has a behavioral intervention plan, the IEP Team shall review the plan and modify it, as necessary, to address the behavior. "

Because the statute requires a functional behavioral assessment when implementing or revising a behavioral intervention plan in response to disciplinary actions, many professionals question whether a functional behavioral assessment is required for all behavioral intervention plans (see Tilly, Knoster, and Ikeda, this volume, for further discussion of the topic). The essential purpose of a functional behavioral assessment is to generate information that would improve the likelihood of creating effective and efficient behavior intervention plans. The results of a functional behavioral assessment identify conditions under which and possible reasons why problem behaviors most often occur and do not occur (Sugai, Horner, & Sprague, 1999). Therefore, it would seem that a functional behavioral assessment should be conducted whenever a behavioral intervention plan is necessary. A strict interpretation of IDEA 97, however, suggests that a functional behavioral assessment is only required when a student with a disability has become the subject of school disciplinary proceedings that have resulted in the student's being suspended or expelled, which constitutes a change in placement.

Some argue that such a strict interpretation may not meet the spirit of the law. For example, Nelson, Roberts, and Smith (1998) identify language throughout IDEA 97 (Individuals with Disabilities Education Act Amendments, 1997) that can be interpreted to mean that a functional behavioral assessment is required whenever a behavioral intervention plan is required to address the needs of a student with disabilities who has behavioral issues. These researchers contend that functional behavioral assessments contribute important decision-making information as a part of the full and individual assessment required for all relevant domains in the evaluation process. As Sugai et al. (1999) state, "if a child's behavior is of sufficient concern that a formal behavioral intervention is developed, that intervention should be guided by basic information about the events that occasion and maintain the problem behavior" (p. 253). This view is shared by many authorities who have written about the IDEA 97 amendments. Perhaps Yell (1998) most clearly expresses this view in his interpretation and summary of both sections of IDEA 97 that discuss behavioral intervention plans:

> To deal with behavior problems in a proactive manner, the 1997 amendments require that if a student with disabilities has behavior problems (regardless of the student's disability category), the IEP (individualized education program) team shall consider strategies—including positive behavioral interventions, strategies, and supports—to address those problems. In such situations a proactive behavior management plan, based on functional behavioral assessment, should be included in the student's IEP. Furthermore, if a student's placement is changed following a behavioral incident and the IEP does not contain a behavioral intervention plan, a functional behavioral assessment and a behavioral plan must be completed no later than 10 days after changing the placement (p. 88).

Indeed, it seems clear that the most defensible interpretation of the 1997 amendments to IDEA compels school-based teams to conduct a functional behavioral assessment before writing a behavioral intervention plan. Therefore, in this chapter behavioral intervention plans are conceptualized as action guides informed by the results of functional behavioral assessment. Although specific detail about conducting functional behavioral assessments is not included in this chapter (see Tilly, Knoster, and Ikeda, this volume), procedures for using the results of the functional behavioral assessment to inform and guide the behavioral intervention plan are described.

In the following sections, considerations for developing, implementing, and evaluating behavioral intervention plans are discussed. Best practice strategies are then identified and professional development implications considered for incorporating behavioral intervention plans into programming for students with disabilities.

CONSIDERATIONS FOR SCHOOL-BASED TEAMS IN DEVELOPING, IMPLEMENTING, AND EVALUATING BEHAVIORAL INTERVENTION PLANS

The need for behavioral intervention plans for many students with disabilities is not new. In many service delivery systems, behavioral intervention plans have been a standard source of best practice for addressing the needs of students with disabilities who display behavioral difficulties. What is new, however, is that the amendments of IDEA 97 have formalized this need for behavioral intervention plans. IDEA 97 mandates the incorporation of behavioral intervention plans for students with disabilities whose behavior interferes with learning, as well as for students with disabilities who undergo disciplinary actions that result in 10 days or more of suspension or expulsion. Moreover, IDEA 97 mandates that behavioral intervention plans incorporate positive behavioral interventions, strategies, and supports to address that behavior. Therefore, the practice of developing and incorporating behavioral intervention plans, which in the past was operationalized from a sense of best practice, has now become prescriptive.

According to the statute, behavioral intervention plans are to be incorporated into IEPs and are to be created by school-based, multidisciplinary teams. The school-based teams are responsible for synthesizing information, identifying appropriate goals and objectives, choosing procedures and interventions that will address the goals and objectives, and monitoring progress toward meeting the goals and objectives. In the following section, considerations for school-based teams in developing, implementing, and evaluating behavioral intervention plans are discussed.

Considerations for Developing Behavioral Intervention Plans

The development of behavioral intervention plans should follow many of the same procedures used to develop IEPs. Behavioral intervention plans should include goals and objectives based on the results of a current battery of assessments, pinpoint specific target behaviors that are associated with the problem behavior, and identify behavioral interventions and supports that will help meet the goals and objectives. Although each of these specific components will not be discussed in detail (it is assumed, that the reader is familiar with basic concepts, such as writing complete objectives with the learner, conditions, behavior, and criteria specified), aspects of the components as they relate to behavioral intervention plans will be described.

Developing Goals and Objectives

Any set of goals and objectives should be developed based on current and useful assessments. Functional behavioral assessments incorporate several methods of assessment and the results provide valuable information about the potential cause of the behavior. Instead of simply focusing on what the behavior looks like, the interventionist can use the results of a functional assessment to begin to understand the underlying purpose of the behavior.

Functional behavioral assessments often include indirect assessments as well as direct observational assessments (Alberto & Troutman, 1999). Indirect assessments may involve behavioral interviews with significant persons, including parents, special education teachers, general education teachers, or the students themselves. Such instruments as *The Functional Assessment Interview* and *The Student Guided Functional Assessment Interview* (O'Neill et al., 1997) provide structure for interviewing informants. Behavioral scales and questionnaires, such as *The Problem Behavior Questionnaire* (Lewis, Scott, & Sugai, 1994), should also be used to gather information that might be related to the function of the behavior. Direct observational assessments involve observing the behavior as it occurs and allow identification of antecedents and consequences of the behavior. Direct observational assessments should occur in different contexts and be conducted over several days (Nelson et al., 1998). By using a variety of both indirect assessments and direct observational assessments allows professionals to develop the goals and objectives based on a comprehensive set of data from different people and settings.

The results of the functional behavioral assessment provide the school-based team with a current level of functioning, information that is important in developing goals and objectives. In particular, the results from the direct observational assessments will provide a baseline level of behavior that can be used to evaluate progress throughout the implementation of the behavioral intervention plan. The baseline level of the behavior, for example, may show that it occurs, on average, 12 times a day. During implementation of the intervention, direct observation of the behavior may reveal that the behavior occurs an average of two times a day. Assessing the magnitude of the discrepancy between baseline and intervention data can provide powerful information to evaluate progress in meeting goals and objectives. It is important, therefore, that someone familiar with data collection techniques conduct the observations in a trustworthy, replicable fashion.

Targeting Behaviors

As was stated previously, the goal of a functional behavioral assessment is to identify the underlying purpose of the behavior. Typically, the underlying purpose, or function, of most behaviors is to provide positive reinforcement (access to something desirable, such as attention, an object, an activity, social engagement), negative reinforcement (escape from something undesirable, such as a difficult task, physical discomfort, social embarrassment), autonomic reinforcement (sensory feedback or stimulation, such as body rocking, mouthing, self-scratching), or a combination of these functions (Alberto & Troutman, 1999). The results of the functional behavioral assessment provide team members with a hypothesis for why the behavior is occasioned or maintained. This information allows the team to target behaviors to address through the goals and objectives of the behavioral intervention plan.

By identifying the function of the behavior, teams can pinpoint behaviors to increase or teach that will serve the same function. That is, rather than simply trying to stop undesirable behavior from occurring, a practice that often suppresses the behavior only for a short time before the behavior reappears or produces a new and equally inappropriate behavior, identifying the function of the behavior allows the team to modify the environment or curriculum to reduce the occurrence of the inappropriate behavior and to teach the student appropriate replacement behaviors; that is, behaviors that accomplish the same function, but in a more socially acceptable manner.

In addition to considering the function of the behavior, Cooper, Heron, and Heward (1987) suggest considering factors such as the following ones to determine the appropriateness of the target behavior: (a) Will addressing the behavior result in higher levels of reinforcement for the student? (b) Will addressing the behavior positively impact the student's skill development and independence? (c) Will addressing the behavior reduce the negative attention the student receives? For target behaviors to be socially relevant and for long-term effectiveness of behavior change, the answers to these questions should be in the affirmative.

Identifying Behavior Interventions and Supports

According to IDEA 97, a school-based team should consider positive behavioral interventions to address behavior that interferes with the learning environment. The specific interventions that are used to address behavior problems must be considered in relation to many resource-related variables (such as cost, time available, and expertise and attitude of the interventionist) as well as behavior-related variables (such as match with function of the behavior and type of intervention that will address the behavior). It is important to note that when addressing specific behaviors, teams may need to identify several interventions.

Research on resource-related variables has often focused on teachers' acceptance of treatments. Teacher acceptance of classroom-based interventions is complex; and the results of the research on treatment acceptability suggest that when choosing an intervention, the team must consider interrelated factors associated with the teacher, the severity of the behavior problem, the type of intervention, and implementation procedures. Tankersley and Talbott (1992) reviewed the literature on treatment acceptability and identified the following implications for teachers' acceptance of interventions:

- Less experienced teachers are more accepting of interventions than more experienced teachers (Witt, Moe, Gutkin, & Andrews, 1984; Witt & Robbins, 1985).
- Special education and general education teachers rate the acceptability of interventions similarly (no significant differences) (Epstein, Matson, Repp, & Helsel, 1986).
- Teachers in different grade levels (K–12) do not significantly differ in their ratings of acceptable interventions (Hall & Wahrman, 1988).
- Interventions implemented by the classroom teacher are rated as more acceptable than interventions implemented by others (Martens, Witt, Elliott, & Darveaux, 1985; Witt & Robbins, 1985).
- Interventions in which students are required to leave the classroom are rated as less acceptable than those implemented in the classroom (Martens, Peterson, Witt, & Cirone, 1986).
- All interventions are rated as more acceptable when applied to severe problem behavior than when applied to mild problem behavior (Elliott, Witt, Galvin, & Peterson, 1984; Martens et al., 1985; Witt, Elliott, & Martens, 1984; Witt, Moe et al., 1984; Witt & Robbins, 1985).
- Teachers are more likely to try new interventions when addressing mild behavior problems than severe behavior problems (Von Brock & Elliott, 1987).
- Teachers are more accepting of interventions that involve short amounts of time to implement than those that are more time consuming (Witt, Elliott et al., 1984; Witt & Martens, 1983; Witt, Martens, & Elliott, 1984).

- Teachers are more accepting of interventions that require high levels of time involvement if the interventions are applied to students with severe behavior problems than if applied to students with mild behavior problems (Witt, Martens, & Elliott, 1984).
- Positive interventions (less aversive) are viewed as more acceptable than negative (punishing) interventions (Witt, Elliott, & Martens, 1984).
- Complex treatments (token economy and time out) are more acceptable if the students have severe behavior problems, and less complex treatments (praise and ignoring) are more acceptable for mild behaviors (Elliott et al., 1984).

By choosing interventions that are more acceptable to teachers, who perhaps are most often the interventionists of behavior plans, teams can increase the probability that interventions will be implemented with accuracy and maintained over time (Reimers, Wacker, & Koeppl, 1987). Interventions that are positive require little time to implement, are implemented in the classroom, and involve the teacher as the change agent are more likely to be accepted. Teams should also be aware of the possible need to directly recruit teachers with more experience into the intervention process and to emphasize the necessity of directly intervening with mild behavior problems.

In addition to considering resource-related variables, such as those associated with treatment acceptability, teams must also consider behavior-related variables when choosing interventions. Behavior-related variables are those that are associated with the function of the behavior and the types of interventions that would address the identified functions. As was previously discussed, the purpose of behavior can be to attain positive, negative, or autonomic reinforcement or some combination of these. In Table 1, examples of targeted intervention activities based on the function of the behavior are provided. Although the table is not meant to provide an exhaustive list of possible interventions, it does provide several standards for positively addressing the functions of behaviors.

In general, when choosing intervention activities, teams should consider ways to reinforce the occurrence or nonoccurrence of the behavior (depending on the goal) and to replace undesired behavior with a more appropriate response. Replacement behaviors are those socially acceptable behaviors that would serve the same function and communicative means as an inappropriate, targeted response (White & Haring, 1980). When choosing replacement behaviors, it is important to ensure that the student knows how to perform the behavior and that the response is adaptable to most situations.

Another point of deliberation for the team in choosing an intervention is the type of treatment that will address the problem behavior. Nelson et al. (1998) suggest four categories of behavioral interventions and supports that should be considered when developing a behavioral intervention plan: (a) ecological factors, (b) longitudinal programming, (c) focused interventions, and (d) responses to

TABLE 1: Examples of Targeted Intervention Activities Based on the Function of the Behavior

Function	Desired Outcome	Examples of Targeted Intervention Activities
Positive reinforcement	Access to desired objects, activities, attention	• Reinforce increased time engaged with non-preferred object, activity, person • Teach and/or strengthen replacement behavior for gaining access to preferred object, activity, person in socially acceptable manner, at appropriate times • Hold preferred objects, activities, attention back as reinforcement for meeting behavioral expectations
Negative reinforcement	Escape from or avoidance of undesirable tasks, activities, social situations	• Reinforce time engaged in undesirable tasks, activities, social situations • Teach and/or strengthen replacement behavior for gaining permission to leave undesirable tasks, activities, social situations in socially acceptable manner, at appropriate times
Autonomic reinforcement	Sensory feedback or self-stimulation	• Reinforce time not engaged in sensory feedback or self-stimulation • Teach and/or strengthen replacement behavior for gaining sensory feedback or stimulation through socially acceptable means, at appropriate times • Reinforce specific competing behaviors
Combination of functions		• Address each desired outcome through a combination of interventions

target behaviors. Examples of these are presented in Table 2. The goal of interventions designed to address ecological factors is to modify the environment to reduce the probability that the target behavior will occur. A major consideration in this area is to match the physical environment and the demands of that environment better to the needs and characteristics of the learner.

Longitudinal programming addresses the skills and competencies needed in order for the student to function successfully by building necessary prerequisite skills (Nelson et al., 1998). Interventions related to the provision of services as well as those related to skill development are included. The third category of behavioral intervention and support, focused interventions, centers on replacing the target behavior with an adaptive skill or socially appropriate behavior. Finally, responses to target behaviors include situational management techniques, such as group contingencies or planned ignoring, that help reduce the teacher's response to the target behavior.

Consideration of resource- and behavior-related variables should help focus the team on specific interventions to address problem behavior. Once these have been delineated, the final consideration of a specific intervention must be on the intervention's effectiveness. Although the research is replete with interventions that have proven effective in specific studies (see Dunlap & Childs, 1996), the field of special education has yet to arrive at a global method for evaluating interventions in terms of their efficacy (Tankersley, Landrum, & Cook, 1999). However, several researchers have begun to address this need by comparing the efficacy of specific interventions. For example, using a meta-analysis technique, Forness, Kavale, Blum, and Lloyd (1997) rated interventions (academic as well as behavioral) based on calculated effect sizes from numerous research studies that investigated the effectiveness of specific interventions. Their results identified interventions that work (e.g., direct instruction, behavior modification, cognitive behavior modification), interventions that show promise (e.g., peer tutoring, reduced class size), and interventions that do not work (e.g., social skills training, modality instruction). Studies that synthesize the results of research investigations will aid team members in identifying effective interventions.

Interventions can be evaluated also on their incorporation of specific elements known to enhance outcomes. Lentz, Allen, and Ehrhardt (1996), for example, advocate designing interventions based on specific principles that enhance effectiveness, including (a) selecting empirically validated or socially significant target behaviors and outcome goals, (b) fitting the intervention into the existing ecologies, (c), ensuring that the environment is conducive to supporting new, acceptable behaviors, (d) providing for continued assistance, and (e) incorporating progress monitoring and data-based decision-making techniques into the intervention process. These elements bring together the sound technical components of effective interventions with consideration of the classroom environment and its influences to create an intervention "package." Several of these elements are discussed in more depth in the following sections.

TABLE 2: **Examples of Behavioral Interventions and Supports**

Category	Examples of Behavioral Interventions and Supports
Ecological factors	• Physical arrangements • Orderliness of room • Positioning of student seating • Adjustment in academic assignments • Clear expectations • Effective monitoring
Longitudinal programming	• Social skills training • Social problem solving • Anger management/conflict resolution • Academic skill development • Counseling services • Medications • Wrap-around services
Focused interventions	• Differential reinforcement procedures • Reinforcement program • Behavioral contract • Self-management
Response(s) to target behavior(s)	• Response cost • Time out • Signal interference cueing • Planned ignoring • Group contingencies

Considerations for Implementing Behavior Intervention Plans

After choosing the interventions to employ, teams must consider how to implement the intervention, who can assist in the implementation, techniques for teaching the intervention to the student, and how to program for the generalization of effects. In the following paragraphs, each of these considerations will be discussed.

Methods of intervention implementation are typically outlined in the literature. The extent to which the intervention methods are followed accurately and consistently during implementation is described as procedural reliability (Billingsley, White, & Munson, 1980) or treatment integrity (Watson, Sterling, & McDade, 1997). Following intervention procedures reliably is important to the efficacy of the intervention. Sugai and Tindal (1993) suggest the following guidelines for delineating the requirements of the intervention in order to implement it accurately: (a) task analyze the intervention into its main procedural steps, (b) identify major decisions that need to be made when implementing the intervention (e.g., What will the interventionist do when the undesired behavior occurs?), and (c) develop a visual display of the intervention procedure (e.g., flow chart, lesson plan, checklist). Teams should strive to enhance the likelihood that interventions are conducted correctly by (a) having more experienced team members assist in training interventionists who are instituting the procedures the first time, (b) monitoring the implementation procedures for accuracy and providing informative positive and corrective feedback, and (c) piloting the intervention in short periods of time before gradually increasing the implementation time (e.g., Sugai & Tindal, 1993; Watson et al., 1997).

When instituting the behavioral intervention, team members should also identify natural supports in the environment that may enhance the implementation of the procedures. Parents, peers, and other professionals within and outside the school may be able to contribute significantly to the implementation of intervention procedures. Parents, for example, may provide opportunities for reinforcement of behaviors that are beyond the scope of school personnel (see Sheridan, Cowan, and Eagle, this volume, for a thorough discussion of parental participation and techniques for working with parents to solve problems). It is important also to note that IDEA 97 requires that general education teachers participate in the determination of appropriate behavioral interventions and strategies. When planning the intervention, the roles of support persons, such as general education teachers, should be delineated and taught to ensure procedural reliability.

Another key factor for implementing the intervention is directly teaching the intervention procedures to the student. Walker et al. (1995) identify eight instructional steps for teaching adaptive behavior: (a) specify the desired behaviors, (b) discuss the goals that provide direction for the behavioral expectation, (c) frequently remind students of behavioral expectations, (d) identify reinforcement procedures and contingencies, (e) plan and institute a strategy for correcting problem behavior promptly, (f) provide corrective and reinforcing feedback on student performance regularly, and (g) develop and implement regular monitoring procedures.

A final consideration in implementing behavioral interventions is to move the intervention toward achieving generalized responding. Perhaps one of the most challenging aspects of instituting behavioral interventions is to ensure that the acceptable behavioral response is demonstrated in a variety of settings, at different times, and in the presence of varying stimuli (Alberto & Troutman, 1999). Indeed, without a generalized response pattern, the acceptable behavior is not functional. For students to achieve generalized responding, the team must actively plan for generalization. In a seminal work, Stokes and Baer (1977) reviewed the literature on generalization and categorized the techniques for programming for generalization. Such techniques include sequentially modifying all settings in which the behavior should occur, introducing natural contingencies into the intervention, and training students using many differing examples.

Considerations for Monitoring and Evaluating Behavioral Intervention Plans

With the details of the intervention and its implementation determined, teams must consider how to monitor and evaluate the effects of the behavioral intervention plan. The first step in monitoring and evaluating the effects of the plan involves establishing criteria by which the team can judge the level of student behavior. Baseline data, collected during the functional behavioral assessment, can provide a beginning level of behavior against which to evaluate later performance. The team may determine, for example, that an increase of a certain number of behavioral displays per observation for a set amount of time would indicate success of the intervention. Another criterion that might be useful is a social comparison of the target behavior with the demonstrated behavior of peers in the classroom. If the target behavior increases to the level of the behavior demonstrated by a peer for whom the behavior is not a problem, then the intervention would be judged as successful. For example, if a typical peer were on task 45% of the intervals during which data were collected, then when the target student increases on task behavior to 45% of the intervals, the intervention would be deemed successful.

Regardless of the criteria that will be employed to determine effectiveness, data must be collected and analyzed throughout the intervention to determine the rate of progress and when the criteria are met. Although a discussion of the various types of data collection procedures are beyond the scope of this chapter (see Alberto & Troutman, 1999, for a complete discussion), it is important that a professional familiar with the methods, advantages, and limitations of each procedure work with the team in determining appropriate procedures for data collection. Monitoring that uses data collected frequently and consistently (some authorities suggest collecting data at least every 2 or 3 days) can be used to create visual representations, such as graphs, of the progress. The current level of functioning of the target behavior can be compared to the level during the baseline condition, prior to beginning the intervention. Such graphic representation is easily interpreted and communicates the effectiveness of the intervention to all members of the team (Alberto & Troutman, 1999).

In addition to identifying progress and determining when criteria are met, monitoring data also can indicate when an intervention is not successful (Alberto & Troutman, 1999). Modification of behavioral intervention plans should occur whenever the intervention is not meeting expectations of change at an appropriate rate, as determined by the team. Other circumstances in which behavioral intervention plans should be modified include (a) when the student has reached his or her criteria level of performance or (b) when the situation has changed (e.g., the behavior is no longer relevant, the interventionists or settings have changed, the priority for addressing the targeted behavior has changed). Behavioral intervention plans should be reviewed, reassessed, and modified within the annual timelines prescribed by IDEA 97. However, it is important to note that the behavioral intervention plan may be reviewed, reassessed, and modified whenever any member of the team believes it is necessary.

BEST PRACTICE STRATEGIES FOR IMPLEMENTING BEHAVIORAL INTERVENTION PLANS

Perhaps the major concern with behavioral intervention plans is creating the documentation that will allow teams to identify goals and objectives, describe interventions and procedures, and track progress in meaningful ways. There are two considerations associated with documenting the plans. First, behavioral intervention plans must be legally defensible. Second, they must be useful to the team. In this section, components of legally defensible behavioral intervention plans are outlined and then other information that would help make those documents most useable to teams are described.

Legally Defensible Behavioral Intervention Plans

IDEA 97 does not go into depth or provide specificity regarding what information must be included in a behavioral intervention plan. Assumptions, however, can be made regarding content based on the requirements for IEPs. Although several requirements of IEPs are not applicable (e.g., statements regarding academic participation in general education settings, statewide or districtwide assessment, transition services), most of the requirements are appropriate to include in developing behavioral intervention plans. Behavioral intervention plans should include the following components that are required in IEPs:

* A statement of present level of performance
* A statement of measurable annual goals and short-term objectives
* A statement of the aids and services to be provided and a statement of program modifications or supports
* The projected date for beginning services and modifications and the anticipated frequency, location, and duration of those services
* How the student's progress toward the goals will be measured, how the child's parents will be informed of their child's progress toward the annual goals and the extent to which that progress is sufficient to enable the child to meet the goals by the end of the year

In addition to these components, Mathur, Nelson, and Roberts (1999) contend that legally defensible behavioral intervention plans must also

* Be based on the results of the functional behavioral assessment
* Include targeted behaviors
* Be included in the IEP goals
* Identify replacement behaviors
* Identify positive and negative consequences
* Detail data collection procedures
* Indicate review dates

In general, the components identified for IEPs address the global identification of goals and services, while the components identified by Mathur et al. (1999) address more specific information surrounding the intervention. In the following sections, these two lists of components are combined to describe the contents of what should be legally defensible behavioral intervention plans. In Figure 1 on page 256 a sample behavioral intervention plan that includes the components listed here is presented. It is important to note, however, that *assumptions* regarding what would be legally defensible at this time are presented and that state and local educational authorities may require further information.

Levels of Performance, Goals, and Objectives

A statement of present level of performance should be created from the data collected during the functional behavioral assessment procedures. The results from indirect assessments (i.e., interviews with significant others, self-reports of the students, and behavioral scales and questionnaires) can provide qualitative overviews of the patterns of behavior as well as descriptions of the behavior and events that are

FIGURE 1: Sample Behavioral Intervention Plan

Student Name:		Phone:	
Address:		Age:	Grade:
Parents' Names:	Emergency Contact:		
Team Members and Roles:			
Annual Goal:			

Objectives	Present Level of Performance	Intervention Techniques and/or Program Modifications	Service Provision	Progress Monitoring	Review Procedures
Objective 1:	Statement of present level of performance	Intervention techniques:	Beginning date of services:	Progress data collection procedures:	Date of review:
					Methods of parental notifications:
			Frequency:	Frequency:	
		Replacement behavior		Intervention implementation data collection procedures:	Statement of progress:
			Location(s):		
Target behavior addressed:	Based on data collected through the following procedures:	Positive consequence:			
		Negative consequence			
			Duration:	Frequency:	

related to the behavior. Results from direct observation assessments provide a quantifiable account of the behavior in different situations. These results also allow for confirmation of antecedents and consequences of the behavior. Taken together, the results from the indirect and direct assessments of the functional behavioral assessment assist teams in identifying target behaviors.

The annual goals and short-term objectives should directly relate to the present level of performance of those target behaviors and provide direction for the teams in creating the remainder of the behavioral intervention plans. Therefore, the annual goals and objectives are built on the results of the functional behavioral assessment, a recommendation of Mathur et al. (1999). The annual goals and objectives should then be incorporated into the IEP. It is important to note that several objectives may be needed to reach the annual goal and that for many students several annual goals may be needed. The sample behavioral intervention plan shown in Figure 1 may be modified to accommodate multiple objectives and goals.

Intervention Techniques and Program Modifications

The intervention techniques and program modifications that will be instituted to address the objective should be identified in a way that is understandable to all team members (Alberto & Troutman, 1999). It may be insufficient to simply list positive reinforcement as an intervention technique without describing the context in which reinforcement will be delivered (e.g., math and science classes), by whom (e.g., math and science teachers), and in what form (e.g., 2 tokens for 80% accuracy on completed work within time limit that can be redeemed in study hall for computer lab time when 20 tokens have been accumulated). In addition to describing the intervention, the team should also identify replacement behaviors that would serve the same function as the inappropriate behavior of concern and what positive and negative consequences can be anticipated as a result of the intervention. This information should help guide the team in identifying the best intervention plans to address the problem behavior.

Service Provision

After delineating the intervention techniques, the team must identify methods of service delivery in the behavioral intervention plans. Teams must decide when the interventions will begin, the frequency (e.g., amount of time per day or week) with which the intervention will occur, the locations or settings in which the interventions will take place, and the length of time the intervention contingencies will be in place. This section may state, for example, that beginning October 17, the intervention will occur each day for 15 minutes (frequency) during math and reading periods (location) for 20 days (length of time).

Progress Monitoring

Mathur et al. (1999) suggest that the behavioral intervention plan include information about two types of data collection. First, data should be collected to assess student progress in attaining objectives and goals. Methods of data collection procedures for monitoring student progress should be delineated, together with the frequency with which those procedures will be employed (see Alberto & Troutman, 1999, for a discussion of data collection techniques). In Figure 2 a sample data collection behavior recording form for collecting event, permanent product, duration, or interval data is provided. To illustrate how data may be collected to assess student progress, the team may decide that time on task will be monitored during independent work in the targeted classrooms 3 days per week for 15 minutes per day using an 15 second momentary time sampling interval recording technique. The results of student progress on targeted behaviors can be graphed daily so that change over time is easily noted.

Second, Mathur et al. (1999) suggest collecting data to assess the fidelity of intervention implementation procedures. Periodic monitoring during the course of intervention can provide information regarding the extent to which the intervention is being implemented as prescribed. Structured observations of the intervention in which the intervention components are delineated and implementation occurrence is rated can help identify the need for additional support (Telzrow, 1995). An example of an intervention implementation observation tool is provided in Figure 3 on page 260. This observation tool allows the incorporation of specific components of the intervention to be defined and assessed. Such a tool would also allow the interventionist to self-monitor the treatment implementation (Telzrow, 1995). Information about how and when these data will be collected should be included in the progress monitoring section of the behavioral intervention plan.

Review Procedures

The final section of the behavioral intervention plan relates to reviewing the plan. A date for formally reviewing the plan should be set and methods for notifying parents should be described. In addition, it is important to include a statement of progress toward the annual goal. Progress toward each objective identified for accomplishing the annual goal may occur at different rates, so a statement regarding each objective will allow teams to identify progress on some objectives and perhaps the need to sustain or redirect effort on others.

FIGURE 2: Sample Data Collection Behavior Recording Form

Student:	Observer:
Classroom:	Teacher:

Target Behavior:

Behavior Definition:

Description of Setting (e.g., instructional grouping, class activity, task requirements):

Start Time:	End Time:	Date:

Type of Data Collection:
- ☐ Event or Permanent Product
- ☐ Duration
- ☐ Interval (Partial, Whole, Momentary Time Sampling)

Record behavior using section below that corresponds to the recording technique used.

Event: Mark a tally for each opportunity for the behavior to occur (if applicable) and for each behavior observed.

Permanent Product: Indicate total number of opportunities and number of correct responses

Number of Opportunities	Number of Behaviors Observed

number of behaviors observed / number of opportunities x 100 = % of behavior occurrence _____

number of behaviors observed / number of minutes of observation x 100 = rate of behavior occurrence _____

Duration: Record the duration of each behavioral event in the boxes.

total duration _____ total number of episodes _____

total duration/total number of episodes = average time per episode _____

total duration / number of minutes of observation x 100 = % of time engaged in behavior _____

Interval:
- ☐ Partial: record a + in each interval in which the behavior occurs at least once
- ☐ Whole: record a + in each interval in which the behavior occurs for the entire interval
- ☐ Momentary time sampling: record a + in each interval in which the behavior occurs at the end of the interval

*Record a − in any interval in which the behavior does not occur

Interval Size: _____ seconds

number of intervals in which behavior recorded / total number of intervals x 100 = % of intervals _____

FIGURE 3: Sample Implementation Evaluation Tool

Date:					
Teacher:	Observer:				
Student:	Classroom:				
Target Behavior:	Intervention:				
Rate each item on the following scale: 1 = very good 2 = good 3 = needs improvement NO = no opportunity to observe NA = not applicable to this intervention					
Materials available.	1	2	3	NO	NA
Student seems to understand procedure.	1	2	3	NO	NA
Student prompted to use the intervention.	1	2	3	NO	NA
Specific components of the intervention addressed:					
1.	1	2	3	NO	NA
2.	1	2	3	NO	NA
3.	1	2	3	NO	NA
4.	1	2	3	NO	NA
5.	1	2	3	NO	NA
6.	1	2	3	NO	NA
7.	1	2	3	NO	NA
8.	1	2	3	NO	NA
Reinforcement available in the environment.	1	2	3	NO	
Inappropriate behaviors addressed quickly and effectively.	1	2	3	NO	
Data collected and graphed.	1	2	3	NO	
Suggestions for improving fidelity of intervention implementation:					
Date of next intervention implementation evaluation:					

Other Useful Information

Including the contents described in the preceding sections when creating behavioral intervention plans allows teams to build legally defensible plans. However, other information also may be helpful in operationalizing the behavioral intervention plans. Specifically, it may be important to delineate further information about how to implement the intervention.

The behavioral intervention plan presented here is based on the information needed to communicate a general plan for addressing behavioral problems. Although the content is informative, it does not typically provide sufficient details for implementing the intervention in a consistent fashion. To communicate such a level of specificity, an intervention implementation plan should be included with the behavioral intervention plan. In Figure 4 on page 262 a sample intervention implementation plan that includes the necessary steps and procedures for carrying out a proposed intervention is presented.

The purpose of the intervention implementation plan is to provide a detailed description of what should occur when instituting the intervention. Many of the considerations outlined in the first section of this chapter were incorporated in developing the implementation plan. In the following sections, the components of the intervention implementation plan are described.

First, the intervention should be task analyzed and broken down into specific steps (Sugai & Tindal, 1993). The steps should identify what the interventionist must do to prepare for and institute the strategy. For example, the steps for implementing a token economy to increase a specific behavior might include the following steps: (a) define the conditions under which the behavior will be reinforced, (b) identify objects or symbols that will serve as the token, (c) create or obtain tokens if necessary, (d) develop a system for storing or recording tokens, (e) select backup reinforcers to be purchased with tokens, (f) obtain backup reinforcers, (g) decide on an exchange rate for purchasing backup reinforcers, and (h) schedule times during which tokens can be exchanged for backup reinforcers (Alberto & Troutman, 1999).

After outlining the steps for implementing the intervention, the team should list any materials that are needed for instituting the intervention or data collection procedures. In the example of the token economy, items such as recording sheets (for data collection), poker chips (to serve as tokens), and gum, puzzles, and books (to serve as backup reinforcers) might be included. Next, supports needed for implementing the intervention should be identified. In particular, roles and responsibilities of team members and others involved in the intervention process should be specified. For example, a backup reinforcer that may be purchased in a token system could be lunch with a peer. Funds may be requested to obtain backup reinforcers. The team members responsible for instituting these supports should be identified.

FIGURE 4: **Sample Intervention Implementation Plan**

Student Name:			Phone:	
Address:			Age:	Grade:
Parents' Names:		Emergency Contact:		
Team Members and Roles:				
Annual Goal Addressed Through this Plan:				
Objective (and Target Behavior[s]) Addressed Through this Plan:				
Intervention Strategy:	Beginning Date:	Where Implemented:	Frequency of Intervention:	Primary Interventionist:
Steps for implementing intervention strategy:	Materials Needed for implementing intervention:	Supports needed for implementing intervention:	Describe procedures for teaching the intervention procedures to the student	Describe procedures for programming for generalization:
1.	1.	1.		
2.	2.	2.		
3.	3.	3.	Describe procedures for addressing inappropriate behaviors:	Describe methods for evaluating student progress:
4.	4.	4.		
5.	5.	5.		

Finally, procedures for teaching the intervention to the student, addressing inappropriate behavior, programming for generalization, and evaluating student progress should also be explained (e.g., Sugai & Tindal, 1993; Walker et al., 1995). Teaching the intervention to the student entails elements of effective teaching, such as direct instruction in performing the appropriate replacement behavior, modeling examples and nonexamples of the desired behavior, and practice using the desired behavior while providing reinforcement and corrective feedback. In addition to deciding how to teach the intervention to the student, teams should also decide upon a course of action to take should the inappropriate behavior occur so that all members can respond consistently when addressing it. Such courses of action may involve a punishment procedure, such as time out or response cost.

When planning the intervention, teams should also incorporate procedures that will facilitate behavior generalization. Systematically incorporating multiple examples of situations in which the replacement behavior should be used, practicing its use in different settings, and reducing the structure of the intervention while incorporating natural contingencies can increase the probability of skill generalization (see Alberto & Troutman, 1999). Additionally, teams should plan for how they will evaluate student progress using the intervention. This may involve restating the data collection procedures outlined in the BIP.

Detailing procedures regarding teaching the intervention, addressing inappropriate behavior, programming for generalization, and evaluating progress should assist team members in instituting the interventions with integrity. Sugai and Tindal (1993) describe other important reasons for detailing the specifics of intervention implementation. First, specificity assists interventionists to be consistent in their response to the target behavior. For example, identifying the steps for implementing the strategy and describing appropriate responses to inappropriate behaviors can ensure that each interventionist involved with the student is responding in the same fashion. Such consistency can enhance more rapid behavior attainment. Second, students will know what to expect in response to both their appropriate and inappropriate behavior. Third, by specifying the procedures, there is a greater likelihood that the intervention will be instituted accurately, reducing the probability of strengthening inappropriate responses and increasing the probability of strengthening desired replacement behaviors.

PROFESSIONAL DEVELOPMENT IMPLICATIONS OF BEHAVIORAL INTERVENTION PLANS FOR EDUCATORS AND SYSTEMS

The IDEA 97 focus on active and sustained intervention for behavioral difficulties is encouraging. However, implementing the provisions surrounding behavioral intervention plans will be difficult for many educators. General classroom management procedures and specific interventions for addressing problem behavior have consistently been areas of concern for new and veteran teachers throughout the years (e.g., Rickman & Hollowell, 1981; Scales, 1994).

Given the increasing behavioral challenges confronting educators, it is disheartening to consider that the teaching and managing of social behavior is among the skills most lacking in all of education. Indeed, the literature suggests that general education teachers are not trained to teach social skills and manage behavior (see Kauffman & Wong, 1991), and even that teachers of students with emotional and behavioral disorders may lack sufficient training in empirically sound practices (Bullock, Ellis, & Wilson, 1994). For example, although there is some evidence validating teaching strategies designed to improve academic and social skills of students with behavioral problems (see Dunlap & Childs, 1996), there is further evidence that these valid procedures are not routinely implemented in practice (e.g., Meadows, Neel, Scott, & Parker, 1994; Shores, Jack, Gunter, Ellis, DeBriere, & Wehby, 1993). Moreover, many teachers do not even modify their instructional or management techniques when teaching students who have behavioral problems (Meadows et al., 1994).

One reason for this is obvious; teachers report that their preservice education programs did not prepare them well, particularly in the area of behavior management (see Gunter & Denny, 1996). In fact, Jack, Shores, Denny, Gunter, DeBriere, and DePaepe (1996) found that only 5% of the teachers studied credited their university coursework as the source of the management strategies they use. Because most teachers and service providers may not have received adequate training in selecting and implementing behavioral interventions, additional resources must be used to bring these skills to the team members.

IDEA 97 supports the contention that school personnel are not well prepared in management techniques and that developing and implementing behavioral intervention strategies is an area in which many teachers and service providers will need additional preparation. Specifically, the statute requires that "States shall address the needs of in-service and pre-service personnel (including paraprofessionals who provide special education, general education, related services, or early intervention services) as they relate to developing and implementing positive intervention strategies."

To ensure that the new requirements for addressing behavioral problems of students with disabilities are being addressed competently, school districts will need to invest in preparing their teams in several areas. First, team members must be competent in identifying and measuring behavior. This requirement would include procedures associated with functional behavioral assessment (indirect and direct observational assessments) as well as on-going evaluation procedures. Second, team members must be able to relate the function of the behavior to a proposed intervention. The results of the functional behavioral assessment should indicate clear paths for choosing intervention activities and categories, as discussed earlier in the chapter. This would require that teams be familiar and proficient with a variety of behavioral interventions from which to choose in meeting the wide range of behavioral goals and objectives set for their students.

Preparation in these areas will require that many schools and districts target resources toward assisting teams through in-service training, workshops, and consultation. Such programs should be designed to provide teams with the information they need to implement techniques and strategies as well as the ongoing technical assistance they need as they institute the procedures in the classrooms. Moreover, implementing intervention techniques are difficult. They require thorough planning, accuracy and consistency during implementation, and on-going record keeping. If teams are to be successful in planning and implementing behavioral interventions, schools and districts must provide teams opportunities to work together to prepare and time to institute the procedures.

SUMMARY

Learning and behavior are often dichotomized. Yet the influence of each to the other is great; and when teaching students with disabilities, the focus must remain on both domains simultaneously. Although professionals have been addressing the behavioral needs of students with disabilities since the inception of P.L. 94-142, IDEA 97 has now prescribed procedures for addressing behavioral problems of students through the development and institution of behavioral intervention plans. Behavioral intervention plans that incorporate features necessary to be legally defensible as well as specified procedures for implementing strategies should provide teams with a course of action that will facilitate classroom environments that are conducive to learning. As teams seek to design and implement behavioral intervention plans, they must consider resource- and behavior-related variables that contribute to the overall effectiveness of the programs. With the new emphasis on addressing behavior in IDEA 97, there is a new optimism that schools and districts will also begin a new focus on systematically addressing behavior problems of students with disabilities.

REFERENCES

Alberto, P. A., & Troutman, A. C. (1999). *Applied behavior analysis for teachers* (5th ed.). Upper Saddle River, NJ: Prentice-Hall.

Billingsley, F. F., White, O. R., & Munson, R. (1980). Procedural reliability: A rationale and an example. *Behavioral Assessment, 2,* 229–241.

Bullock, L. M., Ellis, L. L., & Wilson, M. J. (1994). Knowledge/skills needed by teachers who work with students with severe emotional/behavior disorders: A revisitation. *Behavioral Disorders, 19,* 108–125.

Carta, J. J., Sideridis, G., Rinkel, P., Guimaraes, S., Greenwood, C., Baggett, K., Peterson, P., Atwater, J., McEvoy, M., & McConnell, S. (1994). Behavioral outcomes of young children prenatally exposed to illicit drugs: Review and analysis of experimental literature. *Topics in Early Childhood Special Education, 14,* 184–216.

Cooper, J. O., Herron, T. E., & Heward, W. L. (1987). *Applied behavior analysis.* Columbus, OH: Merrill.

Dunlap, G., & Childs, K. E. (1996). Intervention research in emotional and behavioral disorders: An analysis of studies from 1980–1993. *Behavioral Disorders, 21,* 125–136.

Elliott, S. N., Witt, J. C., Galvin, G., & Peterson, R. (1984). Acceptability of positive and reductive interventions: Factors that influence teachers' decisions. *Journal of School Psychology, 22,* 353–360.

Epstein, M. H., Matson, J. L., Repp, A., & Helsel, W. J. (1986). Acceptability of treatment alternatives as a function of teacher status and student level. *School Psychology Review, 15,* 84–90.

Forness, S. R., Kavale, K. A., Blum, I. M., & Lloyd, J. W. (1997). What works in special education and related services: Using meta-analysis to guide practice. *Teaching Exceptional Children, 29*(6), 4–9.

Gunter, P. L., & Denny, R. K. (1996). Research issues and needs regarding teachers' use of classroom management strategies. *Behavioral Disorders, 22,* 15–20.

Hall, C. W., & Wahrman, E. (1988). Theoretical orientations and perceived acceptability of intervention strategies applied to acting-out behavior. *Journal of School Psychology, 26,* 195–198.

Individuals with Disabilities Education Act Amendments of 1997, 20 U.S.C. § 1400 *et seq.* (West 1997).

Jack, S. L., Shores, R. E., Denny, R. K., Gunter, P. L., DeBriere, T., & DePaepe, P. (1996). An analysis of the relationship of teachers' reported use of classroom management strategies on types of interactions. *Journal of Behavioral Education, 6,* 67–87.

Kauffman, J. M., & Wong, K. L. H. (1991). Effective teachers of students with behavioral disorders: Are generic teaching skills enough? *Behavioral Disorders, 16,* 225–237.

Lentz, F. E, Jr., Allen, S. J., & Ehrhardt, K. E. (1996). The conceptual elements of strong interventions in school settings. *School Psychology Quarterly, 11,* 118–136.

Lewis, T., Scott, T., & Sugai, G. (1994). The problem behavior questionnaire: A teacher-based instrument to develop functional hypotheses of problem behavior in general education classrooms. *Diagnostique, 19,* 103–115.

Lloyd, J. W., Kauffman, J. M., Landrum, T. J., & Roe, D. L. (1991). Why do teachers refer pupils for special education? An analysis of referral records. *Exceptionality, 2,* 113–126.

Martens, B. K., Peterson, R. L., Witt, J. C., & Cirone, S. (1986). Teacher perceptions of school-based intervention: Ratings of intervention effectiveness, ease of use, and frequency of use. *Exceptional Children, 53,* 213–223.

Martens, B. K., Witt, J. C., Elliott, S, N., Darveaux, D. (1985). Teacher judgements concerning the acceptability of school based interventions. *Professional Psychology: Research and Practice, 16,* 191–198.

Mathur, S. R., Nelson, J. R., & Roberts, M. (1999). *Developing behavioral intervention plans: A decision-making process.* Paper presented at the Annual Convention of the Council for Exceptional Children, Charlotte, NC.

Meadows, N. B., Neel. R. S., Scott, C. M., & Parker, G. (1994). Academic performance, social competence, and mainstream accommodations: A look at mainstreamed and nonmainstreamed students with serious behavioral disorders. *Behavioral Disorders, 19,* 170–180.

Nelson, J. R., Roberts, M. L., & Smith, D. J. (1998). *Conducting functional behavioral assessments.* Longmont, CO: Sopris West.

O'Neill, R., Horner, R., Albin, R., Sprague, J., Storey, K., & Newton, J. S. (1997). *Functional assessment and program development for problem behavior* (2nd Ed.). Pacific Grove, CA: Brooks/Cole.

Patterson, G. R., Reid, J., & Dishion, T. (1992). *A social interactional approach: Antisocial boys.* Eugene, OR: Castalia Press.

Reimers, T. M., Wacker, D. P., & Koeppl, G. (1987). Acceptability of behavioral treatments: A review of the literature. *School Psychology Review, 16,* 212–227.

Rickman, L. W., & Hollowell, J. (1981). Some causes of student teacher failure. *Improving College and University Teaching, 29,* 176–179.

Scales, P. C. (1994). Strengthening middle grade teacher preparation programs. *Middle School Journal, 26,* 59–65.

Shores, R. E., Jack, S. L., Gunter, P. L., Ellis, D. N., DeBriere, T. J., & Wehby, J. H. (1993). Classroom interactions of children with behavior disorders. *Journal of Emotional and Behavioral Disorders, 1,* 27–39.

Soodak, L. C., & Podell, D. M. (1993). Teacher efficacy and student problem as factors in special education referral. *Journal of Special Education, 27,* 66–81.

Stokes, T. F, & Baer, D. M. (1977). An implicit technology of generalization. *Journal of Applied Behavior Analysis, 10,* 349–367.

Sugai, G., Horner, R. H., & Sprague, J. R. (1999). Functional-assessment-based behavior support planning: Research to practice to research. *Behavioral Disorders, 24,* 253–257.

Sugai, G. M., & Tindal, G. A. (1993). *Effective school consultation: An interactive approach.* Pacific Grove, CA: Brooks/Cole.

Tankersley, M., Landrum, T. J., & Cook, B. (1999). *Toward a conceptual model of what works in special education.* Paper presented at the Annual Convention of the Council for Exceptional Children, Charlotte, NC.

Tankersley, M., & Talbott, E. (1992). *Treatment acceptability: A review of student and teacher variables.* Unpublished manuscript, University of Virginia.

Telzrow, C. F. (1995). Best practices in facilitating intervention adherence. In A. Thomas, & J. Grimes (Eds.), *Best practices in school psychology* (pp. 501–510). Washington, DC: National Association of School Psychologists.

Thurlow, M., Christenson, S., & Ysseldyke, J. (1984). *Referral research: An integrative summary of findings.* Research Report No. 141. Minneapolis: University of Minnesota Institute for Research on Learning Disabilities.

Tremblay, R. E., Masse, B., LeBlanc, M., Schwartzman, A. E., & Ledingham, J. E., (1992). Early disruptive behavior, poor school achievement, delinquent behavior, and delinquent personality: Longitudinal analyses. *Journal of Consulting and Clinical Psychology, 60,* 64–72.

Von Brock, M. B., & Elliott, S. N. (1987). The influence of treatment effectiveness information on the acceptability of classroom interventions. *Journal of School Psychology, 25,* 131–144.

Walker, H. M. (1986). The Assessment for Integration into Mainstream Settings (AIMS) assessment system: Rationale, instruments, procedures, and outcomes. *Journal of Clinical Child Psychology, 15,* 55–63.

Walker, H. M., Colvin, G., & Ramsey, E. (1995). *Antisocial behavior in school: Strategies and best practices.* Pacific Grove, CA: Brooks/Cole.

Watson, T. S., Sterling, H. E., & McDade, A. (1997). Demystifying behavioral consultation. *School Psychology Review, 26,* 467–474.

White, O. R., & Haring, N. G. (1980). *Exceptional teaching.* Columbus, OH: Merrill.

Witt, J. C., Elliott, S. N., & Martens, B. K. (1984). Acceptability of behavioral interventions used in classrooms: The influence of teacher time, severity of behavior problem, and type of intervention. *Behavioral Disorders, 10,* 95–104.

Witt, J. C., & Martens, B. K. (1983). Assessing the acceptability of behavioral interventions used in classrooms. *Psychology in the Schools, 20,* 510–517.

Witt, J. C., Martens, B. K., & Elliott, S. N. (1984). Factors affecting teachers' judgements of the acceptability of behavioral interventions: Time involvement, behavior problem severity, type of intervention. *Behavior Therapy, 15,* 204–209.

Witt, J. C., Moe, G., Gutkin, T. T., & Andrews, L. (1984). The effect of saying the same thing in different ways: The problem of language and jargon in school-based consultation. *Journal of School Psychology, 22,* 361–367.

Witt, J. C., & Robbins, J. R. (1985). Acceptability of reductive interventions for the control of inappropriate child behavior. *Journal of Abnormal Child Psychology, 13,* 59–67.

Yell, M. L. (1998). *The law and special education.* Upper Saddle River, NJ: Prentice-Hall.

ANNOTATED BIBLIOGRAPHY

Alberto, P. A., & Troutman, A. C. (1999). *Applied behavior analysis for teachers* (5th ed.). Upper Saddle River, NJ: Prentice-Hall.

This introductory text in applied behavior analysis provides the foundation for behavior management procedures and strategies and describes methods of identifying target behaviors, collecting observation data, and graphing behavioral progress. The text also describes specific positive intervention techniques, such as positive and negative reinforcement, group-oriented contingencies, and self-monitoring. Each technique is described in detail to allow for easy implementation. Methods for conducting functional behavioral assessment and promoting the generalization of behavior change are also provided in practical terms. This market-leading text will provide teams with the answers to many questions as they seek to design, implement, and evaluate behavioral intervention plans.

Nelson, J. R., Roberts, M. L., & Smith, D. J. (1998). *Conducting functional behavioral assessments.* Longmont, CO: Sopris West.

This brief manual will assist teams in conducting functional behavioral assessments that lead to behavioral intervention plans. Although the focus of the manual is on conducting functional behavioral assessments, the step-by-step process introduced will promote the subsequent determination of goals, objectives, and procedures identified for the behavioral intervention plan. The authors present a four-stage model of collaborative problem solving for conducting the functional behavioral assessment that addresses the following questions: (a) What is the problem behavior? (b) What is the function of the problem behaviors and what events are related to them? (c) What should be done to address the problem behaviors (development of the behavioral intervention plan)? (d) Did the behavioral intervention and supports work? In addition, the manual includes evaluation materials to use in the functional behavioral assessment: Interview/Self-Report Form, Observation and Analysis Form, Temporal Analysis and Ranking Form, and Summary Analysis Form.

Sugai, G. M. & Tindal, G. A. (1993). *Effective school consultation: An interactive approach.* Pacific Grove, CA: Brooks/Cole.

This practical text provides teams with strategies they can use when collaborating to plan, implement, and evaluate behavioral and educational programs for students with learning and behavioral difficulties. Although the text is divided into two major parts (one for addressing behavior problems and one for addressing instruction), the section devoted to collaborating to address behavioral problems is highlighted here. The text does not focus on the process of collaboration per se, but emphasizes applying a direct approach to intervention selection and decision making. Practical skills for effective collaboration to address behavior problems are discussed in detail. Included are topics such as (a) how to ask for assistance, (b) how to identify problem behaviors, (c) how to collect useful assessment data, (d) how to choose an appropriate intervention, (e) how to program for the intervention, and (f) how to monitor the effectiveness of the program. In addition, examples of informal information-gathering and decision-making forms to use throughout the processes are provided.

CHAPTER 8

Interim Alternative Educational Settings:
Guidelines for Prevention and Intervention

Cathy F. Telzrow
Kershini Naidu
Kent State University

BACKGROUND/PURPOSE OF INTERIM ALTERNATIVE EDUCATIONAL SETTINGS

For over a decade, concerns about the effects of student behavior on safe schools have dominated educators' discussions about collective bargaining and training priorities, as well as the public's views about education (Bader, 1997; Duke & Jones, 1984; Horner, Sprague, & Sugai, 1996). Although available data suggest that the frequency of major school conduct violations, such as those involving weapons and drugs, occur infrequently (Bowditch, 1993; Conoley & Goldstein, 1997; Goldstein, 1999), public concern about such behavior has remained high for several years. Since 1996, "use of drugs," "fighting/violence/gangs," and "lack of discipline" have ranked among the top problems facing schools on annual public surveys (Rose & Gallup, 1998, 1999; Rose, Gallup, & Elam, 1997).

This rising tide of public and educator concern about safe schools has promulgated a trend toward zero tolerance discipline policies and an escalation of reactive, largely punitive responses within educational systems (Bowditch, 1993; Hyman et al., 1997; Imich, 1994; Skiba & Peterson, 1999). Studies that have examined the prevalence of student conduct violations suggest that as many as 41% of students in urban middle schools may have a disciplinary contact annually, and one-third of these resulted in removal from school (Skiba, Peterson, & Williams, 1997). The most frequently cited reasons for discipline referrals and suspensions were fighting/physical aggression, disobedience/talking back, conduct/use of obscene language, and being late to school or class or leaving without permission (Costenbader & Markson, 1998; Skiba et al., 1997). Infractions with the greatest severity (e.g., weapons possession, vandalism, fire setting) were the least frequently cited reasons for discipline referrals and suspensions (Costenbader & Markson, 1998; Skiba et al., 1997). Disproportionate rates of discipline referrals and suspensions have been reported for African-American and Asian-American students, for males, for low income students, and for those with emotional or behavioral disorders (Brantlinger, 1991; Costenbader & Markson, 1998; Skiba et al., 1997).

During the most recent reauthorization of the Individuals with Disabilities Education Act (IDEA 97) (Individuals with Disabilities Education Act Amendments, 1997), increasing concern about the safety of the nation's schools presented an emotionally charged context for discussions about the rights of students with disabilities to maintain their entitlement to services when they violate school conduct codes (Bader, 1997). Unlike nondisabled students, who are often summarily excluded from educational settings following conduct violations, students with disabilities have been afforded special protections that limit the number and proximity of removals and require schools to continue to provide appropriate special education services (Butera, Klein, McMullen, & Wilson, 1998; Yell, Cline, & Bradley, 1995).

Ironically, this theoretical protection of students with disabilities from school removal may not be consistent with actual practice. It has been reported, for example, that students with emotional or behavioral disorders were disproportionately represented among middle school students who received discipline referrals and were subsequently suspended from school (Skiba et al., 1997). In addition, T. L. Rose (1988) reported that more severe punishment for certain offenses was provided to students with disabilities than to nondisabled students. In their investigation of the characteristics of students who were recommended for school removal, Morrison and D'Incau (1997) reported that 22% of their sample were students receiving special education, representing a disproportionate number relative to the population.

Despite these data, the legal protection afforded to students with disabilities who violate school conduct codes was viewed as a dual standard by many educators and the public, which contributed to a 2-year delay in the IDEA's most recent reauthorization (Bader, 1997). Some groups representing school administrators and other educational professionals challenged these students' entitlement to a free appropriate public education (FAPE) when school conduct codes were violated and the behavior was determined to be unrelated to disability. In contrast, advocacy organizations contended that one of the IDEA's inherent principles, the provision of appropriate special education services to all students with disabilities, must not be compromised because of the growing number and complexity of behavioral needs exhibited by today's youth.

Following a lengthy debate, proponents and opponents of the various discipline requirements outlined in the IDEA amendment drafts reached a compromise in the form of the Interim Alternative Educational Setting (IAES) provision. The intent of this requirement in IDEA 97 is to permit the immediate and unilateral removal of students with disabilities from their current educational placement for a designated period in cases of extreme conduct violations, while simultaneously preserving their entitlement to FAPE through the use of educationally effective interim settings (Bear, 1999).

In this chapter, practical information to assist school-based teams in the immediate implementation of the IAES provision is provided. This includes a review of the circumstances when the IAES may be employed, a description of the required features of these settings, and the provision of a decision tree to guide school-based teams in acting in a manner consistent with IDEA 97. Additionally, effective systemic responses to ameliorate student conduct problems are described. Such methods include the use of multi-system prevention programs and proven professional development strategies. It is hoped that this content will guide educational professionals in their work and improve educational experiences for all students.

CONSIDERATIONS FOR SCHOOL-BASED TEAMS IN IMPLEMENTING IAES

Circumstances When IAES May Be Imposed

IDEA 97 describes two applications of the IAES: (a) circumstances when a change of placement is ordered for 10 days or less (identified in this chapter as "short-term IAES placements"), and (b) occasions when a more protracted removal to an IAES is necessary (referred to as "long-term IAES placements"). A decision tree illustrating key considerations associated with IAES implementation is depicted in Figure 1 (see page 275). When a student with a disability violates the school conduct code, the first consideration relative to IAES is whether the offense involves weapons or drugs. If it does not, then short-term placement in an IAES is possible, because school personnel may exercise their authority to unilaterally move a student with a disability to an IAES for short-term placements (i.e., for periods of fewer than 10 days) for any conduct violation. Furthermore, the federal regulations for IDEA 97 specify that there is no absolute limit on the total number of such short-term placements in an IAES. That is, subsequent 10-day placements are permissible for separate incidents of misconduct so long as FAPE is provided and the proximity and pattern of removals does not constitute a change of placement (Individuals with Disabilities Education Act Regulations, 1999). If the offense does involve weapons or drugs, and the school and parents are unable to agree on a permanent alternative to the current placement, then long-term removal to an IAES (i.e., for 45 days) is possible. Specifically, the statute indicates that long-term placement in an IAES may be initiated by school personnel under two circumstances: (a) when a student with a disability carries a weapon to school or to a school function, or obtains a weapon at school or a school function; and (b) when a student with a disability knowingly possesses or uses illegal drugs or sells or solicits the sale of a controlled substance while at school or a school function. Definitions of key terms related to these violations (e.g., weapon, illegal drug, controlled substance, and substantial evidence) are included in Table 1 on page 276.

The two circumstances when school personnel may order students with disabilities to long-term placement in an IAES over parent objections—those involving weapons or drugs—mirror public concern and political reaction to these conduct violations (Yell et al., 1995). It is estimated that 100,000 students bring a weapon to school each day, and that these include such items as heavy belt buckles, false gold chains, boxcutters, pen guns, ammonia-filled spray bottles, and screwdrivers (Goldstein & Conoley, 1997). Cornell and Loper (1998) reported that approximately 13% of over 11,000 seventh-, ninth-, and eleventh- grade students sampled indicated that they had carried a weapon to school during the past month. The most commonly reported sources for obtaining weapons are a friend (38%) or family member (23%), and over half of students indicate that they carry weapons to school or school functions for protection (Goldstein & Conoley, 1997). Several "vulnerability indicators" that significantly discriminated between groups of less violent and more violent ninth graders have been identified (Kingery, McCoy-Simandle, & Clayton, 1997). These include having seen another student with a weapon at school, having been hit or attacked by another student, or having been touched inappropriately by a student of the opposite sex.

With regard to prevalence of substance use, over 20% of students in the Cornell and Loper (1998) survey reported using drugs or alcohol during the previous 30 days. There is evidence that adolescent substance abuse increased more rapidly in the early 1990s than at any time during the previous 15 years (Johnston, O'Malley, & Bachman, 1995). Furthermore, data suggest that students who are at risk for substance abuse are frequently suspended or expelled from school (Brown & D'Emidio-Caston, 1995). Some evidence suggests that violent behavior and drug use may be related. For example, students who had committed more than five violent acts during the past year were more than 10 times as likely to have used cocaine at least once (Kingery et al., 1997), and a relationship between substance use at school and endorsement of aggressive attitudes has been reported (Cornell & Loper, 1998).

FIGURE 1: Decision Tree Illustrating Implementation of IAES by School Personnel

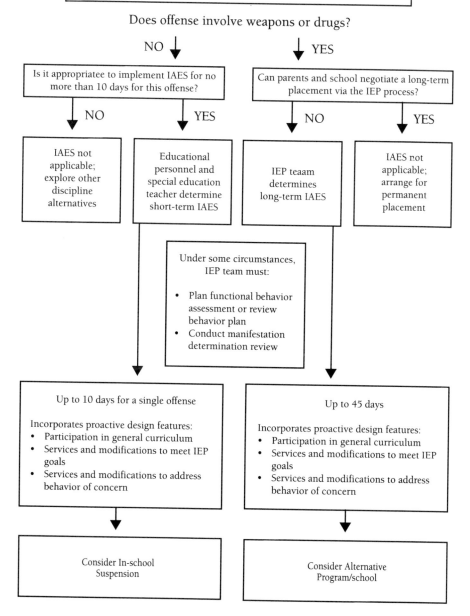

TABLE 1: Definitions of Key Terms Pertaining to IAES

Term	Definition
Weapon	"A weapon, device, instrument, material, or substance, animate or inanimate, that is used for or is readily capable of, causing death or serious bodily injury, except that such term does not include a pocket knife with a blade of less than 2 1/2 inches in length" (Committee on Labor and Human Resources, 1997, p. 34)
Controlled substance	"A drug or other substance identified under schedules I, II, III, IV, or V in section 202 (c) of the Controlled Substances Act" [Section 615(k)(10)(A)]
Illegal drug	"A controlled substance, but does not include a substance that is legally possessed or used under the supervision of a licensed health care professional or that is legally possessed or used under any other authority under that Act or under any other provision of Federal law" [Section 615(k)(10)(D)]
Substantial evidence	"Beyond a preponderance of the evidence" [Section 615(k)(10)(C)]

Selection and Characteristics of IAES Setting

School personnel and the special education teacher may select the IAES for short-term placements. For long-term placements in the IAES, the Individualized Education Program (IEP) team must determine the specific setting (see Figure 1 on page 275). In either situation, the setting must possess three characteristics that are considered central to FAPE. First, the IAES must enable the student with a disability to continue to receive services and modifications to address the goals in the IEP. Second, it must allow the student to continue to progress in the general curriculum, albeit in another setting. Third, the IAES must include services and modifications to address the behavior of concern. A final stipulation pertaining to the IAES provision for long-term placements is that affected students may be served in such settings for a maximum of 45 days at a time. Extensions to the 45-day limit are possible when ordered by an Impartial Hearing Officer (IHO) in response to school officials' contentions that returning the student to the regular placement represents a danger to self or others (Individuals with Disabilities Education Act Regulations, 1999).

Certain of these requirements set the stage for some perplexing challenges for school-based teams. First, it appears that long-term removal to an IAES will occur only in situations when parents and school personnel cannot agree on a permanent placement for a student (see Figure 1 on page 275). However, these same individuals, as members of the IEP team, are required to come together to determine the long-term IAES. It is possible that the specific characteristics of the interim setting (e.g., time-limited, educative orientation) may contribute to a negotiated agreement about an IAES even though the parents and the district are unable to agree on a permanent placement. Nevertheless, this requirement for IEP team designation of the interim setting may result in a continuing impasse.

Second, the statute clearly intends for the IAES to provide an educative function as opposed to serving as a holding place until a more permanent setting can be negotiated (Telzrow, 1999a). However, when students are removed from school as a result of conduct violations, school districts have tended to employ alternative settings (e.g., home-bound instruction) that are unlikely to meet the three conditions outlined for the IAES (Butera et al., 1998; Telzrow, in press). Finally, it is unclear how the IAES may differ from a permanent placement for affected students. This is particularly relevant when one considers the possibility that multiple 45-day extensions of the IAES may result in "interim" placements that extend for a full semester or even an entire school year.

Models of Practice to Inform IAES Provision

Although the requirement in the statute for provision of an IAES to students with disabilities under certain conditions is relatively recent, promising models of practice are available that may help to inform school-based teams' implementation of this provision. Three broad types of approaches that appear to have some applicability to the IAES requirement are described in the literature. These include preventive approaches, in-school suspension programs, and alternative programs or schools. Each of these approaches is described briefly in this section of the chapter. The Best Practices section contains further detail about these three models as they could be used to respond to the IAES provision in IDEA 97.

Preventive Programs

As conceptualized in this chapter, preventive approaches foster conditions to prevent or minimize student misconduct, thus reducing or eliminating the need to use Interim Alternative Educational Settings. The National Longitudinal Study on Adolescent Health reported that a low degree of "school connectedness" is a significant predictor of violent behavior and substance use in grades 7–8 and 9–12 (Resnick et al., 1997). Similarly, personal-social vulnerabilities—including not feeling close to others in school or having a history of consistent problems with teachers—have been identified as predictors of weapons possession at school (Kingery, Coggeshall, & Alford, 1998), and students' weapon use is most frequently attributed to a sense of being disrespected by peers or school personnel (Goldstein & Conoley, 1997). As Morrison, Furlong, and Morrison (1994) have stated, "weapons on campus are not the problem, they are a glaring, powerful symptom of a fundamental interpersonal and structural weakness in the school community" (p. 252).

Experts have identified a number of factors in unsafe schools that contribute to a climate of disconnection with the system and perpetuate student alienation. These include an absence of caring but firm discipline procedures; insensitivity to student diversity; a permissive attitude toward low levels of harassment, such as bullying; and teacher and peer rejection of students who demonstrate at-risk behaviors (Batsche & Knoff, 1994; Conoley & Goldstein, 1997; Hyman et al., 1997; Resnick et al., 1997; Walker & Gresham, 1997). In contrast to such educational environments, schools that have an established track record for safety demonstrate a strong degree of student connection to the educational environment and the process of schooling. Such positive affiliations have been achieved in settings where there are explicit and ambitious expectations for student achievement and behavior and high levels of involvement and participation in the schooling process by students and their parents (Morrison et al., 1994). As Walker and Gresham (1997) have asserted, "ultimately, students need to collectively care about and bond with their school and learn to respect the rights and well-being of other students and staff." (p. 201). Prevention models are designed to promote such conditions.

Although it has been argued that schools have historically lagged behind other social institutions in addressing concerns about youth violence (e.g., Walker et al., 1996), experts are increasingly targeting schools as a critical player in preventive approaches designed to promote safe and drug-free schools (Consortium on the School-Based Promotion of Social Competence, 1994; Gottfredson, 1997; Morrison et al., 1994; Morrison, Furlong, & Morrison, 1997). Depending on the age group and population targeted, such programs may be characterized by primary, secondary, or tertiary prevention methods. For example, Walker, Colvin, and Ramsey (1995) describe a developmental model that progresses from preventive approaches for children in prekindergarten through grade three, remediation in the intermediate grades, ameliorative strategies in grades seven and eight, and accommodation during the high school period. Further discussion about the role of preventive programs in the implementation of the IAES provision is contained the Best Practices section of this chapter.

In-School Suspension Programs

A second approach with relevance for the development of IAES is in-school suspension (ISS). ISS is historically used for students who otherwise would be removed from school following conduct violations. ISS has been described as including three types of programs: punitive programs, therapeutic programs, and academic programs (Garibaldi, 1995; Sheets, 1996; Short, Short, & Blanton, 1994). Punitive ISS programs are characterized by a strict, coercive approach where there is a high degree of adult control and a low degree of student independence or freedom of movement. Therapeutic ISS programs incorporate counseling or other behavior change techniques and are designed to address skill or performance deficiencies in the behavioral area, including social skills deficits or weaknesses in study skills and time management. Academically oriented ISS programs employ individual or small group tutoring and academic goal setting to remediate deficiencies in basic academic areas.

Stage (1997) compared the effectiveness of three different ISS interventions for students with behavioral disorders who were receiving special education in a residential facility. He found no differences in classroom disruptive behavior following students' removal to time-out, time-out plus academic, or problem-solving ISS conditions. However, Stage reported that these results could have been attributed to an absence of necessary reinforcement in the time-in condition (e.g., Shriver & Allen, 1996) or to high levels of teacher disapproval in the classroom, which produced a setting event for student misbehavior to escape to ISS (e.g., Shores, Gunter, & Jack, 1993; Skiba et al., 1997). Although the efficacy of ISS for producing behavior change within permanent settings has not been demonstrated, such programs may meet the IAES requirements outlined in IDEA 97 if they incorporate therapeutic or academic interventions. Further information about potentially effective ISS models is contained in the Best Practices section of this chapter.

Alternative Programs/Schools

A third service delivery model that may have relevance for school districts' implementation of the IAES provision is alternative programs or schools. Three categories of such programs have been described: schools of choice, such as magnet or theme schools; "last chance" programs or schools, where students are assigned for the purpose of modifying their behavior; and programs or schools that have a rehabilitative or remedial emphasis, and target academic deficits, social-emotional deficits, or both (Raywid, 1995). Raywid (1994) asserts that last chance schools do not produce positive change for students unless these also incorporate academic or behavioral supports that are consistent with those in the remedial model. Further information about the features of alternative programs or schools operated within the context of the IAES provision is included in the Best Practices section of this chapter.

BEST PRACTICES FOR IMPLEMENTING THE IAES PROVISION

One response to the IAES provision in IDEA 97 involves implementation of reactive approaches such as the development of alternative schools or programs that comply with the service delivery requirements outlined above. However, the authors argue that more lasting solutions to concerns about student conduct will emerge from a multi-level response. School personnel must provide appropriately for individual student needs as they emerge, as well as invest in the development of long-term preventive systems (Kingery et al., 1998). This section outlines a multi-step, sequential process that reflects such an approach.

Step 1: Employ Decision Tree to Determine Appropriateness of Employing IAES Provision

The first consideration for school-based teams when students with disabilities violate the school conduct code is to determine whether or not the IAES provision applies. As illustrated in Figure 1 (page 275), removal of a student to an IAES by school personnel would be appropriate under two circumstances. The first would occur (a) when the infraction does not involve weapons or drugs and (b) when placement in an IAES rather than the use of suspension or another discipline alternative is deemed to be appropriate. In such instances the student may be served in the IAES for no more than 10 days at a time (short-term placement). The second scenario when school personnel may impose the IAES is one (a) where the offense involves weapons or drugs and (b) where agreement between school officials and the student's parents about a permanent placement cannot be negotiated. In this circumstance, school personnel may unilaterally order a change in placement over parent objections for a period of up to 45 days (long-term placement). Long-term removal to an IAES also may be ordered by an IHO for other conduct violations if, after considering the appropriateness of the current setting and its accommodations to minimize risk, as well as the characteristics of the proposed IAES, there is *substantial evidence* that the current setting is *substantially likely* to result in injury to the student or to others. Because school personnel would not be involved in decisions regarding the IAES in such instances, IHO removals are not addressed in this chapter.

Step 2: Follow Prescribed Procedures to Identify Parties Who Will Determine IAES

For short-term placement in an IAES, school personnel and the special education teacher may determine the IAES without involving the parent or other members of the IEP team (Individuals with Disabilities Education Act Regulations, 1999). For long-term IAES placements, decisions about the specific setting must be made by the IEP team rather than exclusively by school personnel. For all long-term placements, and for any short-term placements that exceed 10 days in a school year or constitute a change in placement, IDEA 97 also requires the IEP team to (a) plan a functional behavioral assessment, if one had not been conducted previously; (b) review the student's behavior plan, if one exists; and (c) conduct a manifestation determination review (Gable, Quinn, Rutherford, & Howell, 1998). The reader is referred to relevant chapters in this volume for further discussion of these requirements.

In cases involving either short-term or long-term IAES placements, individual planning is essential because of evidence of significant variability within populations of students who violate school conduct codes. For example, a recent study of students with recurrent suspensions indicated that this is a heterogeneous group, with 22% demonstrating social skills deficits, 22% academic deficits, 30% a combination of both academic and social skills deficits, and 26% neither of these (Morgan-D'Atrio, Northup, LaFleur, & Spera, 1996). These authors argue, as have others (e.g., Curwin & Mendler, 1999; Gable et al., 1998), that matching alternatives to suspension to identified student needs may enhance the treatment benefits of such approaches.

Step 3: Select Short- or Long-term Settings That Have Proactive Design Characteristics

Regardless of whether the infraction results in a short-term placement or a 45-day placement in the IAES, specific educative features must be incorporated. Specifically, the setting must enable the student to receive services and modifications on the IEP and to progress in the general curriculum, as well as provide interventions to address the behavior of concern. Approaches that school-based teams might consider for addressing these required elements are described in the following sections.

Short-Term Settings

In-school suspension programs that incorporate therapeutic and academic interventions may be appropriate for short-term IAES placements (Center & McKittrick, 1987; Yell et al., 1995). In their review of in-school suspension programs in 10 school districts, Chobot and Garibaldi (1982) concluded that those with the best record of reducing disciplinary referrals are full time, extend for brief periods (e.g., no more than 10 days), and separate students from their peers. ISS approaches that appear to be most consistent with the IAES requirements employ strategies to enhance student skills and behavior; possess adequate program supports, including staffing; and incorporate effective planning and evaluation.

Academic and behavioral supports. The literature consistently identifies ISS programs that incorporate behavioral or academic interventions as superior to coercive or punitive programs (e.g., Sheets, 1996; Sullivan, 1989). Furthermore, such elements are essential for ISS programs to comply with the proactive design features for IAES placements that are outlined in IDEA 97. Student Assignment Centers (SAC) represent a model of ISS that provides academic and behavioral change strategies to enhance motivation, organization, and goal setting for middle school students (Opuni, Tollis, Sanchez, & Gonzalez, 1991). Data reported for the 1990–1991 school year indicated that three-quarters of the students who received services in SACs attended for 2 weeks or less. Over half the students referred to the SAC as an alternative to suspension had no additional referrals. Furthermore, self-report data from students attending the SAC indicated that 57–91%, depending on the specific school, identified the SAC as helpful to them in teaching proactive skills and addressing behaviors that had resulted in the discipline referral.

The majority of teachers (95%) and principals (70%) in Opuni et al.'s (1991) sample identified counseling services as the most vital but missing component of the SAC, and some research suggests that such services may enhance the benefits of an ISS program. Hochman and Worner (1987) compared an ISS program that incorporated a small-group counseling intervention with one that did not. The counseling program emphasized cognitive-behavioral strategies designed to reduce self-defeating behaviors and enhance goal-setting and positive behavior. Relative to matched controls who received ISS only, students who received ISS plus counseling were reported to have significantly fewer office referrals for behavior, fewer referrals for in-school and out-of-school suspension, and lower rates of absenteeism.

Another model of therapeutic ISS incorporates cognitive-behavioral approaches to enhance self-monitoring and problem-solving in students. Zelie, Stone, and Lehr (1980) counseled junior high school students to avoid self-defeating behaviors and to choose adaptive alternatives when referred for disciplinary action. Target students were reported to be referred for conduct problems only one-third as frequently as control students and were rated by teachers as attending more to classwork and homework following disciplinary referrals that incorporated such cognitive problem-solving strategies. A related approach has been proposed by Wilcox, Brigham, and Nicolai (1998), who employed an *ABC Event Frame*, in which students identified the antecedents, behaviors, and desired and actual consequences through writing or drawing following conduct violations. Elias and Tobias (1996) described a computer-assisted approach called the *Student Conflict Manager/Personal Problem-solving Guide*, which helps students to analyze personal and situational variables associated with their conduct violations and to use problem-solving strategies to plan alternative actions. A pencil and paper version (the *Problem Tracker*) that can facilitate student self-monitoring during ISS also is available (Elias, 1998).

Effective ISS programs may emphasize the acquisition of academic rather than behavioral skills. Center and McKittrick (1987) have proposed two curricula for use in ISS programs: (a) a learning skills program that emphasizes strategies such as study skills and time management and (b) a functional academic program that provides instruction in such areas as employability skills and money management. Such approaches may be effective in meeting the proactive design features for IAES placements that are outlined in IDEA 97. It seems likely, for example, that many students with disabilities would have IEP goals that could be addressed by explicit instruction in either learning strategies or functional academics. In addition, either curriculum could incorporate services/modifications to address the behavior of concern through specific environmental and instructional controls (Center & McKittrick, 1987). Finally, continued progress in the general curriculum could be arranged by complementing these stand-alone curricula with general curricular materials (e.g., using newly acquired learning strategies to recall information in a content-area text).

The specific academic and behavioral supports currently employed in ISS models vary. However, these examples suggest that such approaches may have the capacity to address students' IEP goals, to permit their continued progress in the general curriculum, and to incorporate interventions targeted to the behavior of concern.

Appropriate staffing. A second consideration in designing and implementing an ISS program for short-term IAES placement involves staffing. Although some experts assert that a model where full-time staff members are dedicated to the ISS program is preferable to one where teachers rotate into the setting as part of their professional duties (Sullivan, 1989), others contend that the risk of burn out may favor a half-day team teaching model (Chobot & Garibaldi, 1982). The SAC model described by Opuni et al. (1991) provided a student-to-adult ratio of 20 to 1, although many teachers advocated for a reduction in this ratio by at least 25%. Most ISS programs employ certificated teachers, and the value of recruiting the ISS teacher from the school's own faculty has been described as important for fostering acceptance of the program by others (Chobot & Garibaldi, 1982). Specialized training in a related area such as counseling or social work, as well as personal qualities characterized by a commitment to addressing the diverse and intense needs of a population of at-risk students, are frequently emphasized (Chobot & Garibaldi, 1982; Sheets, 1996; Sullivan, 1989). Additional qualities of effective staff members in ISS programs include the ability to relate well to parents and other community systems, to establish a proactive instructional and therapeutic climate, and to champion the program within the broader school environment (Center & McKittrick, 1987; Sullivan, 1989).

Program design, implementation, and evaluation. As with most effective systemic programs, ISS models that are developed through the participation of a broad range of stakeholders appear to have the highest degree of visibility and acceptance within schools. A clearly stated program mission and philosophy that complements that of the larger school or district has been identified as important (Sheets, 1996). Similarly, an absence of well-defined program objectives may detract from effective evaluation and enhancement of ISS programs (Chobot & Garibaldi, 1982). Center and McKittrick (1987) provide several policy suggestions for operating successful ISS programs, including (a) an age span of no more than 3 years, (b) a maximum of 15 students, (c) specifying in advance the number of days in ISS per type of offense, and (d) identifying criteria for returning students to their regular placements.

Fiscal and programmatic supports. A final consideration for establishing ISS programs as a means of providing short-term IAES placement relates to the initial and on-going support for such programs. The literature suggests that ISS programs often receive seed monies from grants or from other community systems such as juvenile court or youth services agencies (Chobot & Garibaldi, 1982). Establishing mechanisms for sustained fiscal support has been described as critical to the operation of ISS programs.

Long-Term Settings

Although in-school suspension programs may represent a satisfactory IAES for short-term placements, these are unlikely to provide the design features necessary to accommodate students for a period of 45 days or longer. In these circumstances, alternative schools/programs may represent a more viable approach.

Alternative schools/programs are not a new phenomenon. Their initial insurgence in the 1960s and 1970s occurred as a means of addressing the needs of a population of learners who were often overlooked by the mainstream educational community (Raywid, 1995). Additionally, such programs have been characterized by an organizational structure that allows flexibility in operation (Raywid, 1994). A recent investigation into the characteristics of alternative schools/programs reported that most are small (e.g., 85% of those responding reported a student population between 8 and 150) and had extended hours (e.g., length of day, week, or academic year exceeded those found in traditional schools) (Lange, 1998). Students attending alternative schools/programs have been described as those who are at risk for not completing school due to such factors as low achievement or delinquency (Cox, Davidson, & Bynum, 1995; Lange, 1998). Although not specifically designed for students with disabilities, significant numbers of such students attend these programs (Gorney & Ysseldyke, 1993; Lange, 1998). For example, Gorney and Ysseldyke (1993) reported that 19% of their sample of students enrolled in alternative schools and learning centers in Minnesota had disabilities, and that emotional and behavioral disorders comprised the largest disability category represented.

Although studies of the effectiveness of alternative schools/programs are few in number and plagued by methodological weaknesses, a recently published meta-analysis suggests that such programs may produce positive outcomes for students, especially in circumstances where a specific population is targeted and the program length is equivalent to a full school day (Cox et al., 1995). The literature pertaining to alternative schools/programs identifies several elements of effectiveness that may have relevance for their use as long-term IAES placements, including an interpersonal focus, academic and behavioral supports, community collaboration, and parent/family involvement (Kellmayer, 1995).

Interpersonal focus. There is evidence that a personal connection with students, such as that provided through a small group setting or through a system of coaching or mentoring, is an important ingredient in effective alternative schools/programs. For example, teachers in alternative settings have reported that there is more one-to-one and small group instruction and more socializing with students than in traditional schools (Lange, 1998). Calgary's Behavior Intervention Centers (Ewashen, Harris, Porter, & Samuels, 1988) provide short-term and long-term alternatives to suspension with a student-teacher ratio of 6 to 1. The 81% success rate reported for these programs (i.e., reintegration into home schools without subsequent suspension) is attributed in part to the staff's empathy for the target students and their attention to individual student needs.

Academic and behavioral supports. As student behavior problems escalate, there is a corresponding tendency to increase teacher control and coercion (Reitz, 1994; Steinberg & Knitzer, 1992). However, research suggests that such approaches may exacerbate the coercive cycle for students with conduct problems (e.g., Shores et al., 1993). Reitz (1994) identified 10 elements of effective classroom-based programs that emphasize academic and behavioral supports rather than authoritarian responses. These proactive strategies, which have been shown to be particularly effective for students with emotional and behavioral disorders, include (a) environmental controls (e.g., consistent classroom schedules and structure); (b) positive instructional strategies (e.g., frequent opportunities for engaged instruction, peer interaction, and individualized treatment); (c) appropriate reinforcement (e.g., the use of token systems and high rates of social reinforcement); and (d) networking and futures planning (e.g., parent-community involvement and reintegration planning).

Consistent with this research, alternative schools/programs that include an educative component—i.e., specific instruction and reinforcement of academic or behavioral skills—appear to offer more promise than those that rely exclusively on control (Raywid, 1994). As Kellmayer (1995) asserts in his guide on establishing an alternative school, *"punitive models are ineffective for all students—whether disruptive or not"* (p. 27, emphasis in original). Fortunately, data suggest that such supports as student employment, and emotional, career, and academic counseling occur with greater frequency in alternative schools/programs than in traditional school settings (Lange, 1998). A recent investigation into school districts' use of IAES placements reported that alternative schools/programs were more likely than other settings to incorporate such interventions as skills instruction, student counseling, parent training, and substance abuse interventions (Telzrow, in press).

Service delivery models. Recent evidence suggests that clustering delinquent or high-risk youth together for therapeutic interventions may be counterproductive to the goal of producing desired behavior change (Arnold & Hughes, 1999; Dishion, McCord, & Poulin, 1999; Gottfredson, 1997). This research identifies a phenomenon referred to as "deviancy training," in which delinquent youths' references to substance use and violent conduct seem to exacerbate such rule-breaking behavior in their high-risk peers. Longitudinal studies have demonstrated that peer-focused interventions for high-risk youth were followed by *increases* in their deviant behavior 1, 2, and 3 years later (Dishion et al., 1999). In essence, the negative effects exerted by high-risk youth on other high-risk youth were more potent than the therapeutic effects of the intervention.

Such findings have significant implications for schools that are endeavoring to provide IAES placements that can facilitate positive behavior change. If Dishion et al.'s (1999) hypothesis that "high-risk peers will support one another's deviant behavior, so group affiliations should be avoided during retraining periods" (p. 757) is accurate, intervention programs, including those provided on an interim basis, should consider mechanisms for reducing deviancy training effects. There is evidence, for example, that the potency of deviancy training is reduced for settings that include prosocial models. This suggests that school personnel may wish to consider the viability of inclusive models when designing alternative programs/schools (Kellmayer, 1995). The effects of deviancy training also are lessened for pre-adolescent groups and when interventions target parents rather than groups of high-risk youth (Dishion et al., 1999). These findings may assist in identifying effective IAES placements for students with disabilities.

Community networking. Alternative schools/programs sometimes are initiated when diverse systems that share a concern about youth violence and substance abuse in the community work collaboratively to develop more effective educational delivery systems (Rabasca, 1999). For example, evidence that increases in community crime are associated with students' out-of-school suspensions has prompted law enforcement agencies in some communities to join with school districts in funding alternative schools/programs. Similarly, hospitals, mental health agencies, and universities have partnered with schools to provide vocational training, employment, mental health or substance abuse services, and program evaluation components for alternative schools/programs (Putnam County School Board, 1996; Reitz, 1994).

Parent/family involvement. Finally, parent/family involvement may be a valuable but underutilized factor in effective alternative schools/programs. A recent study of school districts' implementation of IAES during the first 18 months following the enactment of IDEA 97 reported that 45% of respondents who employed alternative schools/programs for IAES placements had no mechanisms for parent involvement (Telzrow, in press). However, research suggests that family-centered services may be a critical factor in interrupting the trajectory toward antisocial behavior in young children and fostering school completion among high risk students (Reid, 1993; Resnick et al., 1997; Walker et al., 1996; Walker, Severson, Feil, Stiller, & Golly, 1998). Effective methods of parent/family involvement acknowledge members' strengths, avoid blame, and enhance self-efficacy while expanding parenting and personal skills (Borduin et al., 1995; McMahon & Slough, 1996; Reitz, 1994; Walker, Severson et al., 1998).

Step 3: Employ Long-Term Reform-Based Practices Designed to Promote Safe and Drug-Free Schools

Preventive approaches are designed to *eliminate* the need for disciplinary removals. Nevertheless, such methods are recommended as one component of a best-practice strategy for implementing the IAES provision because of their central role in establishing long-term solutions to concerns about student behavior. Indeed, numerous experts have discussed the limitations of a primarily reactive approach to managing student behavior in school settings (Goldstein, 1999; Morrison et al., 1994; Reitz, 1994; Walker & Sylwester, 1991). As Horner et al. (1996) asserted, "punishment and exclusion will neither avert the problem nor improve schools" (p. 718).

In addition to the fact that research on intervention effectiveness demonstrates the superiority of preventive, proactive approaches, both the framing comments in IDEA 97 and the final regulations for implementation of the statute strongly emphasize the need for preventive approaches (Individuals with Disabilities Education Act Amendments, 1997; Individuals with Disabilities Education Act Regulations, 1999). Telzrow (1999a) argued that one aspect of IDEA 97 that offers significant promise for special education reform is the language permitting funds from two federal sources—IDEA and the Elementary and Secondary Education Act (ESEA)—to be combined to support school-wide programs targeting at-risk students. In the following section, examples of such programs are described.

Primary Prevention Programs

Primary prevention programs are generally systemic in nature, in that classroom or building-wide populations are targeted. Such approaches emphasize positive school climate, effective instruction, collaborative problem-solving methods, and recognition of student improvement as strategies to connect students with the school as an institution so that they do not become at risk (Walker et al., 1996). Two examples of primary prevention models to prevent student behaviors that may result in a need for IAES placement are described below.

Invitational Education. Invitational Education emphasizes the interpersonal aspects of the educational process. This approach incorporates four elements symbolized by the acronym TRIO: trust, respect, intentionality, and optimism (Brinson, 1996; Purkey & Novak, 1996; Purkey & Strahan, 1995). In Invitational Education, trust is fostered by a system of rules and regulations that are clear, consistent, and nonintrusive. Respect results from a disciplinary process that emphasizes instruction rather than punitive measures. Intentionality, a core concept in Invitational Education, means that the actions taken by individuals have explicit effects. High expectations for both adults and students in the educational environment are reflected by optimism.

Invitational Education employs a systems change approach that begins with an analysis of the people, places, policies, programs, and processes operating within the educational system. Educators determine the degree to which these are welcoming to all individuals, and endeavor to produce "intentionally inviting" interactions and procedures. Intentionally inviting people, for example, call students and parents by name and treat them with courtesy. Programs that are inclusive and that foster high regard for all individuals are intentionally inviting in contrast to those that promote segregation or exclusion.

Juhnke and Purkey (1995) contend that "providing school success for only a select few is a breeding ground for school violence" (p. 55). Because one of Invitational Education's key objectives is engaging all learners in the educational process, it represents a viable primary prevention model. A number of invitational strategies that may assist in preventing violence in schools have been described (Juhnke & Purkey, 1995). These include teaching specific proactive skills (e.g., conflict management, peer mediation, group guidance programs); creating inclusive and welcoming environments (e.g., celebrating cultural diversity, creating no-cut policies to enable all students to experience success, establishing student mentoring programs); and establishing systems to identify and redirect potential risk factors (e.g., use of permanent name tags, communication vehicles to eliminate rumors).

Although studies examining the effectiveness of Invitational Education are not widespread, the practices promoted are consistent with those associated with successful primary prevention approaches (Morrison et al., 1994, 1997; Short et al., 1994). Descriptions of schools' implementation of Invitational Education have reported increased rates of student recognition and involvement, enhanced school climate, and reductions in student dropout rates, retentions, and failing grades (Hart, 1996; Purkey & Strahan, 1995). The personal characteristics of students and staff, and the physical, social, and cultural environments that are evident in safe schools, mirror those elements in Invitational Education (Morrison et al., 1994). As these authors state, "our real objective is not just to prevent students from being shot on campuses, but to help create campuses that are welcoming and nurturing" (Morrison et al., 1994, p. 252).

Substance abuse prevention models. Possession or use of drugs is one of the two circumstances in which school personnel may unilaterally remove a student with a disability to long-term placement in an IAES. Additionally, it has been demonstrated that substance abuse is a significant predictor of violent behavior in schools (Kingery et al., 1998) and that child psychopathology, most notably conduct disorder and depression, is associated with higher rates and earlier substance use and abuse in both males and females (Costello, Erkanli, Federman, & Angold, 1999). For these reasons, empirically supported models for prevention of substance abuse are included in this section.

In a review of the effectiveness of drug prevention programs, Beck (1998) identified two types: (a) "just say no" programs, characterized by a call for abstinence and a moralistic approach; and (b) "just say know" models, which foster informed choice and a wellness orientation. Although the "just say no programs" date back more than a century and are not empirically supported, more current versions of abstinence-oriented programs are widespread due to their intuitive appeal, popular support, and high levels of government funding (Beck, 1998; Brown & Kreft, 1998; Dusenbury & Falco, 1995).

Despite the popularity of abstinence-oriented substance abuse programs, data suggest that their effectiveness is questionable, which compels schools to consider alternative approaches that have more empirical support (Brown & Kreft, 1998; Gottfredson, 1997; Tobler, 1986). Key characteristics of effective school-based drug abuse prevention programs have been identified (Dusenbury & Falco, 1995). Such programs rely on objective data about substance use and abuse, including an understanding of risk and protective factors (Consortium on the School-Based Promotion of Social Competence, 1994). Studies have reported that risk factors for adolescent substance use include characteristics of individual students (e.g., working 20 or more hours per week, low grade point average, grade retention, and perceiving oneself as older than same-age peers) and families (e.g., homes where there is easy access to substances) (Resnick et al., 1997). Positive affiliations and a connectedness to families and schools represent protective factors for substance use in adolescents (Resnick et al., 1997).

Social-resistance skills training, in which young people are instructed about specific strategies that they can use to resist peers' encouragement to use drugs or alcohol, has been described as an effective feature of substance abuse prevention programs (Dusenbury & Falco, 1995). In addition, programs that incorporate normative education, where students are provided messages that convey that drug use is not typical, also have been shown to be associated with more positive outcomes (Gottfredson, 1997). Combining these skills with other cognitive-behavioral and social skills instruction, such as problem solving, goal setting, and assertiveness, appears to provide an additional therapeutic effect. For example, a meta-analysis of rehabilitation programs for delinquent youth reported that programs that incorporated a cognitive component—characterized by instruction in problem-solving skills or cognitive behavioral modification—were twice as effective as programs without such characteristics (Izzo & Ross, 1990). Finally, drug-abuse prevention programs that employ interactive teaching strategies such as role-playing and discussion are superior to strictly didactic methods (Dusenbury & Falco, 1995).

The Life Skills Training (LST) Program is one example of a promising substance abuse prevention program (Botvin, 1996). The 15-session program incorporates instructional components related to personal self-management skills, social skills, and drug-related information and skills. The program is designed to deliver the primary intervention during the seventh grade year, to be followed by a 10-session booster session in grade eight and a 5-session booster session in grade nine. Research that has examined the effectiveness of the LST Program has reported positive treatment effects for reduced use of various substances, including tobacco, alcohol, and marijuana (Botvin, 1996).

A second substance abuse prevention program with evidence of effectiveness is Project STAR (Students Taught Awareness and Resistance) (Pentz, Cormack, Flay, Hansen, & Johnson, 1986). This multi-system preventive approach incorporates a school-based curriculum targeting students in grades six or seven, as well as a parent training component, community interventions, and public policy and positive media campaigns. Project STAR has been reported to result in reduced use of various substances among both typical and high risk populations (Johnson et al., 1990; Pentz et al., 1989).

Secondary Prevention Models

Secondary prevention models are designed to engage at-risk students early in their development of antisocial behaviors in order to foster their academic and behavioral success (Walker et al., 1995). Such interventions tend to be of a more targeted and intensive nature than primary prevention programs (Walker et al., 1996). Two examples of secondary prevention models are described below.

First Step to Success. First Step to Success incorporates both school-based and family-centered interventions to ameliorate early signs of antisocial behavior in kindergarten age students (Walker, 1998; Walker, Kavanagh et al., 1998; Walker, Severson et al., 1998; Walker & Sylwester, 1991). The 12-week program begins with a kindergarten screening effort designed to identify students who are at-risk for the development of antisocial behavior. Target children receive a structured school-based program to teach adaptive behaviors that can facilitate their positive interactions with teachers and peers and foster academic progress. Group-oriented contingencies and home-school linked rewards are used to enhance learning and performance (Walker, Severson et al., 1998). Concurrently, the children's parents are taught parenting practices designed to facilitate the acquisition of proactive behaviors. Such practices include close supervision of children's activities, friends, and whereabouts; positive strategies for influencing behavior, such as encouragement, praise, and rewards; and the use of discipline approaches that are implemented fairly and in a timely fashion (Walker, 1998; Walker & Sylwester, 1991). These are taught in weekly home-based sessions provided by a program consultant and reinforced between sessions with games and activities implemented by the parent.

The effectiveness of First Step to Success has been reflected in student outcome data. Teacher ratings and direct observation have demonstrated improved adaptive behavior, reduced student aggression, and increased amounts of time spent in teacher-assigned tasks (Golly, Stiller, & Walker, 1998). Furthermore, the power of this intervention system to produce lasting change has been evident from long-term effects reported up to 2 years following the intervention, and generalization to new educational settings (Golly et al., 1998; Walker, 1998). Although the individual components of First Step to Success may be used separately, stronger treatment effects are reported to occur when the comprehensive model is implemented (Walker, Severson et al., 1998).

FAST Track. Although studies examining its effectiveness are still in the early stages, preliminary data suggest that the FAST Track program is a promising secondary prevention model (Bierman et al., 1992; Bierman & Greenberg, 1996; Gottfredson, 1997; Walker et al., 1996). FAST Track targets the elementary school grades, with greatest intensity during the early years of schooling. Consistent with research demonstrating that effective interventions must target children's key socializing agents, the program incorporates school-based, home-based, and individual student interventions. A parent training component, implemented when target children are in first grade, is designed to teach effective discipline and home supports for academic skills (McMahon & Slough, 1996). This component is supported by biweekly home visits to enhance home-school communication and parent effectiveness. The PATHS curriculum (Promoting Alternative Thinking Strategies) (Greenberg & Kusché, 1993; Greenberg, Kusché, Cook, & Quamma, 1995), which fosters the development of self-management, problem-solving, and positive peer interactions, provides a classroom intervention to support the FAST Track objectives. Additional selective interventions targeting high-risk children encompass both social-behavioral (e.g., training in social skills, anger management, and strategies for making and keeping friends) and academic (e.g., reading tutoring) skills (Bierman & Greenberg, 1996).

Early outcome data suggest that, relative to controls, children who have completed the first grade FAST Track interventions have more positive behavioral interactions with adults and peers and lower levels of classroom disruptive behavior (Walker et al., 1996). Of significance, given the necessity to intervene in all children's social systems to alter the antisocial trajectory, early data suggest that warmer, less punitive parenting practices and less aggressive classroom environments are associated with children who had experienced the FAST Track program (Walker et al., 1996).

Tertiary Prevention Models

Tertiary prevention models are those designed to contain a known problem and prevent its escalation. Walker et al.'s (1995) concept of accommodation for secondary level students, in which instruction in survival skills, vocational skills, coping strategies, and transition to employment are emphasized, illustrates this type of preventive approach. Tertiary prevention programs must include critical social forces in the target student's life (e.g., parents, peers, teachers), and often require multi-agency involvement (Reid, 1993; Walker et al., 1996). Such programs tend to be intensive and to occur in specialized settings. For these reasons, tertiary prevention programs are more consistent with models of alternative schools/programs described previously than preventive strategies designed to eliminate the need for removal from school because of student conduct problems.

PROFESSIONAL DEVELOPMENT IMPLICATIONS

The IAES provision in IDEA 97 is deceptively complex. Although this requirement appears to offer schools a straightforward reactive remedy when confronted with serious student conduct violations, closer inspection of the statute and related literature reveals that full implementation of the IAES provision necessitates a comprehensive, systemic approach to discipline that incorporates both prevention and intervention programs. For these to be effective, thoughtful attention must be given to both the content of professional development and proven methods for its successful implementation.

Professional Development Content

Two broad areas of professional development content that are relevant to IAES placements are suggested by research. These include (a) strategies for establishing proactive instructional environments that have been shown to prevent student misbehavior and (b) techniques to assist educators in recognizing low level student disruption and teaching skills and replacement behaviors to prevent its escalation (Bear, 1999; Gettinger, 1988; Gottfredson, 1997; Martens & Kelly, 1993).

Considerable research has identified the importance of instructional variables in preventing student behavior problems and reducing school exclusions (Algozzine, Ysseldyke, & Elliott, 1997; Gettinger, 1988; Gottfredson, Gottfredson, & Hybl, 1993; Imich, 1994; Martens & Kelly, 1993). Examples of such proactive practices include the implementation of systems to (a) avoid down time, (b) establish positive instructional climates, (c) maximize student engagement in learning, and (d) ensure an appropriate instructional match (Gettinger, 1988; Martens & Kelly, 1993). In addition, certain instructional approaches, such as interactive teaching and cooperative learning, have been shown to promote positive attitudinal and behavioral changes among high-risk students, including higher levels of attachment and commitment to school, higher educational aspirations, and a lower rate of suspension and expulsion (Hawkins, Doueck, & Lishner, 1988).

In addition to emphasizing instructional variables and setting events that can prevent student misconduct, professional development also must assist educators in managing and redirecting low levels of disruptive behavior. One effective strategy for achieving this objective involves the use of proven behavioral interventions, particularly those derived from functional assessments (Broussard & Northup, 1995; Dunlap et al., 1993; DuPaul & Ervin, 1996; Gable et al., 1998; Taylor & Miller, 1997). Increased parent-school communication about positive student behavior as well as conduct violations also has been identified as an effective method for redirecting student misbehavior (Gottfredson et al., 1993).

Professional Development Methods

Identifying what educators need to know and do to prevent and ameliorate student conduct problems is essential. However, methods for ensuring that these skills and attitudes are systematically implemented also must be identified. Despite agreement about the importance of acquiring certain instructional and behavioral management skills, teacher in-service programs are often ineffective because of inadequately explained theoretical foundations, poorly defined objectives, insufficient evaluation and feedback provided to implementers, and inadequate communication about the distribution of responsibilities (Colvin, Kameenui, & Sugai, 1993; Gottfredson et al., 1993). As Gottfredson et al. (1993) have stated, "much effort is wasted when training programs are not augmented with school-level support structures to facilitate change" (p. 209).

Morrison et al. (1997) argue that successful efforts to enhance school safety must go beyond "tinkering" to a systemic school-wide approach to school reform. They contend that establishing safe and drug-free schools is a byproduct of educators' systemic efforts to create effective schools. The literature on implementation of education innovations has identified several critical elements that can facilitate such systemic change. These include (a) site-based impetus for change, (b) investment in a unifying theme by a broad range of stakeholders, (c) empowering the implementers of change through such mechanisms as school-based teams, (d) recognition of change as a non-linear and often difficult journey, and (e) utilization of collaborative approaches (Colvin et al., 1993; Curtis & Stollar, 1996; McLaughlin, 1991; Morrison et al., 1997). The reader is referred to Colvin et al. (1993) and Gottfredson et al. (1993) for descriptions of systemic approaches to implementing school-wide discipline programs, and to Curtis and Batsche (this volume) for further discussion of systems change strategies.

SUMMARY

The IAES provision in IDEA 97 permits school personnel to remove students with disabilities to alternative settings over parent objections under certain circumstances. The statute requires that such settings be educative in nature. This chapter suggests that in-school suspension programs, if appropriately designed and implemented, may comply with the guidelines for short-term IAES placement. For long-term placements, alternative schools/programs that incorporate characteristics associated with positive behavior change may be appropriate. Such reactive strategies of response to student conduct violations should be combined with systemic efforts to promote safe and drug-free schools through the use of effective models of primary and secondary prevention.

REFERENCES

Algozzine, B., Ysseldyke, J., & Elliott, J. (1997). *Strategies and tactics for effective instruction* (3rd ed.) Longmont, CO: Sopris West.

Arnold, M. E., & Hughes, J. N. (1999). First do no harm: Adverse effects of grouping deviant youth for skills training. *Journal of School Psychology, 37*, 99–115.

Bader, B. D. (1997). *Schools, discipline, and students with disabilities: The AFT responds.* Paper presented at the Annual Convention of the Council for Exceptional Children, Salt Lake City, Utah.

Batsche, G. M., & Knoff, H. M. (1994). Bullies and their victims: Understanding a pervasive problem in the schools. *School Psychology Review, 23*, 165–174.

Bear, G. G. (1999). *Interim alternative educational settings: Related research and program considerations.* Alexandria, VA: The National Association of State Directors of Special Education.

Beck, J. (1998). 100 years of "just say no" versus "just say know": Reevaluating drug education goals for the coming century. *Evaluation Review, 22*, 15–45.

Bierman, K., Coie, J., Dodge, K., Greenberg, M., Lochman, J., & McMahon, R. (1992). A developmental and clinical model for the prevention of conduct disorder: The FAST Track Program. *Development and Psychopathology, 4*, 509–527.

Bierman, K. L., & Greenberg, M. T. (1996). Social skills training in the Fast Track Program. In R. DeV. Peters & R. J. McMahon (Eds.), *Preventing childhood disorders, substance abuse, and delinquency* (pp. 65-89). Thousand Oaks, CA: Sage.

Borduin, C. M., Mann, B. J., Cone, L. T., Henggeler, S. W., Fucci, B. R., Blaske, D. M., & Williams, R. A. (1995). Multisystemic treatment of serious juvenile offenders: Long-term prevention of criminality and violence. *Journal of Consulting and Clinical Psychology, 61*, 569–578.

Botvin, G. J. (1996). Substance abuse prevention through Life Skills Training. In R. DeV. Peters & R. J. McMahon (Eds.), *Preventing childhood disorders, substance abuse, and delinquency* (pp. 215-240). Thousand Oaks, CA: Sage.

Bowditch, C. (1993). Getting rid of troublemakers: High school disciplinary procedures and the production of dropouts. *Social Problems, 40*, 493–508.

Brantlinger, E. (1991). Social class distinctions in adolescents' reports of problems and punishment in school. *Behavioral Disorders, 17*, 36–46.

Brinson, K.H. (1996). Invitational education as a logical, ethical and democratic means to reform. *Journal of Invitational Theory and Practice, 4* (1), 81–94.

Broussard, C.D., & Northup, J. (1995). An approach to functional assessment and analysis of disruptive behavior in regular education classrooms. *School Psychology Quarterly, 10*, 151–164.

Brown, J. H., & D'Emidio-Caston, M. (1995). On becoming at risk through drug education: How symbolic policies and their practices affect students. *Evaluation Review, 19*, 451–92.

Brown, J. H., & Kreft, I. G. G. (1998). Zero effects of drug prevention programs: Issues and solutions. *Evaluation Review, 22,* 3–14.

Butera, G., Klein, H., McMullen, L., & Wilson, B. (1998). A statewide study of FAPE and school discipline policies. *The Journal of Special Education, 32,* 108–114.

Center, D.B., & McKittrick, S. (1987). Disciplinary removal of special education students. *Focus on Exceptional Children, 20*(2), 1–12.

Chobot, R. B., & Garibaldi, A. (1982). In-school alternatives to suspension: A description of ten school district programs. *The Urban Review, 14,* 317–336.

Colvin, G., Kameenui, E. J., & Sugai, G. (1993). Reconceptualizing behavior management and school-wide discipline in general education. *Education and Treatment of Children, 16,* 361–381.

Committee on Labor and Human Resources. (1997, May 9). *Report [to accompany S. 717].* Washington, DC: Government Printing Office. [Available from Superintendent of Documents, Attn: New Orders, P.O. Box 371954, Pittsburgh, PA 15250-7954. Available on-line from the Senate Reports Online via GPO Access: http://wais.access.gpo.gov].

Conoley, J. C., & Goldstein, A. P. (1997). The known, unknown, and future of violence reduction. In A.P. Goldstein & J.C. Conoley (Eds.), *School violence intervention: A practical handbook* (pp. 493-495). New York: Guilford.

Consortium on the School-Based Promotion of Social Competence. (1994). The school-based promotion of social competence: Theory, research, practice, and policy. In R.J. Haggerty, L.R. Sherrod, N. Garmezy, & M. Rutter (Eds.), *Stress, risk, and resilience in children and adolescents: Processes, mechanisms, and interventions* (pp. 268-316). Cambridge: Cambridge University Press.

Cornell, D. G., & Loper, A. B. (1998). Assessment of violence and other high-risk behaviors with a school survey. *School Psychology Review, 27,* 317–330.

Costello, E. J., Erkanli, A., Federman, E., & Angold, A. (1999). Development of psychiatric comorbidity with substance abuse in adolescents: Effects of timing and sex. *Journal of Clinical Child Psychology, 28,* 298–311.

Costenbader, V., & Markson, S. (1998). School suspension: A study with secondary school students. *Journal of School Psychology, 36,* 59–82.

Cox, S. M., Davidson, W. S., & Bynum, T. S. (1995). A meta-analytic assessment of delinquency-related outcomes of alternative education programs. *Crime & Delinquency, 41,* 219–234.

Curtis, M. J., & Stollar, S. A. (1996). Applying principles and practices of organizational change to school reform. *School Psychology Review, 25,* 409–417.

Curwin, R.L., & Mendler, A.N. (1999). Zero tolerance for zero tolerance. *Phi Delta Kappan, 81,* 119–120.

Dishion, T.J., McCord, J., & Poulin, F. (1999). When interventions harm: Peer groups and problem behavior. *American Psychologist, 54,* 755–764.

Duke, D.L., & Jones, V.F. (1984). Two decades of discipline: Assessing the development of an educational specialization. *Journal of Research and Development in Education, 17*(4), 25–35.

Dunlap, G., Kern, L., dePerczel, M., Clarke, S., Wilson, D., Childs, K. E., White, R., & Falk, G. D. (1993). Functional analysis of classroom variables for students with emotional and behavioral disorders. *Behavioral Disorders, 18*, 275–291.

DuPaul, G. J., & Ervin, R. A. (1996). Functional assessment of behaviors related to attention-deficit/hyperactivity disorder: Linking assessment to intervention design. *Behavior Therapy, 27*, 601–622.

Dusenbury, L., & Falco, M. (1995). Eleven components of effective drug abuse prevention curricula. *The Journal of School Health, 65*, 420–425.

Elias, M. J. (1998). Resolving conflict and preventing violence, school failure and dropout, and related problem behaviors. *NASSP Bulletin, 82* (596), 1–6.

Elias, M. J., & Tobias, S. E. (1996). *Social problem-solving: Interventions in the schools.* New York: Guilford.

Ewashen, G., Harris, S., Porter, D., & Samuels, K. (1988). School suspension alternatives. *Education Canada, 28*(1), 4–9.

Gable, G. A., Quinn, M. M., Rutherford, R. B., Jr., & Howell, K. (1998). Addressing problem behaviors in schools: Use of functional assessments and behavior intervention plans. *Preventing School Failure, 42*(3), 106–199.

Garibaldi, A. M. (1995). Street academies and in-school alternatives to suspension. In M. C. Wang & M. C. Reynolds (Eds.), *Making a difference for students at risk* (pp. 99-118). Thousand Oaks, CA: Corwin.

Gettinger, M. (1988) Methods of proactive classroom management. *School Psychology Review, 17*, 227–242.

Goldstein, A.P. (1999). Aggressive reduction strategies: Effective and ineffective. *School Psychology Quarterly, 14*, 40–58.

Goldstein, A. P., & Conoley, J. C. (1997). Student aggression: Current status. In A. P. Goldstein & J. C. Conoley (Eds.), *School violence intervention: A practical handbook* (pp. 3-19). New York: Guilford.

Golly, A. M., Stiller, B., & Walker, H. M. (1998). First Step to Success: Replication and social validation of an early intervention program. *Journal of Emotional and Behavioral Disorders, 6*, 243–250.

Gorney, D. J., & Ysseldyke, J. E. (1993). Students with disabilities use of various options to access alternative schools and area learning centers. *Special Services in the Schools, 7*, 125–143.

Gottfredson, D. C. (1997). School-based crime prevention. In L. W. Sherman, D. Gottfredson, D. MacKenzie, J. Eck, P. Reuter, & S. Bushway (Eds.), *Preventing crime: What works, what doesn't, what's promising* (pp. 5-1–5-71). Washington, DC: U.S. Department of Justice.

Gottfredson, D. C., Gottfredson, G. D., & Hybl, L. G. (1993). Managing adolescent behavior: A multiyear, multischool study. *American Educational Research Journal, 30,* 179–215.

Greenberg, M. T., Kusché, C. A., Cook, E. T., & Quamma, J. P. (1995). Promoting emotional competence in school-aged children. *Development and Psychopathology, 7,* 117–136.

Greenberg, M. T., & Kusché, C. A. (1993). *Promoting social and emotional development in deaf children: The PATHS project.* Seattle: University of Washington Press.

Hart, M. C. (1996). Identification badges: An invitational approach to school safety. *Journal of Invitational Theory and Practice, 4*(1) 71–79.

Hawkins, J. D., Doueck, H. J., & Lishner, D. M. (1988). Changing teaching practices in mainstream classrooms to improve bonding and behavior of low achievers. *American Educational Research Journal, 25,* 31–50.

Hochman, S., & Worner, W. (1987). In-school suspension and group counseling: Helping the at-risk student. *NASSP Bulletin, 71*(501). 93–96.

Horner, R. H., Sprague, J. R., & Sugai, G. (1996). Positive behavioral support. In *Improving the implementation of the Individuals with Disabilities Education Act: Making schools work for all of America's children* (pp. 711-737). Washington, DC: National Council on Disability.

Hyman, I., Weiler, E., Perone, D., Romano, L., Britton, G., & Shanock, A. (1997). Victims and victimizers: The two faces of school violence. In A. P. Goldstein & J. C. Conoley (Eds.), *School violence intervention: A practical handbook* (pp. 426-459). New York: Guilford.

Imich, A. J. (1994). Exclusions from school: Current trends and issues. *Educational Research, 36,* 3–11.

Individuals with Disabilities Education Act Amendments of 1997, 20 U.S.C. § 1400 *et seq.* (West 1997).

Individuals with Disabilities Education Act Regulations, 34 C.F.R. § 300 and 303. (1999).

Izzo, R. L., & Ross, R. R. (1990). Meta-analysis of rehabilitation programs for juvenile delinquents: A brief report. *Criminal Justice and Behavior, 17,* 134–142.

Johnson, C. A., Pentz, M., Weber, M., Dwyer, J., Baer, N., MacKinnon, D., & Hansen, W. (1990). Relative effectiveness of comprehensive community programming for drug abuse prevention with high-risk and low-risk adolescents. *Journal of Consulting and Clinical Psychology, 58,* 447–456.

Johnston, L. D., O'Malley, P. M., & Bachman, J. G. (1995). *National survey results on drug use from the monitoring the future study, 1975–1994.* Rockville, MD: U.S. Department of Health and Human Service, National Institute on Drug Abuse.

Juhnke, G. A., & Purkey, W. W. (1995). An invitational approach to preventing violence in schools. *Counseling Today, 37* (8)50, 52.

Kellmayer, J. (1995). *How to establish an alternative school.* Thousand Oaks, CA: Corwin.

Kingery, P. M., Coggeshall, M. B., & Alford, A. A. (1998). Violence at school: Recent evidence from four national surveys. *Psychology in the Schools, 35,* 247–258.

Kingery, P. M., McCoy-Simandle, L, & Clayton, R. (1997). Risk factors for adolescent violence: The importance of vulnerability. *School Psychology International, 18,* 49–60.

Lange, C. M. (1998). Characteristics of alternative schools and programs serving at-risk students. *High School Journal, 81*(4), 183–198.

Martens, B. K., & Kelly, S. Q. (1993). A behavioral analysis of effective teaching. *School Psychology Quarterly, 8,* 10–26.

McLaughlin, M. W. (1991). Learning from experience: Lessons from policy implementation. In A. R. Odden (Eds.), *Education policy implementation* (pp. 185-195). Albany, NY: State University of New York Press.

McMahon, R. J., & Slough, N. M. (1996). Family-based intervention in the Fast Track Program. In R. DeV. Peters & R. J. McMahon (Eds.), *Preventing childhood disorders, substance abuse, and delinquency* (pp. 90-110). Thousand Oaks, CA: Sage.

Morgan-D'Atrio, C., Northup, J., LaFleur, L., & Spera, S. (1996). Toward prescriptive alternatives to suspensions: A preliminary evaluation. *Behavioral Disorders, 21* (2), 190–200.

Morrison, G. M., & D'Incau, B. (1997). The web of zero tolerance: Characteristics of students who are recommended for expulsion from school. *Education and Treatment of Children, 10,* 316–335.

Morrison, G. M., Furlong, M. J., & Morrison, R. L. (1994). School violence to school safety: Reframing the issues for school psychologists. *School Psychology Review, 23,* 236–256.

Morrison, G. M., Furlong, M. J., & Morrison, R. L. (1997). The safe school: Moving beyond crime prevention to school empowerment. In A. P. Goldstein & J. C. Conoley (Eds.), *School violence intervention: A practical handbook* (pp. 236-264). New York: Guilford.

Opuni, K. A., Tollis, R. J., Sanchez, K. S., & Gonzalez, J. (1991). *Student assignment centers: An in-school suspension program, 1990–91.* Houston, TX: Houston Independent School District.

Pentz, M. A., Cormack, C., Flay, B., Hansen, W., & Johnson, C. A. (1986). Balancing program and research integrity in community drug abuse prevention: Project STAR approach. *Journal of School Health, 56,* 389–393.

Pentz, M. A., Dwyer, J. H., MacKinnon, D. P., Flay, B. R., Hansen, W. B., Wang, E. Y. I., & Johnson, C. A. (1989). A multicommunity trial for primary prevention of adolescent drug abuse. *Journal of the American Medical Association, 261,* 3259–3266.

Purkey, W. W., & Novak, J. M. (1996). *Inviting school success: A self-concept approach to teaching, learning, and democratic practice* (3rd ed.). Belmont, CA: Wadsworth.

Purkey, W. W., & Strahan, D. (1995). School transformation through invitational education. *Research in the Schools, 2*(2), 1–6.

Putnam County School Board (1996). *P.A.S.T.: Positive Attitude Student Training.* Palatka, FL: Author.

Rabasca, L. (1999). Community-based care gains in popularity. *APA Monitor, 30* (4), 23.

Raywid, M. A. (1994). Alternative schools: The state of the art. *Educational Leadership, 52*(2), 26–31.

Raywid, M. A. (1995). Alternatives and marginal students. In M. C. Wang & M. C. Reynolds (Eds.), *Making a difference for students at risk* (pp. 119-155). Thousand Oaks, CA: Corwin.

Reid, J. B. (1993). Prevention of conduct disorder before and after school entry: Relating interventions to developmental findings. *Development and Psychopathology, 5,* 243–262.

Reitz, A. L. (1994). Implementing comprehensive classroom-based programs for students with emotional and behavioral problems. *Education and Treatment of Children, 17,* 312–331.

Resnick, M. D., Bearman, P. S., Blum, R. W., Bauman, K. E., Harris, K. M., Jones, J., Tabor, J., Beunring, T., Sieving, R. E., Shew, M., Ireland, M., Bearinger, L. H., & Udry, J. R. (1997). Protecting adolescents from harm. *Journal of the American Medical Association, 278,* 823–832.

Rose, L. C., & Gallup, A. M. (1998). The 30th annual Phi Delta Kappa/Gallup Poll of the public's attitudes toward the public schools. *Phi Delta Kappan, 80*(1), 41–56.

Rose, L. C., & Gallup, A. M. (1999). The 31st annual Phi Delta Kappa/Gallup Poll of the public's attitudes toward the public schools. *Phi Delta Kappan, 81*(1), 41–56.

Rose, L. C., Gallup, A. M., & Elam, S. M. (1997). The 29th annual Phi Delta Kappa/Gallup Poll of the public's attitudes toward the public schools. *Phi Delta Kappan, 79* (1), 41–56.

Rose, T. L. (1988). Current disciplinary practices with handicapped students: Suspensions and expulsions. *Exceptional Children, 55,* 230–239.

Sheets, J. (1996). Designing an effective in-school suspension program to change student behavior. *NASSP Bulletin, 80* (579), 86–90.

Shores, R. E., Gunter, P. L., & Jack, S. L. (1993). Classroom management strategies: Are they setting events for coercion? *Behavioral Disorders, 18*(2), 92–102.

Short, P. J., Short, R. J., & Blanton, C. (1994). *Rethinking student discipline: Alternatives that work.* Thousand Oaks, CA: Corwin.

Shriver, M. D., & Allen, K. D. (1996). The time-out grid. A guide to effective discipline. *School Psychology Quarterly, 11*, 67–74.

Skiba, R., & Peterson, R. (1999). The dark side of zero tolerance: Can punishment lead to safe schools? *Phi Delta Kappan, 80*, 372–376, 381–382.

Skiba, R. J., Peterson, R. L., & Williams, T. (1997). Office referrals and suspension: Disciplinary intervention in middle schools. *Education and Treatment of Children, 20*, 295–315.

Stage, S. A. (1997). A preliminary investigation of the relationship between in-school suspension and the disruptive classroom behavior of students with behavioral disorders. *Behavioral Disorders, 23*, 57–76.

Steinberg, Z., & Knitzer, J. (1992). Classrooms for emotionally and behaviorally disturbed students: Facing the challenge. *Behavioral Disorders, 17*, 145–156.

Sullivan, J. S. (1989). Elements of a successful in-school suspension program. *NASSP Bulletin, 73*(516), 32–38.

Taylor, J., & Miller, M. (1997). When timeout works some of the time: The importance of treatment integrity and functional assessment. *School Psychology Quarterly, 12*, 4–22.

Telzrow, C. F. (1999a). IDEA Amendments of 1997: Promise or pitfall for special education reform. *Journal of School Psychology, 37*, 7–28.

Telzrow, C. F. (in press). Interim alternative educational settings: School district implementation of IDEA 1997 requirements. *Education and Treatment of Children.*

Tobler, N. S. (1986). Meta-analysis of 143 adolescent drug prevention programs: Quantitative outcome results of program participants compared to a control or comparison group. *Journal of Drug Issues, 16*, 537–567.

Walker, H. M. (1998). First steps to prevent antisocial behavior. *Teaching Exceptional Children, 30*(4), 16–19.

Walker, H. M., Colvin, G., & Ramsey, E. (1995). *Antisocial behavior in school: Strategies and best practices.* Pacific Grove, CA: Brooks/Cole.

Walker, H. M., & Gresham, F. (1997). Making schools safer and violence free. *Intervention in School and Clinic, 32*, 199–204.

Walker, H. M., Horner, R. H., Sugai, G., Bullis, M., Sprague, J. R., Bricker, D., & Kaufman, M. J. (1996). Integrated approaches to preventing antisocial behavior patterns among school-age children and youth. *Journal of Emotional and Behavioral Disorders, 4*, 194–209.

Walker, H., Kavanagh, K., Stiller, B., Golly, A., Severson, H. H., Feil, E. (1998). *First Step to Success: Helping young children overcome antisocial behavior.* Longmont, CO: Sopris West.

Walker, H., Severson, H. H., Feil, E. G., Stiller, B., Golly, A. (1998). First Step to Success: Intervening at the point of school entry to prevent antisocial behavior patterns. *Psychology in the Schools, 35*, 259–269.

Walker, H. M., & Sylwester, R. (1991). Where is school along the path to prison? *Educational Leadership, 49*(1), 14–16.

Wilcox, T. D., Brigham, F. J., & Nicolai, B. (1998) Increasing self-discipline with the ABC event frame. *NASSP Bulletin, 82*(596), 16–24.

Yell, M.L., Cline, D., & Bradley, R. (1995). Disciplining students with emotional and behavioral disorders: A legal update. *Education and Treatment of Children, 18,* 299–308.

Zelie, K., Stone, C. I., & Lehr, E. (1980). Cognitive-behavioral intervention in school discipline: A preliminary study. *The Personnel and Guidance Journal, 59,* 80–83.

ANNOTATED BIBLIOGRAPHY

Canter, A. S., & Carrol, S. A. (1999) (Eds.). *Crisis prevention and response: A collection of NASP resources.* Bethesda, MD: National Association of School Psychologists.

This publication offers a comprehensive collection of resources related to the prevention of school violence and appropriate responses when crises occur. The brief, topic-focused sections provide school-based teams with practical strategies for implementing both prevention and intervention programs. The loose-leaf binder format and NASP's authorization for copying handouts for educational and home-school collaborative purposes make this an extremely useful and convenient resource.

Goldstein, A. P. & Conoley, J. C. (1997) (Eds.), *School violence intervention: A practical handbook.* New York: Guilford.

This edited volume offers a comprehensive yet practical survey of school violence. Factors that can exacerbate and mitigate the expression of school violence receive thorough treatment by a range of experts in this area. Emphasis is on the application of current research to the creation of effective intervention and prevention programs.

Kellmayer, J. (1995). *How to establish an alternative school.* Thousand Oaks, CA: Corwin.

This practical guide provides a useful resource for educators who are considering creating an alternative school. Though not targeting students with disabilities specifically, the author concludes that alternative schools may offer promise to students with disruptive behaviors. Key characteristics of alternative schools are described (e.g., size, site, access to social services), and 10 alternative models are presented.

Peters, R. DeV. & McMahon, R. J.(1996) (Eds.), *Preventing childhood disorders, substance abuse, and delinquency.* Thousand Oaks, CA: Sage.

This edited volume contains several excellent chapters about high quality prevention programs for childhood substance abuse and conduct disorders. Outcomes associated with models described in this chapter (e.g., Fast Track program, Life Skills training) are summarized. Additional chapters focus on early intervention and family centered treatments.

Walker, H. M., Colvin, G., & Ramsey, E. (1995). *Antisocial behavior in school: Strategies and best practices.* Pacific Grove, CA: Brooks/Cole.

This text provides a review of the research associated with the development of antisocial behavior in children and youth. Effective interventions and classroom management strategies for addressing antisocial behaviors are described. The practical approaches include strategies for managing acting-out behavior, teaching social skills, intervening with problem behavior on the playground, and implementing a schoolwide discipline plan.

ON-LINE RESOURCES

AskERIC Hot Topics: School Safety & Violence Prevention
http://ericir.syr.edu/Qa/hottopics/safety.html

This website provides an annotated database of ERIC print and electronic resources concerned with school safety and violence prevention. Links are provided to related ERIC clearinghouses.

Early Prevention of Violence Database
http://www.csnp.ohio-state.edu/glarrc/vpdb.htm

This database consolidates information on resources related to the early prevention of violence in children from birth to age 6. Categories of information include materials and organizations involved in conflict resolution, materials and programs concerned with early prevention of violence, and relevant conferences.

Early Warning, Timely Response: A Guide to Safe Schools
http://www.ed.gov/offices/OSERS/OSEP/earlywrn.html

This resource guide, targeting school personnel, parents, and community members, is the result of a collaborative effort between the U.S. Department of Education and the U.S. Department of Justice. The guide, which may be downloaded from this site, includes a description of early warning signs of crisis situations in educational settings, together with strategies for prevention.

ERIC/CASS Virtual Library: Substance Abuse
http://www.uncg.edu/edu/ericcass/substnce/docs/tableoc.html

This page provides instant links to a broad array of sites concerning substance abuse. Previously published articles, as well as web sites, are included, and many are suitable for student and parent audiences. Several substances are addressed, including alcohol, crack, cocaine, and smokeless tobacco.

FAST Track (Families and Schools Together) Project
http://www.fasttrack.vanderbilt.edu/

This site provides an overview of the Fast Track Project, including a description of related research projects and a list of pertinent publications.

Institute on Violence and Destructive Behavior
http://interact.uoregon.edu/ivdb/ivdb.html

This site, affiliated with the University of Oregon, provides links to research-based programs designed to prevent antisocial behavior among school age youth. Student populations that are well suited for primary, secondary, and tertiary prevention programs are identified. A products page describes affiliated programs and publications, including First Step to Success.

The Texas Youth Commission Office of Prevention
http://www.tyc.state.tx.us/prevention/

This site contains a directory of programs, research, references and resources related to the prevention of youth problems. Categories of resources include adolescent issues, education, families, alternative education, and delinquency prevention and intervention.

CHAPTER 9

Partnering with Parents in Educational Programming for Students with Special Needs

Susan M. Sheridan
Richard J. Cowan
John W. Eagle
University of Nebraska-Lincoln

From the inception of special education law, parents have been considered an integral component in the identification, evaluation, and program development for children suspected of having special needs. In spirit, parents have been recognized as important contributors in the development and implementation of their children's individualized programs. However, historically there has been a difference between the spirit of federal special education law and its implementation by state-governed school districts. As a result, amendments to federal special education law (Individuals with Disabilities Education Act, IDEA 97) (Individuals with Disabilities Education Act Amendments, 1997) have become more explicit in specifying how and when parents are to be involved in the special education process. The purposes of this chapter are to (a) provide a summary of legal mandates specified in IDEA 97 concerning parental participation, (b) describe the characteristics and benefits of a "partnership" approach to working with parents, (c) present useful models developed to promote problem solving between parents and educators, and (d) discuss details of one empirically supported model (conjoint behavioral consultation) that can be used by practitioners to engage parents and educators actively and constructively in identifying and addressing shared concerns in both pre-referral procedures and on the initiation of special education proceedings.

At the outset, it is important to note that the authors espouse the view that forging working partnerships with parents is an essential component of *best educational practice*, and should be standard in working with all students (i.e., with and without identified disabilities). The mandates of IDEA 97 are specified in relation to formal evaluation, eligibility, placement, and planning decisions; however, constructive relationships with families should be incorporated into the efforts of educating *all* students. Thus, the tenets surrounding parental participation in IDEA 97 should be broadened to promote the establishment of working partnerships with all parents, including pre-referral interactions and those surrounding special education programming. Specific approaches or actions to parental participation vary. However, when a concern is identified by either an educator or a parent, efforts to engage in joint problem solving should ensue at the earliest possible moment, and not only when a formal request for evaluation is made.

BACKGROUND AND PURPOSE OF PARENT INVOLVEMENT IN IDEA 97

In 1975, P.L. 94-142 established the foundations for parental involvement in the special education process. In this regard, it required (a) notification of parents when schools proposed or refused to initiate or change the identification, evaluation, or educational placement of the child, or the provision of a free appropriate public education (FAPE) to the child; (b) attainment of parental consent before a child was evaluated for the first time; (c) parental participation in the development of Individualized Education Programs (IEPs); (d) parental consent for a child's initial special education placement; and (e) parental rights to challenge or appeal special education decisions.

In 1986, P.L. 99-457 semantically altered the law by replacing the phrase "handicapped child" with "child with a disability." This law served as a downward extension of P.L. 94-142 in that it mandated FAPE to children aged 0–3. In doing so, the law also instituted the individualized family service plan (IFSP), reiterating the importance of including parents in the special education process. Specifically, it mandated that educational planning for young students be considered in the context of family services and not simply programming for the individual child.

More recently, the passage of the IDEA 97 included more meaningful and informed parent participation as a major theme, establishing specific regulations for including parents on school-based teams and increasing parental responsibility throughout the special education process. The 1999 Final Regulations of IDEA (Individuals with Disabilities Education Act Regulations, 1999) maintained some of the fundamental mandates of its predecessors. The rights of parents that have remained consistent since 1975 include (a) the requirement of parents to be notified by the school of any initiation or change in their child's identification, evaluation, educational placement, or in the provision of FAPE to their child; (b) the parent's right to inspect and review all of the education records that pertain to their child that are used and maintained by the school; and (c) an independent educational evaluation of their child at the public's expense if they disagree with the determination of the local education agency, unless the local educational agency demonstrates at a hearing that the evaluation is appropriate. Importantly, the definition of "parent" in IDEA 97 was expanded to include (a) "a natural or adoptive parent," (b) "a guardian of the State if the child is a ward of the State," (c) "a person acting in the place of a parent (such as a grandparent or stepparent with whom the child lives, or a person who is legally responsible for the child's welfare)," (d) "a surrogate parent who has been appointed according to criteria established in IDEA 97," or (e) "a foster parent, unless prohibited by State Law."

Procedural Safeguards in IDEA 97

Although the spirit of the law has not changed since 1975, the Final Regulations for IDEA 97 (Individuals with Disabilities Education Act Regulations, 1999) include several modifications and additions regarding parents that attempt to ensure that the law's intentions are carried out. The rights afforded to parents under IDEA according to the 1999 Final Regulations are listed in Table 1 on page 310. Primarily, amendments and modifications of prior laws concern procedural safeguards, including notice, consent, and involvement of parents at various key points in the special educational process.

Notice

A full written explanation of the basic due process safeguards extended to parents under IDEA 97 are articulated in the Procedural Safeguards Notice. This written prior notice must be given to parents in "an easily understandable manner," and in the native language of the parents, on at least four occasions: (a) on initial referral, (b) on each notification of an IEP meeting, (c) on reevaluation of their child, and (d) on receipt of a request for a due process hearing. The Notice requires that parents receive explanation of 10 rights, which are listed in Table 2 on page 311.

Along with a notice informing parents of their due process rights and safeguards, written prior notice is required to keep parents apprised of a school's action in relation to their child's identification, evaluation, placement, or provision of FAPE. The written prior notice must contain a description of and rationale for what the school proposes (or refuses) to do, as well as a description of alternative options that have been considered. Schools are required to provide information in a way that the parents can understand and in a manner consistent with the parents' primary language or mode of communication.

TABLE 1: Parental Rights and Responsibilities Under IDEA 97

Parental Right/Responsibility	Explanation
Input during evaluation	Parental input shall be solicited during the evaluation process.
Input regarding eligibility	Parents are entitled to be part of the group that makes the decision regarding their child's eligibility.
Input regarding placement	Parents are entitled to be part of the group that makes the decision regarding their child's educational placement.
Consent for reevaluation	Parents need to provide consent for their child to be reevaluated.
Participation in all meetings	Parents must be given the opportunity to participate in meetings with respect to the identification, evaluation, and educational placement of their child, and to the provision of FAPE to their child.
Receiving progress reports and revising the IEP	Parents have the right to receive regular re-reports on their child's progress. The IEP would need to be revised to address any lack of progress toward annual goals.
Notification to public agency by parents regarding private school placement	Parents must notify the public agency if they intend to remove their child from the public school and place him or her in a private school at public expense.
Notification by parents of their intent to file a complaint	If parents intend to request a due process hearing, then they must notify the state or local educational agency.

Source: Individuals with Disabilities Education Act Amendments of 1997, 20 U.S.C. § 1400 et seq. (West 1997)

TABLE 2: Rights of Parents Articulated in the Procedural Safeguard Notice of IDEA 97

Based on the Procedural Safeguard Notice, parents have the right to:

1. Written prior notice before a proposal or refusal to initiate or change the child's identification, evaluation, educational placement or provision of a free appropriate public education (FAPE).

2. Give or withhold consent at specific times.

3. Access to their child's educational records.

4. An independent educational evaluation (IEE) of their child.

5. Present complaints to initiate an impartial due process hearing.

6. Mediation prior to a hearing.

7. A due process hearing.

8. A state-level hearing review procedure if the impartial due process hearing is held by a local educational agency (LEA).

9. Appeal the final administrative hearing decision.

10. Attorney's fees.

Consent

Under IDEA 97, schools are required to obtain prior written, informed, voluntary consent from parents at least three times throughout the special education process: prior to an initial evaluation; prior to initial provision of special educational services; and prior to reevaluation. Under prior statutes, parental consent was required only for initial evaluation and placement, and not for reevaluations. It is the state's prerogative to require written, informed consent at times other than those indicated as a mechanism to ensure communication and information sharing with parents. If written consent is requested but not provided at alternative times (e.g., annual development of IEPs), the school is nonetheless required to provide FAPE to the child under IDEA.

Parent Involvement at Key Points in the Process

Under IDEA 97, local education agencies are required to incorporate information gathered from the parents of the child during the identification, eligibility, and placement process. Specifically, they are informed of their right to provide information into the evaluation. This includes solicitation of information about the child (e.g., his or her medical and learning history, strengths and limitations, performance outside of school settings, educational needs), and collection of test information in the child's native language in order to prevent discrimination on the basis of race or culture.

Further, parental participation in meetings where key decisions are likely to be made is specified in IDEA 97. These include meetings where eligibility is determined, the IEP is developed, and placement is determined. Generally speaking, it is believed that parents are in a position to contribute to the annual goals and provide their own perspectives of the special services and supports needed by their child. According to Huefner (2000), "in a nutshell, parents are to be equal participants... (solicitation of their input) furthers the IDEA goal of cooperation between home and school" (p. 177). Before IDEA 97, parents were only ensured to be participants at IEP meetings. IDEA 97 also stipulates that parents retain the right to invite any individual who is determined, by either the school or the parents, to have "knowledge or special expertise regarding the child" to become a member of the IEP team. Thus, IDEA 97 provides parents with the right to determine the qualifications of an outside individual they wish to be a member of the IEP team. IDEA 97 has also extended the services that parents may receive as related services by amending the definition of "parent counseling and training." Parent counseling and training is now defined as not only (a) "assisting parents in understanding the special needs of the child" and (b) "providing parents with information about child development," but it also includes (c) "helping parents to acquire the necessary skills that will allow them to support the implementation of their child's IEP or IFSP."

Summary of Parental Participation and IDEA

IDEA 97 provides several opportunities to envision work with families in cooperative and collaborative ways. Given that the "special education process" is defined as beginning when a concern is first identified (Silverstein, Springer, & Russo, 1992), school psychologists and other educators should begin making efforts to involve parents in their children's educational programs as early as possible. Following the tenets of best practices, parental participation and home-school collaboration should continue throughout the child's educational experience. It also should be noted that the law defines *minimum standards* only. School psychologists and other members of school-based teams are encouraged to engage parents actively *whenever* a concern is identified (i.e., at the earliest opportunity) and not only when eligibility and placement are at issue. Mandates requiring parental participation in special education evaluation and IEP meetings may be conceptualized as opportunities to foster collaborative exchanges between parents and educators. Collaborative problem-solving meetings are useful and important for establishing relationships with parents and partnering around the unique needs of their children. Home-school problem solving models provide the templates and tools by which such constructive partnerships can be operationalized for students with special needs.

CONSIDERATIONS FOR SCHOOL-BASED TEAMS IN IMPLEMENTING PARENT INVOLVEMENT PROVISIONS

Several conceptualizations and procedures for working with parents are possible within the context of constructive parental roles as articulated in IDEA 97. The historic model of interfacing with parents, and to an extent the model that permeated pre-1997 statutes, projected a "school to home" direction and influence (Swap, 1993). It is now recognized that such a model is no longer sufficient when programming for students with special needs. Although the "school-to-home transmission model" (Swap, 1993) endorses the importance of continuous interactions between home and school, it is uni-directional in its nature and influence. That is, parents are enlisted to support the school's mission as its primary goal, with the school's (rather than the parent's) values and expectations as priorities (Swap, 1993).

An alternative approach to working with families known as "family-centered services" has been described in the literature. Family-centered practice is defined as "a friendly, respectful partnership with families that provides (a) emotional and educational supports, (b) opportunities to participate in service delivery and to make decisions, and (c) activities to enhance family members' capacities to carry out their self-determined roles" (McWilliam, Tocci, & Harbin, 1998, p. 207). Family-centered services are those that convey family-oriented attitudes (e.g., concern for and attention to family needs and perspectives). Characteristics of such programs include positiveness (thinking the best about families without passing judgment), responsiveness (doing whatever it takes to address families' concerns), orientation to the whole family (interest in the whole family rather than just the child), friendliness (treating families as friends), and sensitivity (empathizing with families and understanding their needs and concerns) (McWilliam, Harbin et al., 1995; McWilliam, Lang et al., 1995; McWilliam, Maxwell, & Sloper, 1999; McWilliam et al., 1998). The definition of family-centered services as a "partnership" is consistent with the principles promoted in IDEA 97, which require active, meaningful parent involvement throughout the process from initial evaluation through educational planning and monitoring.

Parents and Educators as Partners

A partnership philosophy to working with families considers the bi-directional (two-way) influences of families and educators on children's learning and development. That is, experiences, expectations, and values communicated in homes affect children's performance in schools, and vice-versa. Furthermore, the interdependencies between home and school are recognized, because no one system in isolation can provide for all the needs of a child with a disability. Partnerships can be defined in terms of linkages wherein families and schools "work together to accomplish a common mission ... for all children in school to achieve success" (Swap, 1993, pp. 48–49). Central to this definition is the emphasis on *relationships* between family members and educational personnel, rather than distinct roles that one or the other may play. As such, the responsibility for educating and socializing children is within the shared domains of home and school in relationship with each other. Both families and schools are recognized as essential for the growth and success of children. Additionally, there is a belief in a shared responsibility for educating and socializing children (Christenson & Sheridan, in press). These characteristics of partnerships appear to capture the spirit and intent of parental participation as articulated in IDEA 97.

The characteristics of partnerships may be considered prerequisite conditions to the development of parental involvement practices. Development and implementation of a partnership model for home-school relationships require the presence of several essential elements. These include commitments to collaboration, effective communication, trust, a shared responsibility, mutual support, and joint decision making.

Collaboration

Given the challenges associated with the broad and comprehensive mission surrounding the education and development of students with special needs, collaboration among parents, educators, and community members is essential. Collaboration has been defined in several ways. For purposes of this chapter, home-school collaboration is defined as "a student-centered, dynamic framework that endorses collegial, interdependent, and co-equal styles of interaction between families and educators who work jointly together to achieve common goals" (adapted from Welch & Sheridan, 1995). The goals of home-school collaboration are to enhance the successes and improve experiences for children, including those that are academic, social, emotional, and behavioral in nature.

Collaboration is considered to be an evolving process that enables parents and educators to develop new, creative alternatives. The "collaborative ethic" (Phillips & McCullough, 1990) is a guiding belief, philosophy, or set of values about the importance and essential nature of family participation in educational

314

efforts. It involves both *equality* (the willingness to listen to, respect, and learn from one another) and *parity* (the blending of knowledge, skills, and ideas to enhance positive outcomes for children) (Welch & Sheridan, 1995). When collaborating with parents, there is a commitment to *interdependence*. That is, parents and educators in collaborative relationships depend on one another equally and reciprocally to achieve optimal outcomes for students. Importantly, each individual (parent, teacher, school psychologist, and other members of multidisciplinary teams) defers to the other in their respective domains, works together in a reciprocal fashion, and complements each other's efforts (Power & Bartholomew, 1987).

Collaborative problem-solving meetings are useful and important for establishing relationships with parents and partnering around the unique needs of their children. Certain actions that are desirable when engaging in collaborative interactions related to planning and programming for students with special needs are listed in Table 3 on page 316. Actions that school psychologists and other educators can take prior to, during, and following meetings with parents to enhance their usefulness are presented in Table 4 on page 317.

Effective Communication

Clear communication with parents is at the heart of collaborative exchanges. Parents are likely to be inundated with information from school personnel concerning elements of the special education process. The likelihood of jargon and technical information is apparent when discussing concerns, assessment procedures and outcomes, educational goals and objectives, and programmatic options. There are several considerations for communicating clearly with family members, including ensuring understanding of the language spoken, limiting jargon, and checking frequently for understanding. These and other suggestions for communicating with parents are listed in Table 5 on page 319.

Clear and effective communication assumes that parents and teachers share information honestly, in an open, bi-directional manner. Educators share information about school programs, curriculum, and student progress, and parents convey to school personnel information about their child's background, strengths, and characteristics. Both parties must be willing to share their thoughts and ideas about their respective expectations, goals, and responsibilities. Furthermore, effective communication is dependent on an environment that allows participants the opportunity to voice concerns without being perceived as a "problem" by the other parties (Power & Bartholomew, 1987). When differences arise it is necessary to address conflicts openly and directly. Educators and parents must espouse a philosophy wherein problems in the home-school relationship are not avoided but addressed in an effort to increase mutual understanding. Efforts to withhold

TABLE 3: Actions Reflective of Collaborative Relationships

1. Listening to one another's perspective.

2. Viewing differences as a strength.

3. Remaining focused on a mutual interest (e.g., assessment and planning for students with special needs).

4. Sharing information about the child, the home and school systems, and problems encountered in these systems.

5. Asking for ideas and opinions about the child, problem, goals, and potential solutions.

6. Respecting the skills and knowledge of each other related to the student, source of disability, and contextual considerations.

7. Planning together to address parents', teachers', and students' needs.

8. Making joint decisions about a child's educational program and goals.

9. Sharing resources to work toward goal attainment.

10. Providing a common message to the student about schoolwork and behavior.

11. Demonstrating a willingness to address conflict.

12. Refraining from finding fault, and committing to sharing successes.

TABLE 4: **Actions to Enhance the Effectiveness of Home-School Meetings**

Before the Meeting:

1. Make efforts to establish a relationship with parents before the meeting. Informal social events can be of assistance.

2. Send early notification about the meeting (2–3 weeks prior to its scheduled time, if possible). Try to add a personal note to a formal notice and offer some flexibility in appointment schedules.

3. Schedule an adequate amount of time to cover the concerns or topics in need of discussion.

4. Plan an agenda, which might include a list of questions, concerns, specific information about test scores, report card grades, attendance records, homework completion, or classroom behavior. Be sure to allow at least half of the time for parental input and questions. Prioritize concerns and ideas to discuss, expecting that you will have time to deal with only one or two.

5. Assist parents to plan for the meeting by providing a form on which they can list questions or concerns.

6. Arrange for transportation, babysitting at the school, translators for non-English-speaking parents, evening hours, and meetings for noncustodial parents.

7. Assemble the necessary materials (e.g., paper, writing utensils, student papers, test scores) for easy accessibility during the meeting.

8. Practice in anticipation of difficult moments, particularly if negative information or conflicts are likely. Good listening and communication skills are essential in meetings with parents, especially with those parents who feel angry or threatened or try to make school staff feel that way. In-service training that identifies key skills and provides opportunities to practice difficult situations can be helpful. It might also help to try out ideas and language on a colleague who can provide constructive feedback.

Table 4 continued on p. 318

317

Table 4 continued

9. Set the stage for the meeting by providing a physical comfortable environment for parents. Two or three adult-size chairs and privacy are minimum requirements. If possible, refreshments are a nice touch.

During the Meeting:

1. Clarify the agenda by identifying issues or questions that are important to school staff and to parents. Time the meeting carefully to give each parent equal time.

2. Seek the parents' expertise about their child. Appreciate the uniqueness of each child in a sincere way.

3. Avoid jargon.

4. If shortage of time seems to be pressuring you and the parent during the meeting, then schedule another meeting. The meeting can be continued on a different day, evening, or over the telephone.

5. If the meeting results in plans for action, then decide on how follow-up will occur.

6. Conclude the meeting on a friendly note.

After the Meeting:

1. The parent and school staff should talk with the student about the meeting, emphasizing the positive information that was exchanged and areas in need of improvement.

2. When specific plans for improvement are established during the meeting, continued home–school communication is critical. This may include communication about the student's instructional program, additional work to be completed at home with assistance or supervision, and periodic evaluations of the student's progress.

3. Evaluate the meeting by soliciting information from parents and school personnel regarding satisfaction with time use, quality of information obtained and given, knowledge gained about the family or school, specific plans to

help the student, arrangements for follow through, willingness to attend future meetings, and other suggestions for improving meetings.

4. Monitor the rate of parent attendance, adequacy of scheduled time and space, needs of parents revealed in meetings, and utility of forms used to plan for and evaluate meetings.

5. Administrators can synthesize the evaluation from parents and school staff and discuss suggested changes with staff. School personnel can collaboratively locate, adopt, and redesign procedures to establish meaningful, productive, and effective meeting formats.

Reproduced with permission from: M. Welch & S. Sheridan (1995). Educational partnerships: Serving students at risk. San Antonio: Harcourt-Brace Jovanovich.

TABLE 5: Suggestions for Effective Communication

Strive for a positive orientation rather than a deficit-based or crisis orientation.
* Reframe the child's "problems" as shared concerns, areas for growth, or opportunities for development.
* Point out the child's strengths, and not only his/her limitations.

Consider the tone as well as content of your communications.
* Maintain a friendly, supportive tone of voice while sharing information and concerns.

Develop regular, reliable, varied two-way communication systems.
* Ask parents about the best way to get in touch with them.
* Make sure messages are received by parents by not relying on only one mode of communication such as a home-note or messages on answering machines.

Emphasize a "win-win" orientation, rather than placing blame.
* State a desire to work together toward resolution, rather than making attributions for problems (e.g., "unmotivated," "lacks support").
* Discuss what can be done at home and at school to achieve goals.

Keep the focus of communication on the child's performance.
* Discuss current, observable concerns.
* Solicit information about the child and family only as it relates to child's academic performance or school behavior.

Table 5 continued on p. 320

Table 5 continued

Ensure that parents have needed information to support children's educational progress.
• Refrain from jargon.
• Encourage questions.
• Use parents' native language or an interpreter.
• Check for understanding.

Create formal and informal opportunities to communicate and build trust between home and school.
• Spend time in locations where parents drop off and pick up their children.
• Invite parents to come to the classrooms.
• Establish family gatherings in evenings or weekends.
Underscore all communication with a shared responsibility between families and schools.
• Use terms such as "we" and "us."
• State the importance of positive attitudes and actions at both home and school.
• Invite parents' ideas, perspectives, and observations.
• Use open ended questions and allow parental elaboration.

---

from blaming and fault finding are essential to address differences openly. An excellent discussion of strategies for addressing parent-educator conflict is available in Christenson and Hirsch (1998).

Trust

To engage in honest discourse, elements of trust and reciprocal respect are important. A definition of trust, as related to home-school partnerships, was offered by Adams and Christenson (1998) as "confidence that another person will act in a way to benefit or sustain the relationship, or the implicit or explicit goals of the relationship, to achieve positive outcomes for students" (p. 6). The construct of trust emerges as a central characteristic of several models of home-school collaboration. Key elements of the home-school relationship (e.g., open and honest communication, sharing and working toward common goals) are clearly predicated on trust between partners (Adams & Christenson, 1998). Examples of ways that educators can demonstrate trust include accepting parents' observations of their child's behaviors at home, even if they differ from observations at school, and expressing confidence that parents can help their child.

In reality, interactions in many parent–educator relationships are often brief and infrequent. Further, interactions tend to be focused on problems of the student rather than opportunities for constructive, joint problem solving. The effect this has on the development of trust in the family–school relationship is unclear; however, under such circumstances, it is likely that there is little opportunity to establish higher levels of trust.

Shared Responsibility

A fourth element of a parent partnership model is shared responsibility for learning as it occurs and is enhanced at both home and at school. Development occurs across settings, and various opportunities and practices in each setting support the child's learning in relevant ways. To work in partnership with each other, parents and educators must recognize and accept that they each possess areas of influence and, hence, share in joint responsibility for learning. For example, teachers develop curricula, activities, and relationships with children that create optimal conditions for learning. Likewise, parents can provide structure, guidance, discipline, and assistance to prepare their children to take advantage of learning opportunities. The unique roles and practices occurring across home and school settings contribute in a complementary way to a child's development (Christenson & Sheridan, in press).

As with other partnership approaches, the focus of the relationship is on what parents and school personnel can do *together* to address mutually shared concerns about a child. Problem-solving relationships with families are viewed "as a means for preparing the child for success ... rather than as a mechanism for collecting information from parents that would help educators prepare the child" (Christenson & Hirsch, 1998; p. 325). For this to occur, the nature of such discussions must be constructive (focused on accomplishing a shared goal) and collaborative (cooperative and helpful). For example, if there are problems with a child's daily life skills, school–family teams may jointly identify related activities that can be carried out by teachers (e.g., teaching the child how to distinguish the "walk" from the "don't walk" traffic signals) and by parents (e.g., going for a walk with their child and observing the signals in naturalistic settings) to accomplish a shared goal.

Mutual Support

Mutual support across home and school is an important fifth element of partnerships. Parents can support educators in many ways, including activities such as fundraising, volunteering, or monitoring homework. Teachers can support family members by keeping parents informed of classroom activities, school functions, and student progress and responsibilities (Christenson & Sheridan, in press).

However, it is important to recognize that parents vary in their ability to participate in traditional ways such as these. Work schedules, transportation problems, family commitments, and other personal factors may interfere with parents' abilities to attend school functions or engage in school-determined activities. It is imperative that team members refrain from judging parents based on their visible participation and consider that many other avenues for supporting children's learning are possible. In fact, parents may assist teachers and school personnel to identify meaningful involvement activities. Such supportive gestures demonstrating mutual support among parents and teachers can be instrumental in the establishment of a partnering relationship.

Teaming and Joint Decision Making

Finally, a sixth element of a partnership philosophy allows parents and educators to make joint decisions at various levels. Consistent with IDEA 97, decision making about a child's individualized education program should be a shared responsibility. Toward this end, parents and teachers in partnership with each other can (a) review data pertinent to identified problems, (b) identify respective and shared goals and objectives for a student's education, (c) explore options and opportunities for educational planning to meet the student's goals, (d) discuss roles of each party for implementing components of the educational plan, and (e) monitor progress toward goal attainment over time and in collaboration with each other. The practice of data-based, joint decision making represents a process with ongoing commitment and monitoring and is not limited to a one-time IEP meeting. Under IDEA 97, parents have the right to receive regular progress reports; and, together, parents and educators can make revisions to address lack of progress toward annual goals. Best practices within a partnership orientation suggest more frequent meetings to discuss progress and modify strategies, when necessary.

At a minimum, IDEA 97 requires parents to be included in meetings that concern the identification, evaluation, and placement of their child. Specifically, local educational agencies (LEAs) are required to ensure that the parents of each child with a disability are part of the decision-making group. Further, it is the responsibility of the LEA to ensure that the parents understand both the process as well as the context of the meetings and are also able to participate in group discussions related to the placement of their child. Such decision-making functions carry with them implicit roles that include identification of educational concerns and problem-solving activities.

In sum, school psychologists and other members of school-based teams have much to offer in the development of positive relationships and partnerships with parents in the education of students with special needs. Such individuals are in a unique position to work within and across systems to establish relationships at several levels. Importantly, they can become agents for collaborating with parents to increase conditions for positive learning experiences and student success.

BEST PRACTICE STRATEGIES FOR IMPLEMENTING THE PARENTAL INVOLVEMENT

Home-school problem-solving models emerge as a means for operationalizing a partnership philosophy when working with students with special needs and their families. They provide the templates and tools by which such constructive partnerships can be operationalized for students with special needs. These models are based on at least four common principles: joint responsibility and ownership for problem solution, the child as central, open and direct conflict management, and a focus on solutions (Christenson & Hirsch, 1998). An empowerment orientation is typical; most problem-solving models shift away from diagnosing problems toward developing cooperative relationships with parents (Dunst & Trivette, 1987) to help the child.

Empowerment implies that many competencies are already present or can be possible within families. From an empowerment perspective, a failure to display competence is not due to the deficiencies of families and their children but rather on a failure of social systems, including schools, to create opportunities for competencies to be displayed. Rappaport (1981) has argued that "in those cases where new competencies need to be learned, they are best learned in the context of living life rather than in artificial programs where ... it is really the expert who is in charge" (p. 16). That is, to be "empowered," parents must believe that changes that occur are a result of their own efforts. Therefore, strengths and competencies of families related to their abilities to share in decision making and problem resolution are central. Attention is placed on the shared strengths of the home, school, and child rather than on "fixing" child- or family-centered problems.

It is the authors' beliefs that effective, problem-solving teaming practices empower parents to be meaningful contributors in their child's education. Several models for team-based problem solving are available. Among these are the Family/School Meeting (Weiss & Edwards, 1992), Parent-Educator Problem Solving (PEPS) (Christenson, 1995b), Solution-Oriented Family-School Meetings (Carlson, Hickman, & Horton, 1992), and Conjoint Behavioral Consultation (CBC) (Sheridan, Kratochwill, & Bergan, 1996). Although each of those models is unique in specific procedural protocol, all include four similar procedural elements consistent with a problem solving approach: (a) an introductory phase between members of the school and family environments to set the stage for problem solving, (b) a collaborative brainstorming of concerns, (c) a joint selection of an immediate concern on which to focus discussions, and (d) the implementation of a solution amenable to all parties (see Table 6 on page 324). As such, each of those models relies on effective communication skills and competency in problem solving, and all share a primary goal of empowering parents and creating partnerships between families and schools to promote student competence. One model, Conjoint Behavioral Consultation, will be explored in detail.

CBC is "... a structured indirect form of service-delivery, in which parents and teachers are joined together to address the academic, social, or behavioral needs of

TABLE 6: **Procedural Stages of Home-School Problem Solving Models**

Family/School Problem-Solving Meeting (Weiss & Edwards, 1992)	Parent-Educator Problem Solving (Christenson, 1995a)	Solution-Oriented Family-School Meetings (Carlson, Hickman, & Horton, 1992)	Conjoint Behavioral Consultation (Sheridan, Kratochwill, & Bergan, 1996)
Introduction and overview	Introduction	Introduction	Preconsultation meeting
Finding facts	Identification	Explanation of solution-oriented approach	Conjoint problem identification
Determining a decision	Selection	Joining	Conjoint problem analysis
Arrive at action	Implementation	Negotiating a solvable complaint	Treatment (plan) implementation
Follow-up meeting		Establishing a solution goal	Conjoint treatment (plan) evaluation
		Eliciting multiple solutions toward accomplishing smallest change	
		Gaining agreement on the smallest change in direction of goal	
		Clarifying individual responsibilities and task assignments	
		Follow up	
		Evaluating and recycling if necessary	

an individual for whom both parties bear some responsibility" (Sheridan & Kratochwill, 1992; p.122). The process is guided by a consultant (school psychologist, special educator, or other team member) who shares both technical and interpersonal skill in facilitating the problem solving process. Various process goals of the model are presented in Table 7.

CBC borrows from both ecological and behavioral theories. From ecological theory, CBC espouses Bronfenbrenner's (1977) thesis that children and their be-

TABLE 7: **Process Goals of Conjoint Behavioral Consultation**

1. Increase communication and knowledge about family (e.g., family history, medical information, prior treatments).

2. Improve relationship among the child, family (mother and father), and school personnel.

3. Establish home–school partnership.

4. Promote shared ownership for identified problems and solutions.

5. Establish shared educational goals.

6. Increase parent (mother and father) and teacher commitments to educational goals.

7. Address problems as they occur across, rather than within settings.

8. Encourage consistency in addressing concerns across home and school settings.

9. Promote greater conceptualization of a problem.

10. Increase the diversity of expertise and resources available.

Adapted with permission: Sheridan, S. M., Kratochwill, T. R., & Bergan, J. R. (1996). *Conjoint behavioral consultation: A procedural manual.* New York: Plenum.

haviors are part of at least four nested systems or levels (i.e., microsystem, mesosystem, exosystem, macrosystem). CBC addresses the mesosystem (i.e., interactions among primary systems in a child's life, such as the home, school, and other immediate settings) by involving important primary caregivers (parents, teachers, and other significant individuals) from the essential systems in which the child functions (e.g., home, school). As related to behavioral theory, CBC recognizes the importance of conducting direct behavioral observations, collecting data in a continuous fashion, performing functional assessments, and employing empirically validated interventions as a critical element of educational and behavioral programs.

The CBC model provides a vehicle by which home–school partnerships can be operationalized. It is sensitive to the essential features of home–school partnerships; namely, that home–school collaboration is a process (i.e., a means to an end, and not an end in itself), and "results in a shared responsibility among parents and educators for ... outcomes" (Christenson, 1995a, p. 119). The CBC model allows parents to become actively involved in problem solving and decision making as behavioral, social, or academic problems are identified, defined, analyzed, and treated across settings. Parents' unique knowledge and information, and their active participation in decision making, place them at the center of planning in their child's education. Through mutual and collaborative interactions, parents and school team members identify and explore academic and behavioral problems; analyze functional, contextual/ecological, and/or curricular conditions around behaviors; develop and implement relevant interventions; and analyze the outcome of the intervention (Sheridan et al., 1996).

Consistent with the philosophy of home–school partnerships, CBC can be used early on, at the initial articulation of a concern. Likewise, it is useful in the event of a special education referral, particularly by facilitating the identification of behavioral objectives and strategies in IEPs. Figure 1 presents a schema by which CBC can structure communication and problem solving (a) at the pre-referral stage to address presenting concerns in the general education classroom; (b) throughout the referral and evaluation stages; and (c) at the IEP development, implementation, and evaluation stages.

At the pre-referral level, parental participation is secured as the school team addresses academic and behavioral concerns prior to formal evaluation for special education. If the team can successfully intervene, then formal referral to ascertain special education eligibility may be avoided. Early parental involvement and the documentation of pre-referral interventions represent genuine attempts to meet the letter and spirit of the IDEA 97 legislation. If formal assessment and related intervention procedures become necessary, then the CBC process ensures that the team (a) conducts a complete functional assessment of problematic behavior within the classroom and home settings and (b) develops strategies to intervene at the environmental level through testing hypotheses generated through the consider-

FIGURE 1: Schema for CBC in Pre-referral Interventions and Special Education Programming

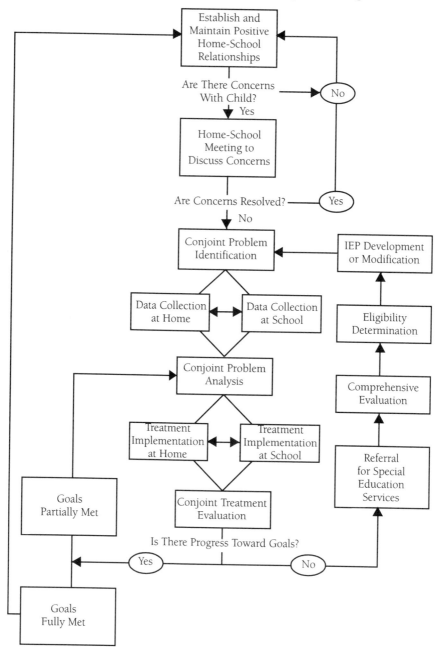

ation of functional assessment findings (see Tilly, Knoster, and Ikeda, this volume; Tankersley, Landrum, Cook, and Balan, this volume). This practice is concordant with the amendments of IDEA 97, stipulating that the team considers positive behavioral interventions, strategies, and supports based on functional assessment findings.

Setting the Stage for Problem Solving by Building Relationships

There are several considerations that should be addressed before initiating formal problem-solving procedures. First and foremost, constructive, positive working relationships between parents, teachers, and the school psychologist consultant (or other facilitator) must be established. It should be noted that establishing relationships between parents and educators is a complex matter that requires time, deliberate efforts, and repeated interactions. There are, how-

TABLE 8: Strategies to Increase the Success of Informal Events with Families

1. Provide a 2- to 4-week notice of upcoming events.

2. Prepare personal invitations in parents' native language.

3. Schedule some events on weekends, evenings, or other times conducive for working parents.

4. Send reminders home.

5. Provide transportation and child care to families in need of these services.

6. Have refreshments available; an informal meal is especially inviting.

7. Plan events carefully (e.g., seating arrangements, open discussions) to promote informal communication between parents and school personnel.

8. Evaluate events by asking parents and school staff their perceptions. Use feedback for planning future events.

Reproduced with permission from: Welch, M., & Sheridan, S. M. (1995). Educational partnerships: Serving students at risk. San Antonio: Harcourt-Brace Jovanovich.

ever, some actions and activities that can set the stage for working effectively with parents. For example, through one or more informal gatherings, parents and teachers can be allowed to interact to increase their familiarity with each other and to share information about themselves, their respective settings, and the child for whom they share responsibility. Suggestions for increasing the success of informal events with families are offered in Table 8.

Communication among parents and school personnel is essential in the establishment of positive relationships (Christenson & Sheridan, in press). All interactions with families can be conducted in ways that prioritize effective communication strategies. For example, open and honest communication can be modeled by discussing the type of and manner in which information will be shared with family members (e.g., through formal meetings, telephone calls, data collection, examination of school records). Likewise, the importance of mutual sharing and continued participation can be conveyed explicitly through verbal statements attesting to the benefits of shared problem solving and implicitly by eliciting information from both parents and teachers throughout the process. Such practices convey the strong message that parent involvement is not only desirable but necessary in the child's education.

Before consultation, the responsibilities of each team member should be made clear. In addition to learning more about their roles in the CBC process, parents and teachers should develop an understanding about how the child's academic or behavioral problem will be identified and addressed through the team-based CBC process.

Stages of CBC Problem Solving

The CBC process consists of four stages, all implemented in a simultaneous, conjoint fashion (Sheridan, 1997; Sheridan et al., 1996). Three of the four stages are initiated through a structured behavioral interview. The stages are (a) problem identification (and the Conjoint Problem Identification Interview; CPII), (b) problem analysis (and the Conjoint Problem Analysis Interview; CPAI), (c) treatment implementation, and (d) treatment evaluation (and the Conjoint Treatment Evaluation Interview; CTEI). The process can be used as a pre-referral procedure, involving parents at the earliest sign of a concern. Likewise, it can be used to structure problem solving as related to specific special educational goals and objectives. The goals of each interview as they relate to pre-referral and to special education (IEP) procedures are presented in Table 9 on page 330.

Conjoint Problem Identification

The first formal stage of CBC is problem identification. This stage is initiated through CPII. Suggestions for this interview are presented in Table 10. As a pre-

TABLE 9: Procedural Goals at Various Stages of Problem Solving in Relation to Prereferral Interventions and IEP Development

Pre-Referral Interventions	IEP Development
Problem Identification	
A. Define the problem(s) in behavioral terms	A. Explore social, behavioral, and academic effects of primary disability
B. Identify important contextual, environmental, and cross-setting conditions that affect the behavior	B. Specify target behaviors in relation to identified disability to be prioritized in special education services
C. Provide a tentative strength of the behavior across settings	C. Determine current level of functioning in relation to target behaviors (e.g., conduct direct observations, examine current assignments, look at grade book)
D. Establish a procedure for baseline data across settings	
Problem Analysis	
A. Evaluate and obtain agreement on the baseline data across settings	A. Evaluate and obtain agreement on current functioning
B. Discuss and reach agreement on a goal for behavior	B. Establish short- and long-term goals and objectives
C. Conduct a functional and conditional assessment of the behavior across settings	C. Conduct a functional assessment
D. Identify setting events, ecological conditions, and other cross-setting variables that may affect the target behavior	D. Explore a range of placement options and determine IDEAA and CBC-51 (i.e., special placement to general class room)

Pre-Referral Interventions	IEP Development
E. Design an intervention plan, including specification of conditions to be changed and the practical guidelines regarding treatment implementation	E. Brainstorm alternative plans to address target behaviors in relation to goals
F. Reaffirm record-keeping procedures	F. Determine roles and responsibilities of the regular education teacher, special education teacher, special education coordinator, parents, school psychologist, counselor, and other team members
	G. Reaffirm record-keeping procedures

Treatment Implementation

A. Monitor implementation of the intervention	A. Monitor the implementation of services as articulated in the IEP
B. Provide training to teachers, parents, and others as necessary	B. Continue to monitor the target behaviors through data collection
C. Assess behavioral side effects and contrast effects	C. Assess behavioral side effects and contrast effects
D. Determine need for immediate revisions in plan	D. Determine need for immediate revisions to the IEP
E. Continue data collection procedures	E. Continue data collection procedures

Treatment Evaluation

A. Evaluate treatment data to determine if the goals of consultation have been obtained goals across settings	A. Evaluate existing data to determine if the IEP goals have been obtained

Table 9 continued on p. 332

Table 9 continued

Pre-Referral Interventions	IEP Development
B. Evaluate the effectiveness of the treatment plan across setings	B. Evaluate services/behavioral plan-as needed (at least once a year)
C. Discuss strategies and tactics regarding the continuation, modification, or termination of the treatment plan	C. Discuss strategies and tactics regarding the continuation, modification, or termination of the treatment plan as as articulated in the IEP
D. Discuss strategies for maintenance and generalization of treatment gains	D. Discuss strategies for maintenance and generalization of treatment gains
E. Recycle through the process to address other concerns	E. Recycle through the process to address additional concerns on the IEP

referral strategy, problem identification targets primary behavioral, academic, or social concerns across home and school that are interfering with a child's achievement and development. If used as part of the special education planning process, then home and school target behaviors related to the child's primary disability and its manifestation are identified. Clear, objective definitions of the target behaviors are developed to help team members (school psychologist or other educational specialist, at least one parent, and at least one teacher) focus educational efforts. Behavioral examples are explored, and priorities for intervention are established. Situations where the concerns are highest (e.g., at what time, in what setting, with what subject matter) are identified and prioritized, allowing for focused observation, analysis, intervention, and evaluation during later CBC stages.

During the problem identification stage, tentative contextual, functional, or skills assessments are conducted. In the absence of direct behavioral data, discussions around environmental influences that may be affecting the target concern are considered tentative. These will be validated (or invalidated) subsequently through the collection of baseline data. Nevertheless, this initial contextual/functional assessment allows the parents and teachers to explore conditions that may be supporting or maintaining the behavior as presented across settings. Detailed descriptions of functional assessment and analysis are beyond the scope of this chapter. Interested readers are referred to Haynes and O'Brien (1990), Larson and Maag (1998), O'Neill et al. (1997), and Tilly et al. (this volume).

TABLE 10: Suggestions for Conducting Conjoint Problem Identification Interviews

1. Begin the interview by eliciting general concerns from the parent and teacher. Ask for specific examples of each general concern as it occurs at home and school.

2. Summarize the general concerns and examples across settings. Try to point out similarities from the parent's and the teacher's examples.

3. Explain that not all problems can be addressed at once. Ask the parent and teacher what they consider a priority. This priority can be determined by selecting the behavior that is of greatest concern or one that can affect other behaviors if targeted. Gain consensus from parents and teachers.

4. Define the priority (i.e., target behavior) clearly and objectively. The definition should be observable and concrete.

5. Keep the discussion focused by restating the target problem and summarizing often. Ask both the parent and teacher for validation to ensure agreement and understanding at both home and school.

6. Ask about antecedents and consequences to the target problem at both home and school. Inquire about any patterns that parents and teachers may see in its occurrence. This information may include day of week, time of day, and other commonalties across instances.

7. Determine both short-term objectives and long-term goals for the student at home and at school. The objectives should be appropriate for the setting (i.e., home and school) based on opportunities and severity. An example of a short-term objective is "Kevin will wait his turn and ask to join in ongoing games with a clear and pleasant voice at least three times during each lunch recess (school) and once a day when playing with his brother (home)."

8. Develop data collection procedures that are simple and practical. Whenever possible, use similar data collection procedures at home and school to allow for direct comparisons. Be sure that the teachers and parents help develop these and that they state whether they will be able to follow through with the collection procedures. Determine the length of baseline data collection.

9. Collect additional data that may be helpful in identifying and understanding the problem, such as work samples, rating scales, self-reports, and sociometric measures.

10. Check in with the parent and teacher midway through the baseline period to monitor adherence to the data collection procedures.

Reprinted with permission: Sheridan, S. M., Kratochwill, T. R., & Bergan, J. R. (1996). Conjoint behavioral consultation: A procedural manual. New York: Plenum.

An additional goal of the CPII includes delineating a valid procedure for collecting baseline data across settings. The goal in data collection is to determine the severity of target behaviors across home and school settings and to identify conditions that may be promoting, maintaining, or reinforcing its occurrence.

Conjoint Problem Analysis

The second stage of CBC is problem analysis, initiated in a conjoint fashion through CPAI. Suggestions for conducting CPAIs are outlined in Table 11. There are two distinct phases of problem analysis: (a) data analysis and (b) plan development (Sheridan et al., 1996). During the data analysis phase, parents, teachers, and the consultant evaluate and obtain agreement on the sufficiency and validity of the baseline data across settings. If the data represent an accurate representation of the presenting behavior across settings, then reasonable short- and long-term goals for behavior change across settings are discussed and agreed on. As a facilitator of the CBC process, it is the consultant's responsibility to encourage parents and teachers to start with reasonable short-term goals before moving toward larger, long-term goals. This is particularly relevant to the development of an IEP, in which educational goals are broken down into specific objectives, with both long- and short-term outcomes identified.

During the CPAI, the CBC team examines the baseline data and conducts a functional assessment of the target behavior across settings (i.e., discusses antecedent, sequential, and consequential conditions of the behavior). In an effort to conduct a thorough functional assessment (per IDEA 97 guidelines; see Tilly et al., this volume), the consultation team seeks to identify setting events (events that are functionally related, but temporally or contextually distal to the target behavior) (Wahler & Fox, 1981); discriminative environmental stimuli across settings that elicit the behavior; factors related to times when the behavior does not occur; and other cross-setting variables (e.g., home and school routines) that may affect the target behavior. Importantly, hypotheses about the function of the behavior or environmental/contextual, functional, and/or curricular conditions contributing to its occurrence are generated by the team before discussing an intervention plan. In the case of academic problems, the child's current level of performance, skills and deficits, details of the curriculum, and instructional procedures are explored. For an invaluable resource in assessing the instructional environment, the reader is referred to Ysseldyke and Christenson (1992).

The second phase of problem analysis is plan development. From the hypotheses generated during the functional/conditional assessment, the team collaboratively develops a program to address the target concern. As a pre-referral strategy, interventions are developed to address target behaviors in the natural settings of the home and classroom. As a strategy to structure IEP development, plans related to specific IEP goals and objectives are specified. In both pre-referral

TABLE 11: Suggestions for Conducting Conjoint Problem Analysis Interviews

1. Start the interview by asking the parent and teacher how the data collection went. Review the data in their presence.
2. Use the behavioral data to structure your questions. Ask about specific instances of the behavior, including what happened before, after, and during its occurrence.
3. Ask about setting events, such as events at home that occurred in conjunction with the target behavior at school, or happenings at school and how they relate to behaviors at school.
4. Try to point out any interesting patterns or trends that are apparent in the data. Highlight similarities, differences, and relationships between the home and school settings if they become apparent.
5. Summarize the data that were collected at home and school and ask if the problem still warrants intervention across settings.
6. Based on the data that were collected and the observations of parents and teachers, inquire about what may be maintaining or reinforcing the problem behavior at home and school. Restate any internal or psychological causes into behavioral or environmental terms.
7. Using the information gleaned from the data analysis and the hypotheses about what promotes or maintains the problem behavior, develop an intervention plan. Use information available regarding empirically validated interventions to select treatment strategies.
8. Involve the parents and teachers as much as possible in the development of the plan. Ask what is reasonable and practical in their setting. Ask for their input about the length of the program and the reinforcers to be used. If feasible, include a home-school communication mechanism, such as a home-note procedure.
9. Suggest that similar programs be implemented in both the home and school settings to increase consistency in the program and maintenance of the behavior change.
10. Ask parents and teachers to continue collecting behavioral data during treatment implementation. Data collection procedures should be identical to those used during the problem identification (baseline) stage.

Reprinted with permission: Sheridan, S. M., Kratochwill, T. R., & Bergan, J. R. (1996). Conjoint behavioral consultation: A procedural manual. New York: Plenum.

and IEP processes, plan strategies are clearly defined, roles and responsibilities of all parties (e.g., parents, teachers, support staff) are clearly delineated, and a timeline for implementing the intervention is constructed.

As related to the ideals set forth in IDEA 97, and to facilitate the process and outcome goals of CBC, it is imperative that all team members participate in treatment plan development. Parents, teachers, and other individuals involved with a child contribute knowledge of their respective contexts (e.g., home/family issues, classroom/curricular–educational considerations). Together with the school psychologist's (or other facilitator's) intervention knowledge base, they together arrive at a reasonable plan. The development and implementation of the consultation plan serves as a vehicle through which the team conducts a meaningful functional analysis (i.e., the manipulation of factors hypothesized to be related to the function of the target behavior). Data collection continues throughout the consultation process, thus promoting a data-driven problem-solving process.

Intervention plans that are implemented across home and school need not be identical in design and structure. It is possible (in many cases, likely) that different behaviors serve similar functions at home and school (suggesting that different behaviors be targeted across settings), that different conditions operate at home and at school to maintain an undesirable behavior, or that functions of similar behaviors vary in different settings (indicating the importance of setting-specific assessment and interventions). Likewise, resources across settings are important to consider in the development of plans aimed at achieving consultation goals. Assuming that the goals are mutually determined and shared across settings, it is possible to focus on one setting (e.g., school) to provide the primary intervention strategy and the additional setting (e.g., home) to engage in complementary roles. For example, when targets for intervention are academic in nature (e.g., reading skill acquisition), a structured peer-tutoring program at school may be appropriate. Rather than invoking an identical tutoring program at home, it may be more desirable to identify supportive practices such as enhancing the linguistic environment at home (Clark, 1988), increasing the amount of reading materials via regular visits to the local library, or interactive parent-child book reading (Taverne & Sheridan, 1995). Other examples of activities in which parents can engage at home to support their child in relation to specific objectives are in Table 12.

There are several intervention variables to consider when designing procedures to be implemented by the consultation team across home and school settings. First, the components of the plan should be based on principles that are derived from empirically validated procedures (i.e., the components should be demonstrated through research and practice to be efficacious as related to similar behavioral concerns within similar settings). Second, the plan should be reasonable (i.e., not too complex) to allow parents and teachers to follow through easily and reliably. Yeaton and Sechrest (1981) argue that the degree of treatment integrity (the degree to which a treatment plan is implemented as intended) is directly

TABLE 12: Suggested Actions for Parents to Support Learning at Home

- Set high but realistic expectations for child's performance, behavior, and achievement.
  Examples: Ensure that homework is completed, help child set realistic goals, make child responsible for his/her own behaviors, state confidence in child's skills and performance.

- Provide structure, organization, routine, and supervision at home.
  Examples: Set rules for behavior, establish a scheduled time and place for homework, supervise child's out of school activities, ask child about school everyday.

- Provide a variety of learning opportunities outside of school.
  Examples: Use everyday tasks to reinforce what child is doing in school, provide a variety of reading materials in the home, tell stories, read to child, go on outings.

- Support child through guidance and interest in his/her activities and school-work.
  Examples: Communicate with child's teacher, problem solve constructively with child when necessary, praise child for good performance, learn something new with child daily.

- Provide a positive climate and maintain a healthy relationship with the child.
  Examples: Use active listening with child, ask child's opinion, encourage child to think positively about him/herself, express affection to child, express affection toward child.

- Model desired behavior and commitment to and value of learning.
  Examples: Communicate effectively with child and others, model a positive attitude about learning new skills, discuss important values such as honesty and learning, read at home, complete high school or college, talk positively about school and learning.

related to the complexity of the treatment plan. If the plan is not feasible in relation to allotted resources (e.g., classroom staff, parent or teacher time to complete the intervention, necessary supplies or materials), treatment integrity is likely to suffer. An additional factor presumably related to treatment integrity is the parent's and teacher's agreement with the plan; that is, whether parents and teachers support the basic principles and strategies required for implementation (this may be related to their motivation, a factor hypothesized to be related to treatment integrity) (Gresham, 1989). Further, active participation of all team members during plan development appears to be important in promoting treatment integrity (Gresham, 1989). Recommendations for improving treatment integrity are beyond the scope of this chapter; readers are referred to Tankersley et al. (this volume) and Gresham (1989, 1996) for a thorough discussion on this matter.

Treatment Implementation

The next stage of CBC in both pre-referral and IEP processes is treatment implementation. During this stage, parents and teachers implement the intervention procedures as agreed on during plan design. This stage does not involve a structured interview; however, there are several practices that are important to ensure effective implementation of the plan (see recommendations in Table 13). It is essential that the school psychologist (or other consultant) remain in close contact with parents and teachers throughout this stage to ensure understanding of the intervention, check for implementation fidelity (i.e., degree to which the plan is being delivered as intended), offer assistance if necessary, provide support and reinforcement for the parent and teachers' intervention efforts, and determine the need for immediate revisions to the plan (Sheridan & Colton, 1994).

In some instances, additional parent or teacher training may be necessary to increase integrity and efficacy of the intervention. For example, a highly structured and systematic behavioral plan requiring high levels of skill in specific behavioral strategies may require instruction to maximize treatment integrity. This is highly consistent with the objectives of CBC, which incorporate development of teachers' and parents' skills and knowledge as an important outcome goal. Further, parent training is defined clearly in IDEA 97 to include aiding parents in acquiring the requisite skills to allow them to support program plans and to help their child attain educational goals. Furthering the knowledge base and skill repertoire of parents of students with disabilities is particularly important for generalization of a child's skills to the "natural" (out-of-school) environment. Practically speaking, this requires the school psychologist consultant (or other facilitator) to assess parents' and teachers' abilities to engage in plan implementation at a level that is commensurate with design tactics and to develop procedures to invoke an instructive element to CBC when necessary.

During the implementation stage, behavioral side effects and contrast effects can also be assessed (i.e., unintended and/or undesired effects of the intervention). This is particularly possible given the inclusion of parents and teachers together, discussing the effects of interventions implemented across settings. If revisions are deemed necessary and appropriate, then the entire team should be

TABLE 13: Suggestions for Treatment Implementation

1. Check with teachers and parents on the first scheduled day of the intervention to ensure that they have the necessary information and materials to proceed.

2. Schedule a time to observe the parents and teachers implementing some intervention components. To minimize resistance, ensure that the purpose of the observation is support and assistance, and not evaluation of their skills.

3. Provide parents and teachers with feedback regarding your observations. Frame the feedback in supportive, facilitative terms.

4. Demonstrate intervention procedures if necessary. In some cases, the consultant may be the primary intervention agent initially (and very briefly) as a model for the parent or teacher. If this training approach is used, fade the consultant's involvement as soon as possible.

5. Check in periodically to ensure that the intervention procedures are progressing as planned and that the data collection continues. Schedule frequent phone calls with parents to ensure that they are supported throughout this consultation stage.

6. Ask parents and teachers for subjective evaluations of how the program is working. If possible, ask to see some preliminary data. If no progress is being made after several days (or if there is behavioral regression), schedule a brief meeting with the parent and teacher to discuss some immediate plan modifications.

7. Confirm the date, time, and location for a formal evaluation of the intervention via the Treatment Evaluation Interview.

Reprinted with permission: Sheridan, S. M., Kratochwill, T. R., & Bergan, J. R. (1996). Conjoint behavioral consultation: A procedural manual. New York: Plenum.

---

informed of the changes to be implemented. Communication is critical during this (and every) stage of CBC.

Conjoint Treatment (Plan) Evaluation

The final stage of CBC is treatment (plan) evaluation, implemented via the CTEI. Recommended considerations for CTEIs are listed in Table 14 on page 341. In pre-referral interventions, it may be determined that the goals established early in CBC have been met; therefore, continuation of educational services in the general classroom may be warranted, with attention to procedures for maintaining treatment gains and the home-school partnership. In cases where progress is made but the goals not attained, revisions to the plan may occur by recycling through earlier stages of problem solving (e.g., the CPAI and modifications to the plan design). In cases where no progress is made after several attempts at problem solving and plan modification, a referral for a formal, comprehensive evaluation by a multidisciplinary team may be in order (see Figure 1 on page 327). According to IDEA 97 and best practices, parents are actively involved at every phase of the evaluation, eligibility, and placement process. The CBC model then provides the structure for establishing IEPs with active, meaningful parental involvement.

During the evaluation stage and the CTEI, the team evaluates the treatment data to determine whether the goals of consultation have been met across settings. This requires feedback from all parents, teachers, and others responsible for the student or elements of the behavioral plan. Depending on whether the goals have been met, the team should discuss strategies and tactics related to the continuation, modification, or termination of the intervention. If the goals are not met, then the team may decide to meet again for another CTEI after modifications are made and a revised plan is implemented for an agreed-on amount of time. If the consultation goals have been met, then the team should discuss strategies for the maintenance and generalization of treatment gains.

Many academic and behavioral problems are complex and multi-componential. Their complexity requires consultation teams to define broad-based behavioral patterns into their sub-components to enhance accurate interpretation and management. This procedure can lead to more thorough functional assessments, which leads to interventions geared toward circumscribed behaviors. As control is gained in relation to one behavior, the problem-solving process can be applied to other behaviors or concerns. In this light, CBC can be seen as a process that can be used by teams in a continuous manner until the over-arching academic or behavioral concerns have been addressed. Because CBC starts with one specific target behavior, it is very appropriate to address issues related to other target behaviors, or other IEP goals. Each IEP goal can be addressed through the CBC process of problem identification, behavior analysis, intervention implementation, and program evaluation.

PROFESSIONAL DEVELOPMENT IMPLICATIONS FOR FACILITATING PARENTAL INVOLVEMENT

The amendments of IDEA 97 provide a foundation for important parental roles in relation to their child's education. However, the provision simply articulates the requirements with which schools and school personnel must adhere. It does not specify how professionals can interface effectively with parents. Although this chapter has outlined a collaborative problem-solving orientation as best practice, it is recognized that not all pre-service or practicing professionals are currently pre-

TABLE 14: Suggestions for Conducting Conjoint Treatment Evaluation Interviews

1. Begin the interview by reviewing the data collected by parents and teachers during the plan implementation stage. Review the data in their presence.

2. Compare the occurrence of the behavior at home and school. Compare the frequency or severity of the target problem during treatment to baseline.

3. Ask for the parent's and teacher's perceptions about the effectiveness of the intervention at home and school. Review the behavioral goals established for each setting during the PII. Ask how they feel about the student's responsiveness to treatment.

4. Ask teachers and parents their preference about what to do next. In general, consultation procedures can be continued or terminated, and treatment plans can be maintained, modified, or faded.

5. If consultation goals have been met and the treatment will be faded, recommend that it be done gradually to increase maintenance.

6. If some progress is seen but modifications are necessary to increase the student's performance, try small changes first.

7. If no progress is seen, recycle through problem analysis and try to determine other conditions that may be maintaining the unacceptable behavior. It may also be necessary to question the adequacy of the problem definition; it may be that the "wrong" problem was selected.

8. In some cases, treatment effects will be seen in one setting and not the other. It may be necessary to make individualized (setting-specific) decisions about the future of the treatment plan based on the student's responsiveness to the program at home and school. Regardless of whether a program is continued across both settings, both the parent and teacher should continue to be involved.

9. Reinforce parents and teachers for their hard work in implementing the intervention, regardless of the outcome!

10. Set up future meeting times to review the student's performance.

11. Encourage parents and teachers to continue communicating and collaborating on the student's behalf.

Reprinted with permission: Sheridan, S. M., Kratochwill, T. R., & Bergan, J. R. (1996). Conjoint behavioral consultation: A procedural manual. New York: Plenum.

pared to develop effective home–school partnership programs. Further, the emphasis in much of the literature remains at a level of *activities* that can be pursued. Much less attention is paid to the *processes* by which relationships with parents can be established and maintained. Therefore, professional development issues in relation to team-based decision making and parental involvement are important for realizing the intent of IDEA 97.

Team-Based Decision Making

The mandates of previous special education law and IDEA 97 have required multidisciplinary teams to cooperate in the evaluation, determination, and placement decisions related to students with special needs. It is the contention of these authors that collaborative problem-solving models are useful tools by which assessment data can be linked to meaningful interventions to address a student's presenting concerns. Consultation-based services are commonly identified as within the repertoire of school psychologists and other educational specialists; however, the practice of team-based, collaborative problem solving presents very complex professional and interpersonal challenges. According to Welch and Sheridan (1995), "effective collaboration requires a number of skills and attitudes, including the ability to take the perspective of others, speak a common language, manage conflict, conceptualize school problems in a broad fashion, and share resources, knowledge, and skills ... however, key individuals involved in partnerships are often not prepared to carry out this role" (p. 383).

It may be beneficial for individuals to learn specific skills and models for effective collaboration at the pre-service training level. Interdisciplinary training at this level can be useful for promoting a common language, knowledge base, and an understanding of the diverse and complex functions of schools. Didactic coursework can provide exposure to the roles and functions of various individuals within schools, and allow students to begin considering complex ecological variables in educational settings. Further, relevant and applied exercises (e.g., role plays) can be structured to provide opportunities to work through cases and issues in a structured, supported manner (Welch et al., 1992).

Similar experiences are necessary at the in-service level. Staff development activities can be organized in a way that allows content information (e.g., stages and procedures of problem solving, data-based decision making) to be presented and practiced through hands-on practice activities (Howey, 1985). Active involvement of the participants during sustained and sequential effort is a key component to successful staff development (Merenbloom, 1984). Planned activities can provide practice, feedback, and support for learning new skills (Jones & Lowe, 1990). To attain generalization to casework with students, at least two additional things must occur. First, specific tasks and responsibilities can be delegated to persons who will follow through on setting up the collaborative problem-solving program. That is, an individual or individuals with clearly established roles for developing the procedures should be identified Second, existing policies may need to be changed to allow collaborative educational partnerships to occur (Welch & Sheridan, 1995). For example, team-based activities (e.g., meetings, data collection) may require modifications to existing schedules and responsibilities, and policy changes may be needed to reflect these modifications.

Preparation in Working With Families

Along with general teaming principles and practices, essential attitudes and strategies for working with families present important training directions. For several years, school psychologists have voiced interest in working more effectively with families as part of their role and responsibility (Carlson & Sincavage, 1987; Christenson, Hurley, Sheridan, & Fenstermacher, 1997). However, this has not been translated readily and consistently into pre-service preparation programs.

There are several content and process domains that represent relevant training agendas for educational specialists working in partnership with families. Given that families represent a potential range of cultural realities that vary on racial, linguistic, socioeconomic, and other characteristics, openness to diversity is an essential prerequisite. Didactic and applied coursework and practica experiences with diverse students, families, and educational settings can facilitate the development of sensitivity and understanding of multiple perspectives. Likewise, meaningful experiences can contribute to an understanding of and respect for diverse values, customs, and cultures.

This type of awareness and openness to differences across families is an important precursor to educators' abilities to reach out to all families. Whereas these attitudes are essential, prospective and in-service educators and service providers also require knowledge of strategies and actions by which to engage families actively in educational decision making. Skills in parent advocacy are among those not typically taught in pre-service programs, but critical to be an effective ally and liaison. Similarly, effective strategies for open and clear communication, conflict management, and portrayal of other family-centered characteristics (e.g., friendliness, family orientation) are central to effective work with parents.

Finally, individuals who are responsible for working with families in educational contexts should be aware of and skilled in delivering a range of parent involvement services. Whereas programs and services cannot be taught irrespective from important family-centered *attitudes* and a supportive, family-friendly *atmosphere* (Christenson & Sheridan, in press), an ability to both identify important idiosyncratic needs of families and develop programs to meet them is crucial for facilitating effective home-school partnerships. Training in processes by which to match needs with services and skills at generating a range of alternative services are among important future directions for pre-service and in-service preparation.

CONCLUSIONS

In this chapter, a partnership orientation was promoted as an overarching framework for working with families. Collaborative, problem-solving practices with families provide a template for "best practices" when working with students with special needs. This includes interactions that occur around general educational planning and decision making, pre-referral interventions, and special education referral, evaluation, qualification, and placement (IDEA 97; Individuals with Disabilities Education Act Regulations, 1999). IDEA 97 provides several opportunities to envision work with families in this regard. However, the law defines *minimum standards* only. School-based teams are urged to engage parents actively whenever a problem is identified and not only when special education placement becomes the issue. For example, parents are entitled to be part of meetings in regard to identification, evaluation, and placement as per IDEA 97. More broadly, it sets a framework for collaborative meetings between parents and educators by inviting their participation around evaluation, eligibility, and planning issues. The meetings are useful and important in the earliest stages of concerns, even before evaluation/placement issues become central.

CBC and other home-school problem-solving models provide the tools by which such constructive partnerships can be operationalized for use with students who have special needs. They can be applied readily to interactions between parents and school staff (e.g., pre-referral intervention meetings, IEP meetings) as they take part jointly in responding to the educational needs of children in a manner consistent with the ideals set forth in IDEA 97.

The spirit of IDEA has always recognized the importance of parent participation during the identification, eligibility, and program development process. In an effort to ensure consistent implementation of the federal legislation by state-governed districts, IDEA 97 further expands the legislative mandates regarding parental participation. It is hoped the new legislation will help promote the original spirit of the law, which surpasses the existing federal mandates.

REFERENCES

Adams, K. S., & Christenson, S. L. (1998). Differences in parent and teacher trust levels: Implications for creating collaborative family-school relationships. *Special Services in the Schools, 14,* 1–22.

Bronfenbrenner, U. (1977). Toward an experimental ecology of human development. *American Psychologist, 32,* 513–529.

Carlson, C. I., Hickman, J., & Horton, C. B. (1992). From blame to solutions: Solution-oriented family-school consultation. In S. L. Christenson & J. C. Conoley (Eds.), *Home-school collaboration: Enhancing children's academic and social competence* (pp. 193–213). Silver Spring, MD: National Association of School Psychologists.

Carlson, C. I., & Sincavage, J. (1987). Family-oriented school psychology practice: Results of a national survey. *School Psychology Review, 16,* 519–526.

Christenson, S. L. (1995a). Families and schools: What is the role of the school psychologist? *School Psychology Quarterly, 10,* 118–132.

Christenson, S. L. (1995b). Supporting home-school collaboration. In A. Thomas & J. Grimes (Eds.), *Best practices in school psychology III* (pp. 253-267). Washington, DC: National Association of School Psychologists.

Christenson, S. L., & Hirsch, J. A. (1998). Facilitating partnerships and conflict resolution between families and schools. In K. C. Stoiber & T. R. Kratochwill (Eds.), *Handbook of group intervention for children and families* (pp. 307–344). Boston: Allyn & Bacon.

Christenson, S. L., Hurley, C., Sheridan, S. M., & Fenstermacher, K. (1997). Parents' and school psychologists' perspectives on parent involvement activities. *School Psychology Review, 26,* 111–130.

Christenson, S. L., & Sheridan, S. M. (in press). *Schools and families: Essential support linkages for student performance.* New York: Guilford.

Clark, R. M. (1988). Parents as providers of linguistic and social capital. *Educational Horizons,* Winter, 93–95.

Dunst, C. J., & Trivette, C. M. (1987). Enabling and empowering families: Conceptual and intervention issues. *School Psychology Review, 16,* 443–456.

Gresham, F. M. (1989). Assessment of treatment integrity in school consultation and prereferral intervention. *School Psychology Review, 18,* 37–50.

Gresham, F. M. (1996). Treatment integrity in single-subject research. In R. D. Franklin, D. B. Allison, & B. S. Gorman (Eds.), *Design and analysis of single-case research* (pp. 93-117). Mahweh, NJ: Lawrence Erlbaum.

Haynes, S. N., & O'Brien, W. H. (1990). Functional analysis in behavior therapy. *Clinical Psychology Review, 10,* 649–668.

Howey, K. R. (1985). Six major functions of staff development: An expanded imperative. *Journal of Teacher Education, 36,* 58–64.

Huefner, D. S. (2000). *Getting comfortable with special education law: A framework for working with children with disabilities.* Norwood, MA: Christopher-Gordon.

Individuals with Disabilities Education Act Amendments of 1997, 20 U.S.C. § 1400 *et seq.* (West 1997).

Individuals with Disabilities Education Act Regulations, 34 C.F.R. § 300 and 303. (1999).

Jones, E. V., & Lowe, J. (1990). Changing teacher behavior: Effective staff development. *Adult Learning, 1,* 8–10.

Larson, P. J., & Maag, J. W. (1998). Applying functional assessment in general education classrooms: Issues and recommendations. *Remedial and Special Education, 19,* 338–349.

McWilliam, R. A., Harbin, G. L., Porter, P., Vandiviere, P., Mittal, M., & Munn, D. (1995). *An evaluation of family-centered coordinated Part H services in North Carolina: Part 1, Family-centered service provision.* Chapel Hill: University of North Carolina, Frank Porter Graham Child Development Center.

McWilliam, R. A., Lang, L., Vandiviere, P., Angell, R., Collins, L., & Underdown, G. (1995). Satisfaction and struggles: Family perceptions of early intervention services. *Journal of Early Intervention, 19,* 43–60.

McWilliam, R.A., Maxwell, K. L., & Sloper, K. M. (1999). Beyond involvement: Are elementary schools ready to be family-centered? *School Psychology Review, 28,* 378–394.

McWilliam, R. A., Tocci, L., & Harbin, G. L. (1998). Family-centered services: Service providers' discourse and behavior. *Topics in Early Childhood Special Education, 18,* 206–221.

Merenbloom, E. Y. (1984). Staff development: The key to effective middle schools. *NASSP Bulletin, 68,* 24–33.

O'Neill, R. E., Horner, R. H., Albin, R W., Sprague, J. R., Storey, K., & Newton, J. S. (1997). *Functional assessment and program development for problem behavior: A practical handbook* (2nd ed.). Pacific Grove, CA: Brooks/Cole.

Phillips, V., & McCullough, L. (1990). Consultation-based programming: Instituting the collaborative ethic. *Exceptional Children, 56,* 291–304.

Power, T. J., & Bartholomew, K. L. (1987). Family-school relationship patterns: An ecological assessment. *School Psychology Review, 16,* 498–512.

Rappaport, J. (1981). In praise of paradox: A social policy of empowerment over prevention. *American Journal of Community Psychology, 9,* 1–25.

Sheridan, S. M. (1997). Conceptual and empirical bases of conjoint behavioral consultation. *School Psychology Quarterly, 12,* 119–133.

Sheridan, S. M., & Colton, D. L. (1994). Conjoint behavioral consultation: A review and case study. *Journal of Educational and Psychological Consultation, 5,* 211–228.

Sheridan, S. M., & Kratochwill, T. R. (1992). Behavioral parent-teacher consultation: Conceptual and research considerations. *Journal of School Psychology, 30,* 117–139.

Sheridan, S. M., Kratochwill, T. R., & Bergan, J. R. (1996). *Conjoint behavioral consultation: A procedural manual.* New York: Plenum.

Silverstein, J., Springer, J., & Russo, N. (1992). Involving parents in the special education process. In S. L. Christenson & J. C. Conoley (Eds.), *Home-school collaboration: Enhancing children's academic and social competence* (pp. 383–407). Silver Spring, MD: National Association of School Psychologists.

Swap, S. M. (1993). *Developing home-school partnerships: From concepts to practice.* New York: Teachers College Press.

Taverne, A., & Sheridan, S. M. (1995). Parent training in interactive book reading: An investigation of its effects with families at-risk. *School Psychology Quarterly, 10,* 41–64.

Wahler, R. G., & Fox, J. J. (1981). Setting events in applied behavioral analysis: Toward a conceptual and methodological expansion. *Journal of Applied Behavioral Analysis, 14,* 327–338.

Weiss, H. M., & Edwards, M. E. (1992). The family-school collaboration project: Systemic interventions for school improvement. In S. L. Christenson & J. C. Conoley (Eds.), *Home-school collaboration: Enhancing children's academic and social competence* (pp. 215-243). Silver Spring, MD: National Association of School Psychologists.

Welch, M., Sheridan, S. M., Hart, A. W., Fuhriman, A., Connell, M., & Stoddart, T. (1992). An interdisciplinary approach in preparing professionals for educational partnerships. *Journal of Educational and Psychological Consultation, 3,* 1–23.

Welch, M., & Sheridan, S. M. (1995). *Educational partnerships: Serving students at-risk.* San Antonio, TX: Harcourt-Brace Jovanovich.

Yeaton, W. H., & Sechrest, L. (1981). Critical dimensions in the choice and maintenance of successful treatment: Strength, integrity, and effectiveness. *Journal of Consulting and Clinical Psychology, 49,* 156–167.

Ysseldyke, J., & Christenson, S. L. (1992). *The Instructional Environment Scale: II.* Longmont, CO: Sopris West.

ANNOTATED BIBLIOGRAPHY

Christenson, S. L., & Sheridan, S. M. (in press). *Schools and families: Creating essential connections for learners.* New York: Guilford.

This book uses eco-behavioral and systems theory lenses to describe ways in which schools and families are connected through the four following components: Approach, Attitudes, Atmosphere, and Actions. Through a discussion of the multi-faceted nature of home–school interactions, the authors describe an approach that considers the shared and unique contributions of both families and schools to the education and development of children. The authors also explore how the attitudes of school personnel are communicated and contribute to family and school connections. Through user-friendly summary tables and a common thread of a process-oriented approach, the authors describe ways that atmospheres affect home–school relationships. The themes presented in the text are concisely summarized in an assessment tool entitled, "Inventory for Creating Family-School Relationships," which allows readers to assess their school communities in relation to the four As (i.e., Approach, Attitudes, Atmosphere, and Actions).

Comer, J. P., Haynes, N. M., Joyner, E. T., & Ben-Avie, M. (Eds.). (1996). *Rallying the whole village: The Comer process for reforming education.* New York: Teacher College Press.

In this book, researchers discuss the history, underlying theoretical principles, and mechanisms of the School Development Program (SDP), a school reform initiative developed by James Comer. Comer and his colleagues believe that a change in a student's behavior, attitude, or achievement requires a change among the interactions within the system or parts of the system that influence the child. The SDP is a process that is designed to empower and unite parents, teachers, and other professionals to make individual and collective differences in the lives of children. Essential within this process is the development of a collaborative and empowering environment involving parents and school staff. The SDP model incorporates several aspects critical in developing collaborative relationships between schools and parents: build trust; plan well; empower parents; continually monitor, assess, and modify as necessary; and build a community through community involvement.

Sheridan, S. M., Kratochwill, T. R., & Bergan, J. R. (1996). *Conjoint behavioral consultation: A procedural manual.* New York: Plenum.

This user-friendly book presents the conceptual, practical, and empirical bases of the conjoint behavioral consultation (CBC) model. In addition to presenting the behavioral consultation model from which CBC is derived, the book provides empirical support and guidelines for working with parents and school personnel, as conceptualized through behavioral, systems, and ecological theories. Through the presentation of practitioner-oriented tables, CBC forms, guidelines, and case-related "tips" for use with consultation, the book guides the reader through the CBC process. The practitioner will be greatly assisted by a chapter devoted to case studies, along with a parallel discussion and relation of the four phases of CBC: problem identification, problem analysis, treatment implementation, and treatment evaluation. Also included in the book is a chapter summarizing empirical support for the CBC model, along with implications for practitioners and future research.

Turnbull, A. P., & Turnbull, H. R. (1997). *Families, professionals, and exceptionality: A special partnership.* Upper Saddle River: Prentice-Hall.

This book, designed for educators and professionals working with children, utilizes theory, research, and best practices in discussing partnerships between families and professionals. The book is organized into three parts: a historical and present day understanding of empowerment, an understanding of families from a systems perspective, and ways to empower families and professionals in a collaborative relationship. The authors discuss partnerships between families and professionals from both general and special education perspectives. Each chapter includes applied techniques used in developing effective partnerships, as well as vignettes describing the experiences of individual families.

CHAPTER 10

Writing and Evaluating IEP Goals and Making Appropriate Revisions to Ensure Participation and Progress in the General Curriculum

Mark R. Shinn
Michelle M. Shinn
University of Oregon

Background/Purpose for Changes in IEPs in IDEA 97

To many educators, the Individualized Education Programs (IEP) is a necessary "procedural evil" that must be completed so that a student with educational needs can receive service. As stated by Bateman and Linden (1998, p. 63) in their latest revision of their book on writing IEPs, "Sadly, most IEPs are horrendously burdensome to teachers and nearly useless to parents. Many if not most goals and objectives couldn't be measured if one tried and all too often no effort is made to actually assess the child's progress toward the goal."

Nearly every study of the limited body of knowledge on IEPs from the past 20 years has concluded likewise. For example, Smith in an extensive review concluded that after more than 10 years of implementation substantive IEP change has not ensued. To too many educators, the field has achieved the IEP nightmare predicted by Rinaldi (1976) in which schools would end up "with paper compliance rather than real or exemplary implementation" (p. 151).

For example, the authors recently noticed this anonymous poem posted prominently on the wall in a special education resource teacher's room. According to the special education teacher, the poem, "IEPs According to Dr. Suess" (author unknown; available at *http://www.hoagiesgifted.org/gftsues.htm.*), was downloaded from the Internet. Excerpts are as follows:

> Do you like these IEPs?
> I do not like these IEPs
> I do not like them Jeeze Louise.
> We test, we check
> We plan, we meet
> But nothing ever seems complete.
> Would you, could you
> Like the form?
> I do not like the form I see
> Not page 1, not 2, not 3.
> Another change
> A brand new box
> I think we all
> Have lost our rocks.

The poem goes on to lament other shortcomings of the IEP process, such as meetings that are too long, the need for lots of goals and objectives, and the emphasis on signatures.

Despite the widespread dissatisfaction with the current state of the IEP process, the authors are confident that this sense of negativism and dissatisfaction with the IEP process in general will be offset if educators take advantage of changes (a) in practice intended by IDEA 97 and (b) in assessment technology derived from research and practice on writing goals and monitoring student achievement that have occurred in the last 20 years. These legal and technological advances are likely to result in more meaningful IEPs with fewer, but more *important* and *measurable* annual goals. With these types of goals, educators *will* be more likely to evaluate student progress. The progress monitoring of important annual goals will result in appropriate IEP revisions, and, as a whole, the achievement of students with disabilities will increase.

The authors see these changes as important for building teams that too often report that the time spent working on the IEP was not important (Joseph, Lindgren, Creamer, & Lane, 1983). In particular, these changes are exciting for school psychologists, who, as a whole, have not played a meaningful role in the development of instructional programs for students with disabilities, other than as a gatekeeper for eligibility. Legal changes with the Individuals with Disabilities Education Act of 1997 (IDEA 97) (Individuals with Disabilities Education Act Amendments, 1997) and technological advances in assessment can facilitate a change in the type of information school psychologists and other team members use to make decisions;

that is from information collected solely to determine eligibility to information that has direct implications for intervention planning as it relates to performance and progress in general curriculum. For school psychologists, this information may facilitate changes in roles as instructional consultants as they work with IEP teams to make decisions about progress toward IEP goals and contribute to IEPs that are revised to address any lack of progress.

The current unsatisfactory state of affairs regarding IEPs is not intended as an indictment of educators for falling short of the ambitious and admirable intentions of the original Education for All Handicapped Children Act of 1975 (EAHCA) and those expressed in subsequent revisions in the Individuals with Disabilities Education Act of 1997 (Individuals with Disabilities Education Act Amendments, 1997). The excessive proceduralism in IEPs that is witnessed today, and its resulting effects on professional practice and attitudes, is most likely due to a combination of variables greater in their sum than in their individual parts. Educators were expected to come into rapid compliance with federal law in 1977 with little pre-service training in writing any form of IEPs, including creating goals and progress monitoring. Quite simply, special education and school psychology programs had not provided pre-service training at the time related to IEPs as they, too, were "learning as they go." At the time of implementation of the original EAHCA, little, if any, validated technology for writing meaningful goals and objectives and monitoring progress toward them existed. Three choices were available: (a) writing behavioral objectives, (b) deriving goals through published norm-referenced tests, or (c) writing broad and vague, but "understandable," goals. A sampling of actual IEP goals that the authors have observed in practice within these three categories is presented in Table 1 on page 354.

Behavioral Objectives

The dominant technology for writing IEP goals was derived from the classic texts on writing behavioral objectives by Mager (Mager, 1962; Mager & Pipe, 1970). Recent variations of these goals are illustrated by Goals 1–3 in Table 1 on page 354. Behavioral objectives are characterized by specifying an observable behavior, the conditions under which it is to be observed, and a criterion for success. This well-intentioned beginning to a meaningful technology for writing goals and monitoring progress had two shortfalls. First, the principal standard for specifying the behavior was that it had to be "observable." The standard seemed necessary, but was also very vague as it did not detail whether the behavior was (a) *important* to measure and (b) *logistically feasible* to measure. Both are necessary for writing and evaluating IEP goals for the purposes of improving outcomes for students.

It appears that that because educators did not know what behavior was important to measure, the practice of writing IEP goals evolved into a "more is better" exercise, in which IEP teams wrote numerous goals for each area of deficit.

TABLE 1: **Sample Goals Observed in Recent IEPs**

Variations on Behavioral Objectives

1. Student will read aloud with 80% accuracy and 80% comprehension.
2. Student will alphabetize words by the second letter with 80% accuracy.
3. Student will read words from the Dolch Word List with 80% accuracy.
4. Student will master basic multiplication facts with 80% accuracy.
5. Student will increase reading skills by progressing through Scribner with 90% accuracy as determined by teacher-made fluency and comprehension probes by October 2001.

Variations on Commercial Achievement Tests and GE Scores

6. To increase reading ability by 6 months to 1 year as measured by the Woodcock Johnson.
7. Student will make one year's growth in reading by October 2001 as measured by the Brigance.

Variations on Pseudo-Goals

8. Student will be a better reader.
9. Student will perform spelling skills at a high third grade level.
10. Student will make one year's gain in general reading from K–3.
11. Students will read one story per week.

Consider a business metaphor. An automaker set its annual goals as (a) makes brakes, (b) installs comfortable interiors, (c) chromes door handles, and (d) guarantees the appropriate amount of oil is placed in the engine. Each of these goals is certainly a task relevant to producing an automobile. However, each one is only one of an innumerable set of tasks in producing an automobile. Arguably, some of the tasks may be more important than others. The automaker could be autocratic and specify that *every* possible task must be included in what would be a long list of goals. A more democratic automaker may allow each team of workers to select which of the goals from the long list would be important to *their* car.

In many districts, the latter, more democratic approach to writing goals appears the norm. The authors call these types of IEP goals an educational smorgasbord. A large pool of possible IEP goals is developed, and teams can select which ones they deem relevant to the specific case. Because there is often little agreement as to which goals are important, more goals are written, and often the choices are arbitrary, driven largely by district or state procedure (e.g., a minimum of four). Outside observers of this process witnessed a widespread problem of lack of linkage between students' educational needs and the services they received , and computers became necessary to make manageable the selection of numerous IEP goals.

The second shortfall of the initial implementation of the behavioral objective technology had to deal with selecting a criterion for success. The hallmark of behavioral objectives was a criterion of 80% accuracy (Bateman & Linden, 1998). Irrespective of the logical sense that this 80% criterion made (i.e., that students should improve but perfectly), this standard appears to be the mode of practice regardless of the behavior. It is unlikely that meaningful outcomes will be produced in reading if students achieve their goal of reading 80% of words correctly. Attaining this goal comes with the unfortunate consequence of *not* reading the remaining 20% of the words correctly. Using this criterion with this goal will not produce readers who understand and learn from the material. Returning to the business metaphor used earlier, should an automaker have as its goal to install brakes with 80% accuracy?

Published Norm-Referenced Tests

The second historical lineage in writing IEP goals was based on the use of commercially available, norm-referenced tests. These tests had a long-standing history of use in special education decision making at the time of implementation of Education for All Handicapped Children Act of 1975 (1975) and a history of summarizing student performance in age- or grade-equivalent (AE or GE) scores. Despite universal agreement on the inappropriateness of these types of scores , it was, and remains, common to describe a student's academic performance as "at the 2.7 level." Given that annual goals were to be written based on current performance information, it was not illogical then, to those who used commercial tests and GE scores, to add some number of months or years to a student's current GE score. How many times in practice has the reader witnessed an annual goal written as the "the student will read at the 3.5 level on the Woodcock-Johnson?" The process seems logical, and the goal is "objective" and most likely would be considered as "understandable" to educators and parents alike.

It is beyond the scope of this chapter to detail the weaknesses in this approach (e.g., lack of sensitivity, regression, lack of equal interval data, differences in AE or GE scores among and within tests) to writing IEP goals. Most of these are attributable to weaknesses inherent in using AE/GE scores. Less obvious to many members of building teams is the limited utility in commercial achievement tests in identifying instructionally relevant skill strengths and weaknesses and in monitoring progress. As will be detailed later in this chapter, this approach to goal setting falls short of the necessary requirements specified in IDEA 97 that IEP goals include statements about participation and progress *in the general curriculum*. It is well established that commercial achievement tests do not meaningfully measure the performance of students in any specific curriculum (Good & Salvia, 1988; Jenkins & Pany, 1978; Shapiro & Derr, 1987). For more detail, see Howell, Fox, and Morehead (1993) or Howell and Nolet (1999) as sources describing these difficulties.

Broad, Vague, But "Understandable" Goals

The third option for IEP teams is to write what the authors call "pseudo-goals." That is, IEP teams write statements that, at first blush, appear to be reasonable goals for students. These types of goals are illustrated in Table 1 on page 354 by Goals 6–7. Like GE goals derived from commercial achievement tests, they are intuitively appealing because they describe growth in terms of annual accomplishments (e.g., 6 months improvement). They appear "understandable." However, when examined more closely, it is often the case that such goals are, in fact, often very difficult to measure, as they do not specify *how* decisions of progress will be measured or what scores will constitute progress. Too often, when the goals are evaluated, they may be assessed by using only professional judgment or turn out to be only a variation of the commercial achievement test/GE score theme. When progress ultimately is evaluated, the team will rely on the standard practice of using commercial tests and GE scores.

Collective Lack of Meaningfulness of Current IEP Goals: Remedies in IDEA 97

Through the authors' work with IEP teams across the country, it is apparent that practitioners are aware of the shortcomings associated with current practices in writing IEP goals. Consequently, writing and evaluating IEP goals becomes a procedural issue, one in which things are done because it is legally mandated instead of because it would improve outcomes. Correspondingly, educators report a lack of confidence in their ability to write goals that can be attained by students with disabilities, and that they will be held responsible if, or when, students fall short. The result of this process then is a smorgasbord of goals in the pseudo-goals category; that is, a number of disconnected goals that are difficult to measure objectively. Because of this lack of measurable goals, there is little ongoing evaluation of progress. And, without ongoing progress monitoring data, IEPs are not revised, until, at best, the annual review. In fact, the limited data available on special education teacher decision making suggests the modal number of significant instructional changes in a year for students not making progress is zero (Wesson & Deno, 1989).

This state of practice is in stark contrast to what is known about writing effective annual goals and monitoring progress. A body of refereed, data-based information, nearly all derived by L. S. Fuchs and D. Fuchs of Vanderbilt University and S. L. Deno from the University of Minnesota, clearly identifies strategies for writing meaningful and socially important goals that are ambitious, that lead to efficient monitoring of progress, and that lead to program modification when progress is below desired rates. The cumulative effect of these goal writing and progress monitoring practices is socially significant achievement gains by students with disabilities (Fuchs, 1986; Fuchs & Fuchs, 1999; Fuchs, Fuchs, Hamlett & Stecker, 1991).

Congress, in examining the state of practice and what is known from school-based research, set forth to remedy this situation. The changes to the content of the IEP in IDEA 97 (see Table 2 on page 358) are more explicit than ever before, especially with respect to (a) student involvement and progress in general curriculum, (b) measurement of progress towards annual goals, (c) how often progress is reviewed and reported, and, consequently, (d) how often and when IEPs should be revised (Yell & Shriner, 1997).

Involvement in General Education

Perhaps the most obvious and comprehensive changes in IDEA 97 with respect to the content of an IEP are the statements of student involvement and progress in the general curriculum. The general curriculum in IDEA 97 is defined as "the same curriculum as for non-disabled children." Clearly, the contents of the IEP now must reflect (a) how a child's disability affects his/her involvement and progress in the general curriculum and (b) annual goals that enable the child to be involved in and progress in the general curriculum. Relatedly, specific services and supports a student needs to access the general education curriculum must be addressed and a general education teacher must be a member of the IEP team.

These expectations represent a departure from earlier versions of IDEA in which the expectation was that the IEP include statements of the extent to which the child will be able to *participate* in regular education programs. In the past, this requirement has been translated into statements such as "the student will spend approximately 33% of time in general education classrooms, participating in music, art, and physical education."

Participation in general education in the past has largely been defined as *placing* a child with disabilities with nondisabled peers for mostly noncurricular activities such as lunch, recess, and physical education. IDEA 97 now demands participation in general education for students with disabilities as more than placement with nondisabled peers, but *meaningful access to the same curriculum* peers would be expected to learn. Access to, involvement with, and progress in the general curriculum has never been a part of any previous legislation and appears

TABLE 2: **Highlighted Language in the Reauthorization of IDEA that Links to the Use of CBM**

In Definitions of an IEP ...
   (i) a statement of the child's present *level of educational performance*, including—
      (I) how the child's disability affects the child's *involvement and progress in the general curriculum*;
Under Evaluation Procedures
(A) use a *variety of assessment tools* and strategies to gather *relevant functional* and developmental information ... that may assist in determining ... the content of the child's individualized education program, including information related to enabling the child to *be involved in and progress in the general curriculum* ...
   (ii) a statement of *measurable annuals goals* ... related to—
      (I) meeting the child's needs ... to enable the child to be *involved in and progress in the general curriculum*;
   (viii) a statement of—
      (I) how the child's progress toward the *annuals goals* ... (ii) *will be measured*; and
      (II) how the child's parents *will be regularly informed* (by such means as periodic report cards), at least as often as parents are informed of their nondisabled children's *progress*
Under Revision of the IEP
   (ii) *revises the IEP* as appropriate to address—
      (I) any lack of *expected progress toward the annual goals and in the general curriculum* ...

to be an attempt to ensure that students with disabilities receive programs that are linked to meaningful outcomes. This translates into the requirement of involvement and progress in the same curriculum as nondisabled peers.

The expectation that an IEP reflect how a student will be involved in and have access to the general curriculum does not mean that the child should be taught using the general curriculum. In the authors' opinions, this concept means that the content of a special education program should produce students learning content that is broader than traditionally conceptualized. For example, in practice, the authors have witnessed IEP goals as reflecting more of "what will be taught" in special education (i.e., the Dolch word list) than goals that suggest "is this important to know?" to be able to progress grade to grade. IDEA 97 explicitly recognizes the need for the *content* of special education programs to produce demonstrable, generalizable skills in the general curriculum.

IDEA 97 also requires that IEP teams include members who are knowledgeable about the general curriculum and can interpret the instructional implications of assessment results. The most natural choice to fulfill this role is a general education teacher. A general education teacher must be present at the IEP meeting along with other members knowledgeable in the areas of suspected disability. Although the general education teacher can clearly be the most knowledgeable team member with respect to the general education curriculum, development of the IEP is a team process. Thus, it is necessary for all team members, including school psychologists, to have at least a working knowledge of the general education curriculum, the expectations for students without disabilities, and how the IEP would be expected to produce results in the general curriculum.

Goals that are Measurable

Before IDEA 97, the language about IEP goals was general; it was expected that the IEP include a statement of annual goals. Now, the law states that the IEP must include a "statement of *measurable* annual goals, including benchmarks or short-term objectives." Of course, one may argue that the addition of one word (i.e., measurable) represents a subtle or even trivial change; however, the addition of this word is a strong attempt to remedy a large problem. Earlier in this chapter, the current problems of pseudo-goals or broad goals were discussed. IDEA 97 sets forth a statement that these types of goals are not sufficient. Furthermore, the addition of this single word, measurable, makes explicit the connection of the goals to a measurement strategy that lends itself to ongoing data collection and decision making regarding the need for IEP revision.

More Frequent Reporting of Progress

In addition to the expectation that annual goals be measurable, IDEA 97 specifies that the IEP include the following statement: "How the child's parents will be regularly informed (through such means as periodic report cards), at least as often as parents are informed of their nondisabled children's progress, of their child's progress toward annual goals, and the extent to which that progress is sufficient to enable the child to achieve the goals by the end of the year."

A time-efficient, ongoing system of data collection and monitoring provides the basis for decision making regarding the effectiveness of programs. When data are collected in an ongoing, efficient manner, there is a greater likelihood that effective programs will be maintained and ineffective programs will be modified *during* the school year. For example, Goal 6 in Table 1 on page 354 states that student reading performance will be measured by the Woodcock Reading Mastery

Test (WRMT), a common norm-referenced test used in schools to measure progress toward IEP goals in reading. Although the WRMT is technically adequate with respect to traditional concepts of reliability and validity, it was not designed for the repeated measurement necessary for more frequent reporting of progress toward annual IEP goals. Among the problems resulting from using this test to measure progress are administration time and the lack of relation to students' performance and progress in general curriculum. Thus, at best, student performance toward this goal is assessed at the *end* of the school year, making it unlikely that the information gained from the test will be used to make changes to the current instructional program.

By using an ongoing and efficient data collection system not only guides the decision-making process regarding the effectiveness of instructional programs but also increases the likelihood that parents will receive more frequent feedback regarding student performance. If students in general education receive progress reports once every quarter, then it is expected that students with IEPs receive progress reports with the same frequency. To accomplish this goal, the measurement strategy must, at a minimum, be efficient and allow for the collection of ongoing data linked to intervention planning. By using the example of the WRMT as a measure of progress, it is unlikely that student performance toward IEP goals would be measured four times per year using this test. At the least, the accumulated time required for repeated administrations would be prohibitive and issues of practice effects would have to be considered due to the lack of multiple parallel forms.

IEP Review and Revision

According to IDEA 97, IEP teams are expected to "review a child's IEP periodically, but not less than annually to determine whether the annual goals for the child are being achieved; and revise the IEP as appropriate to address any lack of expected progress toward the annual goals and in the general curriculum, if appropriate; the results of any reevaluation conducted; and the child's anticipated needs." This change in language represents a more explicit requirement that IEPs be reviewed periodically and, at a minimum, annually to review progress and make changes to address any lack of expected progress.

Prior to IDEA 97, an IEP was to include "appropriate objective criteria and evaluation procedures and schedules for determining, on at least an annual basis, whether the short term instructional objectives are being achieved." These expectations were much more broad and vague as to the expectations for reviewing and revising IEPs, including the need for revisions to address any lack of progress toward annual goals. The addition of more explicit requirements for review and expectations for addressing any lack of progress were written into IDEA 97 to remedy the problem of the IEP's being viewed as more of a "procedural" document versus a "working" document. Specifically, the IEP should be a document that is used by teachers on an ongoing basis to inform instruction, monitor progress, and reflect changes in the program when progress is not being achieved. As many practitioners recognize, all too often, once the IEP is written, it finds its way to a file cabinet in someone's office and, at best, is reviewed and modified when the child's annual review is due.

CONSIDERATIONS FOR SCHOOL-BASED TEAMS IN IMPLEMENTING THE NEW IEP PROVISIONS

As alluded to earlier in this chapter, outcomes of applied educational research on writing IEP goals and monitoring progress will enable educators to meet not only the procedural requirements of IDEA 97 but also the substantive requirements. That is, changes in educational practices relating to the development and implementation of the IEP can make a difference in outcomes for students who receive special education. In addition to the legal criteria for writing goals and objectives specified in IDEA 97 (e.g., measurable, allow statements about participation and progress in general curriculum, frequent reporting to parents, allow for IEP revision), a number of other important criteria to consider have been identified in the literature. Although inter-related, each of these criteria will be discussed individually later in the chapter.

- Annual IEP goals should be ambitious.
- Annual IEP goals must be aligned with either a short-term or long-term measurement strategy to monitor progress.
- Progress should be assessed as frequently as possible.
- Decision rules for IEP revision should be specified.
- Overall IEP goal setting, progress monitoring, and any necessary IEP revision must be feasible.

Most of the professional contributions concerning goal setting, monitoring progress, and program revisions stem from research initiated by the US Bureau of the Educationally Handicapped concurrent with the implementation of the Education for All Handicapped Children Act of 1975 (1975) in a contract awarded to S. Deno as part of the Institute for Research on Learning Disabilities at the University of Minnesota. This research was intended to develop a research-based technology to help teachers write IEP goals and monitor student progress. (For more historical information on this topic, see Deno [1985, 1992] and Shinn [1998]).

The results of this work, Curriculum-Based Measurement (CBM), produced a sound technology for writing IEP goals and monitoring progress. It was not a coincidence that this technology began with an assumption that the best source of assessment materials for evaluating the effects of individuals' special education programs would be the *general curriculum*. Most school psychologists and special educators are now aware that CBM is a set of standard simple, short-duration fluency measures of reading, spelling, written expression, and mathematics computation. CBM was developed to serve as Dynamic Indicators of Basic Skills (DIBS) (Deno, 1985, 1986; Shinn, 1998) or general outcome indicators (Fuchs & Deno, 1991) measuring key indicators or "vital signs" of student achievement in important areas of basic skills or literacy. As will be illustrated in more detail later in this chapter, these key indicators are translated into IEP goals written in a simple but standard format that are individualized based on assessment of student performance in general curriculum.

Goals Should be Ambitious

Regardless of the approach that is used to write goals or monitor progress, the goals that are written should be ambitious (Fuchs, Fuchs & Deno, 1985; Fuchs, Hamlett & Fuchs, 1990; Fuchs & Shinn, 1989). That is, the goals should not significantly underestimate what can be accomplished based on the magnitude of the problem and/or the disability label. When a problem is severe (e.g., a sixth-grade student who is successful reading only a second-grade reader), teams may expect less growth because the student in question has "never made a year's growth in a year's time." The goal, then, might look like Goal 6 in Table 1 on page 354 of "6 months to 1 year on the Woodcock-Johnson." In the case of disability labels, the authors have witnessed statements supporting goals like this with the following rationale: "We could *never* expect that much improvement, because, after all, he is learning disabled." In both instances, these low expectations may be a self-fulfilling prophecy; students with disabilities do not progress very quickly because they are not expected to progress very quickly and consequently, the pace and quantity of instruction is lower. As a result, students with disabilities are not provided opportunity to progress at a quicker rate.

In contrast to such practice, there is evidence of a strong association between goal ambitiousness and student achievement outcome (Fuchs et al., 1985). Teachers who write goals with higher expectations attain greater achievement outcomes. Given this association, high goal ambitiousness is a necessary component to attending to the substance of IDEA 97. Practices for writing ambitious IEP goals have been described in the literature (Deno, Mirkin, & Wesson, 1984; Fuchs, & Shinn, 1989) and suggest that ambitious goals be based on a *minimum* conceptual level of growth of one-month growth in content knowledge for each month of special education service delivery. Less expected growth than this means that even with special education the student would be further behind their general education classmates.

For many practitioners, this ambitiousness may contrast with current goal setting practices. However, the annual goal is an important statement of expectations for a student who receives *special education*. The logic of this minimum growth standard is that the expectation for any student in *general education* is that they would conceptually improve one month for every month of instruction. As the student in question is to receive a special education, with more highly trained teachers, with more intensive programs, and at a higher cost, the expectation is that the student should be expected to learn more rapidly than with "just" the general education program. The U.S. Supreme Court spoke to the issue of IEP goal ambitiousness in the *S. Carter v. Florence School District* (1986) case. The student in question had an IEP with four-month progress goals in reading and math for a 1-year period. The U.S. Supreme Court upheld the District Court ruling that gains such as these failed to meet EAHCA's requirement of more than "minimal or trivial progress." They also concluded that this type of progress was unlikely to permit the student to advance from grade to grade with passing marks. As the Supreme Court summarized in this case, "Clearly Congress did not intend that a school system could discharge its duty under the [Act] by providing a program that produces some minimal academic advancement, no matter how trivial" This judgment suggests strongly that school-based teams consider the ambitiousness of their goals and whether they produce minimal academic advancement.

Annual IEP Goals Must be Aligned to a Short-term or Long-term Focus

Conceptual advances concerning how to assess progress toward IEP goals have taken place in the 25 years since the inception of the EAHCA (1975). Clearer distinctions have been made between simply (a) collecting student outcome information (i.e., testing) and (b) assessment (i.e., using the information for decision making). Arguably, most test data collected to "evaluate student progress" is *not* assessment. No decisions are made with the test results. Consider the case of the end-of-the-week-spelling test, where a student's goal may be to master one unit per week with 80% accuracy. Typically, the data are not used to influence teaching and evaluation decisions. Whether or not the student reaches the 80% mastery standard, the student still typically progresses to the next weekly spelling unit. The instructional plan is not modified and the IEP is not revised based on this test performance.

When *assessment* of student progress toward IEP goals occurs, one of two broad approaches, short-term or long-term measurement (Fuchs & Deno, 1991; Fuchs & Shinn, 1989; Jenkins, Deno & Mirkin, 1979) must be chosen. Short-term measurement (STM), occasionally referred to as mastery monitoring, is a class of progress monitoring strategies where performance on discrete instructional tasks (e.g., addition math facts, sums to 20) or units (e.g., math Chapter 6) is evaluated over time. Ideally, these discrete instructional tasks or units are taught and evaluated sequentially over time. What is measured over time also changes. For example, when a student masters addition math facts, sums to 20, the next task may be mastery of subtraction math facts, from 0-0 to 18-9.

In contrast, long-term measurement (LTM), occasionally referred to as general outcome measurement (Fuchs & Deno, 1992), is a class of progress-monitoring strategies where performance on the *same* general, but important, behavior on curriculum tasks of equal difficulty is evaluated over time. For example, to assess general reading achievement, a student's progress may be assessed using a LTM approach by having the student read aloud for 1 minute from randomly selected passages from a third-grade general education reader with CBM.

Selecting and writing an IEP goal, then, cannot be separated from the measurement approach used to monitor progress. It makes no sense to write an IEP goal in math where the student will complete math homework with 80% accuracy and monitor progress using a LTM approach where the student would complete computations problems for 2 minutes from problems selected randomly from the annual second-grade general curriculum. Conversely, it would make no sense to write an IEP goal in math where the student would be expected to complete 45 digits correctly in 2 minutes when given a set of problems randomly selected from the second-grade general curriculum and monitor progress by assessing weekly mastery of the instructional content using the end-of-chapter tests. Goals and progress monitoring procedures *must be aligned.*

STM and LTM strategies have known different strengths and weaknesses (for more detail, see Fuchs & Deno [1991]). In brief, these advantages can be categorized as relating to (a) social validity and (b) feasibility. Feasibility will be discussed later in this chapter. It is important, however, to devote some attention to social validity, or the degree to which improvement toward the IEP goal is *meaningful.* Consider a goal aligned with a STM approach: In one year, the student will complete 36 reading instructional objectives in the general curriculum. For STM to be appropriate, there must be evidence that (a) the 36 instructional objectives are sequenced appropriately and (b) that adequate rates of progress to typical students have been established. Assuming that these standards are met, 36 separate "tests" would be created. One such test might measure the student's success at reading words with "r-controlled vowels" with 95% accuracy. Each test would be given after instruction on that specific instructional objective. The results of each test would have high "instructional validity." They would tell what a student did or did not do correctly (e.g., reading words with r-controlled vowels). Each test would have little content validity, because it would only assess one small portion of the year's curriculum. If each objective was equally important, and this is unlikely, then each test would correspond to 1/36th of the curriculum.

The social validity of this type of measurement approach is the sum of the skills of the 36 instructional standards. It is important for school-based teams to have some outcome data to suggest that mastery of these 36 instructional standards result in a student's becoming a better reader. For example, is it enough to assume that student mastery of all 36 instructional objectives in the second-grade curriculum means they can successfully read the second-grade curriculum? Although it appears intuitive that this "sum" results in meaningful improvement (i.e., a better reader), typically few curricula offer any empirical support for improving student outcomes. Thus, making an assumption that mastery of the sum of the parts equals better overall reading performance is a high-stakes inference.

IEP goals aligned with a LTM focus are predicated on the *empirical* identification of a valid outcome indicator(s) of general skill proficiency. That is, a behavior(s) must be validated as a measure of the academic construct of interest. CBM was developed to fit within a LTM measurement approach to facilitate writing IEP goals with empirically validated outcome measures. To date, five CBM indicators have been validated for use in writing IEP goals and evaluating progress using a LTM approach:

- In *reading*, students read aloud from passages typically drawn from general education basal readers for 1 minute. The number of words read correctly constitutes the basic decision-making metric.
- In *reading*, maze, a multiple choice cloze reading technique, also has been validated as a CBM testing strategy (Fuchs & Fuchs, 1992). The number of correct word choices per 5 minutes is the primary metric.
- In *spelling*, students write words from randomly selected general education annual spelling curriculum that are dictated at specified intervals (either 5, 7, or 10 seconds) for 2 minutes. The number of correct letter sequences and words spelled correctly are counted.
- In *written expression*, students write a story for 3 minutes after being given a grade-level appropriate story starter (e.g., "Pretend you are playing on the playground, and a spaceship lands. A little green person comes out, calls your name, and ..."). The number of words written, spelled correctly, and/or correct word sequences is counted.
- In *mathematics computation*, students write answers to computational problems selected randomly from general education computational objectives using 2- to 5-minute probes. The number of digits written correctly is counted.

Chapter length limits prevent a detailed description of the technical adequacy of CBM (see Marston, [1989], or for more contemporary perspectives see Good and Jefferson [1998]). A brief illustration of the technical information comes from Reading-CBM. Reliability and validity studies have demonstrated appropriate psychometric properties (e.g., Deno, Mirkin, & Chiang, 1982). Test-retest and alternate form reliability ranges from .82 to .97 with most estimates above .90. Criterion-related validity studies using published norm-referenced reading achievement tests show coefficients ranging from .63 to .90 with most correlations around .80. Reading-CBM is highly related to other measures of general reading achievement, including comprehension (Fuchs, Fuchs, & Maxwell, 1988; Shinn, Good, Knutson, Tilly, & Collins, 1992).

However, more important for use in writing goals and monitoring outcomes is the degree to which an assessment strategy contributes to achievement outcomes. This standard has been described by Hayes, Nelson, and Jarrett (1987) as "treatment validity." Since 1984 (Fuchs, Deno, & Mirkin, 1984) a series of studies have been conducted investigating the effect of using CBM and decision-making features on student achievement. Reflecting the career work of L. Fuchs and D. Fuchs, many of these studies have been conducted with students with disabilities, principally students with learning disabilities. The studies can be divided into three broad approaches: (a) those that use CBM to monitor student achievement with informal decision making or without instruction on how to use the information (Fuchs et al., 1984), (b) use of CBM with systematic rules for making intervention effectiveness decisions (Fuchs, 1988; Fuchs & Fuchs, 1987; Fuchs, Fuchs, & Hamlett, 1989; Fuchs, Fuchs, Hamlett, & Whinnery, 1991), and (c) use of CBM with feedback about how the students' performed on specific required curricular skills or instructional enhancements (Fuchs, 1993; Fuchs, 1998; Fuchs, Fuchs, Hamlett & Allinder, 1991; Fuchs, Fuchs, Hamlett & Stecker, 1991).

As summarized in Fuchs and Fuchs (1986) and Shinn and Hubbard (1992), irrespective of the research focus, the use of CBM improves student achievement outcomes significantly. Average effect sizes typically exceed .5, and they increase when systematic decision-making strategies are used. An effect size of .5 translates to performance at the 84th percentile with the use of CBM in goal setting and monitoring progress compared to performance at the 50th percentile when it is not used. The most powerful achievement outcomes are observed when CBM is used with systematic decision making and feedback and skill analysis. Given the results of these types of studies, school-based teams can be confident that growth or improvement on goals written using CBM will correspond to achieving more in reading, spelling, mathematics computation, and written expression.

Progress Should be Assessed as Frequently as Possible

As was noted earlier, one important change concerning IEPs in IDEA 97 is the requirement for more frequent evaluation of students' progress toward annual goals and the communication of this information to parents on a schedule consistent with that of nondisabled students. The language of "at least as often as …" provides only a minimum procedural safeguard to ensure effective interventions for students with disabilities. For example, if general education students were informed of their progress on a trimester basis, then it would be expected that parents of students who receive special education would be informed of progress on that same timeline. This increase in communication of outcomes is an improvement over current practice and the reporting of progress as part of the annual review. However, from a "quality of program perspective," it could be argued that this type of evaluation of progress and its reporting is still too infrequent.

Within the field of special education, there has been long-standing concern that assessment has been too infrequent. For example, the federal white paper entitled *The National Agenda to Improve Outcomes for Persons with Disabilities* (U.S. Department of Education, 1994) listed among their concerns that the "assessment process is often static rather than dynamic" (p. 21). The authors of this document recommended the use of "continuous progress measures and ongoing assessments to maintain and support appropriate teaching strategies" (p. 21). Increasing the frequency of monitoring and reporting progress to parents to three to four times per year, although better, still only allows for IEP revisions, at best, on two occasions.

As was noted earlier in the chapter, frequent monitoring of student progress has been linked to improved outcomes for students with disabilities, typically with effect sizes of .5 or greater (Fuchs & Fuchs, 1986). Given the potential impact that frequent progress monitoring can have on student achievement, the legal obligation explicit in IDEA 97 for increased monitoring and reporting of progress, and the availability of a validated technology for doing so (i.e., CBM), it seems professionally responsible to set monitoring of progress toward IEP goals on a weekly basis as the standard of practice. With this level of frequency, using CBM and a LTM approach, school-based teams can evaluate the effectiveness of a student's special education intervention reliably within 6-8 weeks (Good & Shinn, 1990; Shinn, Good, & Stein, 1989). This increased assessment frequency can be justified not only by sound professional practice but also for fiscal reasons. Given the significant difference in the cost of special education versus general education, one of the most important "services" that are paid for as part of a special education is that of the cost of frequent monitoring.

Decision Rules for IEP Revisions Must be Specified

Although positive and socially significant effect sizes are associated with frequent measurement of progress, it also has been demonstrated that the systematic use of "decision rules" increases effect sizes further (see, for example, Fuchs [1986] and Fuchs, Fuchs, Hamlett, and Allinder [1991]). Decision rules are a set of specified alarms that are to go off when the expected rate of progress toward the IEP annual goal(s) is not obtained. For example, in a STM approach, a decision rule could be to change an intervention if the student fails to master a unit for 2 consecutive weeks. In a LTM approach, a decision rule could be to change an intervention if three of five consecutive data points (i.e., scores on weekly CBM probes) fall below the expected rate of progress.

Too often, even with systematic STM or LTM evaluation, a student's special education intervention is not changed when progress is insufficient (Fuchs, Wesson, Tindal, Mirkin, & Deno, 1982; Fuchs, Fuchs, Hamlett & Stecker, 1991). As practitioners, the authors have observed this reluctance to change the intervention despite student IEP progress data suggesting the need to do so. Decision rules for IEP revision written into the IEP increase the likelihood of making these changes should the need be evident.

IEP Goal Setting, Progress Monitoring, and IEP Revision Must be Feasible

This chapter began on a more pessimistic note; that is, that practitioners see the IEP, goal setting, and progress monitoring principally as a procedural necessity (Bateman & Linden, 1998). To accomplish the substantive benefits of the IEP process then, IEP process designers (e.g., state departments of education, school district leaders) and teams must attend to issues of feasibility. The process of writing meaningful IEP goals, monitoring progress toward those goals, communicating with parents, and making appropriate revision must be doable (Fuchs & Fuchs, 1999). To make this doable will require abandonment of principles such as "more is better" (e.g., the seemingly exhaustive lists of goals) and of expensive and time-consuming assessment that may not be useful for evaluating progress and participating in general curriculum (e.g., commercial achievement tests). Instead, the authors recommend designing IEP processes that are characterized by (a) fewer but important goals, (b) short but understandable forms and processes, and (c) assessment conducted exclusively to make good decisions. This feasibility, then, can allow team members to focus on providing effective special education programs.

These characteristics are attainable because there are technological, science-based solutions. The problem is not one of having to discover reasonably time efficient ways of writing IEP goals to reflect participation and progress in general curriculum and monitor progress, at least in the basic skills areas. CBM has a substantial body of school-based research support establishing it as a valid technology for accomplishing this mission. The problem then becomes not one of technology discovery but technology *adoption*.

Best Practices Strategies for Implementing the New IEP Provisions

This chapter illustrates how CBM can be used to write finite but important annual IEP goals that are aligned with a LTM approach that is feasible. CBM is used to write annual IEP goals in a simple standard format as shown in Table 3. Most apparent from the descriptions of the CBM measures and the goal formats is the feasibility of the process. Rather than a smorgasbord of reading goals on the IEP, a student may have a single important one. An individualized goal may read: "In 30 weeks, when given a randomly selected passage from MacMillan Level 3.1 (the general curriculum), Craig will read aloud 85 words in 1 minute."

Because each measure is brief (i.e., 1–5 minutes) and some can be administered reliably in small groups, it is possible to assess progress *weekly* toward an IEP annual goal. Information can be collected without a major distraction or diversion from instruction, especially if tests that are no longer relevant to IEP decision making (i.e., commercial norm-referenced tests) are discontinued. Because the skills necessary for administering CBM can be taught to a wide range of school personnel, including trained special education teacher aides, the need for more costly personnel (e.g., school psychologists) to be involved in routine assessment is reduced.

Because goal setting and progress monitoring are feasible, emphasis can be placed on decision making regarding the effects of the special education program and the need for appropriate IEP revision. Students with disabilities who achieve the rate of progress specified in the IEP would have their current IEP maintained.

TABLE 3: Basic Format for CBM Annual IEP Goals in Reading, Math, Written Expression, and Spelling

Academic Area	Conditions	Behavior	Criterion
Reading	In *(number of weeks until annual review)*, when given a randomly selected passage from *(level and name of general education reading series)*	Student will read aloud	At *(number of words per minute correct/number of errors)*
Math	In *(number of weeks until annual review)*, when given randomly selected problems from *(level and name of general education math series)*, for 2 minutes	Student will write	*(Number of correct digits)*
Written expression	In *(number of weeks until annual review)*, when given a story starter or topic sentence and 3 minutes in which to write	Student will write	A total of *(number of words and/or correct writing sequences)*
Spelling	In *(number of weeks until annual review)*, when dictated randomly selected words from *(level and name of general education spelling series)*, for 2 minutes	Student will write	*(Number of correct letter sequences)*

Adapted with permission from Fuchs, L. S., & Shinn, M. R. (1989). Writing CBM IEP objectives. In M. R. Shinn (Ed.) Curriculum-based measurement: Assessing special children (pp. 132-154). New York: Guilford.

Special education programs used with students who are learning at less than desired IEP rate of progress can be detected within 4–6 weeks. IEPs then can be *revised* to produce a more effective instructional program.

The process of writing IEP goals and setting and monitoring progress feasibly consists of four major steps: (a) assessing current performance in general curriculum, (b) writing the annual goal, (c) collecting progress monitoring information, and (d) making decisions about the need to revise the IEP. Each of these steps is discussed in the following sections using the case of Craig to illustrate.

Assessing Current Performance

Craig was a third-grade boy referred by his general education teacher for reading difficulties. Subsequent problem-solving assessment determined his educational needs to be so severe and unlikely to be resolved within general education with supplemental aids and services that he was determined to be eligible for special education.

Part of the data that contributed to this decision was Survey-Level Assessment (SLA) (Shinn, 1989) using CBM. In reading, SLA is the process of having students read multiple samples (usually three) in successively lower levels of the curriculum until an appropriate instructional or normative level is identified (Shinn, 1989). Expected instructional placement typically is considered the level of the general education reading curriculum that corresponds with a student's grade placement (Lovitt & Hansen, 1976). For Craig, a third-grader, his expected instructional placement was Level 3.1 in the *MacMillan Reading Series*, the reading series used for instruction in Craig's general education classroom.

Actual instructional placement is considered the level at which a student can be appropriately placed for instructional purposes. Appropriate instructional materials generally are defined as materials that are not too hard and not too easy for instructional purposes (Taylor, Harris, & Pearson, 1988). Because Craig's performance in the Level 3.1 reader was significantly lower than that of his peers, it was considered too difficult for instructional purposes. Therefore, Craig read three 1-minute passages at successively lower levels of the reading curriculum until an appropriate instructional level was identified. This process was completed in approximately 15 minutes with a school psychologist. The median number of words read correctly per minute (WRC) was used as the summary score for each level and was compared to local normative performance at each level of the curriculum. For example, Craig's score in Level 2.1 was compared to typical second-grade performance in the same materials. His score in Level 1 was compared to first-grade norms. Craig's reading was assessed at each successively lower level in the *MacMillan Reading Series* until his median WRC was above the 25th percentile when compared to local norms.

The results of Craig's SLA are displayed in Table 4. Testing for Craig was stopped at MacMillan Level 1.0 where his median WRC of 36 placed him at the 23rd percentile compared to typical first-grade readers. The discrepancy (three levels in the general education curriculum) between Craig's expected and actual instructional level was large enough to consider him eligible for special education and IEP with an annual goal in reading.

TABLE 4: Survey-Level Assessment Using CBM for Craig

Curriculum and Level	Craig's Median Performance	Grade-Level Median Peer Performance	Craig's Percentile Rank
MacMillan 3.1	33	85	8th
MacMillan 2.2	27		No local norms
MacMillan 2.1	36	72	10th
MacMillan 1	36	66	23rd

Note: Reading scores are reported in the number of words read correctly per minute (WRC).

This extensive sample of Craig's reading skills through multiple levels of the general curriculum was used to (a) conduct a skills analysis, (b) determine appropriateness of materials for instructional purposes (i.e., too hard, too easy), and (c) identify subskill deficiencies. All of this information is useful for planning the instructional content of the IEP.

Writing the Goal

In Craig's case, the IEP team wrote this annual goal: "In 30 weeks, when given a randomly selected passage from MacMillan Level 3.1, Craig will read aloud 85 words in 1 minute." This goal was three curriculum levels higher than his actual instructional placement of Level 1, according to the publisher's scope and sequence chart. The criterion for success was defined by the local normative performance of typical third-grade peers in the Level 3.1 reader. The IEP team wrote this goal because it had high expectations for the special education program and because attainment of this goal would allow consideration of Craig no longer needing extensive special education services in 1 year.

Once an annual IEP goal is written, it is displayed graphically as illustrated in Figure 1 to facilitate progress monitoring and program evaluation. The graph includes (a) time (horizontal axis), (b) unit of measurement (vertical axis), (c) current student performance, or baseline performance, and (d) the criterion for success as written in the long-term goal. The "aimline" represents the intersection between current performance, Craig's median baseline performance in Level 3.1, and expected performance (his goal of 85 WRC in 30 weeks in Level 3.1).

Monitoring Progress Toward the Annual Goal

To evaluate Craig's progress toward his annual IEP goal, he read a different 1-minute passage twice a week with his special education teacher in his long-term goal material, Level 3.1. Each time Craig's scores in the number of WRC were graphed on his progress-monitoring chart as displayed in Figure 1. With practice, this frequency of monitoring is feasible for special education programs.

FIGURE 1: Progress Monitoring For Craig

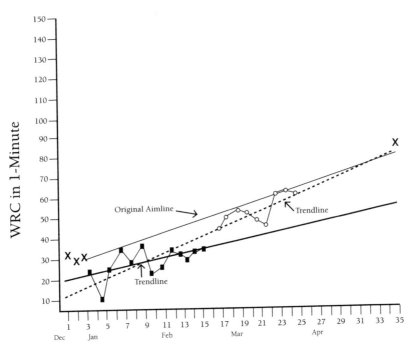

Making Decisions About IEP Revision

After at least 7–10 CBM reading probes were collected over time from Craig, his actual rate of progress was estimated by drawing a "trendline." The trendline is a line of best fit that represents his actual rate of progress toward the IEP annual goal. To determine whether Craig's special education program was working, his trendline, or actual performance, was compared to his aimline, or expected rate of performance. If Craig's instructional program is working, then his trendline will be parallel to, or steeper than, his aimline. In this instance, support would be offered that his current special education program be continued without modification. If his trendline were sharply steeper than his aimline, then the school-based team would be compelled to write a more ambitious goal. A trendline that is *less* steep as the expected rate of progress, "flat," or negative, indicates a need for an immediate change in the instructional program and a revision of the IEP.

As seen in Figure 1, Craig was making gains in his reading achievement after 7 weeks of intervention, as represented by his accelerating trendline. However, this rate of progress, although positive, was below that rate necessary to attain his IEP goal. Thus, his special education program, while resulting in *some* improvement, was not accomplishing what was intended. This type of progress information can be reported to parents at any time without the need to engage in additional time-consuming testing.

Therefore, Craig's IEP was revised to address this lack of progress. This revision included (a) a change in the reading intervention he was receiving in special education and (b) a corresponding revision of the IEP goal to reflect the same rate of progress but an overall lower level of attainment. The fact that a revision was made in his IEP is documented on the graph by a solid vertical line separating Craig's performance during his first program and his performance after the revision was made.

It is important to note that this revision of the IEP need not be a cumbersome process or one delayed by time. Appropriate personnel should meet to problem solve what changes in the special education program may improve Craig's reading achievement. Again, it is critical to have someone present who can interpret the instructional implications of any assessment data. Inviting parents to participate is good practice, but not legally required. Revisions can be made in a timely basis because notification rather than informed consent governs the process.

After the IEP revision of Craig's program, his special education teacher continued monitoring his progress by having him read two 1-minute passages per week from the Level 3.1 book and graphed his scores. After 6 weeks of implementation of the modified program (i.e., after attaining another 10–12 data points), Craig's teacher again evaluated his progress toward his IEP goal. She computed a new trendline (as shown by the dashed line in Figure 1) and compared his slope and rate of progress to his aimline. The slope of Craig's trendline indicated that he *now* was making satisfactory progress toward his annual goal. Therefore, no revisions in his IEP were needed. Again, this progress could be communicated easily and efficiently to Craig's parents.

PROFESSIONAL DEVELOPMENT IMPLICATIONS OF NEW IEP PROVISIONS

The seemingly "simple" changes in IDEA 97 suggest substantial changes in how educators conduct business with respect to writing and evaluating IEP goals (Yell & Shriner, 1997). The professional development implications of improving writing and evaluating IEP goals include both altered and expanded roles for administrators, general and special education teachers, and pre-service trainers as the amendments are enacted. The scope of training, both for pre-service and in-service personnel, should not be underestimated as staff development and systems change efforts will need to focus on both (a) the *acquisition* of new knowledge and skills and (b) *addressing personal concerns* regarding roles and responsibilities. As a starting point, the following suggestions are offered for facilitating the implementation of the provisions related to writing and evaluating IEP goals. Because the development of the IEP occurs as part of a larger evaluation and decision-making process, it is important to recognize that the accomplishment of these professional development milestones will eventually include more than just training on writing better IEP goals.

First, school-based teams will need to shift their assessment focus from one of collecting information primarily for eligibility determination to one of collecting data that will lead to the development of measurable annual goals in the general curriculum. A shift in assessment focus means that writing better IEP goals *begins* long before the IEP is developed with an evaluation process that includes, at a minimum, assessment of student performance in general curriculum and the identification of instructional and curricular variables that impact student achievement. The degree to which student performance in the general curriculum is discrepant from expected performance serves as the basis not only for determining need for special education, but for determining the *content* of the IEP and *writing measurable long-term annual goals* that reflect acquisition of skills in the general curriculum. Permanent products of student performance (e.g., errors made during oral reading, math computation, spelling words) also can be analyzed to determine skills a student does or does not have and provide input into IEP development.

Second, to accomplish changes in assessment practices, educators will need to learn new skills through staff development training and reading. In general, school-based teams will need training *and* on-site coaching during implementation in (a) problem-solving assessment, (b) curriculum-based assessment (CBA) and CBM, (c) instructional design, such as Curriculum-Based Evaluation (CBE), (d) consultation, and (e) the change/reform process.

Items (a) through (d) are specific and necessary to achieving the changes detailed in IDEA 97 for writing and evaluating progress toward IEP goals. Staff development and training in areas (a) to (d) should include a combination of *training* and *on-site coaching*. Training in problem-solving assessment will provide teams with a systematic, question-driven *framework* for collecting data relevant for identifying problems, developing IEPs, writing IEP goals, and evaluating progress toward IEP goals. Training in CBA, CBM, and CBE will provide teams with the *necessary technologies* to collect information within a problem-solving framework. Finally, training in instructional design and consultation will provide teams with knowledge of general curriculum design and consultation skills to work with teachers, students, and parents to develop instructional interventions, monitor progress toward long-term goals, and provide assistance in revising IEPs when students with disabilities are not making adequate progress.

Although training is necessary and provides knowledge and some opportunity for skill development, it alone is unlikely to lead to sustained use of newly acquired skills (Joyce & Showers, 1988). Therefore, an on-site coach is recommended after training to provide teams with opportunities to practice new skills, get immediate feedback, and problem-solve as issues in implementation arise. Without coaching, practice, and feedback, it is estimated that fewer than 5% of trainees will transfer newly acquired skills to the classroom or change practices (Joyce & Showers, 1988). However, when coaching with practice and immediate feedback are used in combination with training, 95% of the trainees transfer new skills into practice. On-site coaches should be knowledgeable in the areas they are coaching (i.e., implementing problem-solving assessment and CBM for special education decision making) and have time to work with teams on-site during implementation of new practices.

Last, training and coaching should be supplemented with reading in areas such as new assessment and intervention technologies, problem-solving assessment, and topics related to instructional design. The authors recommend that reading becomes standard practice for building-based teams and that team meeting time is periodically set aside devoted to scholarly discussion regarding relevant topics.

Finally, as teams acquire new skills and shift the focus of their assessment and problem-solving activities they will need assistance, support, and guidance with implementation at the building and school district levels. The technologies necessary to accomplish the changes in IDEA 97 regarding IEP development have been available to consumers for more than two decades, so gaining knowledge and training for staff and team members will not require reinvention of the wheel. Training goals can be achieved with resources and willing staff.

Most problems arise during implementation of newly acquired skills when *changes* in procedures, roles, and responsibilities begin to emerge. As school-based teams begin working within a problem-solving framework and using better assessment technologies to collect information useful for writing and evaluating IEP goals, they will likely find that implementation of skills into practice requires more than just replacing "old" practices with "new" practices. Rather, teams will find that a paradigm shift is necessary to successfully move toward providing services guided by problem solving (see Reschly and Ysseldyke [1995] for more information on a shift in paradigms). A paradigm shift means a change in professional culture (e.g., degree of collegiality, collaboration, working toward common goals) as well as a change in structure (e.g., different members on the team) (Fullan, 1996). As a result of changes in culture, team members are expected to alter and expand their roles which in turn may create anxiety about (a) job stability (i.e., "Will I lose my job if I no longer give IQ tests?"), (b) ability to learn and implement new skills, (c) doing something illegal, and (d) the time involved to accomplish systems-level change. The questions, or concerns, are frequently encountered by the authors at the school level. However, readers are encouraged to learn more about the change process, as there are plenty of other related concerns and technologies for understanding and evaluating change (Fullan, 1996; Hord, Rutherford, Huling-Austin, & Hall, 1987). In fact, the authors recommend that staff development efforts should provide training to school-based teams in learning about and understanding the change process (Fullan, 1996; Hord et al., 1987) as they acquire new skills and begin implementation to write better IEP goals and evaluate student performance.

School-based teams also are encouraged to contact sites where many of the above-mentioned hurdles, or barriers to implementation, have already been worked out and where successful implementation can be observed. Observing successful implementation provides opportunities for teams to (a) receive feedback about their own practices, (b) observe what works and what does not, and most important (c) see that implementation of problem-solving and assessment technologies at both district and state levels can be done and how they have successfully facilitated the writing of better IEPs and impacted achievement for students with and without disabilities.

Summary

The new requirements pertaining to IEPs that are contained in IDEA 97 provide the field with an opportunity to improve practices for students with disabilities and enhance achievement outcomes further. The changes described in this chapter can result in a feasible yet more valuable IEP process. This part of the law is linked to what has been demonstrated "to work" in school, in school-based research, and to offer remedies to the dilemmas felt by school practitioners. Correspondingly, at least in the areas of basic skills, school-based teams need not search for or invent a process or technology for writing, evaluating and revising IEPs. CBM is a validated, efficient technology, that when used in a long-term measurement approach, not only is consistent with IDEA 97, it is feasible and can result in meaningful improvements in student achievement.

As a profession, then, school-based building team members have the opportunity to identify the problem and work constructively toward resolution. It is the authors' hope that you share their optimistic vision that improving IEPs is a solvable problem that can restore the fundamental faith and importance of providing the best special education programs possible through high quality IEPs. The chapter concludes with an excerpt from the poem presented earlier, but without the original author's sarcasm.

Say! I almost like these IEPs

I think I'll write 6003!

References

Bateman, B.D., & Linden, M.A. (1998). *Better IEPs: How to develop legally correct and educationally useful programs.* Longmont, CO: Sopris West.

Deno, S. L. (1985). Curriculum-based measurement: The emerging alternative. *Exceptional Children, 52,* 219–232.

Deno, S. L. (1986). Formative evaluation of individual student programs: A new role for school psychologists. *School Psychology Review, 15,* 358–374.

Deno, S. L. (1992). The nature and development of curriculum-based measurement. *Preventing School Failure, 36*(2), 5–10.

Deno, S. L., Mirkin, P., & Chiang, B. (1982). Identifying valid measures of reading. *Exceptional Children, 49,* 36–45.

Deno, S. L., Mirkin, P., & Wesson, C. (1984). How to write effective data-based IEPs. *Teaching Exceptional Children, 16,* 99–104.

Education for All Handicapped Children Act of 1975. 20 U.S.C. Sec. 401 (1975).

Fuchs, L. S. (1986). Monitoring progress among mildly handicapped pupils: Review of current practice and research. *Remedial and Special Education, 7,* 5–12.

Fuchs, L. S. (1988). Effects of computer-managed instruction on teachers' implementation on systematic monitoring programs and student achievement. *Journal of Educational Research, 81,* 294–304.

Fuchs, L. S. (1993). Enhancing instructional programming and student achievement with curriculum-based measurement. In J. Kramer (Ed.), *Curriculum-based measurement* (pp. 65-104). Lincoln, NE: Buros Institute of Mental Measurements.

Fuchs, L. S. (1998). Computer applications to address implementation difficulties associated with Curriculum-Based Measurement. In M. R. Shinn (Ed.), *Advanced Applications of Curriculum-Based Measurement*(pp. 89-112). New York: Guilford.

Fuchs, L. S., & Deno, S. L. (1991). Paradigmatic distinctions between instructionally relevant measurement models. *Exceptional Children, 57*(6), 488–500.

Fuchs, L. S., & Deno, S. L. (1992). Effects of curriculum within curriculum-based measurement. *Exceptional Children, 58,* 232–243.

Fuchs, L. S., Deno, S. L., & Mirkin, P. (1984). The effects of frequent curriculum based measurement and evaluation on pedagogy, student achievement and student awareness of learning. *American Educational Research Journal, 21,* 449–460.

Fuchs, L.S., & Fuchs, D. (1986). Effects of systematic formative evaluation on student achievement: A meta-analysis. *Exceptional Children, 53,* 199–208.

Fuchs, L. S., & Fuchs, D. (1987). The relation between methods of graphing student performance data and achievement: A meta-analysis. *Journal of Special Education Technology, 8,* 5–13.

Fuchs, L. S., & Fuchs, D. (1992). Identifying a measure for monitoring student reading progress. *School Psychology Review, 21*, 45–58.

Fuchs, L. S., & Fuchs, D. (1999). Monitoring student progress toward the development of reading competence: A review of three forms of classroom-based assessment. *School Psychology Review, 28*, 659–671.

Fuchs, L. S., Fuchs, D., & Deno, S. L. (1985). The importance of goal ambitiousness and goal mastery to student achievement. *Exceptional Children, 52*, 63–71.

Fuchs, L. S., Fuchs, D., & Hamlett, C. L. (1989). Monitoring reading growth using student recalls: Effects of two teacher feedback systems. *Journal of Educational Research, 83*, 103–111.

Fuchs, L. S., Fuchs, D., Hamlett, C. L., & Allinder, R. M. (1991). Effects of expert system advice within curriculum-based measurement on teacher planning and student achievement in spelling. *School Psychology Review, 20*, 49–66.

Fuchs, L. S., Fuchs, D., Hamlett, C. L., & Stecker, P. M. (1991). Effects of curriculum-based measurement and consultation on teaching planning and student achievement in mathematics operations. *American Educational Research Journal, 28*, 617–641.

Fuchs, L.S., Fuchs, D., Hamlett, C.L., & Whinnery, K.W. (1991). Effects of goal line feedback on level, slope, and stability of performance within curriculum-based measurement. *Learning Disabilities Research and Practice, 6*, 3–12.

Fuchs, L. S., Fuchs, D., & Maxwell, C. L. (1988). The validity of informal reading comprehension measures. *Remedial and Special Education, 9*(2), 20–28.

Fuchs, L. S., Hamlett, C. L., & Fuchs, D. (1990). *Monitoring basic skills progress* [Computer software]. Austin, TX: PRO-ED.

Fuchs, L. S., & Shinn, M. R. (1989). Writing CBM IEP objectives. In M. R. Shinn (Ed.), *Curriculum-based measurement: Assessing special children* (pp. 132-154). New York: Guilford.

Fuchs, L. S., Wesson, C., Tindal, G., Mirkin, P. K., & Deno, S. L. (1982). *Instructional changes, student performance, and teacher preferences: The effect of specific measurement and evaluation procedures.* Minneapolis, MN: University of Minnesota Institute for Research on Learning Disabilities.

Fullan, M. (1996). Professional culture and educational change. *School Psychology Review, 25*, 496–500.

Good, R. H., & Jefferson, G. (1998). Contemporary perspectives on curriculum-based measurement validity. In M. R. Shinn (Ed.), *Advanced applications of curriculum-based measurement* (pp. 61-88). New York: Guilford.

Good, R. H., & Salvia, J. (1988). Curriculum bias in published, norm-referenced reading tests: Demonstrable effects. *School Psychology Review, 17*, 51–60.

Good, R. H., & Shinn, M. R. (1990). Forecasting accuracy of slope estimates for reading curriculum-based measurement: Empirical evidence. *Behavioral Assessment, 12*, 179–193.

Hayes, S. C., Nelson, R. O., & Jarrett, R. B. (1987). The treatment utility of assessment: A functional approach to evaluating assessment quality. *American Psychologist, 42,* 963–974.

Hord, S.M., Rutherford, W.L., Huling-Austin, L., & Hall, G.E. (1987). *Taking charge of change.* Alexandria, VA: Association for Supervision and Curriculum Development.

Howell, K., Fox, S. L., & Morehead, M. K. (1993). *Curriculum-based evaluation: Teaching and decision making.* Pacific Grove, CA: Brooks/Cole.

Howell, K., & Nolet, V. (1999). *Curriculum-based evaluation: Teaching and decision making.* Pacific Grove, CA: Brooks/Cole.

Individuals with Disabilities Education Act Amendments of 1997, 20 U.S.C. § 1400 *et seq.* (West 1997).

Jenkins, J. R., Deno, S. L., & Mirkin, P. K. (1979). Measuring pupil progress toward the least restrictive environment. *Learning Disability Quarterly, 2,* 81–92.

Jenkins, J. R., & Pany, D. (1978). Standardized achievement tests: How useful for special education? *Exceptional Children, 44,* 448–453.

Joseph, J., Lindgren, J., Creamer, S., & Lane, K. (1983). *Evaluating special education: A study to pilot techniques using existing data in Skokie School District 68.* Skokie, IL: Skokie School District 68. (ERIC Document Reproduction Service NO. ED 227 176.)

Joyce, B., & Showers, B. (1988). *Student achievement through staff development.* White Plains, NY: Longman.

Lovitt, T. C., & Hansen, C. L. (1976) Round one: Placing the child in the right reader. *Journal of Learning Disabilities, 9,* 18–24.

Mager, R. F. (1962). *Preparing instructional objectives.* Palo Alto, CA: Fearon.

Mager, R. F., & Pipe, P. (1970). *Analyzing performance problems.* Belmont, CA: Frason.

Marston, D. B. (1989). A curriculum-based measurement approach to assessing academic performance: What is it and why do it. In M. R. Shinn (Ed.), *Curriculum-based measurement: Assessing special children* (pp. 18-78). New York: Guilford.

Pyecha, J. N., Cox, J. L., DeWitt, D., Drummond, D., Jaffe, J., Kalt, M., Lane, C., & Pelosi, J. (1980). *A national survey of individualized education programs (IEPs) for handicapped children.* Durham, NC: Research Triangle Institute. (ERIC Document Reproduction No. 199 970-974.)

Reschly, D., & Ysseldyke, J. (1995). School psychology paradigm shift. In A. Thomas & J. Grimes (Eds.), *Best practices in school psychology III* (pp. 17-32). Washington, DC: National Association of School Psychologists.

Rinaldi, R. T. (1976). Urban schools and P.L. 94-142: One administrator's perspective on the law. In R. A. Johnson & A. P. Kowalski (Eds.), *Perspectives on implementation of the "Education for All Handicapped Children Act of 1975"* (pp. 135-152). Washington DC: Council of Great City Schools.

Salvia, J., & Ysseldyke, J. E. (1998). *Assessment in special and remedial education* (5th ed.). Boston: Houghton-Mifflin.

Shapiro, E. S., & Derr, T. F. (1987). An examination of the overlap between reading curricula and standardized achievements tests. *The Journal of Special Education, 21*, 59–67.

Shinn, M. R. (Ed.) (1989). *Curriculum-based measurement: Assessing special children.* New York: Guilford

Shinn, M. R. (Ed.) (1998). *Advanced applications of curriculum-based measurement.* New York: Guilford.

Shinn, M. R., Good, R. H., Knutson, N., Tilly, W. D., & Collins, V. (1992). Curriculum-based reading fluency: A confirmatory analysis of its relation to reading. *School Psychology Review, 21*, 458–478.

Shinn, M. R., Good, R. H., & Stein, S. (1989). Summarizing trend in student achievement: A comparison of evaluative models. *School Psychology Review, 18*, 356–370.

Shinn, M. R., & Hubbard, D. D. (1992). Curriculum-based measurement and problem-solving assessment: Basic procedures and outcomes. *FOCUS on Exceptional Children, 24*(5), 1–20.

Smith, S. W. (1990). Individualized educational programs (IEPs) in special education: From intent to acquiescence. *Exceptional Children, 57*, 6–14.

Taylor, B., Harris, L.A., & Pearson, P.D. (1988). *Reading difficulties: Instruction and assessment.* New York: Random House.

U.S. Department of Education. (1994). *The national agenda for achieving better results for children and youth with disabilities.* Washington DC: Author.

Wesson, C. L., & Deno, S. L. (1989). An analysis of long-term instructional plans in reading for elementary resource room students. *Remedial and Special Education, 10*(1), 21–34.

Yell, M. L., & Shriner, J.G. (1997). The IDEA amendments of 1997: Implications for special and general education teachers, administrators, and teacher trainers. *Focus on Exceptional Children, 30*(1), 1–19.

ANNOTATED BIBLIOGRAPHY

Bateman, B. D., & Linden, M. A. (1998). *Better IEPs.* Longmont, CO: Sopris West.

This book describes in detail the standards and practices for good IEPs, from a legal perspective and from "what is practical" to allow parents, students, and teachers to work together to develop good programs.

Fuchs, L. S. (1994). *Connecting performance assessment to instruction.* Reston, VA: Council for Exceptional Children.

This short volume from CEC lays out the standards necessary for quality instructional assessment that is linked to interventions. Because quality IEPs cannot be separated from the quality of the data used to set goals, plan instruction, and monitor outcomes, this resource is invaluable.

Fuchs, L. S., & Deno, S. L. (1991). Paradigmatic distinctions between instructionally relevant measurement models. *Exceptional Children, 57,* 488–500.

This article details the distinctions between short-term and long-term progress monitoring systems, providing relevant examples so that the principles can be applied to writing goals and monitoring progress.

Fuchs, L. S., & Fuchs, D. (1999). Monitoring student progress toward the development of reading competence: A review of three forms of classroom-based assessment. *School Psychology Review, 28,* 659–671.

This recent article lays out important principles to be used to evaluate any progress monitoring system and then applies them to three increasingly more frequent measurement systems.

Fuchs, L. S., & Shinn, M. R. (1989). Writing CBM IEP objectives. In M. R. Shinn (Ed.), *Curriculum-based measurement: Assessing special children* (pp. 132-154). New York: Guilford.

This book chapter presents in detail different ways of writing IEP goals using a long-term measurement approach with Curriculum-Based Measurement, including standardized formats and how to set criteria for success.

Authors' Notes. This chapter was supported in part by grant number 84.029D60057 Leadership Training in Curriculum-Based Measurement and Its Use in a Problem-Solving Model sponsored by the U.S. Department of Education, Office of Special Education Research. The views expressed within this paper are not necessarily those of the U.S. Department of Education.

CHAPTER 11

Implementing the IDEA 1997 Amendments:
A Compelling Argument for Systems Change

Michael J. Curtis
George M. Batsche
University of South Florida

Eric M. Mesmer
American Institutes for Research
Washington, DC

Historically, special education laws have been largely procedural in nature, meaning that they have focused, almost exclusively, on process, or "how" things are to be done. For example, laws and associated federal regulations beginning with the *Education of All Handicapped Children Act* (1975) have established mandates relating to such practices as confidentiality, access to educational records, parental permission for evaluation, multifactored evaluations, individualized education programs, decision making related to educational placement, and periodic reevaluations. The principle underlying this approach concerns process accountability, or an assumption that controlling procedure will lead to desirable outcomes.

The Individuals with Disabilities Education Act Amendments of 1997 (IDEA 97) (Individuals with Disabilities Education Act Amendments, 1997) continue to focus largely on procedures. For example, the amendments describe how parents are to be included in evaluations, program planning, and educational placement decision making as means for increasing parental participation in the education of students with disabilities. However, more clearly than in previous federal legislation, IDEA 97 seeks to ensure "results." Rather than just promoting process accountability, there is significant interest in ensuring meaningful education progress for all students with disabilities.

As with prior legislative mandates, it would be possible to address IDEA 97 entirely from a procedural perspective. A school district task force, or perhaps even a small group of district administrators, could analyze the associated federal and state regulations, one section at a time, and ask, "What do we need to do to meet these requirements?" No doubt, this approach has been taken in some districts.

On the other hand, a fundamentally different approach could and should be taken in implementing the mandates of IDEA 97, and more importantly, in addressing the needs of students with disabilities. This approach requires a willingness to engage in and to be committed to systemic change.

PRINCIPLES FOR CHANGE

A comprehensive knowledge base is available regarding principles and practices for effective organizational and systems change, although few school-based change efforts reflect familiarity with this literature. Several principles that are associated with effective change initiatives can be identified (Curtis & Stollar, 1995).

Principle 1: Shared Goals, Philosophy, and Values

Members of organizations often assume that the system's goals are evident, known to, and embraced widely. However, it is apparent that this is not the case. Not only are organizational goals often unknown to some individuals within the system, but many different goals may be held by organizational members, some in direct conflict with one another. In some cases, some who are critical to organizational success have competing goals. It is imperative that explicit goals be agreed on, publicly articulated, and used to focus the energies and resources of the organization. For example, if the primary goal of a school district is to demonstrate meaningful educational progress for each student with an identified disability, then the implications may be markedly different than if the goal is more narrowly defined as being in compliance with state and federal regulations.

It also is important that an organization's activities be based on an agreed on philosophy and set of values. What are those principles that should guide the efforts of all employees regardless of their specific roles? Is meaningful parental involvement in all aspects of the educational process a value inherent in all decision making? Does an empirically based, problem-solving philosophy serve as a foundation for the organization and delivery of services to all students with disabilities? The implications are very different when such a philosophy undergirds service delivery, in contrast to a categorical identification philosophy.

It has been the experience of the authors that many organizations resist investing time and energy in a systemic process to ensure that a coherent set of goals, philosophy, and values is agreed on, broadly accepted, and pursued. Yet, doing so is critical for organizational success.

Principle 2: Systemic Change

In most schools, as in many other organizations, the introduction of yet another new program, curriculum, or activity is met with the attitude, "And this too shall pass." The reason for this sentiment is understandable, because educational professionals are constantly inundated with new initiatives. Each school year is met not with the question, "Will we be asked to implement a new program?" but with, "How many new programs will we have to implement?"

The absence of a coherent overall, systemic approach to change leads to confusion and disillusionment. Once a systemic philosophy, values, and goals are agreed on, attention should be devoted to the design of a service delivery system that is based on that philosophy, reflects those values, and pursues those goals. As was previously noted, it would be possible to simply identify each new requirement established in IDEA 97 and then ensure that each mandate is incorporated into district procedures. However, although such a piecemeal approach may address the procedural requirements of IDEA 97, it probably will not address the mandated emphasis on results. In addition, implementation of the new mandates in such a fragmented manner is likely to be ineffective and to perpetuate the deficiencies of current service delivery models. Rather than simply tinkering with what already exists, efforts should be undertaken to design a comprehensive and coordinated service delivery system that is likely to be effective in achieving agreed on goals. Once such a system is designed, those aspects of the existing system that support these goals can be retained, those that can be changed (e.g., new skills needed) can be developed, and those that do not fit can be eliminated.

Principle 3: Commitment of Key Personnel

Meaningful change will not occur if people in important positions are not in support of the change initiative. The tendency is to immediately think about the superintendent, assistant superintendents, and other administrative personnel when contemplating this principle. Clearly, if those people who control resources and have a great deal of influence oppose, or even fail to publicly support, a change program, then it will be unlikely to succeed. However, roles critical to such efforts extend beyond administrators. Others, such as the heads of teacher unions or parent advocacy groups, also can be influential in determining the outcomes of change efforts, and securing their involvement and support early on is essential.

Principle 4: Involvement of All Primary Stakeholders

The literature on systems change is very clear in emphasizing the necessity of involving critical stakeholders in all aspects of the change process. If those who will be most affected by change do not participate in the process, then they may become obstacles to the effort and, in many cases, will ensure its failure. There are too many examples of school-based change efforts where general education teachers are not centrally involved in, but are merely informed of, a change initiative after it has been developed by administrators and other personnel, including school psychologists. The likelihood for success in implementing such initiatives is low. On the other hand, there are other examples where general education teachers are involved in discussions about potential change programs from the beginning, become advocates for the new program, and are ultimately keys to its success. Given their key role in the delivery of any educational program, general education teachers are critical to school-based change efforts (Fullan & Hargreaves, 1996; Sarason, 1990).

Parents comprise another critical stakeholder group that is often overlooked in change efforts. In attempting to address IDEA 97, it is clear that parents must be meaningfully involved in all aspects of their child's education. As noted by Sheridan, Cowan, and Eagle (this volume), schools must develop relationships with parents as partners in the education of their children. It seems important, also, that parents should be involved beyond just the education of their own children and should be full participants in system-level change efforts to redesign services for all students with disabilities.

Fullan (1995) reinforces the importance of involving key administrative personnel, as well as both general education teachers and parents, by asserting that change must occur from both the top down and the bottom up. All relevant constituencies must be included in all aspects of the change process, from beginning to end ... and there is no end to change.

Principle 5: Collaborative Planning and Problem-Solving Skills

Although personality certainly plays a part in the ability of people to work together, it is abundantly clear that most people do not possess the skills needed to be successful in such efforts. Consequently, formal training in collaborative problem-solving skills is a requisite component during early stages of any systems change process. People must be provided the skills needed to work effectively together not only on a one-to-one basis but in small group contexts as well. It is important to note that these skills are as essential to the successful implementation of IDEA 97 as they are to any systems change effort, regardless of the desired outcome. Clearly, the success of efforts to achieve meaningful education progress for students with disabilities will depend heavily on the ability of school personnel, parents, and community-based professionals to work together collaboratively.

As was asserted previously, the most effective approach to implementing IDEA 97 is through comprehensive system-level change that leads to a redesigned service delivery system for students with disabilities. Each of these five principles is critical to the success of such change efforts.

Last, it is important to remember that *change is an on-going and unending process, not an event or activity*. Change is going to occur, with or without our involvement. The best interests of the children and families are served by planned and sustained organizational change effort that will lead to better educational services and outcomes.

Applying Systems Change to Content Areas of IDEA 1997

IDEA 97 provides members of school-based teams with an opportunity to expand their roles in the delivery of services to students and families. Many school psychologists and special educators may be in a position to provide leadership in their school districts regarding the interpretation and implementation of these amendments. By using skills in consultation, problem-solving assessment, and intervention, professionals can assist districts in systemic change efforts that will both meet the needs of children and families and comply with IDEA 97.

Traditionally, school psychologists have spent significant amounts of time evaluating individual students for purposes of special education eligibility (Curtis, Hunley, Walker, & Baker, 1999; Reschly & Ysseldyke, 1995). Despite their desire for a broader role, school psychological services have been focused on supporting a special education system that has had a "categorical" focus. In this system, students who are struggling academically, behaviorally, socially, or emotionally are referred for an evaluation that determines whether they meet specific requirements for an identified disability. Specific components of IDEA 97 that call for greater emphasis on functional assessment and behavioral interventions provide unique and timely opportunities for school psychologists to shift the focus of their services from categorical placement to collaborative problem solving and intervention. Indeed, of all team members involved in implementation of the mandates for IDEA 97, school psychologists may be in the best position to realize a change in role as a result of the new amendments.

Changing Role of the School Psychologist

IDEA 97 has set the stage for the most significant role change for school psychologists since the passage of P.L. 94-142 in 1975. It has been stated in other chapters of this book and here that these amendments have focused to a great extent on intervention-based service delivery, on a comprehensive responsive assessment system, on collaborative problem solving, and on accountability. Research has indicated a long-standing desire by school psychologists to transform their role from one of assessor for eligibility for services to one who implements and facilitates the implementation of a broad range of services for students, families, and educators (e.g., Curtis et al., 1999; Reschly & McMasters-Beyer, 1991). The same research, however, has indicated that school psychologists continue to spend the majority of their time in assessment activities, particularly assessment for eligibility. Perhaps the continuing gap between the actual and the desired role of the school psychologist results from the way in which school psychologists seek to change their role. A permanent shift in the role of the school psychologist will occur only if the consumers of school psychological services (e.g., teachers, parents, administrators, students) value the services of school psychologists. Consumers of school psychological services will support a role change if the student (family, school climate) outcomes of that role change are clearly visible. The IDEA 97 provides the window of opportunity to facilitate a significant change in the role of the school psychologist that is clear and valued by consumers.

The impact of the IDEA 97 on the role of the school psychologist can occur in four areas: (a) the school psychologist as change agent, (b) supervision in the areas of assessment and intervention development and implementation, (c) implementation of problem-solving models, and (d) program evaluation and accountability. It is clear from these four areas that a significant change will have to occur in training and field-based supervision for these roles to be embraced by school psychologists. Each of these areas will be examined briefly in the following sections.

School Psychologist as Change Agent

Traditionally, school psychologists have provided direct (assessment and intervention) services to students (Reschly & Wilson, 1995). The more recent practice of collaborative consultation has focused primarily on individual student problem solving (Gutkin & Curtis, 1990). Although these have historically provided valuable services, a student-centered delivery system has inherent limitations. For IDEA 97 to be implemented in school buildings across the United States, professionals who work in the schools must begin to organize assessment and intervention services, in part, around building- and system-level change. For example, effective discipline programs for students with disabilities must be implemented within the context of the discipline programs used with other students and by all of the staff within a building. Similarly, a change in the ways that students are assessed, both for eligibility and program development/evaluation, requires a system-level change in assessment practices. To accomplish these (and similar) tasks, team members must redirect the focus of the problem-solving process from individual students to building and system issues.

School psychologists are among the few school-based professionals who have the background and opportunity for training in the skills necessary to assume this role. However, school psychologists must engage in pre- and in-service training to facilitate organizational change and program evaluation, and be provided supervised experience in the application of these skills. This may require that school psychologists receive supervision by professionals other than school psychologists for some of these skill areas.

School Psychologist as Supervisor

Traditionally, school psychologists serve as supervisors of other school psychologists or other student services professionals utilizing a clinical supervision model. IDEA 97 supports comprehensive, multi-faceted, multidisciplinary assessment and intervention programs. The implementation of these programs is complex and requires leadership from those who have skills both in supervision and in the assessment and intervention programs. When conclusions are reached and interventions are developed from a variety of sources and personnel, this process will require individuals to facilitate the integration of these multi-source data and to facilitate the problem-solving process that utilizes these data for the development of interventions. The person who facilitates this process might not be involved in any of the actual assessments of the student. In a parallel manner, the development and implementation of interventions that utilize multiple personnel in multiple settings will require a highly qualified person to facilitate and supervise the implementation of the intervention package. School psychologists have the most extensive and diverse training in assessment and intervention of any professional in the school setting. They would, therefore, be likely candidates for this role. Yet, they would need training in administrative supervision and in strategies to integrate data and interventions from a variety of diverse sources.

School Psychologist as Problem Solver

Traditionally, school-based child study teams have convened primarily to determine eligibility for special education services. The process for determining eligibility is quite different from the process involved in the development, implementation, and evaluation of interventions by problem-solving teams. Performing these roles will require the execution of a significant organizational change process. This process will include developing staff support for the philosophical shift required to move decision making from a diagnostic approach to one of developing interventions, accessing resources for those interventions, and establishing outcomes against which evaluation decisions will be made. Once staff support has been developed, staff training in an agreed upon problem-solving model must take place, and facilitation of problem solving teams is necessary. School psychologists can provide models for training and facilitation, and serve as mentors to others who wish to assume the role of facilitator.

The success of school-based problem-solving teams rests on the belief of consumers (teachers, parents) that the process is effective both for the system (school) and the student. Therefore, a critical component to the role of the problem solver is the extent to which outcome data are shared on a regular basis with the consumers. This feedback can take the form of process information (e.g., how many students were served under this model compared to the eligibility model), outcome information (e.g., student-based outcome data), pedagogical information (e.g., dissemination of intervention strategies for a particular referral problem to the entire staff, not just those involved with the case), and consumer satisfaction information (e.g., staff or parent end-of-year surveys). School psychologists who aspire to the role of problem solver need skills in organizational change processes, facilitating communication among diverse groups, and program evaluation.

School Psychologists as Evaluator

A major outcome of the school reform movement has been a focus on accountability. This emphasis is clear in IDEA 97. The amendments contain an expectation that interventions designed to meet the "unique needs" of students will be evaluated to determine the degree to which these are successful (in terms of regular curriculum standards), not the degree to which the intervention was implemented (process evaluation). This is the most basic form of program evaluation. School psychologists have the pre-requisite training in research and evaluation skills (Reschly & McMasters-Beyer, 1991) to assume a leadership role in developing program evaluation skills and facilitating the implementation of program evaluation practices in school settings. However, program evaluation is equally important at the systems change level. School psychologists can serve as evaluators for the success of building-based discipline programs, student monitoring methods (e.g., curriculum-based measurement), the effects of parent involvement in interventions, and similar building- and district-level change programs. Program evaluation is based on assessment (data collection) and the interpretation of those data for program change. Moreover, program evaluation uses the same problem-solving process (problem identification, data collection, analysis, intervention, evaluation) as the assessment of individual student needs, skills with which school psychologists are very familiar. As the emphasis shifts from assessment of individual students for eligibility determination to assessment that informs and evaluates interventions, school psychologists are the most capable professional to assume leadership responsibility for program evaluation (Knoff & Batsche, 1995).

Developing a Unified System of Prosocial Discipline

In the past 10 years, educators have become increasingly concerned about the behavior of students in school settings. The relationship between student behavior and academic progress has been the focus of applied research in school settings (Knoff & Batsche, 1995). School psychologists and special educators, by virtue of their training, can provide leadership and technical assistance to school districts as those districts attempt to articulate and implement discipline programs. The implementation of building-wide discipline programs facilitates the prosocial behavior development of all students, including those with disabilities.

The application of a school district's Code of Conduct to the behavior of a student with a disability is an area of significant controversy. The degree to which the behavior of the student does or does not relate to his or her disability (manifestation determination; see Kubick, Bard, and Perry, this volume) may determine the degree to which "regular" district discipline procedures are applied to the particular behavioral infraction. Some general education teachers and administrators often may be concerned that a student with a disability appears to be "protected" from the discipline procedures that apply to other, non-disabled students. School psychologists, special educators, and other team members may find themselves in the position of advocating for a student with a disability while potentially alienating the teachers and administrators with whom they must collaborate to develop and implement effective interventions for the student. The IDEA Amendments of 1997 require a "functional assessment of behavior" and the use of the data from these assessments in the manifestation determination hearing (see Tilly, Knoster, and Ikeda, this volume). Unfortunately, the "process" set forth for both the functional assessment of behavior and the manifestation determination provides little guidance unless an effective, systematic intervention system is used to replace the inappropriate behavior with prosocial behavior (see Tankersley, Landrum, Cook, and Balan, this volume).

There are a number of false assumptions that underlie the process by which the majority of discipline decisions are made. These false assumptions apply equally to students with and without disabilities.

False Assumption 1: The Code of Conduct is an Intervention System

The Code of Conduct is, quite simply, a "sentencing manual." The district and school rules are set forth in this manual, student and parent expectations are made specific, and the consequences for violating the rules are described. The Code of Conduct assumes that all students enter school with the same degree of and potential for appropriate behavior, regardless of their socioeconomic status, cultural background, or disability. The Code does not provide for any educational acculturation training (e.g., social skills training) nor for any interventions, other than the stated negative consequences (e.g., Saturday school, suspension, expulsion). Typically, appropriate behavior is expected, not taught. This expectation is the same, regardless of the student's background or ability to demonstrate the expected behavior.

False Assumption 2: Student-Specific Interventions Delivered to Individual Students for Inappropriate Behavior That has Sustained Over Time Will Be Effective

IDEA 97 requires that assessment should "provide information related to enabling the child to be involved in and progress in the general curriculum." It follows, therefore, that interventions should accomplish the same goal. Highly specific interventions for particular students often violates the principles of generalization and transfer of training (see Stokes & Osnes, 1989). The failure to incorporate the variables of setting, teachers/parents, peer group, and instructional factors in the development of interventions may be counterproductive to long-term behavior change. Although the guidelines for the functional assessment of behavior clearly imply the importance of these variables in the assessment process, little is said in IDEA 97 about their importance in the development and implementation of interventions.

False Assumption 3: Discipline Systems That Focus on the Elimination of Inappropriate Behaviors are as Effective as Those Systems That Promote "Replacement" Behaviors

Interventions that seek to eliminate inappropriate behaviors seldom provide components that teach the replacement behavior. The failure to replace an inappropriate behavior with an appropriate one will result in the return of the inappropriate behavior in short order. Many students in school settings have the background (social, behavioral, developmental) to develop a wide range of choices (positive and negative) in their behavioral repertoire. For these students, a discipline system that focuses on providing negative consequences for an inappropriate behavior signals the student to use a more prosocial choice (one already learned) the next time (Knoff & Batsche, 1995).

For many students with disabilities and those students at-risk for behavioral difficulties, the behavioral repertoire is not so rich. For these students, there is a high probability that prosocial choices have not been learned. In addition, with the significant increase in the number of students from diverse cultural backgrounds, there is an increasing probability that behavioral choices reflect the cultural background of the student and not the expectation of the Code of Conduct. The assumption that a student "knows" what to do and simply is not doing it is a dangerous assumption.

Therefore, in the schools of the twenty-first century, the focus of discipline systems must be on "teaching" the behaviors that are expected before "disciplining" students for not demonstrating those behaviors. Unless this philosophy permeates the discipline systems of America's schools, all students who come to school without those behaviors expected in the Code of Conduct, including students with disabilities, are at risk for school failure. IDEA supports the need to focus on assessment and intervention information that teaches replacement behaviors. The focus of discipline systems must be on how to teach students to substitute prosocial choices for inappropriate behavior. When this philosophy guides the development of discipline practices, the entire system of discipline in schools will change.

The application of these false assumptions usually results in the following scenario: A student with a disability violates the Code of Conduct. Initially, the Code may be applied to this student as long as the student is not removed from the educational setting. If removal is desired, then a functional assessment (usually after the removal!) is conducted. At best, an individual intervention is developed, but this is not linked to the general education setting, to a peer group intervention, or one that links school-based and home-based interventions. When this intervention is implemented without consideration for teacher variables, peer group variables, and instructional variables, then the intervention has short-term success or none at all. This scenario occurs primarily because most school-based discipline programs are (a) not educative or focused on teaching replacement behaviors, (b) not building-based and implemented for *all* students, (c) not designed to involve all of the student's teachers and peers in all school settings, and (d) not linked functionally to home-based interventions.

IDEA 97 clearly signals the need for a unified system of prosocial discipline. If students with disabilities (and other students at-risk) are to be integrated fully into the regular curriculum (academic and behavioral), then a unified system is the only effective option that schools have. Increasingly, training programs in school psychology and special education have incorporated curricula that result in school psychologists possessing the knowledge and skills to assist schools in developing a unified system (e.g., Knoff, Curtis, & Batsche, 1997; Walker, Colvin, & Ramsey, 1995). These systems, because they are building-based and apply to all students, can be equally effective with students with disabilities, those students in general education without the repertoire of appropriate behaviors, and those students who choose to violate the behavior expectations of the school. Briefly, a unified system of prosocial discipline would have the following characteristics: (a) the same system would apply to *all* students in a building, (b) the primary purpose of the system would be to increase functionally the number of prosocial behaviors in students, (c) the primary focus of the system would be teaching replacement behaviors, (d) *all* personnel in a building (e.g., teachers, administrators, office personnel, food service personnel, maintenance personnel, substitute teachers, parents, students) would be included in the implementation of the system, and (e) the system would have three "primary" components (prevention, education, and "stopping" procedures). Interestingly, the litmus test of any school-based discipline program is the degree to which students can tell an outsider what the steps of the program are and the degree to which there is inter-student reliability to the recitation of those steps. A school can have a theoretically well-designed discipline program but if the students do not know what it is and are not involved in its implementation, then the program is usually ineffective.

The content of the primary components is critical. Briefly, the prevention, education, and stopping procedures are implemented in a sequential manner in response to student behavior (Knoff & Batsche, 1995). It is important that students are able to predict the next step in the procedure. The prevention component consists of strategies to guide the student in the production of the desired behavior (positive reinforcement, differential reinforcement of other or low rates of behavior, redirection, instruction/gesture/prompt, proximity/prompt/praise). The educative component (e.g., social skills training, direct instruction) is designed to ensure that the student has the skills (academic or social) to be successful with the task associated with the inappropriate behavior. The "stopping" component (e.g., time-out) is designed to stop the inappropriate pattern of behavior long enough to implement a strategy to initiate the prosocial behavior.

By using the systems change procedures outlined in this chapter, a school could develop a prosocial discipline system with the characteristics outlined above. All staff could be trained to implement the system. Typically, the training and implementation of such a system requires 1–2 years (see Knoff & Batsche, 1995). The "systems change" part of the program focuses on securing the commitment of the staff to support the philosophy, the commitment of administrative leaders to allocate sufficient training opportunities and to support the components of the program, the patience of all involved to give the program sufficient time to work, and the trust in the students that they have the ability to learn prosocial behavior.

INTERVENTION-BASED SERVICE DELIVERY SYSTEM

During the past 15–20 years, limitations to the traditional refer-test-place model of delivering services to students who are struggling or disabled have been well documented (Graden, Zins, Curtis, & Cobb, 1989). In response, the National Association of School Psychologists has taken a leading role in advocating for alternative educational delivery systems that meet the needs of all students. Some of these alternative systems include pre-referral intervention teams, consultative services, the use of authentic assessment such as curriculum-based assessment, adaptive instructional strategies, and school reform initiatives (Knoff & Curtis, 1996; Knoff et al., 1997; Shinn & McConnell, 1994). An underlying and critical component of each of these approaches is the emphasis on developing and implementing interventions that directly address the needs of students and families.

Assessment plays an important role within these approaches, but the reliance on standardized test instruments is not presumed. Assessment within a problem-solving paradigm is primarily designed to identify why particular problems exist so that informed decisions can be made regarding potentially effective interventions (Batsche & Knoff, 1995).

Through legislation such as IDEA 97, an intervention-based approach will be supported increasingly as the vehicle through which educational and psychological services are delivered. Intervention services are seen within the context of systemic reform efforts that aim to develop effective and responsive schools. Through integrated and organized efforts, intervention services should effectively respond to the difficulties encountered by students and families, and in many cases prevent problems from occurring.

In the sections that follow, two components of an intervention-based service delivery system are discussed. These components are (a) collaborative problem solving and (b) relevant assessment. Importantly, both of these approaches are either implicitly or explicitly emphasized in IDEA 97.

Collaborative Problem Solving

Collaborative problem solving (also referred to as collaborative consultation) has been extensively discussed as a method for delivering services to individuals and organizations (Curtis & Stollar, 1996; Gutkin & Curtis, 1990; Knoff, 1995; Shapiro, Miller, Sawka, Gardill, & Handler, 1999; Sheridan, Kratochwill, & Bergan, 1996). Regardless of the specific purposes for which the service is intended, the assumptions and stages of each collaborative approach are similar. An extensive discussion of these assumptions can be found in Curtis and Myers (1989). For purposes of this chapter, the following four assumptions are viewed as critical as school psychologists, special educators, and other school-based team members consider IDEA 97.

Assumptions of Collaborative Problem Solving

Assumption 1: Non-hierarchical communication. Collaborative problem solving requires that two or more individuals engage in dialogue for the purpose of addressing a significant area of concern. Critically, neither individual is presumed or intended to be more "powerful" than the other. A nonjudgmental and non-evaluative relationship is required for open communication that occurs in an honest and reciprocal fashion. In this way, ideas and strategies can be shared equally rather than conveyed from one individual to another in a unilateral manner. Although each individual in the process may have significant knowledge or skills that he or she brings to the process, neither individual enters the relationship in the "expert" role.

Assumption 2: Multi-leveled applicability. The problem-solving process can and should be applied in numerous contexts. As was cited previously, systematic collaborative problem-solving processes have received empirical support in addressing concerns about individual students and larger systemic issues. To facilitate the implementation of an intervention-based service delivery system, on-going collaboration will be necessary among key stakeholders to address individual, school-wide, and system-wide issues.

Assumption 3: Linking assessment, consultation, and intervention. The use of collaborative problem-solving methods facilitates the integration of assessment, consultation, and intervention. A collaborative problem-solving structure serves as a scaffold for the provision of services that aim to address problems that arise in the school environment. To understand these problems, assessment techniques require on-going collaboration with teachers, administrators, parents, and others because the factors that influence school-based problems are rarely stagnant. The extension of on-going collaboration and assessment is the development of effective interventions that address the variables that are contributing to identified difficulties (Batsche & Knoff, 1995; Sheridan, Kratochwill, & Bergan, 1996).

Assumption 4: Parental involvement. Collaborative problem solving requires that parental input be solicited and incorporated into any strategy that aims to address the difficulties of that parent's child (Epstein, 1992). As was stated by Christenson (1995) "parents are invited to help solve school-based concerns, and parental input is actively encouraged throughout the process" (p. 261). Thus, parents would not only be involved in developing and implementing interventions once problems have been identified but they also would be involved in defining and understanding the problem and in monitoring the impact of interventions. Consistent throughout IDEA 97 is the mandate that parents are to be involved in all aspects of decision making related to services (and interventions) for their children.

Stages of Collaborative Problem-Solving

Collaborative problem solving is critical to the development of an intervention-based service delivery system. When considered within the context of IDEA 97, the collaborative problem-solving process can be used to assist teams in defining and analyzing student needs and developing, implementing, and evaluating interventions that are contained within a student's Individualized Education Programs (IEP). Bergan (1995) identified four stages in the problem-solving process: problem definition, problem analysis, developing/implementing interventions, and evaluating interventions. Elemental to each of these stages is the four assumptions discussed previously.

Problem definition. During this first stage of the process, the collaborative team is charged with clearly defining the referral concern. Examining records and referral information is just one aspect of this stage. It is critical that face-to-face communication between the referral source and the team (or designated individual) takes place. As Knoff and Batsche (1991) emphasized, the initial face-to-face meeting is critical to developing rapport and a shared level of concern among involved parties. This meeting also can be used to ascertain the commitment of all parties to the process. The objectives of this stage are to clearly define the problem and to gain some consensus regarding the goal(s) of intervention. In the case of individual problem solving, it has been suggested that specific "replacement behaviors" be defined as a way to focus the goal setting task and to define the target of subsequent assessment and intervention (Batsche & Knoff, 1995). Teachers and parents often have difficulty defining the "problem" specifically. They have less difficulty specifying what they want the student to do (replacement behavior). The emphasis on replacement behaviors focuses the problem-solving efforts on reasons why the student is not engaging in the replacement behaviors and organizes interventions around the development of strategies to promote those replacement behaviors. Interventions that result in an increase in replacement (desired) behavior reinforce those persons (teachers, parents) for promoting the intervention each time it is used. Interventions that decrease behaviors reduce motivation to continue the intervention because the target of that intervention is diminishing.

Problem analysis. During the problem analysis stage, hypotheses about why the behaviors of concern exist are developed, and these hypotheses are then confirmed or refuted through collection of data. Emphasis is placed on understanding the function of the student's behavior and the ecological variables that may be contributing to its initiation or maintenance. Inevitably, assessment procedures such as interviews, observations, and informal or formal testing will be required during this stage. This assessment will include collection of baseline data to determine the frequency, duration, and severity of the behavior and the important antecedents and consequences that surround the occurrence of the behavior. Importantly, data should be collected from multiple sources and across multiple contexts (Stanger, 1996). Through consultation with others and on-going data collection, the validity of particular hypotheses is tested. These hypotheses may focus on characteristics of the student, classroom, teacher, peer, school, and/or home and community (Batsche & Knoff, 1995). Once the function of the student's behavior is determined through the confirmation of particular hypotheses, the team will have sufficient information to develop an intervention plan.

Developing and implementing interventions. Elliott, Witt, and Kratochwill (1996) suggest that multiple interventions may be appropriate for any one referral concern. Thus, once specific intervention goals are set, intervention approaches and strategies will need to be selected through collaborative decision making. In selecting an intervention, Elliott et al. (1996) recommend that the following criteria be considered: treatment effectiveness, treatment acceptability, treatment feasibility, and treatment integrity.

"Treatment effectiveness" refers to the research-based validation of a particular intervention. Interventions that have been documented as effective for ameliorating a particular problem should be prioritized over interventions that have little or no empirical support. Importantly, the specific intervention chosen should address the variables that are considered to be contributing to the manifest difficulty. That is, the intervention should address the function of the student's behavior.

"Treatment acceptability" reflects the user's belief that the intervention is appropriate for a particular problem. This aspect of intervention planning is critically important because if the user does not believe in the reasonableness of the intervention then it is unlikely that the intervention will be used (Elliott et al., 1996). Klingner, Vaughn, Hughes, and Arguelles (1999) found that teachers will not sustain the use of a classroom-based intervention if they do not believe the intervention is likely to be successful, regardless of the empirical evidence suggesting its effectiveness.

"Treatment feasibility" refers to the degree to which a particular intervention is judged to be user-friendly. Extensive research has suggested that cumbersome and time-consuming interventions are not likely to be implemented (Gersten & Brengelman, 1996). In addition, interventions that are excessively complicated and require extensive planning may be most problematic for teachers to implement (Gersten & Brengelman, 1996).

"Treatment integrity" is related to the preceding two conditions (i.e., treatment feasibility and treatment acceptability) and refers to the degree that an intervention is implemented as it was intended (Elliott et al., 1996). Obviously, interventions that are neither acceptable nor feasible may not be implemented with sufficient fidelity necessary for its effectiveness. Thus, it is important that the intervention plan includes on-going collaboration to determine treatment integrity and, when necessary, to make needed modifications to the plan.

In addition to these four considerations when choosing interventions, implementation plans should be specific with regard to several factors. Time lines, resources needed, each member's responsibility in implementing the plan, and how the plan will be monitored should all be described in detail.

Evaluation/progress monitoring. Collaborative problem solving will often result in the development of an IEP, a behavioral intervention plan (BIP), or some other type of intervention. It is critical that data regarding the results of these treatments be collected. This information should be used to make needed adjustments if the interventions are ineffective or are not effective to an acceptable degree.

Importantly, IDEA 97 recognizes that a reevaluation does not necessarily require a repetition of the initial evaluation. Within the context of the problem-solving process, reevaluations might include on-going progress monitoring of a student by using less formal measures such as classroom observations and academic skills probes. By examining the direct impact of interventions on targeted student behaviors, progress monitoring can be primarily seen as a way to determine the effectiveness of strategies and interventions rather than as a way to document the on-going existence of an educational disability (see Canter, Hurley, and Reid, this volume).

As was suggested earlier, it is during this stage of the problem-solving process that information also should be collected on the implementation of the designated interventions. Those involved in implementing the plan will require support, and therefore regularly scheduled meetings should be held to address problems that have been experienced. Treatment integrity is enhanced when consultation is available regularly to those individuals implementing the intervention.

In addition to collaborative problem solving, an intervention-based service delivery system will include an assessment process that is responsive and relevant to the concerns of teachers and parents. As was discussed in the preceding sections, assessment is one particular tool that is integrated into the collaborative process; however, for purposes of clarity, specific issues related to relevant assessment are now presented in detail.

Relevant Assessment

Assessment is and will continue to be an important aspect of the school psychologist's role. However, the changes included in the IDEA 97 suggest that assessment procedures and methods will need to become increasingly relevant. From an intervention perspective, relevance suggests that the assessment should provide (a) insight into the reasons behind the referred student's difficulties and (b) a clearer understanding of potentially effective interventions. The increased focus on relevance has implications for the type of assessment information members of the school-based teams collect. This information will need to focus on the functional relationship between the student's manifest needs and the instructional environment, as opposed to underlying processing deficits (Reschly, this volume). On the basis of guidelines provided in IDEA 97 and in accordance with best practices, assessment within an intervention-based service delivery system will need to be educationally valid, comprehensive, functional, accountable, and multidimensional.

Educationally Valid

IDEA 97 requires the provision of a free and appropriate public education based on the "unique" needs of a student as opposed to a "disability" category. In addition, the statute suggests that assessment should "provide information related to enabling the child to be involved in and progress in the general curriculum." Assessment that fails to document the relationship between the student's difficulties and the instructional environment (including the classroom ecology, instructional techniques, and curriculum) will be unlikely to meet the requirements of IDEA 97. It is expected that individualized student goals will increasingly be predicated on local and state standards and priorities that are aligned with statewide assessments. The development of interventions and strategies to facilitate student progress toward meeting individual goals and subsequently local and state priorities can be met only when the assessment process considers the impact of these priorities on the classroom environment. Thus, an assessment that provides insight into methods for helping a child access and progress in the general education curriculum is likely to be considered educationally valid.

Comprehensive

Best practices in assessment have long suggested the need for comprehensive data about a referred student. IDEA 97 increases the legal importance of comprehensive assessment by suggesting that information be collected on all of the child's needs, even when those needs are not "commonly linked" to the suspected disability category. Assessments that solely focus on one aspect of a student's functioning (e.g., IQ test score) may not be adequate to fully understand how functioning in that domain interacts with and impacts other domains (e.g., behavior). Comprehensive assessments should provide substantial information about all aspects of the student, the environment in which he or she functions, and the impact of the on-going reciprocal interaction between the student and the environment.

Functional

IDEA 97 requires that "a variety of assessment tools be used to gather relevant functional and developmental information" about a referred student's difficulties. Aspects of the collaborative problem-solving procedures discussed previously indicate that the collection of functional information is critical in developing effective interventions.

In a training manual developed by KÚpper (1997) regarding the implementation of IDEA 97, it was suggested that individualized assessments answer four critical questions: (a) Does the child have a particular disability? (b) What are the child's educational needs? (c) Does the child need special education and related services? (d) What additions or modifications, if any, are needed to the special education and related services to enable the child to meet annual goals in the IEP and to participate, as appropriate, in the general curriculum?

Importantly, each of these questions can be conceptualized from a functional assessment perspective, as illustrated by the following: (a) What specific difficulties is the child experiencing, and what are the circumstances under which they exist? (b) Where is the child performing independently, instructionally, and at frustration within the general education curriculum? (c) What specific interventions will successfully facilitate the student's educational progress, and are special education resources needed to develop these interventions? (d) Have the designated interventions impacted the student's progress in a manner that was predicted? (e) What changes are needed to increase the student's likelihood of success?

Accountable

Increasingly, individual educators, schools, school districts, and states are being held accountable for the progress of students. IDEA 97 requires that interventions and services be evaluated in an on-going fashion and changed when not successful. Thus, the periodic reevaluation assessment, in particular, provides a formal opportunity to meet this mandate. Further, accountability requires that both IEPs and BIPs be derived from data collected through an assessment. Assessments that are conducted solely for eligibility purposes will not provide this information. Additionally, eligibility evaluations will prove to be of little use during legal proceedings such as manifestation determinations.

Multidimensional

The use of multiple assessment procedures has long been required to assist in determining whether a student has a particular disability. Multidimensional assessment procedures also are considered best practices when developing intervention plans. Thus, multiple procedures will need to be used to assess various aspects of student functioning and of the classroom environment. These procedures are likely to include review of existing data and records, interviews, observations, and formal and informal assessments. Domains of student skills to be assessed might include academic, social/emotional, and behavioral. Domains of the instructional environment might include curriculum, instruction, teacher skills and beliefs, peers, and school level influences.

A MODEL FOR SYSTEMS CHANGE

The implications of IDEA 97 for changes in the practices of school-based teams have been discussed briefly here and are examined in greater depth in other chapters in this volume. In addition to implications relative to individual students, IDEA 97 holds promise for system-level changes that will lead to more effective services for all students with disabilities, and perhaps for all students as well.

Facilitating systems-level change represents a significant expansion of the role for many educators and requires specific knowledge regarding the functioning of systems, principles for change, and systems-change procedures. Several principles, considered critical to any change process, were discussed previously. Each represents a dimension that must be addressed if meaningful change in the way services for students with disabilities are organized and delivered is to occur.

There is an extensive literature available on organizational change (e.g., Senge, 1990) and change strategies (e.g., Senge, Kleiner, Roberts, Ross, & Smith, 1994). In addition, a considerable number of references are specific to organizational change in educational settings (e.g., Fullan, 1995; Goodlad, 1994). Curtis and Stollar (1995, 1996) present one change model and illustrate its application for engaging in a collaborative approach to planning and problem solving for organizational change. Regardless of the specific model adopted or developed, it is important that members of the organization follow a structured, sequential process, while continuing to adhere to the principles outlined previously. It should be noted that a structured problem-solving process could be used to address any goal or concern, including each of the principles for systems change.

Illustrating Systems Change

The model for promoting systems change proposed by Curtis and Stollar (1995, 1996) is presented in this section, using one specific aspect of IDEA 97 to illustrate its application. The example used to illustrate this process involves the hypothetical efforts of a Student Services Improvement Team (SSIT) and relates to the IDEA 97 requirement for parental participation in the educational program of their child.

IDEA 97 promotes increased parental participation in the educational process, primarily by addressing those procedural elements in which they must be involved. However, as argued previously, the involvement of parents should not be viewed in terms of compliance with regulations but in terms of a collaborative partnership for the benefit of students with disabilities, and potentially of all students. Sheridan et al. (this volume) discuss critical elements in the relationship that should exist between parents and school personnel and discuss specific ways that Conjoint Behavioral Consultation can address aspects of IDEA 97. These authors endorse those recommendations and strongly argue that there is a need for a paradigm shift with regard to parents. Even more than being involved in the educational programs of their own children, parents should be members of a collaborative school partnership responsible for determining the philosophy, goals, and values for the educational program for all students with disabilities. In fact, this same paradigm shift should apply to all parents and all students.

For the purpose of illustrating the use of the proposed change model in addressing this hypothetical situation, the following general goal will be used: Create a culture in which parents and school personnel see themselves as members of a partnership whose purpose is to achieve meaningful educational progress for all students with disabilities.

Assumptions

In considering the context within which the hypothetical SSIT is functioning and to understand issues that the SSIT must address, an analysis the school district's consistency with the five principles discussed previously reveals the following:

Principle 1: Shared goals, philosophy, and values. A philosophy, underlying values, and goals for an educational program for students with disabilities needs to be developed, articulated, and widely accepted throughout the school district.

Principle 2: Systemic change. Recognizing the need for and agreeing to seek systemic change, the SSIT has concluded that its purpose is to develop a comprehensive and coordinated educational program for students with disabilities that will be based on the goals, philosophy, and values that are adopted.

Principle 3: Commitment of key personnel. Influential individuals from the school district, parents of students with and without disabilities, and the community are accepting and supportive of the purpose of the SSIT.

Principle 4: Involvement of all primary stakeholders. All primary stakeholders (e.g., parents of students with and without disabilities, school administrators, general education teachers, special education teachers, special services personnel, community-based professionals) are represented on the SSIT and all at-large are included in communication from and to the team.

Principle 5: Collaborative planning and problem-solving skills. The SSIT recognizes the need for collaborative, small group planning and problem-solving procedures, but has not yet been trained in its use.

Stages of Planning and Problem Solving

The model proposed by Curtis and Stollar (1995, 1996) includes six stages. Following the identification and a brief explanation of each stage, the application of that stage in addressing the hypothetical case involving the SSIT is presented. Elements of the illustration are based on the problem-solving efforts of an actual team composed of school personnel and parents.

Stage 1. Describe the goal to be achieved or the concern to be addressed as concretely and in as much detail as possible. To the greatest extent possible, the desired outcome should be stated in operational terms and should be understood by all members of the problem-solving team. Often, the process of developing an operational goal statement leads to the identification of several more specific goals. Specific goals should be addressed one at a time, completing the problem-solving process for each one.

Example: As was noted previously, despite consistency with Change Principles 2, 3, and 4, the team is aware that Principle 1, a shared philosophy, values, and goals, and Principle 5, possessing collaborative planning and problem-solving skills, represent issues yet to be addressed. The SSIT decides that to address Principle 1 effectively, it must first address Principle 5. Consequently, it develops the goal statement, "The SSIT will use effective collaborative planning and problem-solving procedures in all of its work."

Stage 2. Brainstorm in an effort to identify all of those factors and resources that might help achieve the specific goal selected and all of those factors that may serve as obstacles to its achievement. The group should focus on addressing only the specific goal statement agreed on. In addition, brainstorming procedures should be adhered to, emphasizing the involvement all team members in generating as much information as possible.

Example: For the specific goal identified in Stage 1, the SSIT generates lists of resources and obstacles. The resources identified include (a) team members committed to success, (b) people familiar with effective procedures are available, and (c) funds to pay for training are obtainable. The obstacles identified include (a) difficulty finding common meeting times, (b) no experience working as a team, and (c) lack of knowledge of problem-solving procedures.

Stage 3. Select one obstacle that is significant as a hindrance to achieving the specific goal selected. Avoid trying to identify the most important obstacle. Doing so could lead to ownership issues regarding who generated which obstacles during brainstorming and to disagreements regarding the importance of each obstacle. Instead, emphasize that all obstacles will be addressed and lead team to choose one obstacle with which to begin.

Example: The SSIT selects the obstacle, "Lack knowledge of problem-solving procedures" to address first.

Stage 4. Focusing on only the one obstacle selected, brainstorm all possible ideas that might be used to overcome or reduce that specific obstacle. It must be emphasized that this is only an "ideas" stage so that members are encouraged to generate as many ideas as possible and to diminish the tendency to hold back ideas because they may not be feasible.

Example: The SSIT members generates several ideas through brainstorming, including (a) find information about collaborative group planning and problem-solving procedures, (b) identify individuals in district who could talk with or train our team in procedures, (c) locate individuals in other districts or community to conduct training, and (d) identify examples of effective teams.

Stage 5. Using the ideas generated during brainstorming only as a stimulus, develop concrete plans of action that identify who will do specifically what, by when. It is desirable to develop multiple action plans to address each obstacle to increase the likelihood of success in reducing or eliminating that obstacle. Specificity in the statement of action plans increases accountability and therefore the likelihood of success as well.

Example: The members of the SSIT develop several action plans, including the following scenario: (a) Mr. Adams will locate, copy, and distribute an article he read on collaborative group planning and problem-solving procedures to all team members by May 10 and (b) Ms. Baker will contact John Ellensworth, her building school psychologist who has trained groups in problem-solving procedures, by May 3 about conducting training for the SSIT. She will ask him about the amount of time needed for such training and the nature of the training. If he is not available, then she will ask him to provide the names of other persons qualified to conduct the training.

Stage 6. Establish procedures for the promotion of following through with action plans, evaluation of progress, and recycling through earlier stages when necessary. The establishment of regularly scheduled interim reporting dates is often helpful in promoting compliance with action plans. This procedure also allows for the introduction of new or additional resources when necessary. In addition, success in overcoming one or more obstacles allows the team to recycle to an earlier stage, and select a new obstacle to address.

Example: The SSIT developed follow-up procedures for their two action plans, including another scenario: Ms. Charles will contact Mr. Adams and Ms. Baker on May 4 to check on their progress in carrying out their action plans. If either has encountered difficulty or has not been able to follow through, then Ms. Charles will contact Mr. Doan, Ms. Farnsworth, and/or Ms. Gould, team members who have volunteered to provide assistance.

Summary

Although IDEA 97 presents significant challenges for members of school-based teams, they also represent a special opportunity for the facilitation of system-level change. A number of changes reflected in IDEA 97 are consistent with movements that already have merged in school psychology and special education, although those changes have been very slow to influence the practices of school-based teams on a broad scale (e.g., meaningful parental involvement, relevant assessment, intervention-focused services). Most significantly, IDEA 97 seeks to move educational services for students with disabilities from a basis in process accountability to accountability for significant positive results. Rather than attempting to address the mandated changes through the piecemeal adoption of isolated and independent procedures, there is an opportunity and a tremendous need to engage in systemic change in reconceptualizing, reorganizing, and delivering services for students with disabilities.

However, many school-based teams lack familiarity with systems change procedures and the skills necessary to successfully engage in change efforts. This chapter has reviewed some of the systemic changes that are needed to implement the mandates of IDEA 97 as well as principles to guide change efforts and has presented and illustrated one model for organizational change.

References

Batsche, G. M., & Knoff, H. M. (1995). Linking assessment to intervention. In A. Thomas & J. Grimes (Eds.), *Best practices in school psychology III* (pp. 569–586). Washington, DC: National Association of School Psychologists.

Bergan, J. R. (1995). Evolution of a problem-solving model of consultation. *Journal of Educational and Psychological Consultation, 6*(2), 111–123.

Christenson, S. L. (1995). Supporting home-school collaboration. In A. Thomas & J. Grimes (Eds.), *Best practices in school psychology III* (pp. 253–268). Washington, DC: National Association of School Psychologists.

Curtis, M. J., Hunley, S. A., Walker, K. J., & Baker, A. C. (1999). Demographic characteristics and professional practices in school psychology. *School Psychology Review, 28*, 104–115.

Curtis, M. J., & Myers, J. (1989). Consultation: A foundation for alternative services in schools. In J. L. Graden, J. E. Zins, & M. J. Curtis (Eds.), *Alternative educational delivery systems: Enhancing instructional options for all students* (pp. 35-48). Washington, DC: National Association of School Psychologists.

Curtis, M. J., & Stollar, S. A. (1995). System-level consultation and organizational change. In A. Thomas and J. Grimes (Eds.). *Best practices in school psychology III* (pp. 51-58). Washington, DC: National Association of School Psychologists.

Curtis, M. J. & Stollar, S. A. (1996). Applying principals and practices of organizational change to school reform. *School Psychology Review, 25*, 409–417.

Education of All Handicapped Children Act (1975). P.L. 94-142, 20 U.S.C. 1400-1485, 34 CFR-300.

Elliot, S. N., Witt, J. C., & Kratochwill, T. R. (1996). Selecting, implementing, and evaluating classroom interventions. In G. Stoner, M. R. Shinn, & H. M. Walker (Eds.), *Interventions for achievement and behavior problems* (pp. 99-136). Silver Spring, MD: National Association of School Psychologists.

Epstein, J. L. (1992). School and family partnerships: Leadership roles for school psychologists. In S. L. Christenson & J. C. Conoley (Eds.), *Home-school collaboration: Enhancing children's academic and social competence* (pp. 499-515). Silver Spring, MD: National Association of School Psychologists.

Fullan, M. (1995). *Change forces: The sequel*. Levittown, PA: Falmer.

Fullan, M., & Hargreaves, A. (1996). *What's worth fighting for in your school?* New York: Teachers College Press.

Gersten, R., & Brengelman, S. (1996). The quest to translate research into classroom practice: The current knowledge base. *Remedial and Special Education, 96*, 228–244.

Goodlad, J. (1994). *Educational renewal*. San Francisco, CA: Jossey-Bass.

Graden, J. L., Zins, J. E., Curtis, M. J., & Cobb, C. T. (1989). The need for alternatives in educational services. In J. L. Graden, J. E. Zins, & M. J. Curtis (Eds.), *Alternative educational delivery systems: Enhancing instructional options for all students* (pp. 3–16). Washington, DC: National Association of School Psychologists.

Gutkin, T. B., & Curtis, M. J. (1990). School-based consultation: Theory, techniques, and research. In T. B. Gutkin & C. R. Reynolds (Eds.), *The handbook of school psychology* (2nd ed.) (pp. 577–611). New York: John Wiley.

Individuals with Disabilities Education Act Amendments of 1997, 20 U.S.C. § 1400 *et seq.* (West 1997).

Klingner, J., Vaughn, S., Hughes, M., & Arguelles, M. (1999). *Three years later: Do teachers sustain the use of research-based interventions?* Paper presented at the annual convention of the Council for Exceptional Children. Charlotte, NC.

Knoff, H. M. (1995). Facilitating school based organizational change and strategic planning. In A. Thomas & J. Grimes (Eds.), *Best practices in school psychology III* (pp. 239–252). Washington, DC: National Association of School Psychologists.

Knoff, H. M., & Batsche, G. M. (1991). *The referral question consultation process: Addressing system, school, and classroom academic and behavioral problems. The RQC skills workbook.* Tampa, FL: University of South Florida.

Knoff, H. M., & Batsche, G. M. (1995). Project ACHIEVE: Analyzing a school reform process for at-risk and underachieving students. *School Psychology Review, 24,* 579–603.

Knoff, H. M., & Curtis, M. J. (1996). Organizational change and school reform. *School Psychology Review, 25,* 406-518.

Knoff, H. M., Curtis, M. J., & Batsche, G. M. (1997). The future of school psychology: Perspectives on effective training. *School Psychology Review, 26,* 93–103.

Kupper, L. (Ed.) (1997). *Individuals with Disabilities Education Act Amendments of 1997: Curriculum.* Washington, DC: National Information Center for Children and Youth with Disabilities, U. S. Office of Special Education Programs.

Reschly, D. J., & McMasters-Beyer, M. (1991). Influences of degree level, institutional orientation, college affiliation, and accreditation status on school psychology graduate education. *Professional Psychology: Research and Practice, 22,* 368–374.

Reschly, D. J., & Wilson, M. S. (1995). School psychology practitioners and faculty 1986 to 1991–92: Trends in demographics, roles, satisfaction, and system reform. *School Psychology Review, 24,* 62–80.

Reschly, D. J., & Ysseldyke, J. E. (1995). School psychology paradigm shift. In A. Thomas & J. Grimes (Eds.), *Best practices in school psychology III* (pp. 17 – 32). Washington, DC: National Association of School Psychologists.

Sarason, S. B. (1990). *The predictable failure of educational reform.* San Francisco, CA: Jossey-Bass.

Senge, P. (1990). *The fifth discipline.* New York: Doubleday.

Senge, P. M., Kleiner, A., Roberts, C., Ross, R. B., Smith, B. J. (1994). *The fifth discipline fieldbook.* New York: Doubleday.

Shapiro, E., Miller, D., Sawka, K., Gardill, M., & Handler, M. (1999). Facilitating inclusion of students with EBD into general education classrooms. *Journal of Emotional and Behavioral Disorders, 7,* 89 –93.

Sheridan, S. M., Kratochwill, T. R., & Bergan, J. R. (1996). *Conjoint behavioral consultation: A procedural manual.* New York: Plenum.

Shinn, M. R., & McConnell, S. L. (1994). Improving general education instruction: Relevance to school psychologists. *School Psychology Review, 23,* 351– 371.

Stanger, C. (1996). Behavioral assessment: An overview. In M. J. Breen & C. R. Fiedler (Eds.), *Behavioral approach to assessment of youth with emotional/behavioral disorders: A handbook for school-based practitioners* (pp. 5–21). Austin, TX: Pro-Ed.

Stokes, T. F. & Osnes, P. G. (1986). Programming the generalization of children's social behaviors. In P. S. Strain, M. J. Guralnick, & H. M. Walker (Eds.), *Children's social behavior: Development, assessment, and modification* (pp. 407- 443). Orlando, FL: Academic Press.

Walker, H. M., Colvin, G., & Ramsey, E. (1995). *Antisocial behavior in school: Strategies and best practices.* Pacific Grove, CA: Brooks/Cole.

U.S. Department of Education. (1999). *Assistance to states for the education of children with disabilities and the early intervention program for infants and toddlers with disabilities: Final regulations.* Washington, DC: Author.

ANNOTATED BIBLIOGRAPHY

Fullan, M. (1995). *Change forces: The sequel.* Levittown, PA: Falmer.

Following on this well-known author's earlier work, *Change Forces,* this publication examines the pitfalls and opportunities of school-based change strategies. The numerous illustrations, based on actual change efforts in which the author has been involved, make this a particularly helpful work for school-based teams.

Senge, P. (1990). *The fifth discipline.* New York: Doubleday.

In this publication, the author introduces and advances the concept of the "learning organization;" that is, the organization that is continuously engaged in developing the capacity both to respond to current opportunities and problems and to anticipate and prepare for the future. Although well known organizational principles still serve as the cornerstone for much of this work, an intriguing and stimulating new way to think about organizations systems is offered.

Senge, P. M., Kleiner, A., Roberts, C., Ross, R. B., Smith, B. J. (1994). *The fifth discipline fieldbook*. New York: Doubleday.

According to the authors, this publication was intended as a follow-up piece to *The Fifth Discipline* to answer the question, "What do I do on Monday morning?" Numerous pragmatic strategies for systems change are discussed, using a wide range of differing organizations as illustrations.

INDEX

ABC Event Frame: 282

Accommodation: 29, 30, 32, 33, 34, 35, 36, 37, 38, 39, 40, 41, 43, 44, 45, 46, 47, 48, 50, 54, 57

Age-equivalent scores: 355

Alternate assessment: 29, 30, 32, 33, 34, 35, 37, 39, 40, 41, 42, 43, 44, 45, 46, 47, 48, 50, 51, 52, 56

Alternative programs/schools: 201, 203, 275, 277, 279, 284, 285, 286, 287, 292, 294

Applied behavior analysis: 233

Behavior Assessment System for Children (BASC): 111, 141

Behavior intervention: 158, 164, 167, 168, 170, 200, 204, 206, 210, 221, 224, 227, 228, 229, 241, 242, 243, 244, 245, 246, 247, 248, 249, 250, 251, 252, 253, 254, 255, 256-258, 260-265

Benchmarks: 14, 15, 16, 23, 24

Cognitive-behavioral strategies: 282

Collaboration: 312, 314, 320, 322, 326, 342

Collaborative problem-solving: 387, 388, 395, 396, 397, 398, 400

Conflict management: 203

Conjoint Behavioral Consultation: 307, 323, 324, 325, 333, 335, 339, 341, 402

Content validity: 364

Contingency contracting: 203

Decision rules: 361, 367

Diana v. State Board of Education: 67

Direct observation: 158, 161, 165, 171, 172, 173

Division of Special Education: 65, 66, 67, 68, 69, 70, 71, 72, 73, 75, 77, 78, 79, 80, 81, 82, 84, 85, 87, 88, 89, 90, 92, 93, 94, 96

Due process: 202, 204, 220, 229, 230

Dynamic indicators of basic skills (DIBS): 362

Early childhood special education services: 127, 130

Ecological analysis: 218

Ecological factors: 248, 250, 251